BUGATTI

Other books by the author:

NAPIER
The First to Wear the Green

THE RACING 1500S

FIRST AMONG CHAMPIONS
The Alfa Romeo Grand Prix Cars

BUGATTI
A RACING HISTORY

DAVID VENABLES

Haynes Publishing

First published in June 2002

A catalogue record for this book is available from the British Library

ISBN 1 85960 834 5

Library of Congress catalog card no. 2001099292

Published by Haynes Publishing, Sparkford, Yeovil,
Somerset, BA22 7JJ, UK

Tel: 01963 442030 Fax: 01963 440001
Int. tel: +44 1963 442030 Int. fax: +44 1963 440001
E-mail: sales@haynes-manuals.co.uk
Web site: www.haynes.co.uk

Haynes North America, Inc.,
861 Lawrence Drive, Newbury Park,
California 91320, USA

Page layout by Sutton, Stroud, Gloucestershire

Printed and bound in Great Britain by
J. H. Haynes & Co. Ltd, Sparkford

All photographs not otherwise credited are from the collection of the
Bugatti Trust

Contents

Preface

BUGATTI CARS TOOK PART in major motor races for only 19 years and were truly dominant for a mere seven of those years, but the name Bugatti will always feature in any list of the great, immortal racing marques, ranking alongside such giants as Alfa Romeo, Ferrari and Mercedes-Benz. Countless books have been written about Bugatti, and although many of these touched on aspects of the racing exploits, some in much detail, no one has attempted to write a book solely devoted to the motor racing story of Bugatti. In a foolhardy moment, I decided it was a book that needed to be written.

As a small boy, during the Second World War, I spent many hours gazing at a dusty and forlorn T37 standing at the back of a locked and deserted car showroom. I went to my first motor race at Gransden Lodge in July 1947 and among the indelible memories I have of that day, were the sounds, smell and looks of the competing Bugattis. The staccato bark of the engine, the crackle of a cooling exhaust, the smell of Castrol R, the manner in which the alloy wheels became apparent discs at speed and the way in which the most humble amateur driver seemed to take on an aura of glamour at the wheel, generated a fascination that day which has remained with me. I hope I have now been able to impart some of it in this book. It is a complex story with many entwined themes and controversies. It has been suggested that the story is too big to encompass in a single volume, but the size of this book has been dictated by commercial considerations and by my own limitations. Perhaps a multi-volume work will emerge one day, but I feel the enormity of the task could daunt even the most dedicated author and I hope that meanwhile, my efforts will suffice. There is an army of experts, some of whom have made the study of Bugatti a lifetime's work, I await their criticisms with trepidation! I have tried hard to ensure accuracy and if I have made mistakes or trampled on favourite theories, I apologise.

I have received help and advice from many sources and I have found that everyone greeted the project with great enthusiasm and gave me every encouragement. Foremost among those who have helped me is David Sewell. David, who is probably the World's leading authority on Bugattis and the former curator of the Bugatti Trust, has advised and counselled me from the earliest stages. He studied the manuscript as it emerged and made many comments, additions and corrections. I am immensely grateful to him. Guy Griffiths raced, tuned and sold Bugattis in the 1930s. His comments and views on those times, the cars, and the personalities have been invaluable, as has his continuous support and encouragement. He has also provided photographs from his collection. John Maitland has given me a free run of his enormous motoring library, has looked up many obscure points for me and has provided photographs from his collection. Richard Day, Julie Bate and John Bridcutt of the Bugatti Trust have researched many points for me, have allowed me to spend many hours checking facts in the Trust archives and have provided the majority of the photographs. I have also received much help from John Barton, Robert Cooper, Philip Hall of the Sir Henry Royce Memorial Foundation, David McKinney, the librarian and staff of the Royal Automobile Club library, Basil Smith and John Staveley. To all these, I offer my thanks and I apologise to anyone whom I have inadvertently failed to mention.

David Venables
May 2002

Chapter 1

Youthful ambitions, youthful achievements

Bugattis are elite cars intended for the elite; the fact that they may be difficult to maintain, repair and tune, necessitating considerable expense, is therefore of no consequence.
Ettore Bugatti

IN THE HISTORY OF MOTOR racing in the 20th century, the names of two men and the cars they built, became synonymous with the sport. Ettore Bugatti was the dominant figure in the first half of the century, just as Enzo Ferrari dominated the second half. Ettore Arco Isidoro Bugatti was born in Milan on 15 September 1881; he was the first son of Carlo and Teresa Bugatti. The family lived at via Marcona 13 and Carlo had a considerable reputation as a designer and maker of furniture, and also as a silversmith. He was regarded as being a leader in his field and in later years, Ettore said his father was reminiscent of the great men of the Italian Renaissance. A second son, Rembrandt was born to Carlo and Teresa in 1885; according to Ettore's daughter L'Ebé, Rembrandt's birth had a considerable bearing on the direction that Ettore's life subsequently took. As a boy, Ettore went to the art school attached to the Pinacota di Brera, the great gallery in Milan, probably with the intention that he should follow in Carlo's footsteps. Even in childhood, it became evident that Rembrandt's artistic ability greatly exceeded that of his elder brother and he was much more likely to have the qualities that Carlo would have sought in a successor. Rembrandt did not follow his father though, becoming an eminent sculp-

tor, following the school of the French *animaliers*.

Carlo had a friend, Ludovico Prinetti, who with his partner Stucchi, had been making sewing machines in Milan since 1874. They had just begun to make bicycles and were enthusiasts for the newfangled pastime of motoring. They owned a De Dion-Bouton tricycle and at the age of 13 or 14, Ettore Bugatti was permitted to ride this vehicle. The De Dion-Bouton fired his imagination and he realised that this was the field in which he should attempt to make a career. He had already begun to accept that his artistic talent had limitations, and that he would never be the equal of his father or brother. Stucchi must have realised his potential however, and offered to take the youth into his works as a volunteer apprentice. Carlo was not keen though and it probably took some time for Bugatti to persuade his father that he should abandon the Pinacota and join Prinetti e Stucchi. In 1898, Carlo relented and Bugatti joined the firm at an opportune time, as the partners had decided to embark on the manufacture of their own motor tricycle, based on the De Dion-Bouton.

There is some doubt when Bugatti joined the firm. According to his own account and

Carlo Bugatti.

that of his daughter L'Ebé, he was already 17 years of age, so this must have been after his birthday in September 1898, but his name appears in the entry list of the Torino-Asti-Alessandria-Torino road race, held on 17 July 1898, in which he rode a Prinetti e

Stucchi tricycle and retired with engine failure. It is possible the partners already appreciated his enthusiasm and loaned him the machine before he joined them. They had just begun the manufacture of the tricycle and, like most manufacturers in those early days, they appreciated that success in the new sport of motor racing could bring excellent publicity. For the young Bugatti, he had achieved the remarkable distinction of competing in his first race and getting a 'works' drive before his 17th birthday.

Working in the Milan factory, Bugatti learned quickly; he studied the tricycle design and after a year, he had produced his own development, fitted with two single-cylinder engines. It was a comparatively simple conversion, the single engine drove the rear axle by a spur gear on the end of the crankshaft. The second engine, joining the first on the back axle, was turned round and its direction of rotation reversed, this also drove the spur gear. The result was a tricycle classified as 3½hp while the single-engined device was only 1¾hp. The twin-engined machine worked and Ettore drove it in the Verona-Brescia-Mantova-Verona race on 14 March 1899. The course was 100 miles (161km) and Ettore's main opponent among the 19 starters was Count Carlo Biscaretti, later the founder of the automobile museum in Turin, who was driving a De Dion-Bouton tricycle. At Brescia, Biscaretti had a lead of more than five minutes over Bugatti and maintained this lead at Mantova, but on the final leg back to Verona, Bugatti made up the lost time. The two tricycles crossed the line almost together, but Bugatti had started the race two minutes later, so was the winner. His average speed was 24.48mph (39.42kmh) and he collected a prize of 400 lire.

Over a century later it is hard to appreciate the nature of these early races. The cars were unreliable, with minimal brakes and ran on tyres which punctured all too frequently. The races were run over open roads with unmade surfaces which were a

sea of mud or produced blinding dust clouds, with hazards such as ox-drawn carts and pedestrians who knew little or nothing of motor cars. For a competitor to finish at all was a considerable feat, but to win at the speeds being achieved was remarkable; the drivers were men of singular courage and determination.

Bugatti was racing again six weeks later, this time in the 56-mile (90km) Torino-Pinerolo-Avigliana-Torino race on 30 April 1899. He was one of 32 starters and arrived back at Turin in first place, 20 minutes ahead of the 10hp Peugeot car which took second place, having averaged 33.83mph (54.48kmh). A week later, he was out again, on Saturday, 7 May taking third place in a time trial at the Guastalla Hippodrome, then the following day, he won the 52-mile (85km) Corsa Reggio Emilia and was rewarded with a special gold medal. The great French town-to-town races had already become the pinnacle of the sport and the most important in 1899 was the Paris-Bordeaux. This was run on Sunday, 24 May and Bugatti entered the twin-engined Prinetti e Stucchi tricycle. Carlo Bugatti was concerned about the 17-year-old boy going off to race in another country, so the youthful driver was accompanied by Dominique Lamberjack, who had become a friend. Lamberjack had been gaining a reputation first as a bicycle racer, then graduating to motorcycles. He was a few years older than Bugatti and presumably wiser. Bugatti was one of the 37 starters in the motorcycle class in which the tricycle was entered. He assembled with the other entrants at Buc, on the outskirts of Versailles, where the field of motorcycles was released in a mass start at 3.12am, soon after dawn. Unfortunately, the Prinetti e Stucci hit a dog during the race and had to withdraw.

While he had been racing, Bugatti's inventiveness had not lain idle, as he had built a four-wheel competition vehicle. In the spring of 1899, Prinetti e Stucchi had raised their sights and built their first car

which had two engines mounted at the front, driving the rear axle with a belt. It seems likely that Bugatti had adapted a version of this for his machine. It was classified as a quadricycle and Bugatti appears to have added the twin-engined rear axle from the tricycle, although the drive-train arrangements must have been complicated. Whatever its shortcomings, Bugatti made it work and the device had its first outing on 19 June when Bugatti drove it in the Padova-Bassano-Padova race over a course of 108 miles (175km). Once again, he was victorious, carrying off the first prize of 4,000 lire and averaging 27.68mph (44.58kmh).

The quadricycle must have worked sufficiently well to have attracted orders, as at the Brescia speed meeting on 10/11 September, at least three Prinetti e Stucchi quadricycles appeared in the entry list, apparently driven by customers, although these may have been the standard twin-engined model rather than the 'racing four'. The highlight of the meeting, run on the second day, was the Brescia-Cremona-Mantova-Verona-Brescia road race over 138 miles (223km). In this, Bugatti drove a tricycle, and it seems likely this was not a demotion from the quadricycle, as the tricycle was evidently the quicker vehicle. In the race, of the 26 starters, he finished third overall behind two De Dion-Bouton tricycles, while the best Prinetti e Stucchi quadricycle was 20 minutes behind Bugatti. Bugatti's season finished on a slightly muted note, his last event being the two-day meeting at Treviso on 29/30 October. After taking fourth place in a sprint race on the local hippodrome, he ran in the 50-mile (80km) Treviso-Conegliano-Treviso race the following day, but retired with a fuel blockage, although he had already hit a wall, buckled a wheel of his tricycle, and hurt his hand.

In 1900, Bugatti drove in fewer events and although the Italian competition season started at the beginning of April, his first event was the 47-mile (75km) Bologna-Corticella-Bologna race on 28 May. He drove a tricycle and romped home to an easy win by a margin of 11 minutes. He followed this by a class win with the quadricycle in the much tougher 136-mile (220km) Padova-Bassano-Padova race on 1 July. The quadricycle must have finished this race in good fettle, as the following day he took second place overall in a 6.2-mile (10km) sprint outside Padova, pushing a young Vincenzo Lancia, driving a Fiat, into third place. Taking sixth place in this sprint was another name for the future, Carlo Maserati, riding a Carcano motorcycle.

By the summer of 1900, Bugatti was becoming frustrated at Prinetti e Stucchi. The partners were contemplating a return to the simpler world of bicycles and sewing machines, so it seems likely that the firm was not making any money from its internal combustion enterprises. There was little prospect of any opportunity for the burgeoning ambitions of Bugatti, so he entered into a partnership with Count Gian Oberto Gulinelli. The Count had been one of the first customers to race a Prinetti e Stucchi quadricycle, driving it at the Brescia meeting in September 1899 and had driven it in several races in 1900, competing against the youthful Bugatti. The Count and his brother were willing to back Bugatti to enable him to produce a car of his own design. Rather reluctantly, Carlo Bugatti also agreed to provide some capital. Officine Gulinelli was established at Ferrara and in the autumn of 1900, work began on the first Bugatti-Gulinelli. This had a four-cylinder engine with automatic overhead inlet valves, dimensions of 90mm x 120mm, and a capacity of 3,054cc. The chassis was conventional with quarter elliptic springs, there was a four-speed gearbox and chain final drive. The car was fitted with a light, two-seat body and only weighed 1,450lb (660kg). On its first road test the car achieved 37mph (60kmh), a speed which Bugatti was confident could be increased with changed gearing. According to W. F. Bradley, in his biography of Ettore Bugatti, Bugatti did almost all the work on the first

car himself, making the drawings and the foundry patterns, supervising the forgings and doing the assembly himself.

In May 1901, the city of Milan organised a trade fair, the International Breeding and Sport Exhibition, which incorporated the First International Automobile Exhibition of Milan. This had ten classes for motor cars, so the prototype Bugatti-Gulinelli was entered. It won the class for 'the car of private construction proving to be the fastest among those exhibited and which joins to speed, the requirements of simplicity, solidity, optimum functioning and of clever construction' and the constructor received a cup and a diploma. *La Gazetta dello Sport* said in its report of the exhibition that the Bugatti-Gulinelli was 'a simple and most potent motor capable of exacting daily service and of very great speed if necessary'. The writer of this report was not the only one to be impressed by the car. Baron Eugenie De Dietrich, who was making cars at Niederbronn in Alsace, had sent an engineer to look at the machines on show in Milan. He gave a favourable report to the Baron about the Bugatti-Gulinelli, so Bugatti was invited to Niederbronn for discussions. After some protracted negotiations, probably slowed by the need for the intervention of Carlo Bugatti, as Ettore Bugatti was still a minor, and not able to enter into a contract without parental approval, an agreement was signed by the Baron and both Bugattis on 26 June 1902. This gave De Dietrich an exclusive licence to manufacture Bugatti cars and the sole selling rights for all countries except Italy. Bugatti undertook to supervise the design and production of cars for De Dietrich for seven years and was to receive a royalty on every car sold and a lump sum payable in instalments when he started work at Niederbronn. The Italian exception on the sales was probably part of a deal compensating the Gulinelli brothers, who had lost their designer and their motor car.

Bugatti must have taken the Bugatti-Gulinelli with him when he went to

The Prinetti & Stucchi tricycle with two De Dion-Bouton engines. On 14 March 1899, Ettore Bugatti won the Verona-Brescia-Mantova-Brescia race on a similar machine.

Niederbronn and it was probably this car which he drove in the Frankfurt race meeting on 31 August, as his car was reported to be a 20hp De Dietrich-Bugatti which would be the rating of the Gullineri car. It must have been rebodied as he had to carry three passengers. He took part in an eight-mile (12km) handicap race for gentlemen drivers and came second, having received a 250-metre start. In a ten-mile (16km) scratch race, he gained another second place behind a 40hp Mercedes-Simplex. It has been recorded that in October 1902, Bugatti, probably encouraged by his new-found wealth, married Barbara Maria Bolzoni, whom he had met in Milan. Some sources doubt the date of the marriage and suggest that this may have happened in February 1907; in the Bohemian, artistic world of the Bugatti family in Milan, the formality of a marriage would not have been regarded as significant. Bugatti and Barbara Maria took up residence at Niederbronn, in Alsace, which was then a part of the German Empire, having been annexed by the German Emperor as one of the spoils of

May 1901: The Bugatti-Gulinelli.

31 August 1902: Ettore Bugatti at the Frankfurt races with the first De Dietrich-Bugatti.

victory after the Franco-Prussian war of 1870.

As well as the Gulinelli car, he now worked on new designs. There was a twin-cylinder design and two four-cylinder engines destined for De Dietrich-Bugatti road cars. These had the cylinders cast in pairs, each surrounded by a cylindrical aluminium water jacket. The overhead valves were operated by pull-rods. The smaller engine rated at 24hp, had dimensions of 114mm x 140mm and a capacity of 5,308cc. The second engine had a bore and stroke of 130mm x 140mm respectively, a capacity of 7,433cc, and was rated at 42hp. Both these cars had wooden chassis frames, reinforced with steel flitch plates and there were semi-elliptic springs front and rear.

1903: The De Dietrich-Bugatti arrives at the Vienna Motor Show, driven by Ettore Bugatti.

The transmission had a four-speed gearbox with side chain final drive.

Bugatti's third design was much more dramatic. The European motor racing world buzzed with excitement at the announcement of the major road race of the 1903 season. This was to be the most ambitious town-to-town race yet, and would run from Paris to Madrid, on 24 and 25 May, with an overnight stop at Bordeaux. Every manufacturer of note proposed to take part, as well as a multitude of private entrants; Bugatti, already a highly experienced racing driver did not want not be left out. He designed a racing De Dietrich-Bugatti. Little is known

about this car, but photographs show the four-cylinder engine had the blocks cast in pairs with cylindrical water jackets, similar to the road cars. Bugatti said many years later, that the engine had two valves per cylinder operated by an overhead camshaft. There was a tubular chassis frame which carried the cooling water from the radiator to the engine and chain drive transmission. The unusual feature of the car was the low build, with the driver sitting right at the back, above the rear axle and peering over the engine. Like so many competition cars

since, it fell foul of the scrutineers, in this case the French state mining department, which had to ensure the cars competing in the race were of a safe construction. The officials of the department felt that the driver did not have sufficient visibility. The visibility was probably adequate, but the car broke the canons of current orthodoxy and so it was rebuilt with a conventional chassis frame with the driver sitting in a more acceptable position. Two De Dietrichs were entered for the race with Bugatti and Emile Mathis as the drivers, but neither started. As

1903: The car prepared for the Paris-Madrid race and rejected by the scrutineers. Two spare sprockets are strapped on behind.

the race ended in tragedy and was abandoned at Bordeaux, Bugatti lost little by being excluded. A month later, a pair of De Dietrich-Bugattis were entered for Bugatti and Mathis in the Circuit des Ardennes, but again neither started the race.

Bugatti did get a race in 1903, as he drove at the Frankfurt meeting in August. Driving one of the 41hp De Dietrich-Bugattis, he finished in third place in the race for amateur drivers, behind Willy Poege's 60hp Mercedes and Marius Barbarou's 60hp Benz-Parsifal. The town-to-town races had been abandoned after the disasters of the Paris–Madrid and the Gordon-Bennett Trophy had now become the major racing event. This was contested by national teams of three cars, entered by the national automobile clubs. It was a requirement of the race that every component of a competing car had to be made in its country of origin, each country selected its team by eliminating trials and most major manufacturers prepared cars in the hope of being selected. It was reported that a De Dietrich-Bugatti was being made ready for the eliminating trials run by the Automobilclub von Deutschland to select the German team for the 1904 race and the car would be driven by Ettore Bugatti.

Nothing came of the Gordon-Bennett project, which is not surprising, as relations between Bugatti and Baron De Dietrich were deteriorating. The cause was the unreliability of the Bugatti-designed cars, and the Baron terminated the agreement for the employment of Bugatti as his designer. Bugatti seems to have left De Dietrich early in 1904, although Griff Borgeson, in his book *Bugatti*, speaks of a surviving letter of dismissal written in 1905. This left Bugatti out of work, and he now had to support a wife and a young daughter, L'Ebé, who had been born in 1903. His erstwhile team-mate Emile Mathis, provided the answer. Mathis was the agent in Strasbourg for De Dietrich and several other makes. Mathis wanted to become a manufacturer and Bugatti presented him with an opportunity, so by an agreement of 1 April 1904, he was engaged by Mathis to design a range of cars. A drawing office was set up in the attic of the Hôtel de Paris, owned by Mathis's father on the Rue de la Nuée Bleue, in the middle of Strasbourg. A company was established, Société Alsacienne de Constructions Mécaniques with a factory at Illkirch-Graffenstaden in the south western suburbs of Strasbourg where the Bugatti-designed cars were built under the various titles of Hermes, Hermes-Simplex and Mathis. As before, Bugatti was to have a royalty for each car sold.

The first Hermes was shown to the public at the Paris Salon in the autumn of 1904. It was called the 45/60 PS model and had the usual four-cylinder engine with the cylinders cast in pairs and covered with cylindrical water jackets. The curious pull-rods persisted for the inlet valves and there were side exhaust valves, the water pump and magneto were driven by bevel gears from the rear of the camshaft. The dimensions were the same as the 42hp De Dietrich-Bugatti, giving a capacity of 7,433cc. The four-speed gearbox was driven through a multi-plate wet clutch and the final drive was by chain. The chassis was conventional and there were two water-cooled transmission brakes as well as rear wheel braking. A 90hp version with a capacity of approximately 10 litres was announced, but it seems doubtful if any were built. The great Bugatti historian, Hugh Conway, believes that only about 15 Bugatti-designed Hermes were built, but others have suggested the total could be 60–70. Bugatti drove a 45/60 in the 1905 Herkomer Trial which was

intended to develop the touring car. It was run between the 10th and 17 August on a 582-mile (935km) course in southern Germany with the start and finish at Munich; en route the competitors took part in a concours and two speed trials. The Hermes did not appear in the results.

As it had been with the De Dietrich, reliability was a problem with the Hermes and in 1906, Bugatti and Mathis parted. The failure of the De Dietrich-Bugatti had so dispirited the Baron that he abandoned car production altogether, but Mathis was made of sterner stuff and became one of the largest car distributors in Europe and made Mathis cars until 1950. Bugatti was out of work again, so he started on the design for a touring car in the hope that he would be able to sell it to a manufacturer. He obtained financial backing and established a small workshop outside Graffenstaden. Assisted by three draughtsmen, he prepared the drawings and a prototype car was assembled, supervised by Ernest Friderich, a mechanic who had been working for

Mathis, and who had been engaged in the Hermes project. The large industrial firm Gasmotorenfabrik Deutz of Cologne wanted to make cars, so Bugatti produced his design. The directors of Deutz liked it and appointed Bugatti as a consulting engineer to develop the design and put the car into production. His agreement with Deutz was dated 1 September 1907, but it seems that he was working for the company well before the agreement was signed. Bugatti and his family moved to Cologne and took up residence in a villa in the grounds of the Deutz factory, but the agreement did not bind Bugatti to work solely for Deutz, which left him free to seek other consultancies or to pursue projects of his own.

The design was a four-cylinder engine with a monobloc, mounted on an alloy crankcase. It had two valves per cylinder operated by curved banana tappets, with rollers at the end of the tappets, from an overhead camshaft. The water pump, magneto drive and clutch were similar to the Hermes and there was a four-speed

1905: One of the Hermes-Mathis cars entered for the Herkomer Cup.

5–11 June 1907: An historic car – the first to carry the Bugatti name. A pre-Deutz car at the Herkomer Cup/Kaiserpreis trials. Ettore Bugatti stands at the front.

gearbox, a multi-plate clutch and chain drive. The design provided the basis for a range of cars. The initial design became the Type 8A Deutz and had engine dimensions of 145mm x 150mm and a capacity of 9,920cc, it had chain drive and the chassis had a wheelbase of 122in (3,098mm). There were variations on this theme with engine capacities ranging from 6,400cc, down to 2,612cc. There were two significant features of the car, the radiator shape was identical to the first true Bugatti, the

Type 10 which would soon appear, and the radiator badge was an oval, a shape which Bugatti would soon adopt as his own. The similarity of the design to the Hermes in some respects, must have prompted Mathis to write to Bugatti asking if he was interested in buying the unused stock of Hermes parts lying at Graffenstaden.

Bugatti made a second design for Deutz in 1908/9, which had a 92mm x 120mm 3,190cc overhead camshaft engine, with a front cross-mounted magneto and water

pump, with the camshaft driven by bevel gears from the front of the crankshaft. There was a four-speed gearbox, a torque rod to the conventional rear axle and semi-elliptic springs front and rear; the design was beginning to show the hallmarks of those for which Bugatti would soon become renowned. Deutz had problems getting the range of cars into production and apart from prototypes, the first did not appear until 1909. Bugatti drove a Deutz in the 1909 Prince Henry Trial, but as had happened with De Dietrich and Hermes, relations became strained, and in December 1909, Deutz terminated the agreement with

Bugatti and soon afterwards, stopped making cars. The firm survived, making commercial vehicles, later becoming Magirus-Deutz. The breach probably caused Bugatti little concern, as he was already aiming at a bigger and better target.

As the agreement with Deutz permitted Bugatti to tackle other projects, during 1907/8 he began work on the design of a much smaller car, this having a four-cylinder engine with dimensions of 62mm x 100mm and a capacity of 1,207cc. The block was a single casting and was mounted on an alloy crankcase. The overhead camshaft worked the valves through banana tappets, although the camshaft was enclosed, the tappets and valve springs were exposed and were lubricated by oiling felts. The magneto and water pump were driven from a cross shaft at the front of the engine. The crankshaft ran in three plain bearings and drove a small separately mounted four-speed gearbox through a multi-plate cast iron and steel clutch that had become a distinctive Bugatti feature. An open propeller shaft drove to a conventional back axle, with a separate torque stay fastened to the axle and the rear of the gearbox. The front and rear axles were carried on semi-elliptic springs. The wheelbase was 6ft 6¾in (2.0m) and the track was 3 ft 9¼in (1.25m). It is generally accepted by historians that this car was regarded by Bugatti as the Type 10, being his tenth design. (For convenience in this text, 'Type' will be expressed as 'T'.) The car had superficial similarities with the FE model Isotta Fraschini which ran in the Coupe des Voiturettes at Dieppe, a supporting event to the 1908 GP de L'Automobile Club de France, the 'Grand Prix' and the major race of the year. Some historians have suggested that the FE was designed by Bugatti, but this seems unlikely as the FE was a much larger car and, apart from the gearbox, there are few common technical features. Bugatti himself did not claim the design, although it is possible that Bugatti saw the FE, appreciated the qualities of the design and used

1908: The chain-driven Deutz, the T8.

1909: Ettore Bugatti with the T9 shaft-driven Deutz at the Prince Henry Trials.

1910: The T10, Le Homard.

some of the features in the T10. Some aspects of Bugatti's design were developments of those which had already appeared on the Hermes and Deutz.

Bugatti must have realised there was little point in trying again to sell his design to an existing manufacturer: his future lay in making the car himself. The prototype T10 was built in the cellar of the Deutz villa in Cologne; Bugatti, helped by Friderich who was on leave during his military service, had to dismantle it to get it out. Bugatti named the car 'Pur Sang', it had an aluminium bonnet, but the bath-tub body, axles and frame were painted an orange red, so the Bugatti family always called it 'Le Homard' (The Lobster). It is not certain when the T10 was finished, but Bugatti drove it at a race meeting at Frankfurt in August 1909; running in the 6hp or 1,500cc class, he finished sixth. The car was entered at that meeting as a Deutz. In September 1909, the T10 was inspected by

the renowned airman Louis Bleriot who had just achieved fame by being the first to fly across the English Channel. He was attending an air show at Cologne and used the car as his transport during the meeting. He was very enthusiastic about it and confirmed Bugatti's view that he should produce it himself.

Bugatti went to Agustin de Vizcaya, a financier who had been introduced to him in 1905, probably by Count Gulinelli. De Vizcaya, who was Spanish but owned a large estate at Jagerhof, near Molsheim, about 17 miles (28km) west of Strasbourg, suggested that Bugatti should lease an unoccupied dye works at Molsheim as a factory. Bugatti, accompanied by Friderich visited the works, driving the T10. The owner, Mlle Geisser agreed to let the dye works and half the adjoining house to Bugatti for 5,000DM, so he moved in with his family at Christmas 1909. The family was now larger, as a second daughter, Lidia,

had been born in 1907, followed by a son on 15 January 1909. The son was named Gianoberto in recognition of Bugatti's support from Count Gulinelli, but was always called Jean. With support from the Darmstadt Bank, in which de Vizcaya was a substantial shareholder, the equipping of the factory began in January 1910 and Friderich was entrusted with recruiting workers from the locality. Five production cars had been sold to customers by the end of 1910. There were two changes to the design, the bore was increased to 65mm giving a capacity of 1,327cc and the valve gear was fully enclosed and in its revised form, the car became known as the T13, the longer chassis variants with 7ft 10½in (2.4m) and 8ft 4in (2.5m) wheelbases, were known respectively as the T15 and T17.

The first recorded competition of the T13 and thus of the Bugatti, was at the Gaillon hill-climb on 2 October 1910. The course, a straight kilometre on the N15 road was in the Seine Valley, near Vernon, with a gradient of 1 in 10, climbing out of Gaillon village to the north west, on the Rouen side. The competitors were given a flying start. The Bugatti driver was Darritchon, presumably a customer, who recorded a time of 63.8 seconds to take second place in the small touring class. There are reports that Ettore Bugatti drove a Hermes, entered as a Bugatti in the 1905 Herkomer Cup meeting, but this report is unsubstantiated and it seems that the glory of being the first to compete with a Bugatti in a speed event, lies with M Darritchon.

An agent had been appointed in Paris, M Huet at 3 Square St Ferdinand, and in January 1911, the intrepid Huet took a bath-tub bodied T13 through from Paris to Monte Carlo in the first Monte Carlo Rally. Although he finished, Huet was not placed, but he probably showed greater fortitude than Rougier, the winner who had the advantage of a saloon body on his Turcat-Mery. In the summer of 1911 the results began to come. It started with a second place at the Limonest hill-climb, near Lyon in May, but the driver's identity is not known. On 4 and 5 June, two T13s, driven by Agustin de Vizcaya and Gilbert, ran at what would now be called a club meeting at Le Mans, organised by the AC de la Sarthe. De Vizcaya was perhaps getting a drive as a return for the financial support being given by the Darmstadt Bank. The meeting comprised a series of sprints, de Vizcaya was running in the 65mm bore touring class and won the flying kilometre in 41.8 seconds and the standing start half kilometre in 35.4 seconds. Gilbert ran in the 80mm touring class and won over the same distances. It was at Le Mans, a month later, that the big breakthrough came.

The Automobile Club de France had launched the Grand Prix in 1906 and had repeated the race in 1907 and 1908, but in the latter year, much to the chagrin of the French manufacturers, German cars had taken the first three places. The ACF felt there was little point in putting on an event for the benefit of the German motor industry, also, French manufacturers suddenly lost interest, so the race was quietly dropped in 1909 and 1910. In 1911, the AC de la Sarthe decided to organise a free formula race, using part of the circuit on which the 1906 Grand Prix had been run. The ACF, while unwilling to try its hand at the Grand Prix, gave support to the race which was expected to bring back the French manufacturers, and permitted it to have the title of Grand Prix de France. Initially a superb entry seemed likely but by race day, 23 July, this had faded away and the field was reduced to 14 cars, a mixture of older grand prix machines and some modern competitors. Among the number was a T13 driven by Ernest Friderich, by far the smallest car in the field, and was described by Charles Faroux, the famous French journalist, as 'a Lilliputian speedbox'. As an entry which came from Germany, the T13 was painted white, the German racing colour, and for the race, centre lock wire wheels replaced the usual wooden artillery type fitted to the produc-

1910: Prince Henry Trials with Ettore Bugatti in the T12.

21 October 1910: Darritchon with the T13 at the Gaillon hill-climb; the lamps seem to have aerodynamic aids.

23 July 1911: Ernest Friderich with the T10 before the Grand Prix de France.

Grand Prix de France: The mechanic plays his part during the race.

tion cars. When tested before the race, the car was timed at 66mph (106kmh). The gallant Friderich was being thrown in at the deep end, as it seems this was his first race and his task was not easy. The race was over 12 laps of a 33.75-mile (54km) circuit making a race distance of 405 miles (651km). It started at Pontlieu on the outskirts of Le Mans, went south-east on the D304 road, then turned right just short of Le Grande Luce, going on country lanes to Ecommoy and returning to Le Mans on the N138, using what later became the Mulsanne Straight of the 24-hour circuit. It was an immensely hot day, the road surface was poor and soon broke up into stones and dust.

The race began at 8am and the cars were released at one-minute intervals. From the start there was a battle between Maurice Fournier with a 1907 GP La Licorne and Victor Héméry driving a 1910 S61 Fiat. Fournier, a veteran of the early open road races, went off the road between Ecommoy and Le Mans when his front axle broke, he and his riding mechanic were both killed. This left Héméry fighting off Arthur Duray's 1906 GP Lorraine-Dietrich, but the Lorraine's differential broke leaving Héméry in a commanding lead. In the intense heat, all the cars were overheating and stopping with tyre problems, the exception was the tiny white Bugatti which scuttled around the circuit, impervious to the conditions and impressing everyone by its pace and reliability. As the faster cars dropped out Friderich moved up the field; the identity of his riding mechanic is unknown, but he was probably one of the fitters from Molsheim. No provision had been made for a spare wheel, so the long-suffering man carried one in the cockpit for some of the distance as a safeguard against tyre failure. Héméry, who had done the second half of the race with only top gear, came home the winner, the pursuing cars were then flagged off. The Bugatti was second, it had covered ten laps and finished in front of Fernand Gabriel's 6-litre Rolland-

Pilain which had been specially built for the race.

Friderich's drive brought a transformation, the name of Bugatti was now known and respected. The orders were coming in and there were 65 workers in the Molsheim factory, making eight chassis a month. An unknown driver celebrated Bastille Day by winning two classes at the Nancy hill-climb on 14 July and on 11 August, de Vizcaya took a touring-bodied T13 to Mont Ventoux, the formidable 6,000ft (1,900m) hill-climb in Provence. Despite a broken spring and a puncture, he won the 65mm touring class. Dillon Kavanagh seems to have taken over the Bugatti agency from Huet and on 1 October, Kavanagh ran a T13 at Gaillon, winning his class in 63.2 seconds. The T13 was not the only manufacturing activity in the small works. While Bugatti had been working in Cologne, he had designed a four-cylinder 100mm x 160mm, 5,027cc engine. Unlike the T13, this had rockers between cams and valves but was similar to the smaller engine, a vertical bevel shaft driving the camshaft, with a cross shaft driving the Bosch magneto and water pump. This engine had another feature which would become a Bugatti hallmark, with three valves per cylinder, two inlet and one exhaust. There was a single Zenith carburettor. In 1910, this engine was installed in a chain-driven chassis, with strong similarities to the chassis designed for Hermes and it had the first horseshoe-shaped radiator. According to an account given to Griff Borgeson by Roland Bugatti, Ettore's second son, his father chose this radiator design as it was the shape of an egg, which Carlo Bugatti had declared was the perfect shape.

This first car with chain drive was the T11 or T12, the chain assembly having a distinct similarity to that fitted to the Deutz. A second version became the T18, and it is believed that eight of this type were built. One of the customers was Roland Garros, the French pioneer airman who became a close friend of Bugatti, and for

4 August 1911: Agustin de Vizcaya driving a T13 at Mont Ventoux. (*Guy Griffiths Collection*)

this reason, the T18 is sometimes known as the Type 'Garros'. Garros was killed in action in 1918 and when Roland Bugatti was born in 1922, he was named in memory of Garros. Bugatti drove the T12 in the 1910 Prince Henry Trial, but had no success. During 1911, an experimental car was built at Molsheim which used two T13 engines in tandem, apparently in an extended T13 chassis. This had a crude body and artillery wheels, and the engines were coupled by a rubberised leather flywheel. When tested, the car was timed at 86mph (138kmh). It seems to have made one competition appearance when Friderich drove it at Gaillon in October 1912, but third gear stripped, so he did not complete the course. It is possible that Bugatti had conceived the car as a possible

contender in the 3-litre voiturette class, but the venture was abandoned.

Competition successes continued in 1912 with Bugatti himself taking part. He drove a T18 'Garros' at the Limonest hill-climb on 19 May and took first place. A week later he was at the AC de la Sarthe meeting where he won the efficiency award with the T18 while Friderich won the touring and racing classes with a T13. The pair were at Mont Ventoux in July and once again, carried off their classes, Bugatti was fourth overall, his passenger was Alex Schnell, his first racing mechanic. On 6 October Friderich won the racing class at Gaillon, the T13 recording 53.4 seconds, and Tonello won the touring class in 58 seconds. The first foreign sales of T13s were being made. Some had gone to Britain in

26 May 1912: Ettore Bugatti with the T18 at the AC de la Sarthe meeting.

1912/13 and the first British competition success came in 1913 when E. M. Griffiths won his class at the Cardiff MC Rhubina hill-climb on 24 May. South Wales attracted the T13s as P. O. Serck ran at the Caerphilly hill-climb on 19 June.

Although now an established manufacturer, Bugatti was still willing to produce designs for others, perhaps to boost his funds during the first tentative footsteps of his new venture. On 16 November 1911 he signed an agreement to design a small car for Peugeot; this had a 55mm x 90mm,

855cc, T-head (i.e. side valve with separate inlet and exhaust camshafts) four-cylinder engine. There was a two-speed transmission using two concentric propeller shafts, one solid, the other tubular, each driving a separate row of teeth on the crown wheel, with dog engagement. The front suspension used semi-elliptic springs, but the rear used the Bugatti reversed quarter elliptics. The wheelbase was 5ft 11in (1.80m) and the track 3ft 5in (1.05m). This diminutive machine which was Bugatti's T16, became the famous Bébé Peugeot and seemed to

have little sporting pretensions, but during the summer of 1913, two major cyclecar races were held in France. The first, at Amiens had been run over part of the circuit used for the GP de l'ACF and the second, with the imposing title of Grand Prix de l'UMF Cyclecars, was run by the AC de la Sarthe on 4 August over five laps of the circuit used for the 1911 GP de France. Autos et Cycles Peugeot took the 167-mile (268km) race seriously and entered three Bébé Peugeots. The race was an historic landmark as it was possibly the first road race in which a massed start was used. The cars were not quick enough to hold the faster Ronteix and Violet-Bogey which were more sporting machines, but the best Bébé, driven by Bas, was third, and only two minutes behind the winner, who had averaged 46.35mph (74.53kmh). The other Bébés, driven by Chichon and Blanc were fifth and sixth. In August 1913, a Bébé won its class at Mont Ventoux.

The Automobile Club de France had revived the Grand Prix in 1912, it was a resounding success as was the 1913 race. When the 1914 regulations were announced, it was evident that this would bring out the most advanced designs yet seen in racing. Every manufacturer with racing pretensions was likely to have a team in Lyon for the race, which was to be held on 4 July. It would have seemed that the Grand Prix would have been an ideal stage for Bugatti to advance his ambitions, but the more perceptive observer would have already noted that no pure racing designs had emerged from Molsheim. All the racing Bugattis so far, had been developments of existing production designs, thus avoiding the usual crippling expense of building pure racing cars. Automobiles Ettore Bugatti was still a small concern, producing cars in relatively limited numbers and making its way slowly; 175 cars had been built in 1913 and early in 1914, production had increased to 27 cars a month. Bugatti had great racing ambitions, and while the Grand Prix was still out of reach, he was seeking a race which would enhance the prestige of the marque.

It seems that Bugatti had already visited the United States, probably to buy machine tools, and his sartorial tastes had aroused some comment, but in May 1914, he went there again, this time with a T18 which had been entered for the Indianapolis 500-mile race on 30 May. Peugeot and Sunbeam had sent factory entries for the 1913 race and the Peugeot of Jules Goux had won, gaining the French firm much prestige and a useful prize purse. The race regulations permitted a maximum engine size of 450cu in (7,375cc) and a weight limit of 2,300lb

1913: An equestrian Ettore Bugatti at Molsheim with a T13. (Guy Griffiths Collection)

Friderich with the twin-engined lengthened T13.

4 August 1913: Bas in No. 47, the T16 Bébé Peugeot which finished third in the Grand Prix de l'UMF, beside the second-placed Violet.

Friderich in the shaft-drive T18 which he drove in the 1914 Indianapolis 500-Mile Race.

(1,045kg) so the T18 was eligible. A shaft-drive car was prepared for the race, a new crankshaft was fitted, which increased the stroke to 180mm and the capacity to 5,655cc. Continental supplied the 820 x 120 tyres. The car was presumably shipped from Cherbourg to New York and thence to Indianapolis by train. Ernest Friderich was nominated as the driver, and the car, painted white, was regarded as a German entry. A maximum of 30 cars were permitted to start and as there were 45 entries, only the fastest 30 had a place on the grid. The qualifying must have indicated to Bugatti that it was going to be a tough race. Friderich could only qualify in 22nd place at an average speed of 87.73mph (141.06kmh), while the fastest qualifier was the Peugeot of Georges Boillot at a speed of 99.86mph (160.57kmh). The race was run before a crowd of 100,000, which saw French cars take the first four places, led home by René Thomas's Delage, but it was an unhappy race for Bugatti. On the fourth lap, Friderich stopped at his pit as the near side rear tyre had come off the rim, and according to one report, this happened about 12 times during the race, which must indicate there was a substantial mechanical maladjustment. The car retired after 134 laps when a pinion ball bearing broke in the rear axle, by which time, Friderich was 40 laps behind the leader.

Another T18 ran at Indianapolis in 1915. This was not as might have been expected, the 1914 car, left in the USA, but a chain-driven car which had been sold to a Charles W. Fuller of Pawtucket, Rhode Island. Fuller entered the car for the 400-mile (644km) Grand Prize of America race on an odd, 3.8-mile (6.2km) circuit, being part road and part board track, in San Francisco on 27 February 1915. It was driven by Johnny Marquis and only lasted for six laps before being eliminated by ignition problems when in 21st place. Marquis drove the car in the 300-mile (483km) Vanderbilt Cup on the same circuit a week later, on 6 March, but retired again. On 17 March, he took the car to the Venice Grand Prix on the outskirts of Los Angeles and this time it ran well and took fourth place. The performance at Venice impressed Barney Oldfield, who was one of the leading American drivers and he asked Fuller to enter the car for the 1915 Indianapolis '500' on 31 May. The race regulations had been changed and the maximum permitted engine capacity was 300cu in (4,917cc), so the car was taken to the White Motor Co. in Cleveland, Ohio and a new crankshaft was fitted, reducing the stroke to 150mm and the capacity to 4,713cc. Oldfield tried the car in the qualifying trials, but did not like it, and decided he did not want the drive when a connecting rod broke. It was repaired and taken over by George Hill who managed to qualify it in the penultimate place at 81.52mph (131.08kmh). In the race, the white car with black wheels did not distinguish itself, retiring after 20 laps with a broken water pump gear.

Soon after Bugatti and Friderich returned from the United States, in June 1914, Gavril Princip assassinated the Archduke Ferdinand at Sarajevo, and Europe began a six-week slide into war. On 28 July, Austria had declared war on Serbia, and this was followed three days later, on the 31st at 7pm, by a formal declaration of war by Germany on Russia. The 2.7-mile (4.3km) banked Brooklands track had opened in 1907 and was the centre of British motor sport, when the fashionable crowd gathered there for the Bank Holiday meeting on Monday, 3 August. Germany, claiming that French aircraft had flown over its territory, was presenting France with a declaration of war, so those present on that hot summer afternoon knew it would only be a matter of hours before Britain became embroiled in the conflict. A T13 ran at the meeting, driven by Harold Lambert who had a good afternoon as his black and white painted car first won the *Light Car and Cyclecar* handicap, lapping the track at 70.95mph (114.08kmh) then went on to win the

17 March 1915: Johnny Marquis in the chain-driven T18 at the Venice Grand Prix, Los Angeles.

75mph Short Handicap, pushing his lap speed up to 72.71mph (116.91kmh). Lambert, who was the sales manager for Jarrott & Letts, the London Bugatti agents, was the brother of Percy Lambert, who was the first man to cover 100 miles (160km) in one hour at Brooklands, in 1913, driving a Talbot. Another T13 ran at Brooklands in 1914, driven by N. S. Hind and fitted with a polished mahogany body.

In 1914, Bugatti had been redesigning the T13 engine, the aim being to have a competitive car for the Coupe des Voiturettes at Le Mans on 16 August and possibly for the Grand Prix des Voitures Legérès, formerly the Coupe de L'Auto. This would have been held at Clermont-Ferrand on 23 August, over part of the circuit used previously for the 1905 Gordon-Bennett Trophy. The new engine had radical changes: there were roller big ends and the bore was enlarged to 66mm which increased the capacity to 1,368cc. The valve

gear was fully enclosed and pressure lubricated, while the combustion chamber was altered to provide for four valves per cylinder and there were eight sparking plugs, a row of four on each side of the engine.

As war approached, Bugatti's position was anomalous. He was still an Italian national, he was living in Germany but he had decided that his allegiance lay with France. He had adopted a French lifestyle, French was the language spoken in his household, and he spoke it without a trace of his Italian origins, and he was bringing up his children to regard themselves as French. His factory was in Germany, albeit in territory which France yearned to recover, his cars were raced in German colours and as German entries, but he felt no allegiance to Germany and if war came, he had no desire to support the German cause. On the morning of 1 August, Germany announced the mobilisation of her army, this moved units to their war positions and recalled reservists to the colours. It was followed that evening by the German declaration of war on Russia. The Franco-Russian treaty of 1900 guaranteed that France would come to Russia's aid, and during the afternoon of the 1st, it was proclaimed that the French Army would mobilise the following day. War between Germany and France was imminent and was precipitated two days later by the German allegations of violated air space.

Friderich as a reservist, heard the news of the intended mobilisation on 1 August and immediately travelled to Switzerland, just before the frontier was closed, from where he was able to enter France and join his unit, the 8th Artillery at Luneville. Bugatti knew that Alsace was likely to become a war zone, if not a battlefield, when war came between France and Germany. He wanted to go to France but the Franco-German frontier was already closed, so on the same day as Friderich departed, Bugatti took his family to Stuttgart which he knew would be safer than Molsheim. Having ensured their immediate safety, he returned to Molsheim. Five of the 16-valve T13s were being built; two were finished, but before he departed, Friderich removed the camshafts and camboxes from the three incomplete cars, wrapped them in oiled paper and buried them in the garden of the family house. With the help of a friend, Bugatti took the two finished T13s and the 5-litre Indianapolis car to Stuttgart.

The Bugatti family, with the three cars, travelled to Friedrichshafen on the Swiss frontier, then waited for a permit to cross the frontier. Germany was probably reluctant to let him go as his abilities would have been of considerable use to the German war effort, but he was an Italian. Italy had not entered the war and was maintaining a strict neutrality, so to have detained him would have caused diplomatic problems. After a wait of nearly three weeks, the permit was issued and Bugatti passed through Switzerland and thence to Milan. The two T13s and the T18 were stored in a cellar, and Bugatti went to Rome, offering his services to the Italian war ministry. Political unrest had forced Italy to take a neutral stance, but the outbreak of the war had brought an acute economic crisis to the country, so the war ministry was probably in no position to give Bugatti funds to develop a gun which he had designed. When he was told that his services were not required, he asked permission to go to Paris and offer his designs to the French government. The leave was granted and Bugatti arrived in Paris in October or November 1914. It may be surmised that if the Italian war ministry had retained Bugatti's services, the history of motor racing could have been very different.

With the style that was now an innate part of his life, Bugatti immediately established himself at the Grand Hôtel, 2 Rue Scribe where he took a suite of rooms and set up a drawing office, while a workshop was established in the Rue Jean Jaurès, adjoining the Seine at Puteaux, about four miles (7km) from the Grand Hôtel. He was joined by some of the staff from Molsheim. The French Army had realised that the technology of air warfare was leaping ahead and there was a need for a new generation of much more powerful and advanced aero engines. Bugatti was asked by the French Army to design a new engine and shortly after his arrival in Paris, his brother Rembrandt introduced him to the Duc de Guiche, an aristocratic scientist who had a well-equipped laboratory and workshop in the Rue Chaptal. Here, the designs emerging from the Grand Hôtel drawing office were built up into a prototype eight-cylinder engine which was given a 50-hour test in the Delaunay-Belleville factory in 1916. The design was bought by Delaunay-Belleville and by Diatto in Italy, but few were made as there was a demand for more powerful engines. Bugatti responded to this by redesigning the eight-cylinder with a three-valve layout and mounting two of these in parallel on a common crankcase with geared crankshafts.

Throughout this time his work was being backed by the French government, but on 6 April 1917, the United States entered the war and soon afterwards, a US mission was sent to Paris to procure aircraft and aero engine designs suitable for production in the United States. The mission inspected the 16-cylinder engine and watched preliminary tests at the Rue Chaptal workshop, it seemed promising so the prototype was shipped to the United States, accompanied by Friderich who had been released from the French Army to assist Bugatti. He had served with distinction at Nancy and Arras and was awarded the Croix de Guerre in May 1915. Attempts to develop the engine and put it into production at the Duesenberg factory in Elizabeth, New Jersey were disastrous as there were many expensive failures on the test bench. When the war ended on 11 November 1918, only a few pre-production engines had been built and the project was abandoned, but for Bugatti, the outcome had been highly satisfactory as the US Army had paid him $100,000 for the design, a substantial sum at that time.

Chapter 2

A chrysalis in Molsheim

WHEN THE FIRST WORLD WAR ended, the victorious Allied armies advanced to the German frontier and the French army occupied Alsace; in July 1919, the Treaty of Versailles formally returned Alsace to France. Friderich returned from the United States in December 1918 and rejoined Bugatti in Paris. Shortly afterwards, they went back to Molsheim and found that although the factory was neglected, it was undamaged as it had not been in the battle area. Bugatti had been prepared to abandon Molsheim and set up a new factory at La Malmaison, near Paris, but when he inspected the Molsheim works, and found it usable, he decided to return. During the war it had been used for making valves and many of the former workers were still there and anxious to work for Bugatti again. Initially, all the former staff were dismissed, but the best were re-engaged immediately. Bugatti says he received no compensation for the disruption of his business from the French government. This is not wholly surprising as the French attitude to Alsace must have been ambivalent, while it was territory being returned to France, it had been part of Germany to which the inhabitants had owed nominal allegiance during the war. The French government felt there was a need for some indoctrination of the Alsace population. The schoolrooms had the slogan painted on the walls 'France is our country'. Bugatti could comfort himself that although he had not received any compensation from France, the US dollars made an adequate substitute.

The T13 went into production again and, according to Friderich, ten chassis were completed in March 1919; it was announced that the T18 would also be made again, but none appeared. The three incomplete 16-valve racers were still at the factory and the camshafts were exhumed and fitted to the cars. The two cars which had been taken to Milan had been damaged when the cellar was flooded, but had subsequently been sent to Paris and now returned to Molsheim where the ravages of the flood were made good. The Confederation Générale du Travail, the main trade union, attempted to call a general strike in May 1920, but this failed through lack of support and it must have made little impact at Molsheim.

Motor racing in France was slow to start again after the war. The east of the country was in ruins, 1.7 million Frenchmen had died and the people were exhausted. It was a year before thoughts turned again to happier pursuits such as motor racing. The Automobile Club de l'Ouest, which had evolved from the earlier Sarthe club, proposed to run the postponed 1914 race for cyclecars and for voiturettes under 1,400cc, so it was revived in 1920 and became the first major post-war event to be held in France. It was run at Le Mans on 29 August and attracted an entry of 26 cars. Three of the 1914 16-valve T13s were entered and this seems to have been the first time that an entry in an international race was made by 'Automobiles Ettore Bugatti'.

It is not recorded which of the cars came from the cellar or which were the archaeological finds. The drivers were the experienced Friderich, Pierre de Vizcaya, the son of Agustin de Vizcaya, and Michele Baccoli, who worked in the Molsheim factory and was probably a test driver. Baccoli was a long-standing friend of the Bugatti family and had looked after the cars in Milan during the War. The cars retained the 66mm bore, and Friderich's car had two plugs per cylinder, but de Vizcaya's had only one. *The Autocar* reported that the engine developed 29.5bhp at 2,750rpm, which seems somewhat low, with a single Zenith carburettor and a compression ratio of 5.5:1, the output was probably about 40bhp at 4,000rpm. The crankshaft ran in three plain bearings. There was the now-standard multi-plate clutch and a four-speed gearbox with a right-hand gate change. The brakeless front axle was a conventional H-section, the rear brakes with cast-iron shoes were operated by an outside lever, while the brake pedal worked a band brake on the transmission, and the car ran on centre lock wire wheels with 710 x 90 tyres.

The race was held on a ten-mile (17km) circuit, south of Le Mans, starting in the outskirts of the town, at what later became the Pontlieu hairpin on the 24-hour circuit of the 1920s. It ran down the Mulsanne Straight then turned right and went across country towards Arnage, turning right again and returning to Pontlieu. The race distance was 24 laps, a total of 255 miles (410km). During practice, de Vizcaya's engine had overheated and was stripped to inspect the bearings. The race began at 9.30am, the cars were lined up in pairs at the start and released at 30-second intervals. Friderich's riding mechanic was Etien, whom some reports said was only 12 years old; de Vizcaya was accompanied by Emil Mischall, a 17-year-old apprentice from Molsheim, and Baccoli had another apprentice, George Lutz. At the end of the first lap, de Vizcaya was in the lead, 31 seconds ahead of Friderich, Violet's 1,100cc Major cyclecar was third and Baccoli was fourth. The chain driving the distributor of the Major broke, which left the three Bugattis running away with the race, despite having to cope with a road where the crown had been treated with calcium chloride to bind it, but the verges had broken up, thus making overtaking most hazardous.

29 August 1920: The Bugatti headquarters at Le Mans.

29 August 1920: Baccoli and de Vizcaya make pit stops during the Coupe des Voiturettes.

The lead changed among the trio while Ettore Bugatti had an early champagne lunch in the pits. At 20 laps, de Vizcaya who was leading stopped at the pits, the bonnet was opened, apparently to check the oil, the car started again and then Bugatti stepped out of the pit and undid the radiator cap to check the water level. This resulted in the car's immediate disqualification as only the driver and riding mechanic could work on the car. It seemed that bad luck or bad judgment had robbed de Vizcaya of victory. The reality was different, a con rod had broken, by opening the radiator, Bugatti had disqualified the car, but had also concealed the engine failure from the press and public. When the wrecked engine was examined afterwards, it was found that one of the big ends had not been split-pinned when the engine was reassembled after practice. In later years, George Lutz said Bugatti himself was the culprit as he had sent away Emil Mischall, who was reassembling the engine, saying he would complete the task. The easy win seemed even less likely when Baccoli stopped for plugs and his engine would not restart. By the time it was going, he had dropped back to fourth place. Fortunately for Bugatti, Friderich had kept going quickly and steadily and came home to win by 20 minutes from the Bignan in second place. Emil Mischall was sent to England in 1925 to work in the Bugatti depot at Brixton Road, London. He subsequently became a British subject and worked in the aircraft industry for many years. He was awarded the MBE for his services to the industry and died in 1971.

In May 1921, Bugatti sent his cars to race in his homeland for the first time. Two T13s and a T22 were entered for the Circuito del Garda, a 16-lap Formule Libre race run over a ten-mile (16km) circuit at Salo, on the western shore of Lake Garda. The cars were competing in the 1,500cc class and the drivers were Michele Baccoli, Eugenio Silvani, a local driver who had been gaining some successes in Italian sprints and hill-

29 August 1920: Friderich in the victorious T13.

2 May 1921: Friderich in a 2.4m chassis T22, leads Silvani, the winner of the Circuito del Garda in his modified T13.

climbs with a Packard, and Bartleomeo Costantini. 'Meo' Costantini was an Italian who was born in Vittorio Veneto in 1889, and had entered serious competitions in 1914, driving a works-entered Aquila-Italiana, a sporting car built in Turin. He had competed in several events, culminating in the 1914 GP de l'ACF at Lyon, where his car had retired after one lap. Costantini had joined Bugatti at Molsheim where he was regarded as one of the family and had a multitude of responsibilities in the factory, but it has been suggested that he only received a nominal salary as he had a substantial personal income. It is not known if the cars at Salo still had 66mm-bore engines, or if the bore had been enlarged to 68mm. The main opposition

came from a team of three 2-litre Ansaldos, one being driven by a motorcycle racer who was making his debut in a racing car, Tazio Nuvolari. The cars were started at timed intervals and Silvani, whose car had a modified radiator, took an immediate lead followed by Costantini. The Bugattis led not only the other 1,500cc cars, but also the larger Ansaldos, and Silvani went on to win by two minutes from Costantini, with the Ansaldos of Corrado Lotti and Nuvolari another two minutes behind. Baccoli was sixth, 23 minutes behind the winner so presumably had problems, although these are not reported.

Two T13s were entered by Bugatti for the Grand Prix de Boulogne on 3 July driven by René Dely and Deviz, but both retired. The

Italians had recognised the success of the GP de l'ACF and decided to promote a grand prix of their own. The first Gran Premio d'Italia was held at Brescia on Sunday, 4 September 1921. It was the centrepiece of a week of speed events based on Brescia and on the following Thursday, there was a 20-lap voiturette race, the Gran Premio delle Vetturette, held on the very fast 10.75-mile (17.3km) triangular circuit which had been used for the Gran Premio. Like the major race, voiturette entries were only accepted from manufacturers. Four cars were entered by Bugatti, these had the bored-out 68mm engines giving a capacity of 1,453cc. The crankshaft ran in a plain front bearing, with ball bearings for the centre and rear main bearings, while the big ends had roller bearings. Two Bosch magnetos were driven from the rear of the

September 1921: The T13s line up at Molsheim before departing for Brescia.

camshaft and protruded into the cockpit, under the scuttle. A Zenith carburettor was fitted. The chassis remained unchanged with the wheelbase of 6ft 6¾in (2m). The drivers were Friderich, Pierre de Vizcaya, Baccoli and Pierre Marco. The opposition was provided by teams from OM and Chiribiri while there was a solitary SB, which was driven by Silvani and was his modified T13 with a streamlined body. Somehow, Silvani must have persuaded the organisers that he was a manufacturer. The cars started in pairs at one-minute intervals. Friderich took the lead, followed by de Vizcaya and Silvani. When Friderich burst a tyre shortly before half distance, Silvani took the lead and at the halfway point de Vizcaya led Silvani by five seconds. The SB ran its bearing shortly afterwards, which left the four Bugattis leading the field and they ran on to win, Friderich leading home de Vizcaya, Baccoli and Marco. The fifth car was the OM of Minoia which was over five minutes behind Marco.

The Brescia victory was a turning point for Bugatti, the motor racing world now regarded him as a significant racing manufacturer while the T13 and its variants became known as the immortal 'Brescia' model. Ten days after the Brescia race, the AC de l'Ouest organised the premier voiturette race of the year which had a much superior entry to the Italian event, running over the circuit used for the 1921 GP de l'ACF, and the primitive beginnings of the circuit later used for the 24-hour race. Foremost among the competitors was a team of three Talbot-Darracqs. These had twin-cam four-cylinder engines, in effect one half of the Grand Prix Sunbeam engine. They also had front-wheel brakes and were miniature grand prix cars. Bugatti had entered his Brescia team and it was reported that the engines had been bored-out once more to 69mm, making the capacity 1,496cc. A fierce race was expected between the Bugattis and the Talbot-Darracqs and there was a sensation when it was announced almost on the eve of the

race that the Bugatti team had been withdrawn. The excuse was given that there had not been enough time to prepare the cars after Brescia, but some commentators expressed the view that Bugatti realised the T13s were not fast enough to beat the twin-cam, front-braked Talbot-Darracqs. Any publicity gained from the Brescia win would be lost by a defeat at Le Mans.

The Talbot-Darracqs ran away with the Le Mans race, scoring a 1-2-3 victory, but whatever the validity of his excuse for his absence, Bugatti had two cars fully prepared to race four weeks later in Spain. De Vizcaya and Jacques Mones-Maury drove two T13s in the Gran Premio do Penya Rhin at Barcelona. Mones-Maury was a Spanish aristocrat, the Marquis de Casa Maury, who was a strong Anglophile and had flown with the Royal Flying Corps during the First World War. In later life he gained some distinction by becoming the second husband of Freda Dudley Ward, who had been the mistress of Edward, Prince of Wales (later King Edward VIII), until supplanted by Mrs Simpson. It was a 30-lap voiturette race on the 9.2-mile (14.7km) Villafranca circuit. The opposition was thin and after more than five hours racing on a very hot day, the two Bugattis finished in first and second places, with de Vizcaya the victor, nearly one and a half hours ahead of the third-placed La Perle. De Vizcaya and Mones-Maury cannot have tarried in Barcelona, as they had an engagement in England only six days later.

This was for the first long-distance race to be run in England, the Junior Car Club 200-mile race over the Brooklands track at Weybridge, south west of London. The race was to be a real test of the voiturettes as it was a full throttle run, so the absence of front brakes would be no handicap. The Talbot-Darracq team was entered, fitted with much more aerodynamic bodies, as speed would be at a premium. Two T13s, the two cars of the Brescia team which

8 September 1921: The winner's plaque in the Gran Premio d'Italia Vetturette.

had not gone to Spain, were entered by Major Lefrere who was then the Bugatti agent in England. They were still fitted with the two-seat bolster tank racing body and there was no attempt to streamline them in any way. The two drivers only arrived at Brooklands the day before the race, so had little time to familiarise themselves with the track. The race was a Talbot-Darracq demonstration and the team cruised round Brooklands leaving a devastated opposition in its wake, taking the first three places as at Le Mans. The Bugattis led the pursuers and de Vizcaya was fourth, but ten minutes behind Henry Segrave, the winner, while Mones-Maury was sixth. Ironically, Segrave had bought the 1920 Le Mans-winning T13 and had gained some success with it in English hill-climbs during the 1921 season. At the end of that season, Bugatti must have realised that although the T13 had put him on the racing map, it was basically a pre-war design and there would be little prospect of gaining any future benefits from racing the car. As a machine for the amateur driver, it

22 October 1921: Mones-Maury takes his T13 out to the start of the JCC 200-Mile race at Brooklands. (Guy Griffiths Collection)

would continue to score innumerable wins though.

As his company flourished, Bugatti saw the need to move up market and produce larger cars. Over the years a myth has been established that cars were built at Molsheim by highly skilled workers whose talents compensated for the primitive machine tools available in the factory. This legend was manifestly untrue. By 1922, the Molsheim machine hall contained many advanced tools of American origin including Cincinatti grinding machines and a Fellows gear cutter which could produce straight, bevel or spiral gears of a very high quality and accuracy. This equipment contributed to a new design which was shown at the Paris Salon and the London Motor Show at Olympia in the autumn of 1921. This was the T28 which had an eight-cylinder engine, with three valves per cylinder; the dimensions were 69mm x 100mm with a capacity of 2,992cc. The chassis had four-wheel brakes and the gearbox, which had only two speeds, was incorporated in the rear axle. The T28 did not go into production but it was the forerunner of the T30 which appeared during 1922. This had an eight-cylinder, overhead camshaft 60mm x 88mm engine of 1,991cc, using two four-cylinder blocks on a common aluminium crankcase, with the three valve arrangement of the T28, the crankshaft running in three ball bearings, and there were plain big ends. The water and oil pumps were driven by a cross-shaft at the

22 October 1921: Mones-Maury battles on the Byfleet Banking with No. 67, Douglas Hawkes (Horstman) and No. 54, Jack Munday (AC). (Guy Griffiths Collection)

front of the engine. In the initial design, the engine had a capacity of 1,500cc and was known as the T29. The gearbox of the T30 came from the T13. After some initial reluctance, Bugatti had embraced front-wheel brakes which were hydraulically operated, although the rear brakes had cable actuation. The chassis was the well-established T23 with a wheelbase of 8ft 6in (2.55m) running on 765 x 105 tyres. This became an established touring model of which some 600 were built. The sales were encouraged by the French economy which was prospering in 1922, although partially

helped by the terms of the Treaty of Versailles. This required Germany to pay £10 billion over a period of 42 years to the victorious nations. The lion's share went to France and in July 1922, Germany asked for an extension of time to pay.

When grand prix racing was resumed in 1921, the races were run to a 3-litre formula, but this was abandoned at the end of the first season and a new, 2-litre formula was established for 1922. Two-seater bodies

and a minimum weight limit of 650kg were mandatory. Before the touring T30 went into production, an opportunist Bugatti realised that the design could be adapted and modified to become a grand prix car, thus putting the marque right at the forefront of motor racing, albeit with a modified touring car. The engine of this first grand prix Bugatti was little changed from the touring T30; it had two Zenith carburettors, one feeding each block and the compression ratio was probably 7:1. There were two plugs per cylinder fired by two Bosch magnetos driven from the rear of the camshaft, and mounted in the cockpit under the dash. The hydraulic front brakes were foot-operated with 11in (270mm) drums, the handbrake operated at the rear, with 16in (400mm) drums. The chassis was the standard 7ft 10½in (2.4m) T22. The radiator was fully cowled and the car was clothed in a cigar-shaped body which was reputedly designed by Edmondo Moglia, who was later responsible for the unsuccessful land speed record contender *Djelmo*. The cars were completed with bolster tanks, but de Vizcaya persuaded Bugatti that there would be an advantage if a streamlined tail was fitted. This had a hole at the back from which the exhaust discharged.

The premier grand prix of the year was the GP de l'ACF which, in 1922, was run over a triangular circuit of 8.3 miles (13.4km) using the N420 and N422 west of Strasbourg and only four miles (6km) from Molsheim. The 60-lap race was held on Sunday, 16 July and Bugatti entered four cars, choosing his already experienced team of Friderich, de Vizcaya, Marco and Mones-Maury. Using T13s the team had abundant time to practise over the circuit. Before the race, the four riding mechanics had taken driving lessons and gained full driving licences so they could take over the wheel if the need arose. The opposition was impressive with teams from Fiat, Rolland-Pilain, Ballot, Sunbeam and Aston Martin. Practice times showed that the Tipo 804 Fiats were in a different class, being much faster on the long straights of the circuit and also quicker through the corners.

10 July 1922: Friderich with the T30, before the Grand Prix de l'ACF. (John Maitland Collection)

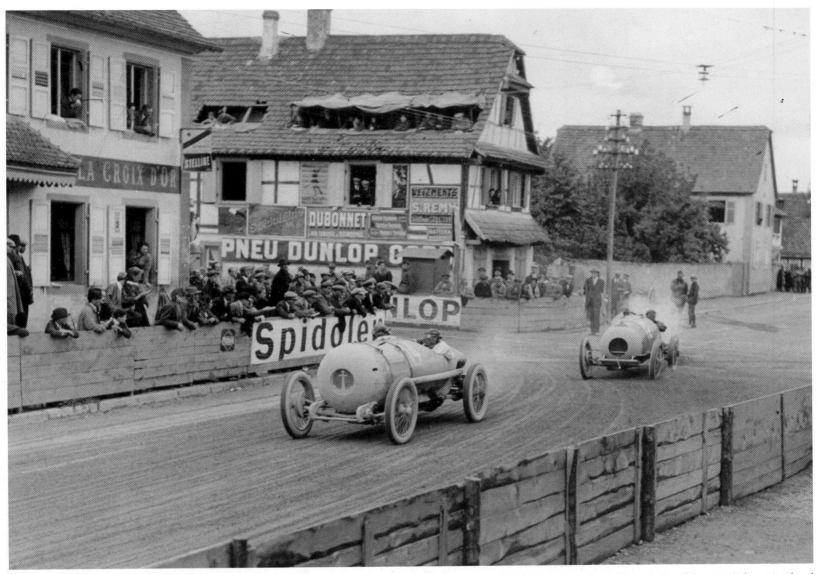

10 July 1922: Pierre de Vizcaya (T30) chases Foresti's Ballot at Duttleheim. (John Maitland Collection)

After a long dry spell, race day was wet and the dusty circuit turned to mud. For the first time, a grand prix would have a massed start and from the rolling start at 8.18am, the grand prix veteran Felice Nazzaro led with his Fiat, Friderich moved into second place and briefly held the lead on the third lap before slowing and then retiring with a misfire caused by defective magnetos. Using their superior performance the Fiats took up a 1-2-3 formation and seemed unbeatable. The three surviving Bugattis were also afflicted with magneto bothers but kept going. On his 51st lap,

Biagio Nazzaro, the nephew of Felice, went off the road while he was flat out on the straight and was killed when the rear axle of his Fiat broke and a wheel came off. With two laps, to go the rear axle of Pietro Bordino's Fiat also broke, fortunately on a slow corner. The surviving Fiat of Felice Nazzaro carried on to take a sad victory. The pace set by the Fiats had played havoc among the pursuers and at the end of the race, the three Bugattis were the only other

cars left running. De Vizcaya was second, but 58 minutes behind the Fiat, Marco was third, 1 hour 20 minutes behind, and Mones-Maury was flagged off having completed 57 laps. He had lost his front brakes at the beginning of the race and could only use the handbrake. Throughout the race, Ettore Bugatti sat on the pit counter, urging-on and encouraging his team. By taking second and third places in the major race of the year, Bugatti had

10 July 1922: Mones-Maury (T30) spins at the Entzheim hairpin. (Guy Griffiths Collection)

become a force to be reckoned with in motor racing and had also become the major French marque in the sport. He was quick to advertise his success, although the distance behind the winner was not emphasised.

Grand prix racing had not yet reached the levels it would attain a few years later and there were only two *grandes épreuves* during the 1922 season. In September, the Monza race track was opened, and to inau-

gurate this venue, the Gran Premio d'Italia was held there. This was the first time a grand prix had been held on a closed purpose-built circuit and from the organisers' point of view it had one outstanding advantage. All the spectators were paying customers, unlike the road circuit grands prix where the majority of the spectators had a free view. The entry list had been opened before the Strasbourg race and had attracted 39 subscribers, so the Reale

Automobile-Club d'Italia (RACI) must have expected an outstanding race. Unfortunately, although only one Fiat had lasted the distance at Strasbourg, the team had shown such superiority, that other manufacturers realised it would be a waste of time going to Monza. Their efforts would merely provide a supporting cast for a Fiat show.

During the eight weeks between the Strasbourg race and Sunday, 10 September, the day of the Monza race, the manufacturers made their excuses and the entries dwindled to a mere eight. Bugatti had entered his Strasbourg drivers with the four racing T30s and kept faith with the RACI, sending the cars by road over the Alps, fitted with mudguards and wooden racks carrying the crew's luggage; a notable contrast with the panoply of a grand prix team 80 years later. The cars ran without the radiator cowls and practice showed that not only were the T30s wrongly geared and were not fast enough, but their tyres were unsuitable for the sustained speeds of the Monza track. Bugatti was going to withdraw the team but, perhaps with some encouragement from the organisers, the Fiat team offered him a set of wheels and tyres which enabled de Vizcaya to run. It has also been suggested that one T30 had been fitted with a roller bearing crankshaft. Sustained high speed running in practice had shown the fragility of the standard crankshaft in the other cars, so the tyres were a useful face-saving excuse. It seems possible, judging from the speed of de Vizcaya's car during the race, that a more suitable back axle ratio had been sent from Molsheim and fitted to the car before the race.

Fiat ran on Pirelli tyres, and presumably Bugatti was running on Englebert but the maker can have had little grounds for complaint at the change. The race was scheduled to start at 9am but it was delayed for 30 minutes so the wheels of the T30 could be changed. It is possible that Bugatti may have needed the time extension to enable his team to complete the protracted task of fitting the higher axle ratio. The race

September 1922: The team of T30s arrives at Monza for the Gran Premio d'Italia.

was over 80 laps of the track, 497 miles (800km). It was a damp day, but despite this a big crowd came to watch. From the start, Bordino's Fiat led, but the Bugatti stayed with it. Unfortunately, this did not last and on the third lap, de Vizcaya stopped at his pit to change plugs and replace his goggles. He had lost a lap, but when he restarted he was running with Nazzaro and kept station with the Fiat and the pair passed and repassed for some time. This duel came to an end when there was a breakage in the Bugatti's carburettor, so there was another long stop while it was replaced. When he started again, de Vizcaya kept going, and towards the end of the race was lapping quicker than the two surviving Fiats which were cruising round. After 5hr 43min, Bordino was flagged off as the winner from Nazzaro, as the Fiats crossed the line, the crowd invaded the course start-

3 September 1922: Gran Premio d'Italia. De Vizcaya's T30 is on the front row of the grid between No. 18, Bordino's Fiat and No. 9, Meregalli's Diatto.

3 September 1922: De Vizcaya makes a pit stop. Ettore Bugatti in a trilby hat looks on.

ing a Monza tradition which has lasted into the 21st century. De Vizcaya, who had covered 76 laps and was the only other driver still running, was flagged off immediately and placed third. According to Laurence Pomeroy in *The Grand Prix Car*, Fiat had raised the compression ratio of the Tipo 804 to 7:1 for the Monza race which increased the output to 112bhp. It is most unlikely that the T30 was producing this power, the best figure quoted for it a year later, being 104bhp which was probably most optimistic. Observers noted that during the race the T30 could almost equal the speed of the Fiat on the straights so the extra speed of the T30 must have been aided by the aerodynamics of the cigar-shaped body.

Although the T13 was now an obsolescent design, it was still a most active competitor in the voiturette class during 1922. With the strange isolation that beset motor racing in Britain for the first 60 years of the sport, the Royal Automobile Club organised the Tourist Trophy, the major British race of the 1922 season, under the 3-litre formula rules that had been abandoned at the end of the previous season. As a result, the major class of the race in the Isle of Man only attracted entries from British manufacturers, but there was also a 1,500cc class. Bugatti had given a licence to the English firm Crossley, to build T13/22/23s, so a team of three Crossley-Bugattis was entered for the Tourist Trophy. The Crossley part was certainly nominal as

22 May 1922: Mones-Maury's mechanic pumps up pressure as his T13 crosses Sulby Bridge during the Isle of Man Tourist Trophy. (Guy Griffiths Collection)

the three cars came from Molsheim and were probably cars from the 1921 team, but for this race were painted yellow. The drivers were de Vizcaya, Mones-Maury and Bunny Marshall. Marshall was a British driver who had driven an Aston Martin in some voiturette races during 1921. Leon Cushman, who worked for Jarrott & Letts, and had gained successes with a T13 in British sprints and hill-climbs, was the reserve driver for the team. The race was held on Thursday, 22 June and there was some doubt if de Vizcaya and Mones-Maury would attend as it was reported they were fully engaged preparing for the Grand Prix de l'ACF, but both arrived for practice. The cars were weighed before the race and the T13s were recorded at 1,260lb (572kg). The drivers and mechanics had to be a minimum weight of 140lb (63.6kg) each. Mones-Maury only scaled 119lb (54kg), and his mechanic 120lb (56kg), so lead ballast had to be added to their car.

The T13s were up against the old rivals, the Talbot-Darracqs and were handicapped by the lack of front brakes. The six-lap race was over the 37 mile (59.5km) Mountain circuit used for the motorcycle TT, it was run in heavy rain and the Talbot-Darracqs took an immediate lead, going on to finish first and second. Moriceau crashed one of the Talbot-Darracqs which let Mones-Maury take third place, while de Vizcaya was fourth having lost time changing a wheel after he hit a kerb. Marshall, very outclassed, was fifth, but the three Bugattis took the team prize.

Four days before the Tourist Trophy, the Italian driver Count Carlo Masetti had scored a win with a T13 in the voiturette class of the tough Circuito di Mugello. This was a six-lap race over a 40.3-mile (65km) circuit in the Appenine mountains between Florence and Bologna. The T13 was still dominating 1,500cc races when the Talbot-Darracq team was absent, but on 19 August, when the 200-mile race was run at Brooklands, the Talbot-Darracq team ran

away with the race as it had done the previous year and Cushman and Marshall driving T13s, entered again by Major Lefrere, could only manage fifth and sixth places. As well as building the fastest grand prix car, Fiat had also built a voiturette, the Tipo 502S and a team of these was entered for the Gran Premio delle Vetturette which was a curtain-raising event at Monza, a week before the Gran Premio d'Italia. Bugatti had entered a team of T13s but he must have realised that there was no chance against the Fiats and withdrew the entry. Such was the reputation of Fiat that even the Talbot-Darracqs were scratched too, leaving the Fiats with an easy but rather hollow victory.

Two T13s and a T22 in racing trim had come to England in the spring of 1922. Cushman had been the first driver to gain success in the many sprints and short hill-climbs which were then held on the public roads; during the 1922 season there were over 70 events. Cushman won his first awards at the Kop climb on 25 March and continued to win throughout the season. At the Laindon hill-climb on 27 May, another T13 driver appeared, this was Raymond Mays, who was then 22-years old and soon to become the leading British sprint driver.

The 1923 season began slowly for Bugatti. There were some appearances by the T13 in voiturette races, but the first important race, the Indianapolis 500, came on 30 May. The race regulations had been changed limiting engine capacity to a maximum of 2-litres (122cu in). At 22 years of age, Martin de Alzaga Unsue was the youthful Bugatti agent in Argentina. He had driven a Miller in the GP d'Italia at Monza the previous September and had been impressed by the performance of the T30. He bought three Strasbourg specification T30s and entered these for the Indianapolis race, and believed he had been told by Bugatti, when he made the purchase in December 1922, that the cars would be fitted with roller bearing crankshafts before being delivered to him.

One of the more colourful figures in motor racing in the immediate years after the First World War was Count Louis Zborowski, a millionaire of Polish-American extraction who had been born and brought up in England. The Count had driven an Aston Martin at Strasbourg and had been impressed with the performance of the T30. He bought one of the Strasbourg cars, and another was sold to a French aristocrat, Prince Bernard de Cystria. They also entered the cars for Indianapolis. The five cars were prepared at Molsheim and fitted with neat offset single-seater bodies with a cowled radiator and a small head fairing, built by Lavocat & Marsaud to the design of Louis Bechereau who had designed the 1914–18 Spad fighter and had previously worked for Bleriot. Four Zenith carburettors were fitted and the compression ratio was raised to 7.5:1. W. F. Bradley says the engine developed 104bhp at 4,500rpm and the drivers used 5,500rpm which would have given a maximum of up to 115mph (185kmh). The cars ran on 29 x 4.5 Firestone tyres. One was weighed at 1,730lb (785kg) before the race.

De Cystria and Zborowski drove their own cars, and de Alzaga Unsue drove one of his entries, the others being entrusted to Pierre de Vizcaya and another Argentinian, Raul Riganti. A tiger motif was painted on the side of de Vizcaya's car by the artist Francis Picabia, before the car left Paris. Riganti set the fastest qualifying speed of the five blue T30s at 95.30mph (153.24kmh) which compared unfavourably with the speed of the fastest qualifier, Tommy Milton, whose Miller recorded 108.17mph (173.93kmh). De Alzaga Unsue was an unhappy customer, and in later years, he said he had admired the superb finish of the Millers while waiting for the T30s to arrive at Indianapolis. When

May 1923: Pierre de Vizcaya outside Bugatti's Paris showroom with the Indianapolis T30. (John Maitland Collection)

30 May 1923: Prince de Cystria makes a pit stop during the Indianapolis 500. The radiator cowling has been removed from the T30 and the Bugatti front shock absorbers have been replaced by Hartfords.

July 1923: The T32 team at scrutineering before the Grand Prix de l'ACF at Tours. Ettore Bugatti shows the engine to Charles Faroux and Costantini approaches from the left.

the crates carrying the cars were opened 'We would have wished to have run away. We were so ashamed. The cars were poorly finished, sloppily painted and a sorry sight. Ettore Bugatti was an unreliable, bad person.' Dissatisfaction with the finish was not the only reason for De Alzaga Unsue's anger. Despite what he had been assured, the cars did not have roller crankshafts and he felt the preparation of his cars had been skimped, too much time had been spent on the other cars, and he had not been told there would be two more entries. In the race, de Alzaga Unsue lasted for only six laps when a con rod broke, Riganti was out after 19 laps with a split fuel tank, and a broken con rod also stopped Zborowski on his 41st lap. De Vizcaya and Cystria were still going and at 400 miles, de Vizcaya had moved up to fifth place, then, on his 166th lap, he too was hit by the con rod scourge. Cystria, who had established the slowest qualifying speed of the five, kept going perhaps driving less forcefully and managed to finish in ninth place at an average of 77.64mph (124.84kmh). The T30's lubrication system, which squirted oil on to the big ends instead of supplying it under pressure, had been inadequate for the constant flat-out running at Indianapolis.

In 1923, the Grand Prix de l'ACF was run over a 14.18-mile (22.83km) triangular circuit, four miles (6km) north of Tours, which used the N158 and N159 roads, joined by a link road, it was narrow and bumpy with a poor surface and a steep camber. The race attracted 17 entries with teams from Fiat, Sunbeam, Delage, Voisin, Rolland-Pilain and Bugatti. The design which Bugatti produced for the race was bizarre, but showed an interesting insight into the trends of the future. Five cars were built at Molsheim, in conditions of secrecy, with only two picked mechanics working on them. The T30 engine was used again, but now had roller big ends, it was reported that parts of two engines came from the unraced Monza cars of the previous September. The chassis, a pressed steel punt with riveted cross members, extended to the outside of the wheels and had a 6ft 6in (2m) wheelbase. At the rear, the usual reversed quarter elliptic springs were used, but remarkably, the same system was fitted at the front. The axles were mounted above the springs, so the punt frame lay beneath each axle. The rear of the engine kept company with the driver and mechanic in the cockpit as there was no bulkhead. The gearbox had three speeds and was mounted in unit with the rear axle, operated by a central change. As before, the brakes were hydraulic.

As well as the technical unorthodoxy, the bodywork was remarkable as it was all-enveloping with a distinct aerofoil shape and was riveted to the chassis punt. In a statement released to the press before the race, Bugatti indicated that he was aware of what later became known in racing as 'ground effect'. He said: 'The more closely a

July 1923: The cockpit of the T32 which the driver and mechanic share with the machinery. The pressure pump is prominent.

vehicle approaches the ground, the less will be its resistance to forward motion. I believe this is due to the fact that a car travels in a more tranquil atmosphere.' It was possibly the first use of an all-enveloping body in racing and came at a time when even land speed record contenders had their wheels exposed to the slipstream. The drivers and mechanics complained that the cockpit was cramped and claustrophobic with poor visibility. The cars which were known at Molsheim as the T32, were functional but not beautiful, and were immediately called 'Tanks'.

The drivers were Friderich, de Vizcaya, Marco and de Cystria. In practice they found that the short wheelbase gave uncertain roadholding and while there was some advantage gained from the aerodynamics of the body, the cars were not fast enough. Bugatti himself, tested the cars

over the circuit, wearing a weird variation of a bowler hat which caused much press comment. The T30 engine was only giving the same power as it had done in 1922, but the rivals had taken a big step ahead. Sunbeam had engaged Vincenso Bertarione, the designer of the 1922 Fiats, to produce a new car and the outcome was virtually a copy of the Tipo 804 Fiat, but faster. Fiat had gone one better and their new car, the Tipo 805 was a straight eight and brought a new element to grand prix racing, as it had a supercharger which gave a 15bhp advantage over the Sunbeam. Race day on 2 July was hot and sunny; the race started at 8am, but the stands overlooking the start and pits were already full and the scent of castor oils as the cars warmed up, would have mingled with the scent of Chanel No. 5, which the designer Coco Chanel had introduced a few months

2 July 1923: De Vizcaya's crash at La Membrolle on the first lap of the Grand Prix de l'ACF.

2 July 1923: Friderich refuels his T32 watched by Costantini and Ettore Bugatti.

earlier. The competitors faced 35 laps of the circuit, 496 miles (797km) and were released in a rolling start. The Fiats and Sunbeams took an immediate lead. On the very first corner of the race, at La Membrolle Hairpin on the junction of the N158 and N159, de Vizcaya misjudged the corner in the cloud of dust, went off the road, hit a tree and severely injured several spectators.

The Fiats and Sunbeams battled for the lead while at the end of the first lap, Friderich was the leading Bugatti in ninth place while the other two trailed along at the back of the field. Marco retired after four laps with unspecified problems. De Cystria lasted until lap 12 when he was lapped by the Sunbeams of Segrave and Divo in La Membrolle. He was not keeping a look-out for the cars behind and went off the road. The T32 was damaged as it struck the palisades lining the track, and de Cystria limped round to the pit and retired. The superchargers of the Fiat were sucking in stones and grit from the road and all three retired, leaving the Sunbeams running 1-2-3. On the last lap, Guinness, in the third Sunbeam, spun when his clutch slipped, this let Friderich up into third place behind the Sunbeams of Segrave and Divo, but he was 25 minutes behind the winner, having taken over seven hours to cover the race distance.

A T32 appeared at Boulogne on 30 August for the Boillot Cup touring car race, driven by the French amateur Count Jean de l'Espée. It is not known if this was a disguised works entry or if the Count was a customer. Apparently, the bodywork was accepted as complying with the regulations, *The Autocar* commented: 'officials discovered mudguards, windscreen and hood', but de l'Espée made a bad start stopping to change plugs about 200 metres after the start and retired when the car slid off the road and hit a heap of stones.

Another T32, the Friderich car, was sold to a Czech banker, Cenek Junek, who lived in Prague, and had bought one of the

2 July 1923: Friderich passes the broken Tipo 805 Fiat of Giaccone.

Strasbourg T30s after the race in 1922. With the T32, Junek set the best time at the Lochotin-Tremosna hill-climb, near Pilsen, on 16 September and repeated the success at the Schober climb, near Prague on 30 September. Bugatti did not send cars to the Gran Premio d'Italia at Monza, a single T32 was entered for the Gran Premio de Espagna but it did not appear, as it was realised the cars were not fast enough and an appearance would do nothing for the reputation of the marque. The T13 was still appearing in the voiturette and touring classes driven by private entrants. Renzo Lenti had picked a number of places in Italian races with his T13, but had not been able to gain a victory. Touring car races were an innovation which had first been tried in Corsica in 1921, other organisers had promoted races and by 1923, a pattern was being established, the races catering for what were becoming known as sports cars although the touring title had not yet been dropped. The greatest race of all, the Le Mans 24-hours was first run on 26 and 27 May 1923. The race was run in tough conditions; there was a hail storm just after the 4pm start, then it rained heavily for four hours. The road surface broke up and turned to mud in many places. Two T22s competed and that driven by de Portales and de la Rochefoucauld finished in tenth place, and was the first 1,500cc car home, the other, driven by Marie and Pichard finished 22nd, but had lost over an hour when it ran out of fuel on the Mulsanne straight and the driver had to run to the pit and collect a spare can. At that time, the strict race regulations about refuelling had not been introduced.

A major race meeting was held at San Sebastian, on the Lasarte circuit, during the last week of July, the main event of which was a race for grand prix cars but there were races for voiturettes and touring cars. San Sebastian was a fashionable resort, and the summer residence of King Alfonso,

it attracted a fashionable crowd during the summer season for whom the racing was an amusing diversion. Two T13s, fitted with mudguards and lamps were entered for the 1,500cc touring car race which was held on Monday, 25 July It was a six-lap race, a distance of 66.3 miles (106km) and the T13s finished first and second, driven by the Spanish driver Patricio Sartrustegui and by Count de l'Espée. De l'Espée then took the road equipment off his T13 and ran the car in the 33-lap 365-

mile (587km) voiturette race five days later. The hard-working T13 did not let him down and won by over half an hour; in second place, driving an Elizade was Ferdinand de Vizcaya, the brother of Pierre. The San Sebastian race was a second division voiturette event, as the major races were those contested by the Talbot-Darracqs, but a new contender had appeared, the Tipo 803 Fiat, a four-cylinder version of the grand prix car. Such was the reputation of the Fiat, that when the Talbot-Darracq team knew the Fiats would be running in the JCC 200-mile race at

26 May 1923. The T22 of de Portales and de la Rochefoucauld before the first Le Mans 24-hour race.

30 July 1923: Gran Premio do San Sebastian Voiturette. Count Jean de l'Espée in his victorious T13 which had already finished second in the preceding touring car race.

Brooklands on 13 October, excuses were made about the cars being unready and their entries were withdrawn. Two Fiats raced at Brooklands and were eliminated by engine failure in the early laps. The race was won by an Alvis, but Leon Cushman took second place in his T13 averaging 91.10mph (146.5kmh), the car's speed aided by a cowled radiator, a streamlined tail with a driver's headrest, and high cockpit sides.

While successes were still coming in the lesser classes, the 1923 season had been a

disappointment to Bugatti in the highest level of grand prix racing. Critics have suggested that the T32 should be accounted a failure and consider Bugatti lost his way aesthetically and technically with this car. The French historian, Serge Bellu, commented that it was evidently the work of an artist, 'head-on it was a perfect rectangle; in profile it was the arc of a circle, drawn with a single flourish of the pencil'.

Bugatti has been accused of being over-conservative with his designs and unwilling to accept technical advances, but the T32 represented a considerable technical advance, and began to explore the benefits of monocoque construction and aerodynamic efficiency. It may not be too fanciful to suggest that with the T32, Bugatti looked into the future and backed away from what he saw.

Chapter 3

The chrysalis opens

THE DISAPPOINTING PERFORMANCE of the T32s at Tours, and the speed of the other competitors made Bugatti realise that he needed a new design for grand prix racing, and in particular, for the GP de l'ACF which was to be held at Lyon on 3 August 1924. It is not known when work began on the new car. In *Grand Prix Bugatti*, Hugh Conway reproduces a letter dated 9 April 1924, from Bugatti to Cenek Junek and his wife, Elizabeth (Eliska) Junek, in which Bugatti describes the salient features of the car and encloses a rough drawing of the body. This seems to indicate that work was already in hand, but in *Memoirs of a Bugatti Hunter*, Antoine Raffaelli says that the earliest drawings of the car are dated April 1924. The new design eschewed the advanced unorthodoxies of the T32, but the result was arguably the most aesthetically satisfying racing car of all time, the Type 35.

Bugatti lacked the financial resources of rivals such as Fiat and Sunbeam, and although the T22/23 and the T30 touring cars were being produced and sold steadily, the firm was still quite small and capital was limited. To have produced a wholly new design would been expensive and fool-hardy, so the new car had to rely on the development of existing components and needed to be relatively inexpensive to produce, as it was intended to be a car for the customer as much as a racer for the works driver. The engine was a develop-ment of the T30, with improvements to make good the shortcomings of the earlier

unit. The grand prix formula was unchanged in 1924, so the engine capacity and dimensions remained unaltered. The change came at the bottom of the engine where there was a new crankshaft built up in sections and aligned with cotter pins. This permitted the use of roller big ends running in bronze cages and one-piece connecting rods. The double ball-bearing centre, front and rear main bearings of the T30 were retained, but there were two addi-tional roller main bearings between the second and third cylinders and the sixth and seventh cylinders. Despite the prob-lems at Indianapolis, the oil jet system still lubricated the crankshaft. The basic design of the T30 crankcase was used, but it was now split along the centre line. The T30 cylinder blocks were retained, but the two inlet valves were enlarged by 2mm and the exhaust valve by 4mm. Bugatti rejected the new-fangled supercharger which had been adopted by all his grand prix rivals and still used two Zenith carburettors. In 1924, the power output was about 90bhp. The engine drove a modified T13 gearbox through the now standard wet multi-plate clutch. There was an open propeller shaft and the rear axle also followed what had become standard Bugatti practice, with a pair of aluminium castings split on the centre line with the half shafts carried in a pair of steel trumpets.

The chassis frame was new, this being a channel section of tapering depth with a riveted rear cross member and additional bracing provided by the engine mountings and the cross tubes supporting the gearbox. The front axle was also new. Bugatti must have looked carefully at the axle of the Tipo 804 and 805 Fiats, this being circular in form and hollow with the springs passing through an eye in the axle. Bugatti had improved on the Fiat design as his axle was a single piece and stronger than the Fiat, which was in two parts bolted together in the middle. The rear axle was supported on splayed reversed quarter elliptic springs. There was a torque arm between the differ-ential housing and gearbox, and a tubular torque arm on each side running forward from the axle to the outside of the frame. The wheelbase was 7ft 10½in (2,400mm) and the track 3ft 9in (1,143mm); the complete car weighed about 1,430lb (650kg). The car had a small horseshoe (or egg-shaped) radiator and a neat and beauti-fully proportioned body with a pointed tail, enclosing the fuel tank, which offered a low wind resistance. There was a full-length undertray only broken by the bottom of the sump. Bugatti had reverted to cable brakes with a carefully designed compensating mechanism. The crowning glory of the design was the wheels. These were cast aluminium with eight broad flat spokes, one flange of the rim was detachable to aid tyre fitting and the brake drums were incor-porated in the wheel, with a shrunk-in steel liner. In adopting a cast alloy wheel, Bugatti preceded the rest of the grand prix world by some 35 years.

At least six T35s had been built by the middle of July 1924 and Bugatti entered five for the GP de l'ACF. The drivers were Pierre de Vizcaya, Friderich, Costantini, Jean Chassagne, who had previously been a member of the Sunbeam team, and Leonico Garnier, an unusual choice, as he had little or no racing experience and was an agent for Talbot in San Sebastian. Friderich had left Molsheim during the summer, as he had opened a Bugatti agency in Nice, at 21 Rue de Rivoli, but had been asked to return for this event and Chassagne had already been engaged by Bugatti to do some of the testing of the first T35. The race was held on part of the circuit used for the 1914 Grand Prix and was situated about 12 miles (19km) south of Lyon. The circuit was 14.4 miles (23.12km) and the race was over 35 laps, a distance of 503.4 miles (809.5km). The official practice was from Friday, 18 until Tuesday, 22 July, between 5.30am and 8.30am, after that further practice was forbidden, so all the competitors used the same stretch of Route Nationale for testing and checking their cars. The Bugatti team arrived at Lyon the day before practice began, six T35s were driven from Molsheim with the drivers at the wheel, and Bugatti himself driving the reserve car. The appearance of the cars was a sensation and brought forth universal praise. Bugatti had invested heavily in the race, and the team was housed in a large encampment. A huge tent with a wooden floor was erected to house the cars and the camping equipment came in three railway wagons and two lorries pulling trailers. There were sleeping cabins, each with running water, for the 45 team members, showers and electric light. The cooking was done in a wooden hut and there were two refrigerators. Bugatti and his family lived in a separate large caravan.

The team practised without any problems, although mesh stone guards were fitted to the radiators and to the cowl in front of the driver, the magneto drive was altered and thermometers were fitted to the radiator caps. It was evident that the oppo-

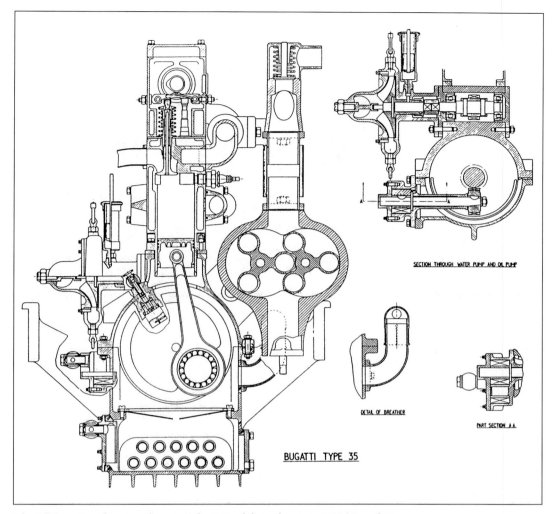

SECTION THROUGH WATER PUMP AND OIL PUMP

DETAIL OF BREATHER

PART SECTION A.A.

BUGATTI TYPE 35

The T35 engine showing the supercharger of the subsequent T35B and C.

sition was formidable. All the manufacturers had produced new designs and a new generation of grand prix cars had emerged. It seemed that the race would lie between Fiat and Sunbeam, but there was an impressive V-12 Delage team, while the dark horse of the race was a team of P2 Alfa Romeos; it was the first time that the marque had competed in a grand prix. Sunbeam and Alfa Romeo had joined Fiat in embracing the supercharger, without this aid, the T35 showed that it was reasonably competitive during practice, but unable to challenge the faster cars.

In the days before the grand prix, there were races for bicycles, motorcycles and touring cars and on the day of the big race, a crowd of 200,000 arrived to watch in superb weather. The cars were lined up in a two-by-two grid for a mass start led by two motorcycles. Immediately it became a race between Fiat, Sunbeam and Alfa Romeo. The Sunbeams were held back by magneto problems and the pace of the new Alfa Romeos gradually wore down the Fiats. It was a pace that the T35s could not match, after the first lap, Chassagne and Friderich were in eighth and ninth places while Costantini, de Vizcaya and Garnier were at the back of the field. Lack of pace was the least of the team's problems. It seems generally accepted that the straight-side

August 1924: Ettore Bugatti presents the T35 of de Vizcaya to the scrutineers at the Grand Prix de l'ACF.

Dunlop 28 x 400 tyres fitted to the cars were badly vulcanised and thrown treads resulted, although Borgeson has suggested, following talks with S. C. H. (Sammy) Davis, the great writer and driver, who was riding mechanic in Zborowski's Miller during the race, that an error had been made in the machining of some of the new alloy wheels which were waiting as spares in the pits and the integral brake drums were too small to fit over the brake shoes. De Vizcaya was able to change a punctured tyre at the end of the first lap and also changed a burst tyre on lap three. On lap 10 he went off the road and bent the rear axle and frame of his car. Costantini had worked up to seventh place, but a thrown tread had bent his gear lever and he lost

Above: *August 1924. The Bugatti team testing on the Route Nationale before the race.* Below: *August 1924: The T35s line up at the Grand Prix de l'ACF: No. 7, de Vizcaya; No.13, Chassagne; No. 18, Costantini; No. 21, Friderich and No. 22, Garnier. (Guy Griffiths Collection)*

3 August 1924: De Vizcaya follows Garnier down the descent to Les Sept Chemins.

August 1924: The wheel and front brake of the T35 with the controversial Dunlop tyre.

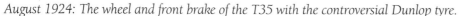

second and top gears, so he retired on lap 16. Chassagne and Friderich were told to slow down to preserve their tyres and they finished the gruelling race in seventh and eighth places, although over 40 minutes behind the winning car, Campari's Alfa Romeo. Garnier was flagged off having done 33 laps.

Lyon must have been a great disappointment to Bugatti, although the reception accorded to the T35 must have gratified him and he had the consolation that none of the team had been eliminated with mechanical trouble. It seems he decided not send any cars to Monza for the Gran Premio d'Italia, which should have been run on 7 September but was postponed for a month when the bulk of the entry was unready, but three T35s were sent to Spain for the Gran Premio do San Sebastian on 25 September. While strictly not a *grande épreuve*, as well as the three T35s, it attracted full teams from Sunbeam, Mercedes, Delage and Rolland-Pilain; the Bugatti drivers were de Vizcaya, Costantini and Chassagne. Although the race was on his doorstep, it is unsurprising that no drive was given to Garnier, a fourth car being entered for a local driver Ogniben Avera, but it did not start, and it seems he blew it up in practice. One change had been made to the cars, the Dunlop tyres had been replaced by beaded-edge Michelin 710 x 90s. The race was over 35 laps of the tough, 11.02-mile (17.73km) Lasarte circuit, the road running through open country and also through two towns. In Oria, the road was little more than 7ft (2m) wide between the buildings. Race day was wet and the course was treacherous, the touring car race the previous day had broken up the surface and inadequate repairs were made, using gravel and packed clay. A crude deflector was fitted to Chassagne's T35 to protect the riding mechanic but it seems that Soderini, who rode with Costantini, had to take his chance with the elements. Giulio Masetti (Mercedes) led initially followed by Benoist's Delage and Segrave's Sunbeam.

Costantini was coping with the conditions, but de Vizcaya and Chassagne were running at the back of the field, both slowed by misfiring. Benoist crashed and Masetti stayed ahead of Segrave and Guinness in the second Sunbeam, but Guinness crashed and was seriously injured, while Barratt, his mechanic, was killed.

At half distance, Segrave led the race, but Costantini was up into second place and duelling with Divo's Delage; he was now the fastest driver in the race, was coping with the conditions better than his rivals and was gaining on the leading Sunbeam. Segrave won after six hours racing, but the T35 was only a minute behind at the finish. In the closing laps, Costantini had made several stops to fill the radiator which had been leaking from the overflow pipe joint. So many cars had dropped out that de Vizcaya and Chassagne were fifth and sixth, although half an hour behind. After the race, the drivers were presented to Queen Victoria Eugenie and received their prizes from her. Costantini had made the fastest lap of the race, so Bugatti had the satisfaction of knowing that even without a supercharger, he had a competitive car. The T35s had been driven from Molsheim to San Sebastian, after the race they were driven to Paris and were used as demonstrators at the Paris Salon; potential customers were allowed to drive.

The Gran Premio d'Italia was held on Sunday, 19 October without any Bugattis and was another win for the P2 Alfa Romeos, this time a 1-2-3, but the race was marred by the death of Zborowski, when he crashed his Mercedes. On the same day, there was a minor meeting at Montlhéry, the new banked track south-west of Paris. The principal race on the track was for voiturettes over 180 miles (289.4km). Not unexpectedly, it was another Talbot-Darracq victory, but Cushman took fourth place with his T13. De Vizcaya ran a T35 in a ten-lap race for 6-litre cars. The favourite was the 7.2-litre Leyland-Thomas of the British driver Parry Thomas, who was the virtual

25 September 1924: Costantini sits in the T35 in which he finished second in the Gran Premio do San Sebastian. Soderini, his mechanic, sits beside him, Ettore Bugatti looks thoughtful and Pierre de Vizcaya gazes at the camera.

champion of Brooklands. To get the car into the capacity limit of the race Thomas removed the rockers from two cylinders. De Vizcaya held Thomas, who averaged 111.22mph (178.84kmh) for almost the whole race, only losing by 100 yards (90m).

Although obsolete, the T13s were still getting results; in Italy, on 13 July, Luigi Spinozzi won the 158-mile (254km) Coppa Acerbo Vetturette at Pescara, a race which would soon achieve a much greater status. Bunny Marshall, who had driven an unhappy race in the Isle of Man two years earlier, found the Boulogne circuit much more to his liking and won an easy victory in the Grand Prix de Boulogne on 30 August, then right at the end of the season, on 9 November, when most racing cars had been put away for the winter, Count Aymo Maggi, who would later become the founding father of the Mille Miglia, won the

Circuito del Garda. There were two more T13s in the race, Roberto Malinverni was third but Decimo Compagnoni went out of the race when he overturned on lap five. Later examples of the T13 were fitted with front wheel brakes of a type almost identical to those fitted to the T35. It is possible that some cars had been fitted with these brakes before the end of the 1924 season. The lack of front brakes was making it hard for the T13 to keep up with the faster opposition. A team of four T22s had been entered for the Le Mans 24-hour race, but the entries were withdrawn shortly before the race, the reason given was that there had not been sufficient time to prepare the cars as the preparation of the Lyon cars had taken precedence at Molsheim. A T30 ran in the Georges Boillot Cup sports car handicap at Boulogne on 30 August. The conditions were bad, with heavy rain, but Chandon de

30 August 1924: Bunny Marshall, seen here at Brooklands, was the victor in the Grand Prix de Boulogne with his T13. (John Maitland Collection)

Braille kept going and finished third behind a pair of Chenard Walckers.

Count Zborowski had kept his Indianapolis T30 and took it to Brooklands in 1924. He entered for the Easter meeting on Monday, 21 April and won the Private Members' Handicap on the Outer circuit, lapping the track during the race at 107.57mph (172.97kmh). He would have won the 90mph Short Handicap, but made the error of failing to turn into the Finishing Straight to take the flag and was disquali-fied. G. Blackstock, driving a T13 belonging to J. O'Day, picked up two second places. At the Whitsun meeting on Monday, 26 May, the blue T30 was taken over by George Duller, who shared his time between driving racing cars and riding race horses. Duller took second place in the 100mph Short Handicap and it was left to Blackstock to win the 90mph Short Handi-

27 May 1924: George Duller at Brooklands in the Zborowski Indianapolis T30 with which he broke class records. (John Maitland Collection)

cap lapping at 92.57mph (148.85kmh). At the summer meeting another T13 appeared which was declared in the programme with the engine dimensions of 69mm x 120mm, a printing error as the T13 would not take a crankshaft with a stroke of this size. Driven by a naval officer, Lt P. D. Du Cane, it was second in the 75mph Short Handicap, while Duller also took a second place with the T30 in the 90mph Short Handicap, lapping at 109mph (175kmh). Until the end of 1924, there was no fully established formula for international class records and Brooklands maintained a local system.

On 27 May, Duller took out the T30 and broke the class B (1,639cc to 2,048cc) standing and flying start half-mile, kilometre, mile and ten-mile records. Before the attempt the T30 was weighed at 1,820lb, (827kg).

In British hill-climbs, Raymond Mays was the man to beat. He had been most successful in 1923 and his T13 broke the record for the major British hill-climb, Shelsley Walsh. Bugatti was so impressed

with Mays's results that he was invited to Molsheim during the winter of 1923/24, his car was rebuilt and a second car was sold to him at a very favourable price. A whole page of the 1923/24 catalogue was devoted to the results gained by Mays. In 1924, Mays secured one of the first motor racing sponsorship deals with G. H. Mumm, the champagne growers of Reims. The first car, which had a ball bearing engine, was called *Cordon Rouge*, after the

1924: Raymond Mays sits in the T13 Cordon Rouge. Amherst Villiers is on the left and Harold Ayliffe is peering at the carburettors. Ayliffe worked for Mays's father, a wool broker, but later became Mays's full-time mechanic.

brand of champagne and had a red sash on the bonnet. The second car, also with a ball-bearing engine, retained its road equipment, and was named *Cordon Bleu*, the title of the Cognac marketed by Martel, and was painted with a blue sash. The cars had been

highly developed by the engineer Amherst Villiers, *Cordon Rouge* was driven to a meeting running on petrol, then at the meeting, compression plates were removed from the bottom of the cylinder block and the fuel was changed to alcohol. It was reported

that both engines had a compression ratio of 8:1 and the engine of *Cordon Rouge* went up to 6,700rpm, while that of *Cordon Bleu* went even higher, to 6,900rpm, although these were only flash readings for sprints and could not have been sustained.

Chapter 4

The golden years begin

BUGATTI BEGAN SELLING T35s to the public within a month of the Lyon race, the first sale being to Eusebio Bertrand, the Bugatti agent in San Sebastian; the car, driven by Garnier in the race, was dispatched from Molsheim on 24 August. Cenek Junek, bought the car driven by Friderich at Lyon, paying 90,000FF, having been given a 10 per cent discount as a good customer. It is difficult to give this a sterling equivalent as the franc/sterling rate fluctuated wildly during 1924; in March it was 117FF to the £1 and by July, the French government had stabilised the rate at 65FF to the £1. Taking the mid-point it would have been aproximately £950, which at the prices of 2000, would be £23,000. The T35s that were sold, were built to the same specification as the cars kept for the works drivers, so for the first time in motor racing history, a private entrant could buy equipment the equal of the factory teams. Within a year, this would change the face of motor racing and especially of grand prix racing, which would no longer be the preserve of the factory teams.

Bugatti's relationship with his customers, particularly those who went racing, was unusual. It was not the normal salesman/buyer relationship of the motor trade, but was more akin to the attitude of the proprietor of a fine art gallery to the purchaser of a painting. The more favoured customers were entertained in a specially constructed hotel adjacent to the Molsheim factory, where Bugatti had, by the mid-1920s established himself more as a minor aristocrat than a car manufacturer. He had bought the Molsheim factory from Mlle Geisser, and had also acquired the adjoining château and built another elegant house where he lived with his family in the style of a French landowner. The ageing Carlo, had moved from Milan and lived with the family, showing a proprietorial interest in his son's products. Bugatti's house was elegantly furnished and he kept a stable of thoroughbred horses which he rode round his estate; his alternative form of transport was a bi-cycle he had designed himself. The bicycle was the accepted mode of transport for everyone in the factory and on the estate. The factory itself was beautifully appointed, with such refinements as varnished oak doors and wood-block floors; Bugatti regarded his workers as part of an extended family over which he showed a paternal solicitude. W. F. Bradley gives a description in his biography of Bugatti: '. . . this is the Bugatti factory. The term seems inappropriate, for it is not a factory in the ordinary acceptance of the term. It is Ettore Bugatti's

The Molsheim factory in the mid-1920s.

April 1925: Louis Chiron at the start of his career with a T22 in the Cannes speed trials.

estate, and his interests cover car design and construction, riding, hunting, fishing, dog breeding, farming, sculpture, architecture, the fine arts, naval construction, fine wines and dishes, aviation and the whole gamut of mechanical arts, it is impossible to class it with the ordinary type of car factory.'

Bugatti seems consciously to have modelled his life on the Renaissance princes of his homeland. Bugatti was known to all as 'Le Patron' and his control over the company was absolute. His rule extended not only to the running of the company, but to the design and development of the cars and the management of the racing team. He had a number of talented engineers working for him, notably Felix Kortz and Edouard Bertrand, who worked on engines, but such was his control, that to the world at large, all the creativity came from him alone. Much of the inspiration must have come from Bugatti, who relied on his engineers to put his ideas into concrete form. Equally, the engineering subordinates must have made suggestions and had ideas of their own, but all aspects of their work came under the penetrating gaze of Bugatti himself, who had the innate ability of recognising those which should be adopted and developed. Those that were, became Bugatti's ideas and innovations, although with most, he must have made his own improvements and alterations, thus adding the inimitable stamp and signature of his own work. Bugatti's paternal solicitude towards his employees had an autocratic side. In this he had been helped by the virtual collapse of the trade union movement in France after the abortive general strike in May 1920. In the 1920s probably only 10 per cent of the French labour force belonged to a trade union.

The motor racing season began early in 1925, and the weather in Rome during February was more clement than that north of the Alps. A T35 had been sold to the rich Florentine amateur, Count Carlo Masetti, and on 22 February he entered the 40-lap Premio Reale di Roma on the 6.6-mile (10.6km) Monte Mario circuit outside Rome. It was a Formule Libre race wth a strong field including the star of the Alfa Romeo team, Antonio Ascari, although he was driving an RLSS model and not one of the formidable P2s. To the shock and probably the chagrin of the other Italian drivers, Masetti ran away with the race, leading from start to finish and giving the T35 its first victory. The T35 had sold well to customers and two weeks after the Rome race, the cars took first and second places in the unlimited class of the GP de Provence on the unbanked oval track at Miramas in the Camargue, the drivers being Marcel Vidal and the British driver Glen Kidston.

Kidston, a lieutenant in the Royal Navy and later a member of the Bentley team, was the first driver to bring a T35 to Britain. He raced the car at the Brooklands Easter meeting winning the 100mph Short Handicap and lapping the track at 104.63mph (168.24kmh). Strict silencing regulations had come into force at the track and the T35 had a crude and ugly outside silencer. Kidston also took the T35 to Shelsley Walsh in May and made a rather wild and spectacular climb. At the Brooklands Whitsun meeting, he lapped at 110.68mph

13 April 1925: Glen Kidston in his T35 at Brooklands with which he won the 100mph Short Handicap. The car is fitted with a crude silencer to comply with the Brooklands regulations. There are two tail pipes above and below the axle.

(177.97kmh) while taking second place in another handicap. Duller continued to race the Indianapolis T30 at Brooklands during 1925, sharing the car with Woolf Barnato, who would later finance the Bentley team, the pair picking up several places, and at the Essex MC meeting in October, Duller won the Junior Long Handicap at an average speed of 105.74mph (170.02kmh).

On 10 April, the Exposition Internationale opened in Paris and ran until October. This was the great cultural event of the year, the theme being art deco and the exhibition was established in halls and pavilions on both banks of the Seine. With such diverse subjects as the glass of Lalique, the high fashion of Chanel and Lanvin, and the textile designs of Raoul Dufy, it must have been a magnet for Ettore Bugatti who could have reflected that his T35 was a fitting example of the main theme. He must also have reflected that his brother Rembrandt had played no part in the exhibition, having taken his own life in January 1916.

When the open road races had been abandoned after the Paris-Madrid disaster, racing moved on to long and arduous circuits, often with unsurfaced roads. Gradually, the length of the circuits shortened and the surfaces improved, but there was one race, the Targa Florio which maintained the tough traditions of earlier years. The race had been established by Count Vincenzo Florio in 1906 and had become a legendary event, thanks to the heroic feats of the drivers who raced over a circuit

5 May 1925: Costantini and Soderini with their T35 before the Targa Florio. The wheels are painted with identifying numbers.

1925

Souvenir de la Targa
à l'ami Walter

Fernand de Vizcaya

5 May 1925: Fernand de Vizcaya in his T35 which retired on the third lap. The arduous nature of the course is evident.

which wound through the Sicilian mountains. At first it had been a lap of 90 miles (148km), and the course was described by W. F. Bradley in his book *Targa Florio*: 'More than 90 miles of the most crazy highway it was possible to imagine, with the road struggling painfully to attain altitude, twisting, doubling back on itself as if giving up in despair, then resolutely attacking the vertical mass in a rage of determination to reach the fortified village above it.'

By 1925, the lap had been reduced to 67 miles (107.7km) but little else had changed. It was a Formule Libre event and in the early 1920s had been the scene of immense struggles between Alfa Romeo, Ballot and Mercedes. Giuseppe Campari and Antonio Ascari, the aces of the Alfa Romeo team, had sharpened their skills in the Targa Florio.

Two T13s driven by Italian drivers had run in the 1923 event; Domenico Antonelli had retired and Renzo Lenti had finished 7th, nearly two hours behind the winner. In 1925, the entry was not as powerful as it had been in the preceding years. Alfa Romeo had decide to keep their cars only for grand prix events and Mercedes had withdrawn from racing as their 1924 grand prix car had gained a reputation as a vicious handler. Bugatti entered three T35s, for Costantini and the Vizcaya brothers, and the main rivals were a team of four 4-litre Type 174 Peugeots, rugged cars based on a touring model which had gained a number of racing successes. The Peugeot drivers,

Christian d'Auvergne, Louis Rigal, Louis Wagner and André Boillot, were all experienced and had driven in the Targa Florio in previous years, so knew what to expect.

The race was held on 5 May, and was five laps, 335.5 miles (539km). It was a fine day, but the course was in poor condition after the winter. The cars were started at timed intervals and at the end of the first lap Peugeots held the first three places led by Boillot, with Costantini in fourth place. On the second lap, Boillot was slowed with tyre problems, then d'Auvergne went off the road and overturned, his riding mechanic was thrown clear but he was trapped under the car which caught fire.

26 July 1925: At the Grand Prix de l'ACF, Montlhéry, Costantini and the long-suffering Soderini show that the controversial cowling allows some room for a passenger.

Wagner who was following stopped and dragged the badly burned d'Auvergne clear, losing his lead to Costantini. Wagner restarted, but was not able to make the time he had lost, so Costantini, with Soderini as his riding mechanic, came home as the winner, five minutes ahead of Wagner who was second. Boillot was third, followed by Pierre de Vizcaya, while Ferdinand had retired on lap three. It was perhaps a slightly lucky win for Costantini, but the event proved that the T35, while

not as fast as some of the opposition, was rugged and had road holding which was probably better than any of its rivals. The Targa victory had also shown that the new-fangled alloy wheels had confounded the critics and were capable of standing up to the most adverse conditions.

The Grand Prix de l'ACF was to be held at Montlhéry on Sunday, 26 July on a circuit which used part of the banked track and a new artificial road course which had

been constructed during the winter. The GP de l'Overture was held on 17 May to mark the official opening of the new road circuit, although the main event of the day was a 200-lap voiturette race on the banked track. Bugatti entered two cars, but only one appeared at the meeting. This was a remarkable machine. Taking advantage of a new regulation which banned riding mechanics in racing cars, he had designed a

26 July 1925: Pierre de Vizcaya has a brief moment of glory and leads Ascari (Alfa Romeo P2) and Segrave (Sunbeam) at the start. (John Maitland Collection)

26 July 1925: Costantini makes a pit stop supervised by Ettore Bugatti.

single seater, the T36, that broke most accepted rules. It had a slim frame, the front axle was a straight tube mounted in sliding guides and sprung by forward-facing semi elliptics. At the rear, there was no suspension at all, a conventional axle was bolted straight to the rear of the frame, the axle incorporating the gearbox in a similar manner to the T32. The brakes and wheels were standard T35 and the car was covered with a neat single-seater body. The detailed drawings of the design were made by Edouard Bertrand. The engine was a standard T35 which Hugh Conway believes was sleeved down to 52mm, giving a capacity of 1,495cc. It was reported that Bugatti drove the car himself from Molsheim to Montlhéry, and during the drive he must have realised that although the principles of the T36 worked in theory, on the road it was a different story. After a few practice laps, Pierre de Vizcaya reported that it was

virtually undriveable so it was withdrawn from the race and taken back to Molsheim, where it was put on one side, for another day.

The Grand Prix de l'ACF was being joined by other *grandes épreuves* as the sport gained momentum, in 1925 the Grand Prix de Belgique was added to the calendar and was given the additional and imposing title of Grand Prix d'Europe. It was run on 28 June, over the Spa-Francorchamps circuit, which in a reduced form is still used today, although it bears little resemblance to the circuit used in 1925. To the dismay of the other manufacturers, the Alfa Romeo team was entered, which had the effect of melting away the entry list. The Sunbeams were withdrawn and Ettore Bugatti, who had entered three T35s, said the cars would not be going to Belgium as he could not afford to take part. It is not known if the Royal Automobile Club de

Belgique offered financial inducements, but the T35s remained at Molsheim. The race became a straight fight between the Alfa Romeo and Delage teams and the Italian cars dominated the race.

In the Grand Prix de l'ACF which followed four weeks later, on Sunday, 26 July, at Montlhéry, the rival manufacturers had summoned up enough courage to face Alfa Romeo and full teams appeared from Sunbeam and Delage while Bugatti entered five T35s, driven by Costantini, Pierre and Ferdinand de Vizcaya, and Jules Goux, a veteran who had raced successfully for Peugeot in grands prix and voiturette races before the war, winning the Indianapolis 500 in 1913. He was born at Valentigney (Doubs) in 1885 and had raced for Ballot in the post-war years, winning the 1921 Gran Premio d'Italia; in 1924 he had driven for Rolland-Pilain. The fifth driver was Giulio Foresti, who had been a teammate of Goux with Ballot and Rolland-Pilain. The grand prix regulations had changed in 1925 and riding mechanics were banned. This was a sensible move, so often the mechanic came off worst in an accident, and the change also made life more comfortable for the driver as there was little room for two men in a cockpit during a six-hour race.

Taking advantage of the new rule, the passenger's seat was cowled over on the T35s, but this was forbidden in the race regulations. The Delage team had wanted to fit cowls, had checked with the ACF and been told they were illegal, so lodged a protest against the Bugattis during the evening before the race. Bugatti argued that the regulations only specified a cockpit width of 31in (800mm) so the cowls were not a transgression, and that if he was forced to remove them, the team would be withdrawn. After more argument, the matter was compromised and the cowls were partially cut back.

As required by international regulations, the five T35s were painted their customary blue; Borgeson says Bugatti blue was

18 July 1925: The touring T39s are lined up in Strasbourg before departing to Montlhéry for the Touring Car Grand Prix.

derived from the colour of the Gitane cigarette packet which was always in the pocket of Mme Bugatti's apron. As the colour of the packet varied, so did the colour of the cars. In July 1925, the packet must have been most anaemic as *The Autocar* reported that the cars were finished in a pale, pastel shade. Mme Bugatti's habit may have been stimulated by the declaration of some Parisian scientists a few months earlier, that smoking was beneficial to the health, as the nicotine killed harmful bacteria.

The race over 80 laps, 621 miles (1,000km), began at 8am with a rolling start led by a Peugeot and a Mathis saloon. For a few metres, Pierre de Vizcaya held the lead then he was overwhelmed by the field and at the end of the first lap, the five

Bugattis were in the last five places, lacking the power to keep up with the supercharged rivals. Once again, the P2 Alfa Romeos showed their superiority, while the Delages and Sunbeams gave chase, one Alfa dropped back, but Ascari and Campari were pulling away from the rest when it began to rain. On lap 20, Ascari misjudged a corner and his car overturned, he was thrown out and died shortly afterwards. The two surviving Alfa Romeos were withdrawn from the race at half distance which left Robert Benoist's Delage leading the sister car of Louis Wagner and the only surviving Sunbeam of Giulio Masetti.

Behind the Sunbeam, the five T35s were still running well. The President of the Republic, Gaston Doumergue, a troubled man, as the franc had fallen sharply the previous Friday, arrived to watch the closing laps and the race finished in a downpour of rain with a Delage 1-2, Masetti's Sunbeam was third, and then came the five T35s. With the death of Ascari, there was no celebration at the end of the race, but Bugatti must have had quiet satisfaction that all five cars had finished intact.

In August 1925, the Alliance Internationale des Automobile Clubs Reconnus (AIACR) met in Paris and announced, as

19 July 1925: Costantini drives on to victory in the Touring Car Grand Prix passing an empty enclosure, highlighting the lack of public interest in the race.

expected, that the 2-litre grand prix formula would cease at the end of 1925 and be replaced by a formula with a maximum capacity limit of 1,500cc. There was a minimum weight limit of 700kg (1,543lb) and the cockpit width of 800mm was retained despite the riding mechanic ban. It was felt that the supercharged 2-litre cars were getting too fast, and the change may also have been prompted by the rising number of fatalities in grand prix racing. When a grand prix formula is changed, there are always objections from the manufacturers and this change brought forth the usual protests. The T36 may have been Bugatti's first tentative steps towards the new formula, but he made a much more positive step in the Touring Car Grand Prix which was run at Montlhéry, a week before the GP de l'ACF on 19 July. This was a testing event run in capacity classes and Bugatti entered five cars in the 1,500cc class which had to cover 75 laps of the grand prix course, a distance of 590 miles (948km).

There is some doubt about which cars were entered. In appearance these were T35s with a wider body, long wings and running boards and full lighting equipment. It seems the engines were the eight-cylinder T35 units, with a dimensions of 52mm x 88mm giving a capacity of 1,493cc, but Hugh Conway suggests that the cars had new, four-cylinder engines of 69mm x 100mm, the prototype of the T37 which would appear some months later as a replacement for the T13/22. However, Antoine Raffaelli is emphatic that the cars ran with the eight cylinder engines. The cars were required to carry sandbag ballast to simulate passengers, two sandbag passengers were stipulated in the 1,500cc class and the cars had a minimum weight limit of 1,433lb (651kg). There was also a fuel consumption limit and the Bugattis were limited to a rate of 24mpg (34.7 litres per 100km); no refuelling was allowed during the race.

The five Bugattis, driven by the Vizcaya brothers, Costantini, Foresti and Goux, were only completed the day before the race and were driven to Montlhéry. The field was towed out to the 8.30am start where the engines had to be started on electric starters; the Bugattis were reluctant to go. The first lap had to be covered with the hood erected and the five Bugattis, running on Michelin tyres, soon went to the front of the class, the 1,500cc opposition coming from three Mathis, three Darracqs and two EHPs. Ferdinand de Vizcaya was eliminated by a leaking radiator, but the other four carried on to win the class convincingly, Costantini leading home de Vizcaya, Foresti and Goux. The race was run in fine weather, but hardly anyone came to watch, at midday *The Autocar* correspondent counted 59 spectators in the main grandstand.

To encourage manufacturers to try their new 1,500cc cars before the next formula began, the RACI included a 1,500cc class in the Gran Premio d'Italia on 6 September. Bugatti, realising that the T35 could not hope to offer any real resistance to the P2 Alfa Romeos or the V-12 Delages, took up this alternative with enthusiasm. Five cars were entered, and it has been suggested that three had sleeved T35 engines, and were now known as the T39, while the other two were the first of the T37s. It

5 September 1925: Paul Mongin takes his T30 round the St Martin Hairpin in the Coupe Boillot, on the Boulogne circuit, before retiring from the race. (John Maitland Collection)

6 September 1925: The T39s line up at the back of the grid for the Gran Premio d'Italia.

seems likely that all were T39s, and were the Touring GP cars fitted with the standard racing bodies and having an auxiliary fuel tank in the place of the mechanic's seat. The cars were driven by the Montlhéry team again. The Gran Premio had a particular significance, as at a meeting on 19 March, the AIACR had declared that a World Grand Prix Championship would be contested during the 1925 season. This was the forerunner of the later Formula One Constructors' Championship, the qualifying rounds were at Spa, Montlhéry, Indianapolis and Monza. Delage, Alfa Romeo and Duesenberg had each won a round, so the marque which won at Monza would clinch the Championship. Delage expected the P2 Alfa Romeos would be unbeatable so admitted defeat and withdrew from the race, but two works Duesenbergs were entered. At the start of the 80-lap race, Peter Kreis took his Duesenberg into the lead for two laps then

went off the road. This left Campari's Alfa Romeo in front and it stayed there for the next 30 laps until the refuelling stops began. When Campari stopped, Tommy Milton with the second Duesenberg took the lead.

The P2 Alfa Romeos were not going as well as expected. Campari had a long stop with magneto problems and while Gastone Brilli-Perri's Alfa Romeo took up the lead when Milton made his stop, the delays to Campari and to Peter de Paolo with the third P2 enabled Goux to move up into fourth place, followed by Costantini, who then lost some ground with a long stop to change plugs. Goux retired after 64 laps with a leaking fuel tank and Costantini was able to take third place when De Paolo made a long stop to repair a broken exhaust and Milton stopped to mend a broken oil pipe. Milton and De Paolo chased Costantini during the closing laps, but he was too far ahead to catch and finished

third behind the Alfa Romeos of Brilli-Perri and Campari. Ferdinand de Vizcaya, Foresti and Pierre de Vizcaya took sixth, seventh and eighth places in their Bugattis. The two Chiribiris and the Eldridge which made up the opposition in the voiturette class had fallen out in the early laps, so the race was a convincing class win for Bugatti and showed once again that the T35/39, although not quite fast enough, could last out a 500-mile (800km) race.

The final grand prix of the season and also of the 2-litre formula was the Gran Premio do San Sebastian, which was a Spanish Grand Prix under another name. This was held two weeks after the Monza race; Alfa Romeo having won the World title had nothing more to prove, so stayed away and the race became a straight fight between the Delage team and four T35s driven by the de Vizcaya brothers, Goux and Costantini. The Delages ran away with the race taking the first three places, although the fourth Delage crashed and the driver, Paul Torchy, was killed. Pierre and Ferdinand de Vizcaya took fourth and fifth places, Goux was still running at the end but was unclassified, and Costantini fell out with a holed radiator, although he had the consolation of the fastest lap; the T35s were not capable of sustaining a fast enough pace to tackle the serious opposition. There was one other car still running at the finish, a T13 driven by Marcel Lehoux who, although French-born, ran a garage in Algeria. At 37 he was older than most of his rivals and had made a late start in the sport, but with the T13, he had already gained his first victory, in the 1924 Circuit d'Anfa at Casablanca. He showed his ability by keeping in front of Goux and Ferdinand de Vizcaya for over 30 laps, until he dropped back after a long stop. He would appear again.

Count Aymo Maggi had replaced his T13 with a T35 and repeated his 1922 Circuito di Garda win, but others were still racing the T13 and probably waiting expectantly for the new T37. In Italy, Croce won the 1,500cc class at Rome while Zaniratti scored a class win at Mugello. Bunny Marshall beat off Frazer Nash and Aston Martin opposition at Boulogne to win there for a second time, but the biggest impact made by a T13 during the 1925 season was in England. Raymond Mays had sold *Cordon Bleu* to an inexperienced driver, Francis Giveen, who took the car to the Kop hill-climb in Essex on 28 March. Unfortunately, the crowd control was bad and Giveen hit and injured a spectator who was standing too close to the road. This accident resulted in an immediate ban on hill-climbs and sprints being held on public roads in Britain, a restriction which had a most detrimental effect on British motor sport. For the next eight years the sport on the British mainland would be restricted to Brooklands, Shelsley Walsh and some minor sprints on private ground. Giveen was so upset by the accident, it is reported that this contributed to him taking his life some years later.

The T37 went into production in the autumn of 1925 and the first car was sold

6 September 1925: Goux consoles himself with a cigarette after his T39 has retired with a split fuel tank. (John Maitland Collection)

19 September 1925: Costantini at Lasarte before his T35 retires from the Gran Premio do San Sebastian with a holed radiator.

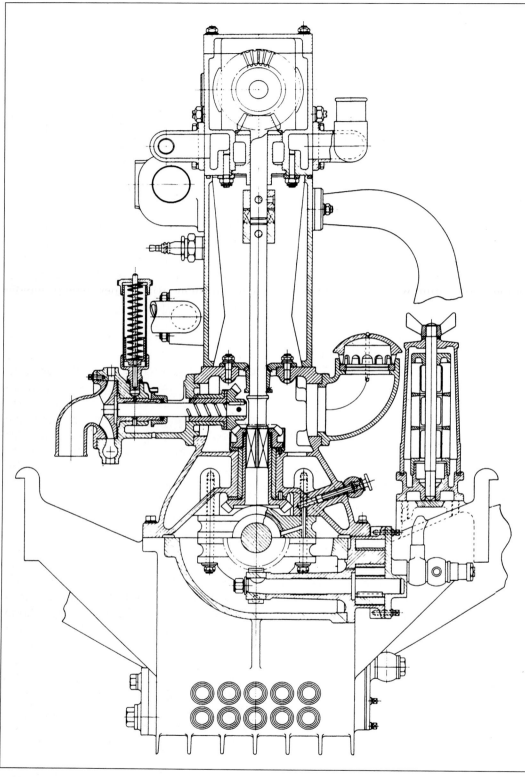

A front view of the unsupercharged T37 engine.

in November that year. This went to Malcolm Campbell in London. Campbell was an agent for Bugatti and at that time was one of the leading British drivers. He was the holder of the World Land Speed Record which he had established at 150.86mph (242.73kmh) driving a Sunbeam at Pendine, in Wales the previous July. The T37 was truly a grand prix car for the amateur, the more so as the new formula would be for 1,500cc cars. Apart from the substitution of wire wheels with 27 x 4.4 tyres, for the alloy-spoked wheels of the T35, the chassis was identical to that of the larger engined car. The four-cylinder engine had dimensions of 69mm x 100mm and a capacity of 1,496cc. The overall design was almost identical to the T35, except that there was a one-piece crankshaft running in five plain bearings, while the connecting rods also had plain bearings. Coil ignition replaced the magneto of the bigger engine. Using one Solex carburettor, the output of the early engine was probably about 50bhp at 4,700rpm. In the next four years, some 280 examples of the T37 and the supercharged version, the T37A, would leave the Molsheim factory. A detuned and modified version of the engine would be fitted to the T40, a touring car which would replace the touring versions of the T22 and T23 in 1926.

The introduction of the T37 was not the only significant event in November 1925. The American performer Josephine Baker had arrived in Paris and was appearing at the Folies Bergères in her show *Le Revue Nègre*. Her half-clothed act delighted one half of Paris and outraged the other half; the novelist Anita Loos commented that 'She had a witty rear end'! Josephine Baker was not the only threat to French morality that was being denounced. The fashion houses had decreed that hem lengths were to be drastically curtailed and women's hair was to be cut short. The age of the flapper had arrived and was regarded, along with dashing young men in sporting cars, as evidence of an accelerating moral decline.

Chapter 5

Champion of the World

JUST AS HE HAD BEEN reluctant to fit front brakes, Bugatti was just as reluctant to adopt the supercharger, an item of equipment which his rivals had regarded as essential since 1923. Recent research has revealed that Bugatti filed a patent for a vane-type supercharger in January 1924, but more positive steps towards supercharging were taken at Molsheim sometime during the summer of 1925 and the first drawings were dated August 1925. Edoardo Moglia was engaged to pursue the matter. An Italian, Moglia who had already designed the body for the 1922 Strasbourg T30, had worked with his fellow countryman Vincenso Bertarione, on the design of the Talbot-Darracq voiturettes so was already well-versed in the problems and advantages of supercharging. He was almost certainly engaged by Bugatti as a consultant and was not an employee. During the winter of 1925/26, experiments continued and the Bugatti supercharger was developed; this was the Roots type, but had triple lobe rotors, unlike the conventional Roots used by most manufacturers with double-lobe rotors.

At first, Bugatti cannot have been wholly convinced of the merits of the Roots, as experiments were done, possibly for comparison, with the Cozette supercharger. This was a proprietary vane-type unit which was popular with some French and British manufacturers. By May 1926, bench tests had shown the advantage of the Bugatti-Roots supercharger and had also shown the optimum engine dimensions. The supercharger was mounted on the off-side of the engine and driven by a short shaft from the gear train at the front of the engine. The compressed mixture went via a short vertical pipe to the inlet manifold and a pressure relief valve was mounted above the manifold, which discharged through a hole set high in the bonnet side, a distinguishing feature of the supercharged T35/39 series cars. The carburettor was mounted underneath the supercharger. Alternative engine dimensions were tried with the supercharger. The T36 52mm x 88mm version was compared with the T39 60mm x 66mm engine. The T36 unit gave 120bhp at 5,500rpm but had the disadvantage that the smaller bore limited the size of the valves. The T39 breathed more freely and gave 125bhp at 6,250rpm, so it became the choice for the 1,500cc *grandes épreuves* of 1926 and with the supercharger fitted became the T39A. Work was also done on the T35; a new crankshaft was produced with a longer throw, this increasing the stroke to 100mm which gave a capacity of 2,262cc.

T35s had been selling well, nearly 70 had been sold by the spring of 1926 and almost 80 T35A had also found buyers. The T35A was known as the 'imitation' T35 or 'Tecla' after a popular make of imitation pearl which was being sold in Parisian boutiques. The T35A was a T35 using the crankshaft and con rods of the T30 engine, and fitted with wire wheels. It was the ideal mount for the well-to-do sportsman who wanted the glamour of the real thing without the maintenance problems. It was a very profitable venture for Bugatti. A number of T35s had gone to Italy where they would rapidly become the backbone of Formule Libre racing. The Italian organisers found that there was a substantial number of old cars which were still being raced and had no difficulty in getting good-sized fields without bothering over the niceties of a particular formula. At the end of 1925, Alfa Romeo had withdrawn from racing for economic reasons. Ostensibly, the all-conquering P2s had been sold to private entrants. In reality, the cars were probably still owned by the factory and were being leased or loaned to the most competent drivers, but the arrangement satisfied Alfa Romeo's political masters.

The European season began with two Formule Libre races in Italy. The first, at the Circuito del Pozzo, Verona on 21 March was a win for Alessandro Consonno in a T35, after another T35 driven by Filippo Tassara had gone off the road while in the lead. A week later Tassara took his T35 to the outskirts of Rome for a much more important race, the Premio Reale di Roma, where he joined another six T35s and six T37s to take on two ostensibly private P2 Alfa Romeos driven by the Monza winner Brilli-Perri and by Giovanni Bonmartini. The P2s headed the field and Aymo Maggi with the fastest of the T35s gave chase. He caught Bonmartini and then with two laps

28 March 1926: 'Williams' waits beside his T35, No. 17, before the start of the third heat of the Grand Prix de Provençe at Miramas. No. 16 is the T30 of Robert Savon. (John Maitland Collection)

to go, Brilli-Perri, who had a commanding lead, stopped to change a wheel. The P2 restarted just in front, but on the last lap, the T35 passed the P2 to gain an impressive and unexpected win.

On the same afternoon that Maggi was upsetting the Alfa Romeo applecart, the first French race of the season, the Grand Prix de Provençe, was being held on the flat, featureless Miramas oval in the Camargue. This race was a trial run of the circuit for the Grand Prix de l'ACF that would be held there three months later. The race had a big field and the entrants ran in ten-lap capacity class heats with the fastest qualifiers battling it out in a 50-lap final. The favourites were the three Talbot-Darracq 70 voiturettes led by Segrave with the serious opposition coming from six T35s. The extra 500cc of the T35 almost matched the supercharger of the Talbot-Darracq; Segrave won the final but in second place was a T35 driven by an unknown driver, 'Williams', who had first disposed of the Talbot-Darracq of Bourlier, then chased Segrave

throughout the race and lost a likely victory by making two stops for tyres. Moriceau's Talbot-Darracq was third and in fourth place was another T35 handled by a newcomer to the upper echelons of the sport, Louis Chiron. In the 2-litre heat, Marcel Lehoux, who had abandoned his T13 for a T35, had been the victor, beating 'Williams' and Chiron.

'Williams' was a pseudonym for William Grover-Williams, often referred to as the 'Anglo-French enigma'. Only in the years since the Second World War has his story emerged and parts are still uncertain. He was born in 1903 of an English father and a French mother and was brought up in France. In the early 1920s he was engaged by the British artist Sir William Orpen as a chauffeur. Orpen was a fashionable portrait painter and was then at the peak of his fame. He lived in Paris with his mistress Yvonne Aubicq and was seen with her, in Paris and fashionable resorts such as Deauville and Le Touquet, being driven by 'Williams' in a Rolls-Royce Silver Ghost.

'Williams' was also seen driving a Rolls-Royce around Paris with other passengers, so it is possible that he was 'moonlighting' or was permitted by Orpen to use the car for his own purposes. It has been suggested that 'Williams' owned the Rolls-Royce and drove Orpen under contract, but a search in the Rolls-Royce archives shows that Orpen bought two Silver Ghosts, the second in 1923, but there is no record that 'Williams' was an owner at the time when he was driving Orpen. It seems that 'Williams''s father owned a car-hire business in Paris so he may have been driving for him as well as for Orpen. His father may have helped in the purchase of the T35 which 'Williams' drove at Miramas. It is also possible that some support was given by Yvonne Aubicq, who may have already been closer to 'Williams' than his employment suggested. 'Williams would soon find that driving a Bugatti was more profitable than driving a Rolls-Royce.

Louis Chiron was born in 1899 at Monte Carlo, the son of a French father and an Italian mother. He served in the French Army during the First World War, driving the car of Marshal Pètain, who commanded

25 April 1926: André Dubonnet (T35) makes a pit stop, on his way to fifth place in the Targa Florio.

the French armies of the north in 1918. When the war ended, Chiron returned to Monte Carlo and worked as a dance partner to rich women guests at the Hôtel de Paris, where his father was *maître d'hôtel*. He started his competition career in 1923 with a T22, getting some support from Friderich and used the T22 again during the 1924 season; his first victory was at the Côte du Barbonnet at Menton. One of his dancing customers was a rich American widow who bought him a touring T30. This was fitted with a lightweight body and Chiron raced it in hill-climbs and sprints on the Riviera in

1925, gaining several successes and becoming the champion of the Moto Club de Nice. Chiron then met Alfred Hoffmann, the heir to the Hoffmann-La Roche pharmaceutical empire. 'Freddy' Hoffmann was a keen motor racing enthusiast and with his wife Alice attended many races. Before her marriage, she was Alice Trobek and had been born in Connecticut of Swedish parents, and was to have a significant influence on the motor racing world in the years to come. Hoffmann had started a small

company, Nerka, making racing sparking plugs and it was agreed that Nerka would sponsor Chiron, buying him a T35 for the 1926 season.

The first outing for the new long-stroke T35, which became known as the T35T, was the Targa Florio on 25 April. Bugatti entered three cars for Costantini, Goux and Ferdinando Minoia. Minoia, who was 41 years old, had experience of the Targa Florio which went back to 1907 and he had won the 1908 Coppa Florio with an Isotta

27 June 1926: The T39As of Costantini, Goux and Pierre de Vizcaya line up for the start of the Grand Prix de l'ACF at Miramas.

Fraschini. Since the war he had been a journeyman driver, turning out for such diverse teams as Mercedes, Steyr, Benz, OM and in the 1924 GP d'Italia, for the P2 Alfa Romeo team. The T35Ts were backed up by four private T35s and several T37s. Ranged against the Bugattis was the team of three V-12 Delages driven by Divo, Benoist and René Thomas with the additional privately entered Delage of Giulio Masetti. Little noticed among the entries was a new car, a Maserati, making its racing debut, driven by Alfieri Maserati, one of five brothers who were its originators. Despite the much more powerful supercharged engines of the Delages, practice showed that the T35Ts were faster round the tortuous Madonie circuit, the balanced chassis and the exemplary roadholding of the Bugatti chassis was ideally suited to the conditions.

From the start, the Bugattis dominated the race with Costantini leading Minoia and Goux. Masetti went off the road on the first lap and was killed when his Delage rolled on him, the three surviving Delages gave chase in vain and when the drivers learned of Masetti's death, they retired, having no heart for a race which they knew they could not win. Costantini covered the five 55.9-mile (89.9km) laps in 7hr 20min 45sec,

and was ten minutes in front of Minoia, and 15 minutes ahead of Goux. The three T35Ts had dominated the race and shown an absolute mastery of the hardest circuit in Europe. Costantini, a driver whom history has always under-rated, showed that he was the equal of any of his rivals, but the celebrations for the 1-2-3 victory were muted by the death of Masetti who had been a popular and highly regarded driver. Probably almost unnoticed, and a pointer to the future, was the victory of the Maserati in the 1,500cc class.

A week after the Targa Florio, François Eysermann, who lived in Tunis, took his T35A to the Gran Premio di Tripoli, an important occasion for the Italian colony in North Africa. This was still a minor event and had not achieved the eminence it would have subsequently, and was run in its earlier years on a 16.3-mile (26.1km) circuit that was almost double the length of the legendary circuit used in the 1930s. Eysermann proved that even a T35A could have its day, as he won, beating Vittorio Astarita who had brought his T35 from Naples for the race.

The GP de l'ACF at Miramas was the first *grande épreuve* of the new 1,500cc formula. It attracted entries from Bugatti, Delage and

Talbot, but when the organisers prepared the circuit for practice during the week before the race on 27 June, they were distressed to find that only three cars had arrived, the T39As of Costantini, Goux and Pierre de Vizcaya. The other teams had stayed away as their new cars were still being built. To add to the mortification of the organisers, a big crowd arrived to watch on race day. Fortunately, the supporting 1,100cc cyclecar race had a somewhat better entry, so the timetable was changed and the three-car Grand Grand Prix was run in the morning. The T39As had been running on methanol in practice, but before the race, Costantini's and de Vizcaya's cars were filled with a fuel with a high benzole content. De Vizcaya led from the start, was passed by Goux on lap five, then stopped with a broken piston. Goux who was running on the methanol blend used in practice and supplied by BP, carried on happily, taking 4hr 38min to reel off the 100 laps to win, while the crowd watched patiently. The car had a 13 x 54 final drive ratio which at the agreed limit of 5,700rpm, would have given the car a maximum of 118mph (190kmh). Costantini kept going, but realised that to match Goux's pace while running on the suspect fuel would be disastrous, so had only done 85 laps when Goux was flagged off. After the race, Bugatti sought out Emile Petit, the patron of

18 July 1926: Costantini and Goux in their T39As flank Benoist's Delage on the starting grid of the Grand Prix d'Europe at San Sebastian. Soderini checks the front of Costantini's car while the driver walks round the Delage.

Salmson and suggested that it would be undesirable if the Salmson team, which were expected to win the cyclecar race, put up a higher average speed than Goux. In the afternoon, the crowd were entertained to a battle between the Salmson team and a trio of the new C6 Amilcars, until the latter blew up, leaving the Salmsons to cruise home, setting a lower average speed than Goux, doubtless to Bugatti's gratification!

The second *grande épreuve* to the new formula was in Spain. This was given the GP d'Europe title and this additional grandeur did attract more starters than the Miramas fiasco. The race was held on Sunday, 18 July, over 45 laps of the San

Sebastian circuit and the three T39As driven by the same drivers as in the French race, were matched against three new Delages. These were straight eights, with a notably low build, driven by Bourlier, Benoist and André Morel. The Delages were the faster cars, but in the race were in continuous trouble with fumes in the cockpit and with an exhaust system that burned the drivers' feet, the problem exacerbated by the intense heat of the day. While the Delages were in and out of the pits, the

drivers cooling their feet and handing over to the reserve drivers, Goux took the lead. When he stopped for fuel, soaking his cap in water to cool himself, Costantini went to the front and had a lead of nine minutes over Goux when valve problems set in. Costantini made several stops, which let Goux go on to win and the fastest Delage also went by to take second place. Costantini had to settle for third, and Minoia was fifth behind the second Delage, having had what was said to be plug problems, but more likely the same valve troubles, throughout the race. The Delage team had swapped drivers among the three cars to keep running and had asked Robert Sénéchal, who had never driven the car, to take one over for several laps to give the burnt drivers a longer rest. Bugatti even offered the services of Louis Dutilleux, a Molsheim test driver, who was in the pit, assisting with the timekeeping. This was probably not a wholly altruistic gesture as a few laps by Dutilleux in a Delage could have given Bugatti useful intelligence material. After the race, the organisers disqualified the Delage team but following a protest, supported by Ettore Bugatti, the Delages were reinstated in second and fourth places.

The Spanish organisers, fearing the GP d'Europe would be a fiasco, had arranged a 40-lap Formule Libre race over the San Sebastian circuit a week later. To ensure its importance, it was entitled the Gran Premio de Espana and three T35s were entered for Goux, Costantini and Minoia; these were driven on the road from Molsheim. It is surprising that T35Ts were not entered, but one was there; 'Williams', perhaps with parental or Orpen help had entered the Targa Florio-winning car which he had bought after the race. The opposition came from three 2-litre V-12 Delages and a 4-litre V-12 Sunbeam driven by Segrave. This remarkable car had broken the World Land Speed Record on Southport Sands on 16 March at 152.33mph (244.94kmh). The race was attended by King Alfonso and the drivers were presented to him before the start. Benoist's Delage led for the first five laps, then Wagner's Delage took over the lead, but as the Delages made brief stops, Costantini went to the front and stayed

18 July 1926: Goux prepares to top up the radiator at a pit stop. It seems that he and Costantini swapped cars for the race as No. 10 was Costantini's official number.

18 July 1926: Goux keeps well away from the tramlines as he passes under the Lasarte railway bridge, on his way to victory.

there. He kept pulling away from the field and went on to win by the enormous margin of 17 minutes. Goux was second and a Delage, shared by Wagner and Benoist after the latter's car had retired, was third; Minoia was fourth. 'Williams' was still running at the end and the Sunbeam had stopped when its front axle broke. Once again, Costantini had shown his ability.

On that Sunday afternoon when Costantini was winning in Spain, a small meeting was held outside Reims in the Champagne district of France. This was the GP de la Marne and was run on the Reims-Gueux circuit, a fast triangle of roads running across one of the major 1914–18 battlefields. The shell craters had been filled, the buildings rebuilt and the circuit was lined with poplar saplings, replacing those destroyed by shellfire. The race was won by François Lecot, an amateur driving a T35. Within a few years the Reims-Gueux circuit would be a much more important place. The following weekend, Louis Chiron scored his first significant victory when he drove his Nerka-sponsored T35 in the GP du Comminges over the 16-mile (26km) St Gaudens circuit, which ran alongside the River Garonne in south-west France. The entry was not strong, and Chiron dominated the race, winning by a margin of 21 minutes.

Stimulated by the new formula, the RAC decided that it was time for Britain to have a grand prix, so 20 years after the first grande épreuve, the first British Grand Prix was held at Brooklands on Saturday, 7 August 1926. This had the best entry yet for the new formula with full teams from Delage and Talbot, but surprisingly, Bugatti stayed away altough a T39A had been sold to Malcolm Campbell which he entered for the race. He received the car the day before the race and was only able to do a few practice laps on the circuit which used the Finishing Straight with artificial bends formed with sandbanks, the Railway Straight and the Byfleet Banking. Campbell felt that the standard alloy wheels would not survive the harsh Brooklands surface, so the car was fitted with the hubs and wire wheels of a touring T30; during practice, he was unhappy with the brakes which were relined overnight. The race was a fierce battle between the Delages and the new straight-eight Talbots. Once again, the Delages burned the drivers and the Talbots had various problems, one broke a front axle and the other two retired with supercharger problems. Campbell never ran lower than fourth profiting from the difficulties of his rivals. In the latter part of the race, the leading Delage, shared by Wagner and Sénéchal, was slowing with a split exhaust, which was not only burning the drivers but also setting the car alight. Campbell tried hard to catch it, but the T39A had gone off tune with broken valve springs, perhaps caused by over-revving in the early stages and he finished second at the end of the 110-lap 287-mile (461km) race.

Campbell ran the T39A at Boulogne three weeks later and a con rod broke. The race was won by another British driver, George Eyston with a T39, alleged to be Costantini's winning car at Monza the previous year, as Costantini's name was written in pencil on the back of the seat squab. Eyston nursed the car home in the closing laps as an axle tie rod had broken. He would later achieve great fame by breaking the World Land Speed Record. A small piece of motor racing history was made at Boulogne as it was the first race complying

with a grand prix formula to be led by a woman; Ivy Cummings leading the race in her T37 for four laps until she went off the road.

The Gran Premio d'Italia at Monza on 5 September was another event during the 1926 season which suffered from the reluctance of maufacturers to race their cars. Delage withdrew to design a new exhaust system and Talbot went away to find a stronger front axle. This left three T39As driven by Goux, Costantini and a newcomer 'Sabipa', the pseudonym of Jean Charavel, an engineer from Paris. He had little experience and it may have been a rent-a-drive, or Bugatti had agreed to enter a car he had bought. It was very difficult for an amateur to get an entry in a *grande épreuve*. The race was over 60 laps of the full Monza course using the road and the shallow banked track, a distance of 372 miles (600km). The opposition was thin, a pair of T26 Maseratis and a Chiribiri, together with six 1,100cc cyclecars. The latter only had to do 40 laps. Costantini took the lead at the start followed by Goux and 'Sabipa', then Emilio Materassi went up into second place with his T26 Maserati and pursued Costantini, staying there until lap 36 when his engine expired and he joined the other Maserati which had already stopped. Costantini went on increasing his lead until three laps before the end when the car staggered into the pits with the engine on the point of seizing. He restarted and spluttered round the remaining laps, but was caught by 'Sabipa' who won the race. Costantini nursed his car across the line to take second place. It was a result reminiscent of Miramas and the two T39As were the only finishers as Goux had fallen out on lap 36 with a broken oil pump. Once the cyclecars stopped, having done their 40 laps, it was a dismal race for the crowd and the organisers, but for Bugatti, it was a triumph as the result gave him the World Championship.

A week later, it was evident that Bugatti's antipathy to the supercharger had been

wholly overcome. Much as the Spanish organisers had done, a 40-lap Formule Libre race was held at Monza seven days after the Gran Premio and entitled the Gran Premio di Milano. It attracted a much larger entry, albeit that cyclecars and voiturettes made up the bulk of the entries. The battle for the major honours lay between Segrave's 4-litre V-12 Sunbeam and two T35s entered for Costantini and Goux. These were fitted with superchargers and thus became the T35C model. The supercharger was similar to the T39A, having a 150mm casing and giving a boost of 6psi (0.4 bar) with the supercharger running at engine speed. This gave approximately 120bhp at 6,000rpm. Shortly afterwards, a 185mm casing became standard for all the supercharged T35/39 engines. Perhaps influenced by Campbell's decison at Brooklands, the cars were fitted with T30 hubs and wire wheels. The Milanese crowd were once bitten, twice shy, so stayed away, probably expecting another dull race and sadly, their expectations were confirmed. Segrave, who had found in practice that he could improve his lap time by four seconds by holding the Sunbeam on the lip of the shallow banking, went straight into the lead and seemed uncatchable until his gearbox leaked away all its oil and he was out of the race at half distance. This left Costantini and Goux running on happily to win. Once more, Costantini showed his superiority, being 11 minutes in front of Goux at the finish. Two T35s were third and fourth driven by Arturo Farinotti and Louis Chiron, who was having his first race outside France. Costantini set the fastest lap, an improvement of five seconds on his best lap at the Gran Premio d'Italia. Among those who dropped out, was a motorcycle racer, Achille Varzi, driving a T37. He had been the 1926 500cc champion of Italy riding a Sunbeam and was taking part in his first major car race. Costantini's T35C was left in Italy after the race as it had been sold to Count Maggi who used it to

score an easy win in the Circuito del Garda on 17 October.

As the former voiturette class had become the grand prix formula, there were no voiturette races as such and in the minor 1,500cc events, the T37 had taken the place of the T13. The cyclecar or 1,100cc class had virtually taken the place of the voiturette class, although the title of cyclecar had become wholly inaccurate as the cars had come a long way from the spidery machines which had competed in the class only four years earlier. The GSC 'San Sebastian' Salmsons and C6 Amilcars which were battling fiercely for the honours were miniature grand prix cars and as the Salmsons had shown at Miramas, were nearly as fast. Bugatti threw a large pebble into the 1,100cc pool in May 1926. Following its disastrous debut at Montlhéry, the T36 had been put on one side at

30 May 1926: Pierre de Vizcaya in the monoposto 1,100cc T36 before the Grand Prix d'Alsace.

Molsheim. After an interval of 12 months, Bugatti decided that it was worth another airing and substantial alterations were made. A T35 rear axle was suspended on conventional reversed quarter elliptics, although the unusual front suspension was retained. A new engine was built with a bore of 51.3mm giving a capacity of 1,092cc. This engine was known as the T39B and was fitted with a supercharger similar to that which had been tried on the experimental T39 engine. A conventional T35 gearbox replaced the original axle-mounted unit. Three engines were built, two were installed in the single-seater T36 chassis and the third was put into a standard two-seat T35.

The three cars were entered for the GP d'Alsace on 30 May. This was run over the

1922 Grand Prix circuit at Strasbourg; it was a 35-lap, 287-mile (461km) race and as it preceded the GP de l'ACF at Miramas on 27 June, it was the first race in which a supercharged Bugatti competed. André Dubonnet, the aperitif heir, had the two-seater, while Aymo Maggi and Pierre de Vizcaya had the monopostos. Dubonnet was an experienced driver who had raced for several seasons and a month earlier had taken fifth place with his T35 in the Targa Florio. The three cars ran faultlessly, but sadly the Salmson, Amilcar and BNC opposition stayed away, already the reputation of Bugatti was feared, so Dubonnet, Maggi and de Vizcaya scored a 1-2-3. Bugatti must have felt it was not worth bothering with the 1,100cc class again, the cars were sold, one went to Malcolm Campbell and the

30 May 1926: De Vizcaya, Count Maggi and Dubonnet in the T36s before the start of the Grand Prix d'Alsace.

others later disappeared, though one raced in Switzerland in 1931.

In England, the T35s and T37s had been selling well and a number appeared at the BARC Brooklands meetings during the season. George Duller, driving a T35 belonging to 'Babe' Barnato, the Bentley sponsor and driver, won a handicap at the Easter meeting, as did Harold Purdy with a T37. At the Whitsun Brooklands meeting there was a two-lap Bugatti handicap over the Outer circuit for which Ettore Bugatti presented a cup and a £40 first prize. Five T35s and four T37s were entered and victory went to Chris Staniland with a T35A, Duller was second, lapping the track at 110.19mph (177.18kmh). At the same meeting, Malcolm Campbell driving the ex-Costantini T39, won a handicap by a length from Jack Douglas's T37. Purdy scored again with his T37 at the summer meeting, while at the August

Bank Holiday meeting, there was a 100-mile handicap in the programme. In this, Eyston's T37 had lubrication problems, Campbell and Staniland both stopped with thrown tyre treads, which left Douglas to win with his T37 at the excellent average speed of 94.75mph (152.35kmh). The flat-out racing at Brooklands probably gave a better indication of the outright performance of the cars than the averages achieved in European road races. Before the autumn meeting Purdy modified his T37, fitting an extra plug to each cylinder, fired by a second distributor and raising the compression with higher crown pistons. The modifications paid off and he won two handicaps lapping the track at 103.33mph (166.15kmh). During the season, Bugattis broke several international class records on the Brooklands track. In June, Staniland set new class E (2-litre) records for five and ten kilometres and

Eyston shared his T39 with Jack Douglas in October to take the class F (1,500cc) records for three hours, six hours, 500km, 500 miles and 1,000km at speeds from 86mph to 89mph.

Although 1926 saw Bugatti rising to the highest pinnacles of motor racing, for France it had been a year of mixed fortunes. An economist has described France during the inter-war years as 'A wealthy country, chronically on the verge of bankruptcy'. After the 1924 elections, the 'Cartel of the Left' was formed between the Socialists and the Radicals. It was accepted that economic reforms were needed, but agreement could not be reached on what reforms should be adopted. There were continuous political crises, and six ministries were formed in six months. For two years the franc fell steadily and during the summer of 1926, reached its lowest point since the end of the war; it was worth one-tenth of its 1914 value. While this inflation helped Bugatti to sell cars to foreign customers, it was wiping out the savings of the middle-classes in France

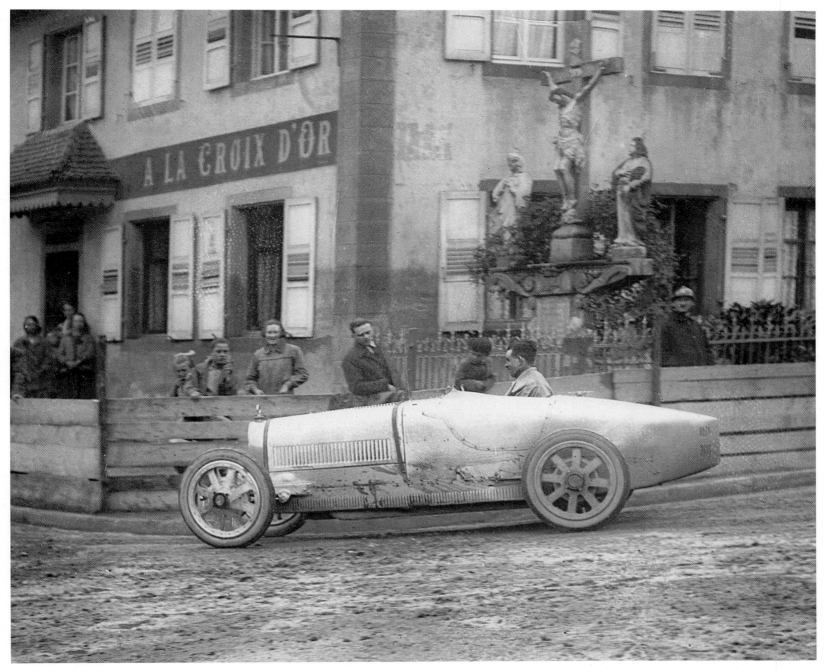

30 May 1926: On his way to victory in the Grand Prix d'Alsace, André Dubonnet takes Duttleheim Corner in his T35 with the T36 engine. (John Maitland Collection)

and also destroying the domestic market. A coalition was formed between the Radicals and the Moderates and on 23 July, the former President, Raymond Poincaré, became premier. He brought in immediate reforms and in particular, pegged the franc at one-fifth of its 1914 value, it rose rapidly and the other measures, raising taxes and cutting government expenditure, brought economic stability within a few months. The foundations had been laid for several years of prosperity.

Chapter 6

Mixed fortunes

THE ECONOMIC STABILITY brought by the Poincaré reforms came at an opportune time for Bugatti. At the beginning of 1927, he was about to launch an ambitious programme with three new models. Foremost was the incredible T41, the Royale, intended to be a fitting carriage for the crowned heads of Europe. With an eight-cylinder engine of 14,726cc, it was a car bordering on fantasy and the prototype was running early in the year. On a more practical theme, the T44 was about to be announced to the public. This was a touring car with a 69mm x 100mm 2,992cc eight-cylinder engine, which would replace the T38 that had been a short-term successor to the T30. The T44 had all the 'standard' Bugatti design features. The third car was the T43, this was virtually a long chassis grand prix car, which had the 2,262cc engine but was fitted with the T35C supercharger and would carry a 3/4-seater touring body. It was intended to be an ultra-fast touring car, but would also be suitable for sports car racing, a branch of the sport that was just beginning to emerge as a fiercer kind of touring car racing.

Bugatti must have realised that his chances of retaining the World Championship in 1927 were slim. The T39A was going into battle again with some alterations, although not perhaps improvements. The Delage and Talbot had been worked on during the winter, and once the Delage had been persuaded not to cook its drivers it was likely to be uncatchable. Bugatti's main hopes of success in 1927 lay with the T35 in Formule Libre races and to make the most of these chances, a supercharger was fitted to the T35T. Initially this was probably the T39A supercharger with a 150mm casing, while the inlet valves were enlarged from 23.5mm to 25.5mm. The car was known by the factory as the T35TC but this title was soon shortened to T35B, and the new model became the most famous of the T35 series. The first T35B was completed in November 1926 and the cars started to reach customers in the following spring. A 135mm supercharger had also

Spring 1927: Roland Bugatti drives an electric T52 at Molsheim watched by his father. (John Maitland Collection)

A T35B engine showing the supercharger.

been fitted to the T37, using the same drive as the T35C, this becoming the T37A, the first of these also going to customers in the spring of 1927. With the supercharger, the output was allegedly 90bhp at 5,000rpm.

In *The French Grand Prix*, David Hodges makes the much-quoted observation that the T35 '. . . can be rated the finest second-rate Grand Prix car ever built'. In his classic work *The Grand Prix Car*, Laurence Pomeroy makes a more detailed analysis, which is probably a very accurate critique of the T35 series. '. . . there was something about the Bugatti design enabling each horse-power to be utilized to far better advantage than on other racing cars of its period. The secret of this maximum realisation of power is to be found in the extraordinary controllability, roadholding and general stability of the Bugatti cars.' Pomeroy continues: 'Sixty b.h.p. per litre is no outstanding feat for a supercharged power unit and certainly cannot be held to justify the complicated construction of the engine. There are however, some points to be put forward in extenuation. Bugatti in this engine clearly expressed his choice of simple machining operations backed up by highly skilled handwork in fitting and assembly, as against a type that requires a great deal of expensive tooling and jigging, but can be easily put together by ordinary labour. Finally, although the engine was of moderate output it was, when driven within the limits for which it was designed, exceedingly reliable.'

Meo Costantini had not been well, so retired at the end of the 1926 season and became the racing manager at Molsheim. He is probably one of the most under-rated racing drivers of all time. Describing his Targa Florio victories, W. F. Bradley says: 'It was under such conditions that Costantini and his Bugatti were at their best. The driver approached his corners at terrific speed; but at precisely the right moment his brakes went on, he swung round without any trace of a skid, he left no rubber behind, and his gear changes were marvels of precision. Costantini appeared to make no physical effort, but the drivers who tried to follow him admitted that he was their superior in both physique and skill. The more difficult the road conditions, the more he drew away from his rivals by reason of his absolute and mathematical precision.'

With Costantini's move from the wheel to the pit, new blood was recruited. The first major race was the Gran Premio di Tripoli on 6 March. This was beginning to achieve a status, possibly as it paid good prize money, and Bugatti entered two T35Cs for Emilio Materassi and Renato Balestrero. Both were experienced: Materassi had driven for Itala, Diatto and Maserati with some success, while Balestrero had driven for OM. The main opposition came from a P2 Alfa Romeo driven by Maggi, who retired after two laps leaving Materassi to lead Balestrero home in an easy win. Freddy Hoffmann had bought Louis Chiron a T35T, which he collected from Molsheim on 19 March and drove down to the Riviera. Factory records show this was a T35T, but a supercharger was fitted either before it was handed over, or as soon as Chiron took it back to Monte Carlo, so it became a T35B. This was entered for the GP de Provençe on 27 March. The race looked promising on paper but turned into a farce. 'Williams' had been entered with a T35B by Bugatti, but the car did not turn up, so he accepted the offer of a 'works' Talbot. The race was run in capacity class heats, there was a full Talbot team and a solitary 1,500cc Delage for Benoist. It rained heavily on the morning of the race and the start of the heats was postponed and these were reduced to five laps.

The Talbots took the first three places in the 1,500cc heat with Benoist back in sixth place and conserving his Delage for the final. Chiron won the 3-litre heat from Lehoux who also had a T35B. The rain was still falling, and the Talbot manager considered the course was dangerous, so the team was scratched from the final. As the cars came round on their warming-up lap, Benoist spun off and collided with an Amilcar already waiting on the back of the grid. He and the Delage were slightly damaged so he was out of the race. Chiron took the lead at the start of the final but the crowd felt cheated, expecting a better field, and invaded the course. The race was stopped and Chiron was declared the winner. The crowd tried to storm the Talbot pit and had to be dissuaded by a bevy of *gendarmes*!

On that Sunday afternoon, when the angry Provençal crowd was trying to demolish the Miramas pits, weary competitors were racing across the northern Italian plain towards Brescia, on the closing stages of the first Mille Miglia. This event had been the brain child of Count Aymo Maggi, and three friends, Franco Mazzotti who had raced a T35 in 1925, Renzo Castagneto and the motoring writer, Giovanni Canestrini. They had wanted to promote an Italian event that would be a rival to the Le Mans 24-hour race and thought initially of a race from Brescia, their home town, to Rome, but Mazzotti, who had just returned from the United States and was perhaps under the influence of Anglo-American measurements, suggested the distance of 1,000 miles and it was agreed that the race should be that distance and go from Brescia to Rome and back again. The first race was run on a figure-of-eight course going as far north as Feltre on the edge of the Dolomites, and passed through Bologna and Florence. The roads were poor for much of the course and there was little crowd control; it was a return to the heroic open road races which had ended with the Paris-Madrid disaster. It was a great success, the victor was Nando Minoia, who had forsaken Bugatti to drive an OM, but the only Bugatti entered for the race shared a small piece of the laurels. Two amateurs, Giulio Binda and Atilio Belgir, who had previously raced Fiat and Amilcar, drove a T40 in the 1,500cc sports class and defeated a factory-supported team of Ceiranos. It was a hard day's drive for the pair who took 23hr 18min to finish the course, beating the fastest Ceirano by ten minutes.

There was more serious racing a month later in Sicily. With the prospect of a hattrick, Bugatti had entered three T35Cs for the Targa Florio on 24 April, the drivers being Materassi, Minoia and Dubonnet. There was a large supporting cast of T35s and T37s, running under the eye of Costantini who was also responsible for the customers' cars as well as the factory team. Among these was a T35B driven by Elizabeth Junek, the wife of Cenek. She had collected the car in T35T trim from Molsheim the previous September and a supercharger had been added during the winter. She had already gained many successes in hill-climbs in Czechoslovakia, driving her husband's Bugattis, and she took the Targa Florio very seriously. She drove round the circuit every day, using a T37 as a practice car, sometimes covering five laps. She and her husband also walked the entire course of 67 miles (107km) covering about 12 miles (19km) each day. Unlike many women racers of that era, Elizabeth Junek was noted for retaining her charm and femininity. The opposition to the Bugattis came from a 4-litre Peugeot, driven by André Boillot, and a team of Tipo 26 Maseratis. Minoia led for the first lap, followed by Materassi, Dubonnet and Mme Junek. On the second lap, Minoia dropped out with a broken torque arm, while Mme Junek's steering box broke and she hit a wall. Materassi took the lead, but went off the road on his third lap. He was able to retrieve the car and carried on to win, followed by Count Caberto Conelli who had driven an excellent race with a T37A and was only four minutes behind at the finish. Alfieri Maserati was third with one of his own cars, while Dubonnet came sixth.

Mme Junek received a special gold medal to honour her performance and in recognition of the hat-trick, Ettore Bugatti was presented with a donkey by Count Florio. This was named *Totosche* and taken back to Molsheim where it lived happily, keeping company with the horses on the estate, but sadly, was killed in 1940 when German forces occupied the factory. Conelli's speed with the T37A showed that it was an ideal car for the ambitious amateur and it became a first racing car for many drivers.

Throughout the early summer, the T35Bs and Cs knotched up victories in Formule Libre races on both sides of the Alps. On 8th May the strength of Italian racing was shown when there were full entries for two races. With a T37A, Antonio Caliri won the Coppa Messina, a local Sicilian race held

after the Targa Florio, securing victory when Balestrero had ignition troubles with his T35C, and Gaspare Bona won at Alessandria with a T35B. Three weeks later, Raymond Leroy showed endurance as well as speed winning the Six Heures de Bourgogne at Dijon with his T35C. There was a much more significant win in Rome on 12 June, when the Premio Reale di Roma was won by Tazio Nuvolari with a wire-wheeled T35. He had started racing in 1922 with an Ansaldo and had achieved some success with Bianchi and Chiribiri in the 1,500cc class but had devoted most of his energies to motorcycle racing. He had

been the Italian 500cc champion in 1924 riding a Bianchi. At Rome he was starting to show the extraordinary ability which was to set him apart from his racing rivals. The other contenders in the race had T35Bs or T35Cs, and Nuvolari saw off such drivers as Materassi and Balestrero, and hounded Maggi who was leading until Maggi's clutch broke. Nuvolari then took the lead and stayed in front to win in his unsupercharged T35 by nearly a minute from the supercharged cars of Lepori and Balestrero.

Nuvolari was out of luck a week later at Bologna. He led the race for two laps, then the car objected to the treatment he was

2 July 1927: At the start of the Course de Formule Libre de l'ACF at Montlhéry, George Eyston (T35C) and Louis Chiron (T35B, No. 16) lead the ill-fated Guyot of de Courcelles (No. 2) and the V12 Sunbeam of 'Williams' (No. 12).

giving it and he dropped out, which left Materassi to lead home a Bugatti clean sweep. Over the weekend of 2 and 3 July, all eyes were on Montlhéry. The major event was the first *grande épreuve* of the year, the GP de l'ACF on Sunday, 3rd, which was expected to be a three-cornered battle between Bugatti, Delage and Talbot. The organisers must have feared the 1,500cc grand prix cars would not be a crowd-puller, so the previous day, two lesser races were staged, the ten-lap, 77.6-mile (124.7km) Course de Formule Libre de l'ACF, and the Coupe du Commission Sportive, a 32-lap race for cars running on a 97lb (44kg) allowance of fuel and oil, which included the oil in the transmission. It was raining very heavily on the morning of Saturday, 2 July and the start of the Formule Libre race was delayed for two hours to await an improvement in the weather. Dubonnet and Eyston had T35Cs and Chiron had a T35B and were racing against two 4-litre V-12 Sunbeams driven by 'Williams' and Wagner, while Divo had a 1,500cc GP Talbot, the spare car of the team which would be racing in the Grand Prix the following day. Eyston had been advised by the Molsheim mechanics not to exceed 5,400rpm and noted that Chiron was using a lower axle ratio. 'Williams' led initially but was passed by Divo and Chiron, then dropped out with gearbox problems. On the third lap, de Courcelles crashed his Guyot and was killed, Chiron was closing rapidly on Divo, but an ambulance sent to the accident was travelling the wrong way of the course. Divo and Chiron encountered it where the track joined the road circuit. Divo was able to get by, but to avoid an accident, Chiron had to drive on to the infield of the track and spun, he restarted but his chances of passing Divo had gone and he came second, 30 seconds behind the Talbot with Eyston finishing third. In the fuel consumption Coupe du Commission Sportive, Bugatti entered two T37As for Goux and Conelli, while Dubonnet had entered a third car. The

drivers had to balance speed against consumption and the winner was a 2.6-litre Type 176 Peugeot specially constructed for the race and driven by André Boillot. The finish was close and Boillot was only 11 seconds ahead of Doré's La Licorne at the end. Conelli was fourth, almost three minutes behind, Goux was sixth and Dubonnet was eighth.

Bugatti had entered three T39As for the Grand Prix with Goux, Materassi and Dubonnet as the drivers. He had been concerned that the 60mm x 66mm engine had too short a stroke, equally, the original 52mm x 88mm had a stroke that was too long, so for Montlhéry, he produced a compromise, an engine of 54mm x 81mm which was called the T39C. Bugatti said that he had been too busy preparing cars for the Targa Florio and the other Italian races to devote sufficient time to the T39As for the GP de l'ACF and these were only finished just before the race. The cars were driven to Montlhéry from Molsheim and arrived on the Thursday night. When the cars went out for the final practice session on the Friday, it was evident that they were not fast enough to offer any opposition to the Delages and Talbots, so Bugatti scratched the entries. The withdrawal was announced as the cars were being pushed out on to the starting grid and there were catcalls and booing from the 100,000 crowd. In the Grand Prix, the Delages set a pace that the Talbots could not match and took the first three places, the only surviving Talbot was fourth. The dominance of Delage, the failure of Talbot and the reluctance of Bugatti, would soon bring the end of the 1,500cc formula.

New drivers were emerging and on 10 July, Philippe Etancelin, a wool and goose-down merchant from Rouen, who was always known as 'Phi-Phi', driving a T35 in his first major race, won the GP de la Marne on the fast Reims-Gueux circuit, by a margin of two laps. Etancelin had moved on to the circuits after a successful 1926 season in hill-climbs with the T35. After

the hyper-inflation and financial collapse in Germany in 1920/21, the Weimar government was gradually establishing economic normality. Among the schemes to reduce unemployment, building work had begun in 1925 on a big artificial road circuit in the Eifel mountains, west of Koblenz. This was intended to provide a test track for the German motor industry and also to be a race track. The Nürburgring was completed in the spring of 1927, an inaugural race meeting was held on 18/19 June, and the first major event, the Grosser Preis von Deutschland was held on Sunday, 17 July over the combined North and South circuits, making a lap distance of 17.58 miles (28.26km). Mercedes and Benz had amalgamated in 1926 and the new concern was not making racing cars, so to encourage the S Model sports cars that Mercedes-Benz were building, the race was an 18-lap sports car race with capacity classes. Four T35s ran in the 1,500cc to 3,000cc class, fitted with road equipment, and driven by Mme Junek, Kappler, von Kalnein and Baader, while Cleer ran a T37 in the 1,500cc class. The Junek car had the high-sided touring body. The eligibility of the cars was not in doubt as the T35A was sold as a sports car with road equipment, as was the T37.

The T35s were not fast enough to challenge Mercedes-Benz for the outright lead but had little opposition in the 3-litre class. Kappler led the class for six laps, followed by Mme Junek who was troubled with a leaking oil pipe. He stopped with a boiling engine and Mme Junek passed him. Kappler set off in pursuit and spun off at the South Curve with a jammed throttle, then Mme Junek made a long stop to mend the oil pipe and lost over a lap to Baader. She chased him and was six minutes behind at the finish, but Baader was disqualified for a technical infringement so Mme Junek won the class, the only finisher. Some sources have suggested that she drove a T35C, but this seems unlikely as in the supercharged car she would surely have

10 July 1927: Etancelin's wife holds the bouquet after his first major win in the Grand Prix de la Marne, driving his T35. (John Maitland Collection)

been fast enough to challenge the leaders. The band engaged by the organisers did not have the music of the Czech national anthem to mark her success, so played an excerpt from the overture to Smetana's *Bartered Bride*! In the 1,500cc class, Cleer took second place.

The fashionable high season at San Sebastian coincided with a week of motor racing. This opened on Monday, 25 July with a Formule Libre race, the 40-lap, 430-mile (690km) Gran Premio do San Sebastian, for which Bugatti entered Materassi, Dubonnet and Conelli with T35Cs, backed up by Chiron with his Nerka-sponsored T35B. The T35B should have been the more powerful car, but at that time, Bugatti seems to have favoured the smaller engine for the works cars, which probably indicates that in terms of performance, there was little to choose between the two models. Bugatti himself came to

the meeting, bringing the prototype of the T41 Royale which he showed to King Alfonso. This was fitted with a body from a Packard tourer, the King was impressed and placed a provisional order. There was little opposition to the Bugattis in the race as the team of 1,500cc GP Talbots had been withdrawn. Materassi led all the way, at first he was pursued by Chiron who dropped back after his eye was cut when his goggles were broken by a flying stone, but while chasing Materassi, he set fastest lap. Dubonnet and Conelli were second and third with Chiron in fourth place. The 1,500cc formula Gran

25 July 1927: A slightly bashful-looking Ettore Bugatti watches as King Alfonso of Spain talks to Count Caberto Conelli before the Gran Premio do San Sebastian.

Premio de Espana was held the following Sunday, 31 July. Bugatti entered three T39As, this time with the usual 60mm x 66mm engine. Once again, Materassi, Dubonnet and Conelli were the drivers, but as an indication of his rising stature, Chiron was nominated as the reserve driver for the team. The Talbot team had been withdrawn as the company had financial problems, so the race was a straight fight between the Bugattis and the three Delages with only a

solitary Maserati with a walking-on part. With the previous form of the season, it seemed an inevitable Delage walk-over, but although Benoist took the lead at the start of the 40-lap race, Materassi held on and Conelli was running third in front of the other two Delages.

The Delage was much faster on the straights, but Materassi made up ground on the twisting parts of the circuit and when the cars stopped to refuel at half distance,

the Bugatti pitwork was better and Materassi set off with a lead of 27 seconds. It was now Benoist who had to chase, and he closed up on Materassi who held on to a slender lead for another ten laps. Soon after the start of lap 31, as the cars ran alongside the River Oria, Materassi spun and hit a retaining wall, and the two off-side wheels were knocked off the Bugatti, but Materassi clambered out unhurt. When he spun there was a big cloud of dust and Benoist, who was unsighted, also spun but missed the wall and the Bugatti. Bourlier who had been lapped just avoided the accident in his

Delage. Benoist stopped to make sure Materassi was unhurt before carrying on to win. Chiron had taken over Dubonnet's car and moved up to second place behind Benoist, but had to stop on lap 35, so Conelli was second and Bourlier, the only other finisher, was third. Although the T39As had not won, the performance must have been gratifying to Bugatti and helped his sales promotion among the Spanish grandees. He must also have pondered on the wisdom of his decision to withdraw at Montlhéry.

The Formule Libre races continued during the holiday season; in Italy, Materassi having an easy win with a T35C in the Circuito di Montenero on the long and hilly circuit outside the seaport of Livorno. Nuvolari should have provided

fierce opposition but the organisers were reluctant to let him race. He had fallen off his 350cc Bianchi in the Coppa del Mare over the same circuit the previous week-end, and had been taken to hospital with an injured arm. He only proved his fitness to race by winning an arm-wrestling contest in front of the race officials but he could only manage fourth place. George Eyston won on the sands at La Baule on 25 August, with his T35B, in front of a fashionable crowd. He drove the car from England accompanied by his mechanic with a T35, which was used as a practice car. Bourlier's Delage was the main opposition, but retired, showing

that the 1,500cc Delages were not wholly invincible.

The Reale Automobile Club d'Italia (RACI) had been granted the honour of promoting the 1927 GP d'Europe, but must have felt unsure about the crowd-pulling attractions of a 1,500cc Gran Premio, so as well as the formula grand prix, a Formule Libre GP di Milano was held at Monza on Sunday, 4 September. Despite the results at San Sebastian, Bugatti was unwilling to take on the Delage team again, so no T39As were entered for the GP d'Europe. As it turned out, this was probably a mistake. The GP di Milano was run in five lap capacity class heats with the

6 August 1927: A group of T37s leads the 1,500cc class at the start of the Coppa Acerbo, Pescara. The eventual class winner, Tonini's Maserati (No. 52), comes up behind.

qualifiers going into the final. The wet day began with the combined heat for the 1,500cc and 2-litre cars. Among the 1,500cc runners was the remarkable new V-12 Tipo 806 Fiat appearing for its only race. It ran away with the heat leading home Maggi's T35C and Giuseppe Campari's P2 Alfa Romeo which swapped places several times, and Materassi's T35C. Nuvolari, who had acquired a T35C, dropped out. The next race on the day's programme was the 60-lap, 372-mile (598km) Grand Prix d'Europe; Delage were so confident of victory that only one car was entered for Benoist. The other five cars in the field were two Millers and a Duesenberg from the USA, and two OMs. Benoist duly ran away with the race, winning by 23 minutes from Morandi's OM. A T39A would surely have put up a better fight. To confuse the crowd, the first four cars at the completion of the first five laps of the Grand Prix were

regarded as qualifying for the final of the GP di Milano. In the five-lap final, Maggi led Campari and Bordino but the Fiat was soon in front and went on to win. Campari was second ahead of Maggi while Materassi pulled into his pit, having a sulk and protesting that Campari was baulking him!

On 1 October, the RAC promoted another British Grand Prix at Brooklands. The race was expected to be the best race yet of the 1,500cc formula as a team of Tipo 806 Fiats was entered to oppose the three Delages, while Bugatti had entered three T39As. Conelli and Materassi were joined in the team by Chiron, whose performances during the season had impressed Bugatti. With the disappearance of Talbot, 'Williams' was unemployed so he was engaged as the reserve driver to the team. The T39As had revised engines with modified blocks to provide better cooling, larger valves and modified valve gear, and were

fitted with bigger radiators. These engines were known as the T39D. Bugatti had realised that with the greater power of the supercharged engines, the T35 series needed improved brakes, the 10½-inch (270mm) brakes which had served the car since its debut were no longer up to the task. Larger drums with a diameter of 13in (330mm) were developed during 1927 for the T43 and photographs seem to show that these brakes were fitted to Chiron's car at Brooklands, although the other cars of the team were still using the small drums. If there were problems, it was better that the new boy should be afflicted rather than the experienced hands. Unfortunately, the Fiats were withdrawn so it was left to the Bugatti team to offer what challenge it could to the mighty Delages.

There were 11 starters in the race, the only time a field for a *grande épreuve* run under the 1,500cc formula attained double figures and it would be the last *grande épreuve* of the formula. The race was run on a typical British autumn day, cold and wet. For half a lap Materassi and Chiron led the Delages, but the trio swept by into the lead and the Bugattis were left with a fruitless chase. Materassi made a long stop to cure a water leak and Conelli took up the chase until he ran out of fuel and had to push the car over a mile back to the pits. When it was filled up, 'Williams' took it over. The three Delages reeled off the 125 laps and finished the 327-mile (525km) race in 1-2-3 order. The result secured the World Championship for Delage; Benoist had won every round and received the Legion d'Honneur in recognition of the achievement. Chiron was the only member of the Bugatti team to complete the race distance, taking fourth place, 27 minutes behind the winner. Materassi had done 118 laps and the Conelli/'Williams' car was flagged off. The three privately entered T39As of Eyston, Campbell and Prince Ghika dropped out.

Two weeks after the British Grand Prix, the JCC held the 200-mile race at

14 August 1927: Nuvolari, nursing a damaged shoulder, is flagged away in his T35 in the Circuito del Montenero by an elegant starter.

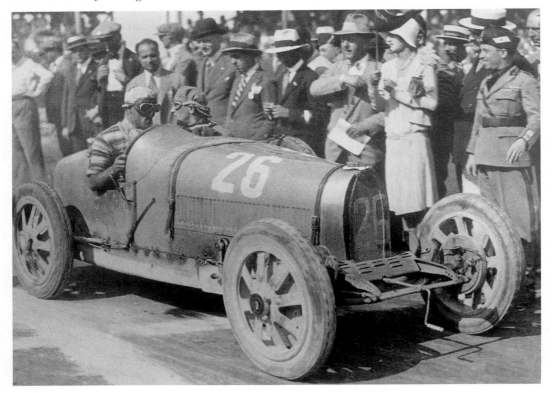

8 June 1927: His mechanics gaze at George Eyston in his T35B which was first in the Gold Vase Handicap at Brooklands. (John Maitland Collection)

Brooklands over the same course. Malcolm Campbell won with his T39A after Eyston's similar car had dropped out with burnt valves. Campbell had a reasonably easy victory, but had to keep looking over his shoulder at a cohort of pursuing C6 Amilcars which took the next three places ahead of all the other 1,500cc cars. On 9 October, Nuvolari won the Circuito del Garda with his T35B. Minoia held the lead with the T37A used by Conelli in the Targa Florio but after three laps, was passed by Maggi and Nuvolari. Maggi's T35C stopped with problems on lap nine, and after that, Nuvolari was unchallenged reeling off the 25 laps to win by 11 minutes.

Apart from the British Grand Prix, England was a motor racing backwater, but Brooklands was active throughout the 1927 season with the BARC events. At the Easter meeting, Malcolm Campbell won a handicap with his T36, which had been returned to Molsheim to have a T35B engine fitted,

lapping the track at 119.15mph (191.59kmh). A week later, on 24 April, Purdy won the JCC Junior Grand Prix for 1,500cc cars with his modified T37 on the Brooklands 'Mountain'. The Brooklands authorities would not permit the faster cars to run on the track in heavy rain, so some of the races at the Whit-Monday meeting were postponed although Eddy Rayson won a handicap with a best lap at 101.85mph (163.77kmh) with a T35. The faster cars had to wait and the postponed races were run on Tuesday, 8 June; the principal race, the Gold Vase Handicap going to Eyston with a T35B, who averaged 106.74mph (171.63kmh) and lapped at 115.29mph (185.38kmh). Bad weather forced the cancellation of the August Bank Holiday meeting but at the beginning of September, the Surbiton MC, one of the

smaller clubs which also held meeting at the track, ran a 150-mile (240km) sports car race wth a combined class and fuel consumption handicap. Malcolm Campbell ran a T43, one of the first competition outings for the model, and took second place having been allowed 8.5 gallons (38.6 litres) for the distance. At the closing meeting, Eyston brought out his T39A and lapped at 108.27mph (174.09kmh) to win a handicap, while Campbell also scored a win with his T35C.

Eyston was also busy at Brooklands during the 1927 season, attempting international class records. In April he used his T35B to take the class D (2-litre to 3-litre) records for the flying kilometre at 188.40kmh, the flying mile at 113.81mph, the standing start kilometre at 115.06kmh (31.3sec) and the standing mile at

The 13-inch (330mm) brakes which appeared on the T35 at the end of the 1927 season.

81.26mph. He went on to take the five, ten and 50-kilometre and one-mile records. Record breaking could be a profitable pastime, as the oil, fuel tyre and accessory manufacturers would pay bonuses for each record broken. The guileful driver would break a record by a narrow margin, leaving enough in hand to break it again shortly afterwards, thus collecting bonuses on each occasion. A month later, Eyston was back at Brooklands, setting new figures for the 50-kilometre record and also establishing figures for the 50-mile, 100-kilometre and one-mile records and taking the class one-hour record as well, the latter at 108.48mph (174.43kmh). In September, Eyston collected more bonuses when he broke his own class D records for the five kilometre and five miles and the ten-kilometre and ten-mile distances. In October he brought out the T39A and took the class F (1,500cc) one-hour record at 115.56mph (185.82kmh), collecting the 100-mile record en route.

In the autumn of 1927, Louis Delage announced that he was withdrawing from racing. The cost of building and racing his complex grand prix cars had been crippling and he would have endangered his company if he had carried on. To be fair, there was little point in Delage continuing to race, the 1,500cc formula was dying on its feet and it seemed that if it continued into 1928, apart from Bugatti and Maserati, there would be no contestants. The AIACR accepted the inevitable and announced that the formula would be changed for the 1928 season. It would become virtually Formule Libre, the only restrictions placed on the cars being a minimum weight limit of 550kg (1,212lb) and a maximum of 750kg (1,650lb) with a requirement that a race should exceed 600km (375 miles). The whole concept of grand prix racing changed at the end of 1927. Previously, the *grandes épreuves* and in particular, the Grand Prix de l'ACF had been restricted in the main to manufacturers' teams, private entrants were unwelcome. The teams had been expected to race for glory only, little or no prize money had been paid and there had been no starting money. Henceforth, for the next three or four seasons, the private entrant would be the backbone of grand prix racing and all entrants would expect to be paid starting money and to compete for a reasonable prize fund.

For Bugatti, the change was welcome and a further justification of his decision not to design and build new cars for the 1,500cc formula. His racing programme in 1926 and 1927 had not caused financial problems, unlike Delage and Talbot, and he knew that the T35B and T35C were likely to be fully capable of tackling any opposition in 1928. Their extra engine capacity balanced the superior performance of the Delages, the major rivals, which were sold off to private buyers at the end of the 1927 season. In the hands of the better drivers, the Bugattis could beat the 1,500cc Talbot 700, the Type 26 Maserati and the P2 Alfa Romeo. Furthermore, Bugatti was still the only manufacturer offering racing cars for sale to the public, and as the cars were already competitive, there was no need to spend large sums on developing new designs. Any capital cost in producing the original T35 design had long since been written down and the sale of each car represented a substantial profit to him. Mild improvements could be made to the cars raced by the factory team and these improvements could subsequently be passed on to the customers. The running of a factory team was relatively inexpensive as the team cars were sold after the team had no further use for them and were sometimes sold to unsuspecting buyers as new cars after a full overhaul! In the context of Bugatti's costs and profits on competition cars, a 1927 factory costing analysis calculates the overall cost of building a T37A with alloy wheels at 51,630FF or £417 at the rate of exchange then current. The car was sold at 83,000FF, ex-Molsheim, or £670 in London, so the mark-up was 61 per cent.

Chapter 7

Vive la Formule Libre!

AT THE BEGINNING OF THE 1928 season there was a reshuffle among the Bugatti works drivers. Emilio Materassi, whose efforts in 1927 had made him Champion of Italy, departed as he had bought the four Type 700 1,500cc Talbots from the cash-embarrassed STD combine in the autumn of 1927. He intended to run these as the Scuderia Materassi, based in his home town of Florence, although he was given no works backing. Although probably not acknowledged as such, Louis Chiron had become the No. 1 driver in the team. With the departure of Delage and Talbot from the racing scene, Ettore Bugatti had a strong pool of talent available to back up Chiron. He was now the only manufacturer who was running a full professional team, Alfa Corse, the racing division of Alfa Romeo was entering cars but these entries were irregular and the small Maserati firm was competing, but frequently the cars were driven by one of the Maserati brothers. Bugatti was able to call on the services of the unemployed Benoist, Divo and 'Williams', as well as the veteran Minoia.

The joker in the pack was Nuvolari, whose reputation and ability were burgeoning. According to René Dreyfus, in his autobiography *My Two Lives*, Bugatti offered Nuvolari a contract at the beginning of 1928 and it was agreed that he would drive the works cars in the major races, being free to run his own T35C in other races. He would also continue his motorcycle racing when this did not clash with the motor

racing commitments. Nuvolari formed Scuderia Nuvolari and to sponsor this he sold some farming land, then he persuaded Achille Varzi to join forces with him and race a second T35C which Nuvolari would have had prepared by his mechanic, Decimo Compagnoni. It seems that Nuvolari owned the second T35C and Varzi was only paying for his drives. Varzi was then 23 years old, the son of a rich textile manufacturer from Galliate, near Milan. After his motor racing debut with a T37 in the 1926 GP di Milano, he had gone back to motorcycles in 1927, racing for the Moto-Guzzi team, but was now intending to concentrate his efforts on driving cars. A third T35C was prepared for Cesare Pastore an old friend and supporter of Nuvolari, who may have paid for the car, and who certainly paid for the running costs.

From his earliest childhood, Ettore Bugatti's eldest son Jean had been fascinated by the cars that his father manufactured, and particularly, their racing exploits. Jean's interest had been encouraged by his father and while he had been given no formal engineering training, he had spent almost all his time in the Molsheim factory since his childhood, had been taken to many of the major races and had developed considerable skills including much of his father's flair for design. Jean's status as 'Crown Prince' was evident to all who worked at Molsheim. By 1928, while Ettore Bugatti was still wholly absorbed in the design and production of the racing cars

and the problems these posed, he was taking less interest in the organisation of the racing team. The responsibility of running the team had been delegated to Meo Costantini who now had the 19-year-old Jean as his assistant, although major decisions, including the programme for the season and the recruitment of drivers were still taken by Ettore Bugatti himself.

The first important event of the season was across the Mediterranean in Tripoli, on 11 March, where the Gran Premio, over 16 laps of the Mellaha circuit, a distance of 260 miles (418km) was beginning to assume a greater significance. Nuvolari and Pastore were entered by Scuderia Nuvolari, while Varzi had entered a T35C in his own name. AIACR regulations for races other than *grandes épreuves* still required that a riding mechanic should be carried or the car should carry ballast of 120kg. Materassi had entered two Talbot 700s and refused to carry the ballast, arguing that the cars had been designed as off-set single seaters. He asked Nuvolari to support his stand but Nuvolari refused, insisting the Talbots should carry the extra weight. The organisers asked the RACI to annul the rule but the request was refused, so Materassi withdrew the cars from the race. This left an emasculated field and Nuvolari led from the start, Pastore went off the road on the first lap and overturned, he and his mechanic escaping with minor injuries. Nuvolari stayed in front for 12 laps then dropped behind Varzi when he stopped for fuel. He

11 March 1928: Varzi fills the radiator of his Scuderia Nuvolari T35C before the start of the Gran Premio di Tripoli.

31 March 1928: Pietro Bordino (T43) at the start of the Mille Miglia. (Guy Griffiths Collection)

caught Varzi after two laps and went on to win easily. Towards the end, Varzi slowed and finished in third place.

Two weeks later, Nuvolari was at Pozzo, near Verona for the local Gran Premio. The 25-lap, 191-mile (307km) race was run in heavy rain and the course was covered in mud, so Nuvolari took a riding mechanic with him to wipe his goggles and the aero screen. He led for two laps then lost seven minutes with a puncture. Once going again, he retook the lead and went on to win by over a lap. Nuvolari's first works drive for Bugatti came on 31 March. Three T43s were entered for the Mille Miglia, although only a year old, it had already established itself as a major sports car race, ranking with Le Mans. Aymo Maggi had suggested to Ettore Bugatti that he should enter a team and he responded enthusiastically. As well as Nuvolari, the cars were driven by Gastone Brilli-Perri, a former member of the P2 Alfa Romeo team and Pietro Bordino, the Fiat ace who had won the 1922 GP d'Italia and beaten the field with his Tipo 806 Fiat at Monza the previous September. Nuvolari had driven a Bianchi and Brilli-Perri an Alfa Romeo in the 1927 event, while Bordino was a rising star at Molsheim, as he had bought a T35C which he had collected from the factory on 14 March. He had driven it at Pozzo, but fell out with minor problems. The opposition to the T43s was strong; there were full teams from Alfa Romeo, Lancia and OM. Alfa Romeo had a new model, the 6C/1500, the work of Vittorio Jano, the designer of the championship-winning P2. The first competitors left Brescia at 8am. The Bugattis were among the last cars to be flagged away and immediately led the field on time. At the end of the first leg to Bologna, via Parma, Nuvolari who had averaged 77mph (124kmh), led by 5min 30sec from Brilli-Perri, who was a minute ahead of Bordino in third place.

From Bologna, the course ran over the Futa Pass to Florence and then to Rome. The new 1500 Alfa Romeo was more nimble in the mountains than the T43 and the trio could not maintain their pace. At Rome, Giuseppe Campari's Alfa Romeo was leading, five minutes ahead of Nuvolari in second place and ten minutes ahead of Brilli-Perri, who had dropped back to fourth. Beyond Rome the T43s ran into trouble, Bordino had a jammed throttle, he and Nuvolari had to stop and change worn out brake shoes and all three had to make many stops to change plugs, but they made it to the finish at Brescia. Brilli-Perri was sixth, 31 minutes behind the winning Alfa Romeo of Campari and had the slight consolation of taking second place in the 3-litre class. Nuvolari and Bordino trailed in much later, taking 13th and 16th places. Varzi had entered a T35, but retired in the early stages.

While the three T43 drivers were changing plugs and brake shoes and having a miserable day, Louis Chiron was performing with his T35C at Cannes in the Circuit de la Riviera. The South of France was changing; it was still fashionable for the well-to-do to winter in one of the resorts and the popularity of the region as a summer playground was just beginning to grow. The race was a minor event, and provided a distraction for the visitors who would soon be departing.

31 March 1928: Nuvolari on the Futa Pass. His T43 has an extended stone guard over the radiator and lights. The tread on the spare tyre has been shredded.

Chiron was beaten in his six-lap heat by 20-year-old Edward Bret, driving another T35C, who was racing on home ground as his father owned the Hôtel des Anglais in Cannes. Chiron put the upstart in his place and dominated the ten-lap final. He was

1 April 1928: Left to right, Bret (T35C), Dreyfus (T37A) and Chiron (T35C) come out for the start of the Circuit de Riviera.

9 April 1928: Waiting for the start of the Grand Prix d'Antibes, Juan-les-Pins, Bret and Chiron are on the front row and 'Williams' (T35C No. 6) is behind. The course is little more than a country lane.

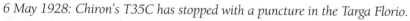

6 May 1928: Chiron's T35C has stopped with a puncture in the Targa Florio.

chased home by Bret and in third place was another local driver with a T37A, René Dreyfus, a 23-year-old paper merchant from Nice who had already gained some successes in local events with a T22. The T37A was not fast enough to challenge Chiron and Bret, but Dreyfus's driving impressed the onlookers. A week later a second Riviera race was held. This was at Juan-les-Pins and was over 75 laps of a 2.5-mile (4km) course in the woodlands on the Cap d'Antibes; the road was narrow and passing was difficult. Chiron and Bret resumed their previous battle, Chiron led but spun on the ninth lap, then stopped to inspect the car. He restarted at the rear of the 16-car field, meanwhile Bret led from 'Williams' and Dreyfus. Bret retired with valve troubles and Chiron caught 'Williams', going on to win by two laps, while Dreyfus was third. Soon afterwards,

Bret gave up motor racing and became a keen pilot. He was an agent in the Special Operations Executive during the Second World War and was decorated with the OBE.

There was a lull until 22 April when many of the leading Italian drivers took part in the Circuito di Alessandria over eight laps of the tough 20-mile course on the Lombardy plains. There was a tragic accident in practice when Bordino hit a dog which jammed the steering of his T35C, the car hit the parapet of a bridge and fell into the River Tanaro; Bordino was drowned before he could be rescued. According to Dreyfus's autobiography, when he heard about the accident, Costantini asked Nuvolari to withdraw from the race, either as a mark of respect, or as he feared Nuvolari could also have an accident. Nuvolari was a tough professional who, apart from other considerations, raced for the money. He ignored the request and raced. He dominated the race and led all the way after seeing-off a challenge from Materassi's Talbot. Varzi was second in his T35C, despite taking two long stops to change plugs. If he had not been delayed, the result would probably have been much closer.

Bugatti sent a full team to Sicily for the Targa Florio on 6th May. If Dreyfus is correct, Nuvolari had expected a works car for the race, but was told that as he had disregarded Costantini's wishes, the offer had been withdrawn and his services were no longer required. Usines Bugatti entered T35Cs for Chiron and Giulio Foresti, a T35B for Divo and a T37A for Minoia. When it was bench-tested at Molsheim before the race, the engine of Divo's car developed 130bhp at 5,100rpm. Deprived of his drive, Nuvolari had entered his own T35C, supported by Pastore. Among the many other entrants of private Bugattis, Elizabeth Junek was prominent; she had taken delivery of a new T35B a few weeks before and the car, painted in the Czech racing colours of yellow and black, was getting much support from the Molsheim mechanics.

6 May 1928: Elizabeth Junek in her T35B. (Guy Griffiths Collection)

6 May 1928: Elizabeth Junek after the race; Count Florio is on her right. (Guy Griffiths Collection)

16 May 1928: Janine Jennky (T35C) leads Chiron in the Coupe de Bourgogne.

There was a second woman driver, the German Countess Margot Einsiedel, with a T37A. The main opposition to the Bugattis came from works teams of 1,500cc Alfa Romeos and Tipo 26B Maseratis. During practice the Bugatti drivers used a T40 fitted with a truck body, to become familiar with the circuit. It was a hot day and dust rather than mud, was the main hazard. The cars were started at one-minute intervals so Campari led the works Bugattis on the road, but at the end of the first lap, Divo was in the lead followed by Elizabeth Junek and Campari. Mme Junek increased the pace on lap two and took the lead; undaunted she maintained this lead on the third lap and even passed Divo on the road.

At the end of lap three, Junek was still in front followed by Campari and Divo. Campari put on a spurt and at the start of the fifth and final lap, he led by a minute from Junek who was only nine seconds ahead of Divo and followed by Conelli, Chiron and Minoia. Soon after the start of the lap, Campari had a puncture and had to drive nearly 12 miles (20km) to reach his depot. This should have given Junek her chance, but the water pump of her engine was leaking and she stopped while her mechanic found water to top up the radiator. The delays to his rivals gave Divo his chance and he went on to win by nearly two

minutes from Campari, Conelli was third with his own T37A, Chiron was fourth and Mme Junek, despite her long stop was fifth. She had put up what is arguably the finest performance ever by a woman driver and may well be regarded as the greatest woman racing driver of all time. Nuvolari had retired after one lap with a broken piston and Countess Einsiedel was 12th despite hitting a wall en route. Despite his long racing experience, the 33-year-old Divo, who had served as a fighter pilot with the Armée de l'Air during the war, was probably under-rated by his contemporaries. At that time his true name was Diwo and this was changed to Divo by a decree of the Tribunal Civil de la Seine in December 1928.

On the same day that Mme Junek was demonstrating her remarkable ability, across the Mediterranean in Algeria, Marcel Lehoux was having an easy win in the GP d'Algerie with a T35C which had been sold to him the previous January; four weeks later he repeated the win in the GP de Tunisie. Women drivers were in the ascendant in the early summer of 1928, and Mme Janine Jennky, with a T35C carried off the Coupe de Bourgogne at Dijon on 16 May. This was a race of four hours duration and catered for both sports and racing cars. Initially, Chiron led with his Nerka-entered T35C but went off the road after 22 laps, leaving Jennky to win having covered 28 laps of the 10.8-mile (17.4km) circuit by the finish. In 1927, she had been the first woman to win a European hill-climb by setting best time at Gaillon with the T35C. In her private life, she was the long-standing mistress of Albert Divo.

The new grand prix formula had little appeal to race organisers and the national clubs were unwilling to make a commitment to the financial outlay of a *grande épreuve*, so lesser events now assumed a much greater importance. On 10 June, the Premio Reale di Roma on the Tre Fontana circuit, attracted an impressive entry and for Bugatti the race justified sending four cars all the way to Rome. There were T35Cs for Brilli-Perri and Chiron, a T39A for Minoia and an unusual T35 for Foresti. They faced the Materassi Talbots, several Maseratis and a large contingent of independent Bugattis, including Nuvolari's. It was noticeable that Pastore had abandoned the Scuderia Nuvolari and had bought a Tipo 26 Maserati. Brilli-Perri led for the first 12 laps then stopped with a puncture which let Chiron into the lead. He held this to the end and pulled out a five-minute lead over Brilli-Perri at the flag. Minoia was fourth just behind Materassi's Talbot and took second place in the 1,500cc class; Foresti without the urge of a supercharger,

was eighth. After his meteoric start to the season, Nuvolari had hit a bad patch; he retired four laps before the end with a broken piston, while holding third place.

There was some consolation for the failure of the T43s in the Mille Miglia when the Tre Fontana circuit was used again on 16 and 17 June for the 20-hour-duration Premio Romano del Tourismo; one T43 was entered, driven by Foresti and Minoia, and saw off challenges by several 6C-1500 Alfa Romeos to secure victory. Having rebuilt his engine after the Premio Reale, Nuvolari had some consolation at Cremona two weeks later. The Circuito di Cremona was an unusual race run over the imperial distance of 200 miles and comprising five laps of a 40-mile (64km) circuit, much in the tradition of the Targa Florio. It was a four-cornered fight between Nuvolari, the Talbots of Materassi and Arcangeli, and the P2 Alfa Romeo of Campari, ostensibly a private entry, but with much evidence of factory support. The race was against the clock and all four had tyre problems caused by the rough course. Campari fell right to the back but Nuvolari and Materassi fought to the finish. Tyres decided the outcome, Arcangeli had driven a slightly slower race and with fewer tyre stops, was the winner, but Nuvolari took second place just ahead of Materassi.

Possibly with an eye to the publicity value, and also perhaps as a reward to loyal drivers, Bugatti conceived the idea of an all-Bugatti Grand Prix over the Sarthe circuit at Le Mans, a week after the 24-hour race. This was open to amateur drivers and comprised eliminating heats and a handicap final. In the final, the T35Bs were on scratch and the limit T37s received a 34-minute start. The race for the lead became a hard battle between the T37s of Dubonnet, Baron Philippe de Rothschild, a member of the banking family, who raced under the pseudonym of 'Philippe' and 'Williams'. 'Williams' was delayed by a broken fuel line and Dubonnet pulled out a good lead but stopped to change plugs. His

Janine Jennky. (John Maitland Collection)

car refused to start and he got away just in front of de Rothschild and held a narrow lead to the end. 'Williams' was caught on the line by the T37A of Delzaert. The winner's prize was a new T35C covered in plaques noting the marque's successes, the second prize was a T37A and the third prize was a T37.

The Automobile Club de France wanted to promote the Grand Prix for the new formula, but by the time the entry list closed only six entries had been received. With a rapid change of heart, it was decided that the race would be held for sports cars, and would be on the 16.3-mile (26.2km) St Gaudens circuit at Comminges in south west France, on 1 July. The race comprised four ten-lap capacity class heats, the qualifiers would run in a ten-lap final which would be a handicap based on the times in the heats. Pit stops, mechanics and refuelling were barred and all tools and spares had to be carried on the cars. Bugatti

24 June 1928: The T37s line up after the Bugatti Grand Prix at Le Mans. No. 50 is the winner, Dubonnet. No. 53 is 'Philippe' who was second and No. 52, Delzaert, who was third. Ettore Bugatti in a characteristic bowler hat talks to Dubonnet.

entered 'Williams' with a T35C suitably equipped with wings and lights. He ran in the second heat for cars between 1,500cc and 3,000cc and qualified in second place behind Guy Drouet's T35. The only car to qualify in the 1,500cc heat was 'Sabipa''s T37A. The organisation was somewhat haphazard as Mme Jennky, who had not qualified in the heat, decided to run her T35C in the final and when the first group of 1,100cc cars was started in the final, Drouet started with them, so the group had to be stopped after a lap, then restarted

minus Drouet. 'Williams' had 32min 8sec to make up on the smallest cars. Drouet and 'Sabipa' retired and at half distance 'Williams' was in ninth place, two laps later he was fourth and as he started his last lap, he was in sight of Rousseau in the leading 1,100cc Salmson. Halfway round the lap, 'Williams' took the lead and came home to win by over two minutes.

A new racing car design had been intended for the Grand Prix de l'ACF and when the grand prix formula race was abandoned and the sports car race was substi-

tuted, the design was shelved. Much of the detail work was done by Adolphe Nuss, one of the Molsheim draughtsmen, and it was designated the T45. The remarkable feature was the power unit which was two engines, broadly similar to the T35, connected together by a gear train at the front. Each engine had a separate crankcase, but unlike the T35, there were nine roller main bearings and plain big ends with dry sump lubrication. Each engine had its own supercharger mounted at the rear. Two versions were produced, that intended for the grand prix car having dimensions of 60mm x 84mm and a capacity of 3,801cc. The second version was intended to power a sports racing car having dimensions of 60mm x 66mm and a capacity of 2,986cc, which became the T47. The T45 developed 250bhp and the T47, 200bhp, both peaking at 5,000rpm. The engine drove a separate four-speed gear box through the usual Bugatti clutch. The chassis was similar to the T35 but had slightly larger dimensions, with a wheelbase of 8ft 6in (2.6m) and a track of 4ft 1in (1.25m).

The Royal Automobile Club de Belgique had been running a 24-hour race for sports cars over the Spa-Francorchamps circuit since 1925, but this did not attract any Bugatti entries until 1928 when the race took place over the weekend of 7/8 July. Two T43s were entered by Belgian drivers, there was a T35 driven by Bouriano, a T37 and a T30. George Bouriano was a colourful personality, born in Rumania in 1901 of well-to-do parents, he had worked in Italy as a tester for Fiat before settling in Brussels. He did not fancy running for the full 24 hours so made bets totalling 10,000 Belgian francs that he would lead the race at the end of the first lap, which he knew would cover his expenses of preparing the car. At the 4pm start, Bouriano took the lead, he held it for six laps, so winning his bet, until he was passed by the T43 of Reynaerts, which began to pull away from the field. It stayed in front until dusk when it was slowed with tyre problems then the car caught fire while the co-driver, Freddy Charlier, was at the wheel; he stopped safely and the fire was extinguished but the car's race was run. Bouriano had stopped earlier with broken gears and the cylinder block had lifted on the second T43 driven by Delzaert. As the T30 had also shown incendiary tendencies and the T37 had stopped in the early laps, the first appearance of Bugatti sports cars at Spa was not a noteworthy success.

Chiron had been entered at Comminges with the Nerka car but did not attend. He took a factory T35B to Reims for the GP de la Marne on 8 July and had a fast, determined drive on the rolling plains of the

1 July 1928: 'Williams' checks over his T35C before the final of the Grand Prix de l'ACF at Comminges. The T35 of Guy Drouet is on the right.

7 July 1928: The T30 of Dethier and Mans de Zenica which retired after it caught fire during the Spa-Francorchamps 24-hour race.

7 July 1928: The T43 of Delzaert and Carels which retired from the Spa race when the cylinder block lifted.

change wheels, the heat of the day and the intensity of the race had made the wheels so hot they were very difficult to handle and he lost valuable time. Brilli-Perri put on a spurt and passed two of the Mercedes-Benz to take third place, then dropped back to fifth when he stopped for tyres. The pace and the conditions had been so demanding that at the end only ten cars were left running. The Mercedes-Benz team took the first three places led by Caracciola, and Brilli-Perri was fourth in front of the other Mercedes-Benz. Chiron and Minoia were sixth and seventh, leading Birkin's Bentley. The only other finishers were the two surviving T37As of Hans Simons and Kersting. The two T35Cs and the T35B carried off the 3-litre class and the T37As were the only finishers in the 1,500cc class. The death of Cenek Junek and also an Amilcar driver, von Halle, marred the race and understandably, Elizabeth Junek decided that she would never race again. In 1929/30, she acted as a travelling representative for Bugatti and took a T44 on a sales tour of India. She subsequently became a director of Bata, the Czech shoe company, and died in Prague on 5 January 1994, aged 93.

Champagne country. The opposition was amateur, the only real threat coming from Etancelin's T35C which dropped out at half distance and at the finish, Chiron had a lead of six laps. It was a different story a week later. Taking a cue from the ACF, the Automobilclub von Deutschland ran the Grosser Preis von Deutschland as a sports car race for a second year, no doubt with the aim of encouraging Mercedes-Benz. The 18-lap, 316-mile (508km) race was run over the full Nürburgring circuit using both north and south loops. The entry was divided into capacity classes. In the unlimited class there were four works SS Mercedes-Benz and a single works 4½-litre Bentley driven by Henry Birkin which had raced at Le Mans three weeks before. Bugatti brought out sets of wings and lights and entered two T35Bs for Minoia and Conelli, and two T35Cs for Chiron and Brilli-Perri. These ran in the 3-litre class with six privately entered T35s. Prominent among these was the yellow and black

T35B being shared by Elizabeth Junek and her husband Cenek.

In the 1,500cc class there were seven privately entered T37s. The race attracted 45 entries of which 41 started on a very hot day, watched by a crowd of 90,000 in a temperature of 40° with melting tar making the course treacherous in places. The classes were released at two-minute intervals, led by the largest cars. Mme Junek led the 3-litre class followed by Brilli-Perri, but on the second lap Chiron was leading the class, with Brilli-Perri still in second place. Chiron was trying very hard to keep up with the Mercedes-Benz team, Rudolf Caracciola was leading the race followed by Christian Werner, Georg Kimpel and Otto Merz, while the Bentley was in fifth place and being harried by the Bugatti. At the end of the fourth lap, Elizabeth Junek handed over to her husband, but halfway round the fifth lap he went off the road at the fast Breidscheid bend, the car overturned, and he was killed. Chiron stopped to refuel and

In the last week of July, the racing circus moved to San Sebastian where the usual fashionable speed festival took place. Following fashion, the Spanish club ran the Gran Premio de España as a sports car handicap, this taking place on Sunday, 29 July but the previous Wednesday, a 40-lap, 391-mile (498km) Formule Libre race was run over the Lasarte circuit. It was an indication of the state of the sport, or equally of the dominance of Bugatti, that the field of nine which started was all Bugatti. The rest, of whom the most prominent was Caracciola with a Mercedes-Benz, were non-starters. Bugatti entered four cars: a T35B for Benoist and T35Cs for Divo, Chiron and 'Williams'. Chiron led from the start but stopped after a lap with carburettor problems. He got going again at the back of the field which was being led by Divo who retired after 12 laps. This left Goffredo Zehender, an Italian amateur, to benefit from the refuelling stops of the faster cars and led with his T37A for a short while, but he was caught by Marcel Lehoux (T35C), who was battling with Benoist. Benoist passed Lehoux but Chiron was climbing through the field; he overtook Lehoux on lap 22 then set off after Benoist. He passed him with several laps to spare and went on to win by over two minutes. Benoist was second, followed by Lehoux and Zehender. Despite the one-marque field, the race had entertained the crowd and had also shown that Chiron could perhaps be regarded as the finest driver in Europe. To emphasise the point he defeated the field and the handicap to win the sports car Gran Premio the following Sunday.

After eliminating heats, there were 44 starters in the 15-lap final, the road was wet and Chiron starting from scratch gave a start of 23 minutes to the limit car. He came right through the field and at the finish, had a lead of five minutes over Bouriano who was second in another T35C. It also emphasised the reliability and strength of Bugattis that Chiron used the same T35C which had already done 40 laps four days before; fitted with wings and lights, it did all that was needed once more.

The Bugattis were dominating the sport north of the Alps, but in Italy the P2 Alfa Romeo was still capable of giving as good as it received and the only active car, driven by Campari was formidable. On 4 August, Campari took it to Pescara for the Coppa Acerbo, run on the 15.8-mile (25.4km) triangular circuit, with a long straight alongside the Adriatic and two legs running into the Apennines. He dominated the race, leading from start to finish, Nuvolari chased hard in his T35C but made two long stops which dropped him back to fourth at the finish. Once again, Varzi's T35C retired. The next day, the Targa Abruzzo for sports cars was run over 15 laps of the Pescara circuit, Foresti brought out a T43, presum-

15 July 1928: The T35Cs dominate the start of the 3-litre class of the Grosser Preis von Deutschland. The ill-fated Junek car (No. 9) is on the extreme left.

ably the car which had won at Rome and scored again, beating off a challenge from Ernesto Maserati's T26 Maserati and winning by five minutes from two 6C-1500 Alfa Romeos.

For Varzi, the season had been a disaster, his only finish had been at Alessandria in March. He was very ambitious and knew that his string of retirements in Nuvolari's cars was not advancing his cause. After the Pescara race, he told Nuvolari that he was terminating his agreement with Scuderia Nuvolari and went off to buy Campari's P2 Alfa Romeo. The manner in which their agreement was ended is not known, but it sparked off a bitter rivalry which was to last for many years and was to produce some electrifying motor racing in the seasons to come. Perhaps being relieved of the responsibility of maintaining Varzi's car, gave Decimo Compagnoni and the other mechanics more time to look after

their employer's car as the next time he raced, Nuvolari's T35C was running better. He ran in the Circuito do Montenero on the 14-mile (22.5km) circuit in the hills outside Livorno on 19 August. Materassi's mechanics, aided by the cars' designer, Bertarione, had done a lot of work on the Talbot 700s since their arrival in Italy and the cars were much faster than in 1927. Materassi ran away with the race driving one of the Talbots, but Nuvolari held on to him all the way and was a good second. The winner of the 1,500cc class was Carlo Tonini's T37A, which had taken third place at Pescara.

After the wet and dismal Isle of Man event in 1922, the RAC had refrained from promoting the Tourist Trophy for six years, but in 1928, it was revived in Northern Ireland, on a demanding, 13.6-mile (21.8km) circuit running between Newtownards, Comber and Dundonald on

18 August 1928: Malcolm Campbell's T43 on fire in the pits during the Ulster Tourist Trophy. The Boy Scouts are doing a good deed.

the eastern outskirts of Belfast. It was held on Saturday, 18 August and like the French and Spanish *grandes épreuves*, it was a sports car handicap, the larger cars having to carry four-seater bodies. Three T43s were entered, two were entered and driven by Malcolm Campbell and Lord Curzon respectively. Campbell was at the pinnacle of his fame as he held the World Land Speed Record, which he had taken the previous February at Daytona in his Napier-Campbell *Bluebird* at 206.95mph (332.99kmh). Curzon was 44 years old, and after a distinguished career in the Royal Navy and as a Member of Parliament, he had taken up motor racing at the beginning of the 1928 season. He and Campbell had raced their T43s in the Six-Hour race, another sports handicap at Brooklands in May, but both had retired early in the race. The following month, Curzon had taken second place in a 150-mile (240km) fuel

handicap for sports cars on the Brooklands track. The third T43, entered by Leo d'Erlanger, a member of the Anglo-French banking family, was probably a disguised factory entry and was driven by the Molsheim tester Louis Dutilleux. The three Bugattis ran in class D for cars from 2-litres to 3-litres. Each class had a distinguishing stripe painted on the bonnet; as class D was blue, the T43s needed no extra paintwork. It was an unhappy race; the cars had to do the first two laps with hoods erected. During the opening laps, the fuel tank of Campbell's car had split and when he stopped to lower his hood after the requisite two laps, fuel ran on to the exhaust pipe, the car burst into flames and burnt out completely, in front of the pits. Campbell shouted to the firefighters 'Save the engine, save the engine'.

This disaster received much attention in the daily press and many photographs were

published. The tank of Curzon's car also split and he was out of the race after 20 laps. Dutilleux carried on but the engine was misfiring and he finished in ninth place and third in class D. The tanks of Campbell's and Howe's cars had been modified in England, whereas Dutilleux's car had the original Molsheim tank. Dutilleux drove a T37A in the Coupe Georges Boillot on the Boulogne circuit on 8 September. This was a 12-lap sports car handicap on the 23.2-mile (37km) circuit. It was a sad event for him as the night before the race, he received a telephone call from Molsheim telling him that his eight-year-old son had died of typhoid. Ettore Bugatti suggested he should return immediately, but Dutilleux said he would honour his commitment to race. He took the lead on lap six, then hit a kerb on the last lap and a wheel collapsed.

Unlike the other national clubs, the RACI had the courage to run the Gran Premio d'Italia to the new grand prix formula. As the only race to be run to the formula during the 1928 season, the race was given the additional honour of being nominated as the Grand Prix d'Europe. It took place over 60 laps of the combined track at Monza on Sunday, 9 September, and if it had not been marred by a terrible accident, it would have been the outstanding race of the season and would have justified the organisers' enterprise. Surprisingly, Bugatti only sent 'Williams' and Chiron with T35Bs; Divo and Benoist were left at home. The pair were opposed by the Materassi Talbots, the Varzi P2 Alfa Romeo, a full team of the rapidly improving T26 Maseratis, a pair of the 1925 2-litre Delages and a large number of private entrants, mostly with Bugattis and led by Nuvolari. Twenty-two cars were on the balloted grid and 'Williams', who was on the front row, took the lead at the start followed by Nuvolari and Materassi. 'Williams' held the lead for four laps then stopped to change plugs and his race was run. This left Nuvolari in front while Materassi stopped to tighten a wheel.

Nuvolari was caught by Varzi and Brilli-Perri with one of the Talbots and the three began a slipstreaming battle. Chiron, who had started from the back row, was gradually coming through the field and at ten laps had tacked on to the leading group. Brilli-Perri stopped for plugs and Chiron and Varzi began to ease away from Nuvolari, then on lap 17 the whole character of the race changed. Materassi had rejoined the race in 12th place, but had worked his way up to fifth; on lap 17, he swerved while passing Foresti's T35C on the grand stand straight and the Talbot hit the barrier at the side of the track. Materassi was thrown out and killed instantly, and the cart-wheeling car went into the packed crowd, 22 spectators were killed and many more injured. The organisers decided that to stop the race would cause greater problems, so it continued. Chiron and Varzi seemed unaware of the tragedy and fought on fiercely, and on lap 20 Chiron took the lead and began to pull away from Varzi. When Varzi stopped to refuel he handed the car over to Campari who had been helping the injured spectators and had little inclination to race. He carried on but the challenge to Chiron was over and he reeled off the remaining laps to come home the winner, over two minutes in front of the P2 Alfa Romeo, Nuvolari was third, but 14 minutes behind Chiron.

British enthusiasts were providing the best market outside France for Bugattis, both racing and touring models. During the 1928 season T35s and T37s were prominent at Brooklands, which apart from the Shelsley Walsh hill-climb and a sand racing course at Southport, was the only racing venue in England. At the Easter meeting, Chris Staniland, a test pilot for Fairey Aviation won two handicaps on the outer circuit with his T37A lapping the track at 108.51mph (174.48kmh). At the Whitsun meeting Staniland lapped even faster, at 113.19mph (182.00kmh) although un-

placed in a handicap, but Dr Dudley Benjafield, the 1927 Le Mans victor, won a handicap with his ex-Campbell Boulogne-winning T37A, instead of his more customary Bentley, as did W. B. Scott with a T35. Scott's best lap was 110.68mph (177.97kmh). Scott and his wife gained several victories at minor Brooklands club meetings during the season. Staniland continued to win, although his successes meant that he received a stiffer handicap each time he raced. At the August Bank Holiday meeting he won two handicaps, one at an average of 108.57mph (174.58kmh). At the closing meeting of the season, on 22 September, Staniland took two second places in handicaps and while doing so, lapped the track at 121.47mph (195.32kmh) the fastest lap ever by a T37A at Brooklands and an indication of the potential of the car. Some international class records were broken at Brooklands by Bugattis during the season. In July, Kaye Don, the winner of the Ulster Tourist Trophy, used a T35B to take the class D (2-litre to 3-litre) five and ten-kilometre and five and ten-mile records at over 121mph (195kmh) and the standing start kilometre in 29.3sec 72.2mph (116.19kmh).

The following day, he took the car out again and took the standing start mile in 42.28sec (85.14mph/136.99kmh), the flying start kilometre at 196.98kmh (122.4mph) and the flying mile at 121.08mph (194.82kmh). He finished his day by taking the 50 kilometres at 178.32kmh (110.8mph) and the 50 miles at 110.9mph. This was a useful clutch of records that would have collected him the usual bonuses. In September, Staniland used his impressive T37A in an attempt on Eyston's class F (1½-litre) one-hour record, but failed by a narrow margin, although he had the consolation of taking the 100-mile class record at 115.82mph (186.23kmh).

The season had been triumphant for

Bugatti, the cars had dominated both Formule Libre and sports car racing. The only real set-back was in the Mille Miglia, as the defeat by the much bigger-engined Mercedes-Benz at the Nürburgring was not unexpected. The touring cars were selling well, production of the T38 had been tailed-off and it had been replaced by the T44 during 1928; it was a popular car, and the T40 was still finding willing customers. Trading conditions in France were still favourable and the depression which was starting to emerge in the other major countries of the world would take longer to bite in France. Poincaré had led the moderate right-wing parties to victory in the April 1928 elections, the economic changes introduced when he became prime minister in 1926 were working, despite the ominous signs of problems in the future. French sales in overseas markets had dropped as the franc had become over-valued so there was a mild devaluation in June. In the autumn, the radical wing of the governing coalition broke away, but unusual for France, the government did not fall; things would get worse, but not yet. In Germany, there had been a gradual return to prosperity after the collapse of the mark in 1921, but fears of a slump were helping to increase the membership of the National Socialist German Workers Party, under its leader Adolf Hitler. In his political testament *Mein Kampf*, Hitler called for the repudiation of the Treaty of Versailles, but any possibility that this posed a threat was ignored by the French government. France had not recovered from the crippling losses of the war and pacifism had gripped the French people. The period of compulsory military service was reduced to 12 months in March 1928 which brought general acclaim. Among those who benefited was René Dreyfus, who had been called up for military service shortly after he had competed in the Targa Florio in May.

Chapter 8

1929 – another year of triumph

LOUIS CHIRON WAS NOT available to race for Bugatti at the beginning of the 1929 season. His results in 1928 had made him the Champion of Europe and he had ambitions to gain further glories on the other side of the Atlantic. He went to the United States during the early months of 1929 to test several American cars at Indianapolis with the aim of winning the 500-mile race on 30 May, which was still being run to the 91cu in (1,500cc) formula. It seems Chiron was not happy with the cars he tried and agreed with Freddie Hoffmann, who was sponsoring the venture, that the ideal car

for the race would be a 1,500cc GP Delage. Although three of the cars had been sold, Delage had retained one of the 1927 team and this was either bought by Hoffmann or leased by him for Chiron to drive at Indianapolis. Chiron would probably have been better suited by a Miller or a Duesenberg, as the Delage took seventh place in the race and never offered a serious challenge. Alice Hoffmann accompanied her husband and Chiron to the race and unknown to Hoffmann, a relationship was beginning to form between her and Chiron.

The AIACR decided that the grand prix

formula needed modifying for the 1929 season, although the motor racing world took little notice as Formule Libre racing in the form that had become established in 1928, was generally accepted as providing the racing that everyone wanted. The new formula was probably doomed by its impracticality; there was a minimum weight of 900kgs (1,980lb) and a minimum body width of one metre (3ft 3in). Fuel and oil consumption was limited, 14kg per 100km were allowed, which assumed a fuel consumption of 14/15mpg. More bizarre, a standard size cylindrical fuel tank had to be carried on the car and left exposed, without any bodywork covering it.

Nuvolari had two T35Cs and also a large pile of spare parts. He realised the T35Cs would probably not be competitive in 1929 and he needed a new car, so he engaged a young engineer, Alberto Massimimo to design a single seater from the parts. The construction was done by Compagnoni, assisted by Amadeo Bignami and the result was an ugly, quasi single-seater with the engine offset to the left, a narrowed frame and a large misproportioned radiator. Massimimo was at the beginning of a long learning curve, the result was unsuccessful and the car known as a TN, was rejected by Nuvolari when he tested it at the end of December 1928. In a letter to Masssimimo, he said: 'it needs very major adjustment in

24 March 1929: Nuvolari, in a Fair Isle jersey, before the start of the Gran Premio di Tripoli.

connection with its stability'. Massimimo went on to join Enzo Ferrari as one of the design team for the Tipo 158 Alfa Romeo, later worked for Maserati designing the A6GCM and, after doing some work on the 250F, ended his career as Ferrari's technical director in the 1950s, so perhaps the TN was an invaluable experience. Nuvolari took one of the T35Cs to Tripoli for the first major race of the season on 24th March. Despite Materassi's death, his Scuderia continued to race the Talbots and one of these, driven by Brilli-Perri, ran away with the race after a fierce battle with Borzacchini's Tipo 26 Maserati and Varzi's P2 Alfa Romeo. Nuvolari was in the battle for a while, then dropped back with misfiring and finished third.

As in 1928, the closing Riviera season was entertained by two races at Antibes and Cannes. The Antibes race was led by 'Georges Philippe', otherwise Baron Philippe de Rothschild, who had bought three T35Cs through Guy Bouriat, a Bugatti agent in Paris. When 'Philippe' crashed at half distance, victory went to the T35B of Mario Lepori, a Swiss driver living in Lugano, who had bought Divo's winning car in the 1928 Targa Florio. A week later, on 7th April, the second race was held at Cannes and Edward Bret, probably revelling in the absence of Chiron, had a runaway win in his T35B, followed by an ever-

improving Dreyfus with his T37A. With the aim of getting some sales-boosting publicity, a T44 with a saloon body was taken to Montlhéry during April. Under the supervision of Jean Bugatti and Costantini, it did a 24-hour timed run on the track, driven by Divo, Marco and Dutilleux and covered 3,000km at an average speed of 75mph (125kmh).

Since 1911, the annual rally had made Monte Carlo a centre of motoring endeavour, but Anthony Nòghes, the rally organiser wanted to have a motor race in the Monaco principality. Furthermore, he wanted this race to have the full status of a grande épreuve as the Grand Prix de Monaco. This seemed impractical to most observers as the locality was wholly built-up and there appeared to be no possible venue for a race. Undaunted Nòghes decided upon a circuit in the centre of Monaco, running through the streets. Even the officials of the AC de Monaco were sceptical at first, but they were swayed by Nòghes's arguments, not least by the suggestion that there could be economic benefits for the principality. Nòghes then persuaded the equally sceptical officials of the AIACR that Monaco should be permitted to stage a street grande épreuve; there had been races where the circuits ran through towns, but there had never been a race where all the action took place in a town, and this became the first 'round the houses' race. Thus the Grand Prix de Monaco, to many the most romantic and attractive motor race of all, came about and the AIACR agreed that the first GP de Monaco should be held on 14 April 1929.

Surprisingly, the race did not attract any official entries from Molsheim, but 'Williams' had entered a T35B, which was painted green in recognition of his nationality. Records seem to indicate that the car was still registered in the name of Ettore Bugatti Automobiles, so it may have been a disguised factory entry. 'Williams' was supported by some of the stronger independents such as Etancelin and Lehoux, who had won the GP d'Algérie the previous week. The opposition came from several 6C-1750 Alfa Romeos, the new enlarged 6C and expected to be well-suited to the street circuit. Most unusually, Caracciola had entered an SSK Mercedes-Benz, a new short chassis version of the Nürburgring victor, but even in its abbreviated form, it was a seemingly impractical car for the circuit. The starting grid was balloted which made Caracciola's task even more difficult as he was on the back row. The notable absentee was the local hero and European Champion, Chiron, who was in the USA. Race day was warm and fine, and Prince

14th April 1929: 'Williams' (T35B No. 12) races Etancelin (T35C No. 4) for the first corner. (John Maitland Collection)

14 April 1929: 'Philippe' (T35C) is in third place ahead of Caracciola's SSKL Mercedes-Benz at the Tabac.

Louis of Monaco toured the circuit in a Voisin before the field of 15 was released. Lehoux led for the first two corners, then 'Williams' went to the front, while Lehoux crashed on lap two. Caracciola was storming through the field and was up to second place by lap five. He stalked 'Williams', the gap fluctuating between two and six seconds, and took the lead on lap 30 between the Tunnel and the chicane, but the Bugatti went to the front again on lap 35. 'Williams' then stopped for fuel which let Caracciola, who was only two seconds behind, into the lead. When Caracciola made his stop, it lasted over four minutes while the huge tank was filled and the rear wheels were changed and he was back in fourth place behind the T35Cs of Bouriano and 'Philippe' when he restarted.

Bouriano then had his problems when he spun and hit the wall at Mirabeau Corner on lap 65. He stalled and bent the starting handle, but was able to restart the engine by coasting the car down the hill. This left 'Williams' with a commanding lead and he went on to win by over a minute from Bouriano, while Caracciola caught 'Philippe' to take third place. Anthony Nòghes's faith had been fully justified and the critics, who prophesied that the field would be eliminated by crashes, were confounded; Lehoux had the only accident, and probably just as satisfying, the race made a minimal loss of FF610. It was run on the same day as the Mille Miglia, but after the disappointments of 1928, no Bugatti team had gone to Brescia; there were three private T43s, but the only finisher was the car of Ricchetti/Ferlunga which completed the course in 24th place, over five hours behind the winning Alfa Romeo. Richetti had been racing a T35 and was the victor in the 1926 Trieste-Opicina hillclimb.

The first outing for the works Bugattis was in Sicily at the Targa Florio on 5 May. It was probably a relief for the team that Varzi had not entered with his P2 Alfa Romeo, as after a setback in Tripoli, he had been unbeatable in the early Italian races of the

5 May 1929: A famous photograph showing Minoia's T35C being refuelled in the Targa Florio.

season. T35Cs were entered for Divo, Wagner, Minoia and Conelli and the opposition came from an Alfa Corse team of 6C-1750 Alfa Romeos and several Maseratis including two factory entries. Mme Junek, who had come to give support to the team, was acclaimed wherever she went on the island. Campari was expected to give Alfa Romeo a long-awaited win so his team was dismayed when he had an off-day and offered no challenge to the Bugattis. After a lap, Minoia led followed by Borzacchini (Maserati) and Divo. On lap two Divo, who had the spur of following Campari on the road, speeded up and took second place. W. F. Bradley, who was watching the race, went to the Bugatti replenishment depot at Polizzi in the mountains, halfway round the 67-mile (107km) course. The depot was managed by Costantini and Bradley was impressed by the rapid, well-drilled refuelling stops. Divo kept up the pressure and took the lead from Minoia on lap four, going on to win. Minoia was second and Brilli-

Perri, who had rejoined the Alfa Corse team, took third place. Wagner retired with a broken piston and Conelli hit a rock which had rolled into the road. Foresti, who was driving one of 'Philippe''s T35Cs finished in fifth and last place behind Campari, over two hours after the winner, having stopped with a multitude of troubles on the way.

On the Wednesday after the Targa Florio, 'Philippe' was at Dijon for the GP de Bourgogne with two of his T35Cs, he drove one himself and entrusted the other to Bouriat. The pair came first and second, Bouriat dutifully following his sponsor home. The importance of the Prix Reale di Roma justified a T35C being sent to Italy on 26 May for Divo. He was up against the cream of the home runners including Varzi and an additional factory-entered P2 for Brilli-Perri. The two P2 Alfa Romeos ran away from the field and Nuvolari with his T35C chased them, followed by Divo. Nuvolari dropped out with the almost inevitable mechanical problems, leaving

Divo to take third place, ten minutes behind the two Alfa Romeos. The P2 Alfa Romeo was still a potent car, with the reviving interest of Alfa Corse in preparing and entering the cars and the advance in the stature of Varzi, it was becoming unlikely that any foray by Bugatti into Italy would yield a dividend.

The success of the Bugatti Grand Prix in 1928 encouraged Ettore Bugatti to sponsor the race again in 1929. It was held on Sunday, 2 June and became the first of a series of events over the Sarthe circuit at Le Mans, which would run throughout June. It was a Formule Libre race, each competitor was given 54kg (118lb) of fuel and oil, the relative combination being left to the driver. The race was over 25 laps of the circuit, which had been shortened since 1928 by the elimination of the Pontlieu Hairpin in the suburbs of the city. The race distance was 254 miles (408km). There were 15 starters, flagged away by Ettore Bugatti

and the winner was Juan Zanelli, the Chilean, who was the Vice-Consul of Chile in Nice, with a T35C. He was followed by Robert Gauthier with another T35C and 'Sabipa' was third with a T37A. Zanelli had burst the engine of his T35C in practice and to get a drive in the race, he bought one of 'Philippe''s T35Cs on the morning of the race. This was the car raced by 'Philippe' at Monaco. There were only five finishers and 'Philippe', who drove a T43 was one of the retirements. The first prize was a new T43 Grand Sport valued at 130,000FF, at the rate of exchange fixed the previous summer; this was £1,075. Second prize was a T44 chassis valued at 60,000FF and the third place earned a T40 chassis worth 36,000FF. There is some doubt if Zanelli took the T43, as Antoine Raffaelli says he received one of the factory-entered T35Bs which ran in the Grand Prix de l'ACF later in the month, and was overhauled before delivery to him.

The 24-hour race was held on the Sarthe circuit on 15 and 16 June and resulted in a victory for the Bentley team, the third in a row. The British cars took the first four places, followed in fifth place by a Stutz shared by Bouriat and 'Philippe'. Ettore Bugatti attended the race, which was the occasion of his apocryphal comment, 'Mr Bentley is a very clever man to make his lorries go so fast'. When this appeared in the press, Bugatti was deeply concerned, he wrote to W. O. Bentley immediately, dissociating himself from the remark, which he was emphatic he did not make and apologised to Bentley for any distress that the report might have caused. Not everyone was at Le Mans that weekend. The minor GP de Lyon was held on a small triangular circuit at Quincieux, north of the city and now bisected by the Autoroute du Soleil. It proved an easy win for the German driver Hans Simons with his T35, after he had seen off a challenge from Dreyfus who crashed his T37A.

The Grand Prix de l'ACF was held at Le Mans on 30 June and was run to the fuel consumption formula. Bugatti entered three T35Bs for Divo, Conelli and 'Williams'. The cars had an ugly bolster fuel tank replacing the usual tail, with a large dial gauge mounted on it and a spare wheel strapped behind. Probably in the interests of fuel consumption, an interim 150mm supercharger was fitted. The cockpit sides were widened to conform with the one metre width regulation and as the cars had to comply with the minimum weight limit of 900kg, ballast must have been carried. When weighed at Molsheim before the race, one car scaled 910kg. The cost of the tank, the gauge and the fuel supplied, was met by the ACF from the entry fee of 5,000FF. The race was over 37 laps of the circuit, a distance of 607km (377 miles) to comply with the formula's requirement of a minimum race distance of 600km (373 miles). There were four independent Bugattis led by 'Philippe'. Remarkably, the Peugeot company had entered two of the

26 May 1929: Nuvolari in his T35C during the Premio Reale di Roma. Perhaps the tow rope draped over the front was a premonition, as he later retired.

elderly 174S models which had first appeared in the 1924 Targa Florio. These were driven by André Boillot and by Guy Bouriat who had abandoned a 'Philippe' drive for this race. Jean Chassagne led the field at the start with an old Ballot, but at the end of the first lap it was Boillot's Peugeot in front, being pursued by 'Williams' and Conelli. Despite 'Williams''s efforts, including a new lap record, Boillot stayed there for six laps, then the Bugatti took the lead, but Boillot was back in front on lap nine. A lap later 'Williams' was back in front and pulled out a small margin which increased when Boillot made a brief pit stop and lost second place to Conelli for a short while. 'Williams' went on to win by 1min 19sec and Boillot just staved off Conelli by eight seconds to take second place. Divo was fourth, Robert Sénéchal (T35B) was fifth and Robert Gauthier (T35C) was sixth and last. During the race 'Williams' had averaged 17 litres per 100km (15.5mpg) and had taken 20 seconds off the lap record set two weeks earlier by Henry Birkin's 6½-litre Bentley.

It was an indication of the strength of racing in France that on Sunday, 7 July there were two grands prix only 135 miles (220 km) apart and both attracted reasonable fields, while over the same weekend, across the frontier in Belgium, the 24-hour sports car race was run at Spa with an impressive entry of 38 cars. At Reims, there were ten starters in the GP de la Marne. Etancelin led with his new T35C which he had collected from Molsheim ten days earlier. He was chased by Zanelli, whose spare wheel fell off as he was passing the main stand, injuring a spectator, but Zanelli continued his chase and took the lead when Etancelin refuelled. Zanelli then made his stop and Etancelin went to the front again, staying there to the end. Zanelli was second and Lehoux, with a new T35B, was third. In the GP de Dieppe there were 24 starters, but none troubled Dreyfus who had an easy win with a borrowed T35B. He was driving the car raced by 'Williams' at

30 June 1929: Conelli in the T35C which finished third in the Grand Prix de l'ACF at Le Mans. The bolster tank and the fuel gauge are prominent.

Monaco, still painted green, which had been sold after the race, to Albert de Bondelli, a friend of Dreyfus. Dreyfus's talent had been noticed, as he was supported at Dieppe by Ernest Friderich.

At Spa, Charlier had a T43 and there was also a T44 and a T37. The race was honoured by the presence of Prince Leopold, the heir to the Belgian throne, accompanied by his wife, the much-admired Princess Astrid. Leopold was a keen Bugatti owner and had become a personal friend of Ettore Bugatti. It was overcast when the race began, and soon afterwards it rained. On the opening lap, Charlier collided with the Minerva of Lamarche, bending a wing and breaking a brake cable on the T43. He was in the pits for 50 minutes while repairs were made, then he set off to chase the field. He was timed on the Masta Straight at 113mph (183kmh), the highest speed recorded in the race, but during the evening, the T43 went off the road and hit a tree; Charlier

30 June 1929: 'Williams' the winner. (John Maitland Collection)

6 July 1929: The T44 shared by Barthelemy and Porta, which was fourth in the 3-litre class of the Spa-Francorchamps 24-hour race.

was killed instantly. The race was won by the 1750 Alfa Romeo of Robert Benoist and Attilio Marinoni. The T44 of Barthelemy and Porta, fitted with a lightweight fabric body, kept going and came fourth in the 3-litre class, while the T37 took second place in the 1,500cc class behind the Alfa Romeo of Eyston and Ivanowsky.

Louis Chiron returned to the fold on Bastille Day, 14 July when he led the team of three T35Cs at the Nürburgring for the Grosser Preis von Deutschland. His team mates were 'Philippe' and Bouriat, both getting a works drive for the first time. It is possible that 'Philippe''s two cars were incorporated into the team and prepared at

Molsheim. The race was for sports cars again, so the T35Cs ran fully equipped. In addition to the factory entries, there were three private Bugattis in the 3-litre class and four running in the 1,500cc class. There were four works-entered SSK Mercedes-Benz led by Caracciola. Practice times showed that the Bugattis were faster than in 1928, which seems to indicate that either the contemporary press reports were wrong and the cars were T35Bs, or a larger supercharger was being used. Race day was fine and a crowd estimated at 78,000 turned up to watch.

The big car class was the first to be flagged away, followed two minutes later by the 3-litre class. Caracciola led the race in the opening laps, but by lap four, Chiron had made up the two minute deficit, passed three Mercedes-Benz and was on Caracciola's heels. The pressure was too much for the German car and it was out a lap later with a broken con rod. Bouriat passed the three remaining Mercedes-Benz to take second place behind Chiron and took the lead when Chiron stopped to refuel, change tyres and refresh himself with a glass of champagne. Suitably fortified, Chiron went back into the lead, followed by 'Philippe' and Bouriat, but Rosenstein and Momberger speeded up their Mercedes-Benz and went past Bouriat. On the last lap, Rosenstein's car was in trouble and slowed, he was passed by Bouriat and Mario Lepori, whose T35B was the fastest of the private entries. Chiron won by 11 minutes, or nearly a lap and drank a lot more champagne, 'Philippe' was second and Momberger was third, followed by Bouriat and Lepori. The 1,500cc class was won by Ernst Burggaller, the Berlin driver with a T37A. The defeat of 1928 had been avenged, but the reason for the Bugattis' extra speed remains unknown. Chiron had taken eight minutes off Caracciola's 1928 race time and had set a fastest lap that was 13 seconds quicker.

Costantini must have been satisfied with the performance of 'Philippe' and Bouriat at the Nürburgring, as they were engaged for the Gran Premio do San Sebastian on Friday, 25 July. They were supporting Chiron in the second race of the 1929 season which was run to the unpopular grand prix formula. 'Philippe' and Bouriat had T35Cs, which again gives rise to the surmise that 'Philippe''s two cars had been absorbed into the factory team, while Chiron had a T35B. The wide bodies and bolster tanks were taken out of the stores and fitted to the three cars to comply with the regulations and presumably the 150mm superchargers were fitted too. The 14-car field was all-Bugatti, except for a 1925 2-litre Delage and a 6C-1500 Alfa Romeo. It was a 430-mile (690km) race over 40 laps of the Lasarte circuit. The race began in a drizzle and 'Philippe' took the lead at the start and stayed in front for two laps, he was passed by Zanelli, but was back in the lead on lap five. The rain was falling heavily and Chiron was biding his time in third place. Zanelli spun off the road and retired,

14 July 1928: Seibel in a T37A; he did not finish the Grosser Preis von Deutschland.

17 August 1929: Count Conelli in his T43. He was still running at the end of the Ulster Tourist Trophy, but was not classified as a finisher. (Guy Griffiths Collection)

but Etancelin who had move up to third, was coping well with the conditions and passed Chiron. When the drivers made their refuelling stops at half distance, 'Philippe' handed over to Bouriat who had dropped out with a lack of brakes on lap seven. Etancelin had led for a lap until he stopped, and after the stops Bouriat was in front, but Chiron speeded up and went into the lead on lap 24. Bouriat was being followed by Etancelin who was caught out by the conditions on lap 30 and rolled his car into a ditch. He was unhurt, but this left Chiron with a commanding lead from Bouriat. Chiron eased off near the end letting Bouriat close the gap, but he won by five minutes. Lehoux was third, only a minute behind Bouriat while the improving Dreyfus was fourth in the Bondelli car.

Etancelin soon made repairs to his car, and to show that the accident had not left any after-effects, on 18 August, he won the 2-litre class at Comminges, after Lehoux crashed and Zanelli retired. Four days later he must have impressed the holiday makers when he romped home to an easy win on the sands of La Baule in the Loire estuary in the local Grand Prix. The day before Etancelin's victory at Comminges, Bugatti had sent four T43s to Northern Ireland for the Tourist Trophy; the size of the entry and the drivers engaged, indicated this was a serious venture. The team comprised Divo, 'Williams', Conelli and Baron d'Erlanger. There were two private T43s driven by Earl Howe, the former Lord Curzon who had recently succeeded to the earldom on the death of his father, and J. F. Field. D'Erlanger arrived too late for practice and was excluded, but the race was a failure for the other T43s, which were delayed by a multitude of problems such as broken oil pipes and exhausts. All were flagged off at the end

and none was classified as a finisher. This was the second Irish failure for the T43 in 1929. On 13 July, Field and Basil Eyston, the brother of George, had driven in the Irish Grand Prix on the Phoenix Park circuit in Dublin. Both cars 'did a Campbell', catching fire while being refuelled at the pits.

The golden days of Bugatti in Italian races had been ended by the resurgence of the P2 Alfa Romeo, the increased speed of the Materassi Talbots and the growing stature of Maserati. Renato Balestrero had won the Coppa di Camaiore in July with a T35C but otherwise the results had been negligible. Since the Rome race in May, Nuvolari had abandoned his T35C and had been driving a 6C-1750 Alfa Romeo and one of the Talbots. The last major event of the Italian season was the Gran Premio di Monza on 15 September. The Reale Automobile Club d'Italia decided it would not organise a *grande épreuve* under the formula rules and invited Count Florio to run a Formule Libre event at Monza. Florio knew that good racing was needed to attract the crowds and decided upon a meeting using only the fast, banked track. The race was run in three 22-lap qualifying heats of 61.5 miles (98.9km) with cars running in capacity classes and a 22-lap final. Bugatti and Costantini must have realised that the T35B or C would not be fast enough in a race that would need sheer speed, so no cars were sent from Molsheim. Zanelli ran a T35B and T35Cs were entered by Clemente Biondetti and Foresti, who presumably had one of the 'Philippe' cars. The three Bugattis ran in the second heat for the 3-litre cars and the drivers watched the two P2 Alfa Romeos and the Tipo 26B Maserati disappear into the distance. Zanelli retired, while Biondetti and Foresti were fourth and fifth, so did not qualify for the final which was won by Varzi with his P2 Alfa Romeo.

The sensation of the meeting was the American driver, Leon Duray. His real name was George Stewart, but he had adopted the name of Duray as it had a better sound for the American crowds. Duray had been racing on the American board track circuits for most of the decade. He had the reputation of being a hard, unyielding driver, he had led the Indianapolis 500 on several occasions, but his car had broken under him. During the qualifying trials at Indianapolis in 1928, he covered four laps of the track at 122.391mph (196.80kmh) and did one lap at 124.018mph (199.42kmh) with a front-drive Miller 91, setting a qualifying record that stood until 1937. Later in 1928 he set a World Closed Circuit Record on the 2½-mile (4km) Packard testing track in Michigan at 148.17mph (238.25kmh). He had scored several important wins on the wooden board tracks where speeds were maintained that were regarded as almost impossible in Europe. In 1929, his racing was sponsored by the Packard Cable Co. and he came to Europe in the late summer with two front-drive Miller 91s. Duray took one car to the speed trials at Arpajon on the N20 between Paris and Orleans and broke the class F (1,500cc) record for the flying kilometre at 138mph (222kmh).

The second car was taken to Montlhéry where, in the cool of the evening to save the tyres, Duray broke the World ten-mile record at 135.55mph (217.96kmh) and the class F five-mile and five-kilometre records at 139.22mph (223.86kmh). These records caused a sensation in the French motoring world as the speeds were unattainable by any European 1,500cc car and the twin-camshaft eight-cylinder engine was setting wholly new standards of performance. At Monza, Duray drove both cars. He went to the front of the 1,500cc heat passing the Materassi Talbots with ease, but after 15 laps the car pulled off with big end failure. This seems remarkable in a car designed for sustained high speed, but all the American tracks ran anti-clockwise, unlike the clockwise Monza. It is likely that centrifugal force was forcing the oil in the dry sump tank away from the pick-up sited for the

18 December 1929 Montlhéry. 'Hellé-Nice' in her T35C after breaking local class records.

American tracks. The second car was alleged to be 1,502cc and ran in the 3-litre heat, but it dropped out for the same reason, although some reports state it had transmission problems. For Bugatti, the Millers were a catalyst which began a technical revolution at Molsheim.

Bugattis were not quite so prominent at Brooklands in 1929. George Eyston brought out his T35B on the Thursday before Easter and took the class D five-mile and ten-mile and one-kilometre records, the five-kilometre speed being 124.57mph (200.30kmh). On Easter Monday, 1 April, he used the T35B to win the Founders' Gold Cup Race at 114.17mph (183.58kmh) with a best lap of 122.07mph (196.28kmh). On 10 and 11 May the Junior Car Club organised the Double-Twelve-Hour Race, a sports car event in which the competitors ran for 12 hours on each day. Earl Howe drove a T43, but in

typical T43 form, was beset with problems and although still running at the end, was unclassified. At the Whitsun meeting R. C. Stewart won a handicap with his T37A, lapping at 110.92mph (178.35kmh), after Staniland's much faster T37A had dropped out of the race. At the autumn meeting, C. R. A. Grant lapped the track at 109.22mph (175.62kmh) in his T35, an impressive speed for an unsupercharged car, when winning the 90mph Short Handicap.

During 1928, Sir William Orpen had tired of the charms of Yvonne Aubicq, so they parted. The parting was amicable and Orpen made her a generous settlement and presented her with his Rolls-Royce Silver Ghost. On 27 November 1929, Yvonne Aubicq married 'Williams' at Montrouge, the Paris suburb where he had been born; they settled at La Baule where they soon established a reputation as leading breeders of Aberdeen terriers.

Chapter 9

Two camshafts

THERE HAVE BEEN MANY accounts of the events which led to the appearance of the first twin overhead camshaft Bugatti engine in 1930. Studying these accounts it seems possible to deduce that Jean Bugatti's influence was growing and played an important part in these events. Although only 20 years old, at the beginning of 1929, he had realised that the days of the T35B and C were numbered. It was becoming more difficult for the cars to win races and if grand prix racing was restored to its former glories, newer and faster designs would appear. Early in 1929, Vittorio Jano had started work on a new eight-cylinder engine for Alfa Romeo which would replace the P2. As Jano wrote to the British Alfa Romeo concessionaire about the design in September 1929, its existence was probably an open secret in the closely knit motor racing world, soon after the design work began. Jean appreciated the limitations of the three-valve T35 design and began urging his father that a new twin-camshaft engine was needed. Although inherently conservative, Ettore Bugatti appreciated his son's arguments, then a most fortuitous turn of events came to his aid.

Like the rest of the French motoring world, Bugatti had been most impressed with the performance of Duray's Millers at Montlhéry. It is not certain if he was at Monza in September to watch Duray racing the cars, but either at Monza, or shortly afterwards, Bugatti agreed to buy the two Millers. Some reports suggest that Duray was penniless and needed to sell the cars to pay for his tickets back to the United States, but the reality seems rather different. Duray's racing, and presumably his trip to Europe, had been paid for by his sponsors. The American 91cu in racing formula was to be abandoned at the end of the 1929 season in favour of a 'junk car' formula using stock car parts. The Millers would be obsolete, particularly as the wooden board track era was coming to an end and most of the tracks had closed, forced out of business by the cost of maintenance. A sale of the cars made good business sense to Duray who was paid by Bugatti, not with cash, but with three T43 chassis which were delivered to California. Bugatti had the most advanced racing engine in the world to study and dissect. He also had a most effective front-wheel-drive transmission to ponder upon.

In the autumn of 1929 and the spring of 1930, there were big changes in the range of touring Bugattis offered to the public. A new luxury chassis was announced, the T46. This had a 5,359cc engine and a three-speed gearbox in unit with the rear axle. It was in many respects, a small Royale and was aimed at the upper end of the market. The final touches were being put to the T49 which would be announced in July 1930. This was to replace the T44 and had virtually an enlarged T44 engine with the bore increased to 72mm, giving a capacity of 3,257cc. To many Bugatti connoisseurs, the T49 was the finest touring Bugatti of all and marked a break with the past as it was the last single-cam engine to be produced.

The first fruits of the Miller purchase appeared not in a racing engine, but in another touring car, the T50 which was marketed in parallel with the T46. The wheelbase of the T50 was 10ft 2in (3.1m) and the track was 4ft 7in (1.4m). It was aimed at a different market and the engine had many indications of being a racing unit, something it would become. It had a twin-overhead camshaft fixed-head engine which showed strong connections with the Miller. There were two valves per cylinder, inclined at 90° and operated directly by the camshafts via cups, which was standard Miller practice. The crankshaft ran in nine main bearings and the dimensions were 86mm x 107mm giving a capacity of 4,972cc. It was supercharged and a vertical shaft at the front of the engine, driven from the crankshaft by bevels drove the pressure and scavenge pumps of the dry sump lubrication system through spur gears. An intermediate pair of bevels drove a short cross shaft and a further pair of bevels from this shaft drove the supercharger mounted alongside the engine and running at twice engine speed and drawing from two Schebler carburettors. The top of the vertical shaft drove the camshafts through five spur gears and idlers and a pair of bevels. The supercharger gave a boost of 6–8lb (0.4–0.5 bar) and the engine in touring form developed 220bhp at 4,000 rpm. The chassis was identical to the T46 with the

6 April 1930: The start of the Grand Prix de Monaco: No. 34 Borzacchini (T26B Maserati), No. 28 'Williams' (T35C), No. 14 Zanelli (T35B), No. 18 Chiron (T35C), No. 16 Bouriat (T35C), No. 20 Dore (T37A), No. 42 Zehender (T35B), No. 26 Lehoux (T35B) and No. 24 Etancelin (T35C). (John Maitland Collection)

three-speed gearbox in the rear axle. There was a milder version, the T50T which developed 200bhp and had a longer wheelbase of 11ft 2in (3.5m).

It was not an auspicious time to introduce new luxury cars. On 24 October 1929, the American stock market had collapsed in the notorious Wall Street Crash. This was the most obvious manifestation of a depression which had been creeping up on the major economies of the world. The United States and Britain suffered worst from the immediate effects, while Germany was also affected. In France, the downturn was not so sharp, but a gradual decline began, industrial production fell and unemployment began to rise. It has been observed cynically that the rich are seldom richer than when the poor are poor, and the depression hit hardest at those who would never be in the market for a luxury or sporting car. Bugatti's market was affected but motor racing continued and there were still enough customers to keep manufacturing going at Molsheim. Work on the new design to replace the T35 was slower than expected and the T35B and C were still at the forefront at the beginning of the 1930 racing season. Up to the end of 1929, 191 racing variants of the T35, excluding the T35As, had been built and sold, and the car had been the backbone of European motor racing. It is not fanciful to suggest that without the T35, there would have been no motor racing. The motor racing scene was changing, the Maserati brothers had undertaken further development on the Tipo 26M, which in 2½-litre form, developed 185bhp, and Alfa Romeo, realising their new 8C would not be ready for the 1930 season, had revamped three P2s. The engines had been uprated to give 175bhp and the cars had been given new chassis frames and axles. It is difficult to make comparisons between quoted power outputs and the figures declared by the Italian manufacturers may have been optimistic or their horses may have been a lighter breed, but by the start of the 1930 season, the T35B and C Bugattis were at a power disadvantage. Nuvolari had abandoned his T35C and had signed with Alfa Corse and also with the Scuderia Ferrari. The Scuderia had been founded by Enzo Ferrari at Modena in the autumn of 1929, the sponsors being some rich amateur drivers with support from Alfa Romeo and Pirelli. Its purpose was to prepare Alfa Romeos for customers and to race Alfa Romeos in the lesser events, leaving Alfa Corse to devote its efforts to the major races. The Scuderia operated very efficiently and gradually took over the reins from Alfa Corse.

6 April 1930: Chiron leads 'Williams' round the Gasometer Hairpin in the early laps. The cars have twin fillers and well-base wheels for the first time.

The first race of the season was at St Raphael on 2 March and it gave Dreyfus an opportunity to exercise his new T35B. He collected the car from Molsheim and drove it direct to St Raphael. He had bought it in collaboration with Friderich, each paying half the price, and as the Bugatti agent in Nice, Friderich took the car with a 50 per cent discount. The race was a useful debut for the car and Dreyfus had an easy win. The first important race was across the Mediterranean at Tripoli three weeks later, where surprisingly, Varzi, who was signed up with Alfa Corse, appeared with a T35C. Brilli-Perri was racing one of the Scuderia Materassi Talbots, and during practice, he went off the road on a fast bend, the car overturned and he was killed. A member of an aristocratic family in Florence, he assumed the title of Count although not entitled to it; at 37 years old, he was a highly regarded driver who had scored some major victories including the 1925 GP d'Italia. He had only driven a factory-entered Bugatti in a few races, but had given most worthwhile performances at Rome and the Nürburgring. Varzi only lasted a lap in the race which was a win for Borzacchini with the V4 Maserati, a fierce machine designed for the fastest circuits with two Tipo 26 engines geared together. Arcangeli was second with a normal Tipo 26B.

Only one P2 Alfa Romeo was entered for the Grand Prix de Monaco on 6 April. The driver was Enzo Ferrari, but neither he nor the car appeared. Apart from the Alfa Romeo, every car and driver of note was in Monte Carlo for the race, which after only a year, was already a major event. Three T35Cs were entered, for Chiron, Bouriat and 'Williams'. There were two evident changes to the cars, the fuel tanks had been fitted with two fillers, presumably to speed up refuelling, one acting as an air vent, while the cars of Chiron and 'Williams' had well-base one-piece wheels. It is hard to discern if Bugatti had an established policy about the merits of the T35B and the

T35C, and the suitability of the car for the course. It seems that the T35C may have given more power with its ability to rev higher, but the T35B may have had more torque. The main rivals to the Bugattis were two works T26B Maseratis and two works SSKL Mercedes-Benz, one driven by Caracciola. To general astonishment, the AC de Monaco refused to let Caracciola run, stating that his car was too heavy and unsuitable for the course. The decision was more mystifying as the second car, driven by Count Arco, was allowed to start. Prominent among the independents were Dreyfus, Etancelin and Zanelli. Dreyfus, abetted by Friderich, had removed the passenger's seat from his T35B and fitted a large extra fuel tank which he hoped would let him go through without a stop. The three works T35Cs were on the front two rows of the balloted grid and Chiron took an immediate lead at the start followed by 'Williams' and Bouriat. 'Williams' soon stopped with mechanical problems which let Borzacchini's Maserati into third place, but he too stopped, lacking brakes. 'Williams' restarted but had to abandon his car at the Gasworks Hairpin and walk back to the pits. Chiron was establishing a big lead, but Dreyfus who had started from the fifth row, was up into third place on lap 16 and passed Bouriat into second place on lap 30. At half distance Chiron led Dreyfus by two minutes and all the non-Bugattis had dropped out, Etancelin in fourth place was followed by Zanelli and the German driver, Hans Stuber. Chiron was having trouble with a sticking throttle and on lap 83 he stopped for fuel, plugs and attention to the throttle and clutch. He restarted only a few seconds in front of Dreyfus and on lap 85 Dreyfus took the lead, Chiron with the defective throttle could do nothing about it. Dreyfus carried on to win after a non-stop run, an angry and disappointed Chiron was second, 22 seconds behind, Bouriat was third and Goffredo Zehender (T35B) was fourth. The extra fuel tank had paid off, but without the throttle troubles Chiron would surely have won. According to Dreyfus, Chiron was in an ill-temper after the race. He personally supervised the preparation of his cars, so probably blamed himself for the failure.

Three weeks after Monaco, Dreyfus and Etancelin were in Algeria for the GP d'Oranie on the 5.6-mile (9.0km) Arcole circuit. There must have been a local magneto malady as it put Dreyfus out of the race on the first lap, it then eliminated Lehoux who had been battling with Etancelin and had taken the lead when Etancelin crashed. Etancelin's T35B was still quite new, having collected it from Molsheim on 24 March, but it was only mildly bent in the accident. With the serious runners by the wayside, Jean de Maleplane won with his T35C. The previous day there was a 30-lap 168-mile (270km) sports car race on the same circuit which saw Count Stanislas Czaikowski take the race with a road-equipped T35B; T44s took second and third places.

There were reports that the rebuilt P2 Alfa Romeos had suspect handling and the cars were to be scratched from the Targa Florio on 4 May. Varzi intervened and pointed out that his contract provided for him to drive a P2 in the race and he expected the contract to be honoured. Although Varzi had the only P2, he was backed by Nuvolari and Campari on Alfa Romeo 6C-1750s, so Chiron, Divo, Conelli and 'Williams' driving T35Bs, faced stern opposition. The cars were started at three-minute intervals and Varzi went ahead immediately, followed by Campari and Nuvolari. Chiron rose to the challenge and moved up into second place, pursuing Varzi. The spare wheel of Varzi's P2, which was mounted in the tail, broke away cracking the fuel tank and at the start of the fifth and last lap, Varzi led Chiron by only 23 seconds. Realising that he could run out of fuel, Varzi stopped at a refuelling depot in the mountains and topped up the tank, continuing with his mechanic carrying a spare can of fuel. Chiron realised he could

27 April 1930: The T35Bs of Lehoux (No. 26) and Zehender (No. 28) lead the field at the start of the Grand Prix d'Oranie.

4 May 1930: Chiron (T35B) during his chase of Varzi in the Targa Florio.

catch Varzi, but his mechanic, Ernst Zirn, fearing that the excessive revs that Chiron was using could result in disaster, started to pump more oil into the engine. Chiron, believing this would oil a plug, knocked Zirn's hand off the pump and in doing so, lost control. The car swerved into the rocks beside the road and two wheels were broken. It was carrying two spares and the damaged wheels were changed, losing valuable time. Such was the haste that the Bugatti set off again, leaving the two broken wheels and the jack lying in the road.

A few miles short of the finish, the engine of the Alfa Romeo stammered with fuel starvation. Varzi did not stop but the mechanic poured the contents of the can into the tank. Some fuel splashed on the exhaust and the car caught fire, but still Varzi did not stop and the mechanic beat out the flames with a seat cushion. Varzi won the 335-mile (538km) race by 1min 50sec from Chiron after nearly seven hours racing. After six years the Bugatti hold on the Targa Florio had been broken in a race which has become one of the all-time legends of motor racing. Conelli took third place

ahead of Campari and Nuvolari, while 'Williams' was seventh, having handed his car over to Divo after Divo crashed on the third lap. Ernst Zirn had joined Bugatti as an apprentice in 1919 at the age of 14. He was Baccoli's riding mechanic at Brescia in 1921, rode with Mones-Maury in the 1922 Grand Prix de l'ACF at Strasbourg, with Marco at Tours in 1923 and with Garnier at Lyon in 1924. When Chiron joined the team in 1928, Zirn became his personal mechanic.

Chiron and Varzi were able to fight again in the Premio Reale di Roma on 25 May, which still held its place as one of the major races of the Italian calendar. Chiron had the T35B used by 'Williams' in the Targa Florio, which probably had an easier race than his own car and he was accompanied by Bouriat with a second car. He was up against Varzi and Nuvolari with P2s and a works Tipo 26B Maserati driven by Arcangeli. Chiron and Arcangeli took the lead from the front of the grid, but Chiron pulled into the pits after a lap and retired. Bouriat was called in and handed his car over to Chiron who set off 55 seconds

behind Arcangeli who led the race. Varzi, who was running second, soon dropped out with clutch problems, and Nuvolari challenged Arcangeli, taking the lead on lap seven. By lap nine, Chiron was up to third place and the pair in front were exchanging the lead on almost every lap. On lap 17, with three to go, Nuvolari slowed and was passed by Chiron. Believing he had the race in hand, Arcangeli eased off and was caught by Chiron, who was on his tail at the start of the last lap. Chiron squeezed by into the lead and held it until the very last corner, when Arcangeli with a do-or-die effort overtook and just held off Chiron in the dash to the line, winning by 0.4 seconds, while the partisan Italian crowd went mad with excitement.

Chiron did not go to Le Mans on 1 June for the third Bugatti Grand Prix. There was a good entry but only eight cars came to the line for the handicap race in which the scratch car had to do 32 laps, 352 miles (566km) of the 24-hour course. It rained heavily and Zanelli (T35C), who had to cover 30 laps was the winner from Fourny's T37A. The Bugatti family arrived at Le Mans as walking wounded. Ettore had his arm in a sling as he had broken a collar bone in a fall from his horse, while Jean was walking with two sticks. One report said he had fallen down stairs, another that he had crashed an unnamed American roadster that he was testing. As his prize, Zanelli collected a second T43. All the regular Bugatti drivers were in action at Lyon on 15 June for the second GP de Lyon over the Quincieux circuit. Chiron entered a T35C in his own name, although presumably a factory car as the Nerka arrangement had come to an end, affected by his relationship with Baby Hoffmann. Dreyfus led from the start followed by Lehoux and Etancelin, while Chiron bided his time in mid-field. Dreyfus broke his engine and Chiron moved up taking the lead when Lehoux dropped out, going on to win by nearly six minutes from von Morgen, the German driver with a T35B, while Etancelin was

21/22 June 1930: The T40 of Marguerite Mareuse and Odette Siko which finished seventh in the Le Mans 24-hour race. The front wing stays were designed to withstand the rigours of the race.

third. After a break of seven years, a Bugatti ran in the Le Mans 24-hour race on 21 and 22 June when a T40 was driven by the women drivers, Marguerite Mareuse and Odette Siko; they drove steadily and came seventh, taking second place in the 1,500cc class. The race was the fourth successive triumph for the Bentley team. It was the last time that Bentley would race at Le Mans as the company was in serious financial trouble, partly caused by the cost of going motor racing.

The Bugatti 'circus' moved to Reims for the GP de la Marne, a week after the Le Mans race. *Motor Sport* summed it up: 'It must be great fun to be the owner of a fast Bugatti in France. You enter it for every one of the provincial Grands Prix and when you get to the start there are all your old rivals ready to do battle. If you think that so-and-so beat you in one race because you had a bit of real bad luck – well you can always have another scrap with him in the next.'

Reims, with its long straights running across the open Champagne country, was the archetypal French racing circuit of the late 1920s and early 1930s. Race day was hot and cloudless and the large crowd watched a fine race with 19 starters. To the disappointment of the spectators, Chiron offered no challenge to his rivals and made several pit stops before retiring, but Dreyfus continued to show the form that was taking him to the forefront. In the opening laps Etancelin and Lehoux fought for the lead only lengths apart, while Dreyfus watched and waited. After seven laps he passed them both, Lehoux dropped back and on lap 13, Etancelin slid on melting tar at La Garenne Corner and broke a wheel. Despite the heat, he ran back to his pit for a spare, returned to the car and changed it. Cheered on by the crowd he set off again, now 13 laps behind Dreyfus who was uncatchable. Lehoux closed slightly near the end of the 250 miles (400km) but Dreyfus took the flag with a lead of two minutes. The dogged Etancelin was fifth and last, the pace had accounted for the rest. After the race

Dreyfus was embraced by a delighted Friderich. As *Motor Sport* said: 'Reims, the capital of Champagne land is not a bad place to celebrate!'

Having shunned Le Mans, Bugatti entered a T43 for the 24-hour sports car race on the Spa-Francorchamps circuit on 5/6 July. This race had been given the title of the Grand Prix de Belgique and the apparent downgrade in its status was to accommodate the Grand Prix d'Europe which was to be a proper formula race on the same circuit two weeks later. The entry was made at the last minute and was much against Ettore Bugatti's wishes as there had been little time to prepare the car. Chiron was very keen to drive in the race as he wanted to familiarise himself with the circuit before the *grande épreuve*. The T43 was taking on a factory team of three 6C-1750 Alfa Romeos which, although staying away from Le Mans, had gained some impressive results in 1929 and in the first half of the 1930 season. The race began at the traditional time of 4pm and Chiron, who was sharing the car with Bouriat, went into the lead and held it for the first 24 laps, followed by the three Alfa Romeos. When Chiron made his first stop and handed the car over to Bouriat, it was found the dynamo drive had broken. This took some time to repair, but when the car restarted Bouriat put on the pace and pulled back five minutes before he handed the car back to Chiron again. After six hours, the T43 was third, a lap down on the two leading Alfa Romeos. Chiron continued to pull back the lost ground, but as darkness fell, he came into the pits as the drive had broken again and the car had no lights. Another repair was not possible, so the car was withdrawn from the race.

The Alfa Romeos ran on for the remainder of the 24 hours and took the first three places. A privately entered T43, fitted with wire wheels, was fourth, driven by Pierre-Louis Dreyfus and Antoine Schumann; Dreyfus, a banker who was no relation to René, sometimes raced under the pseudo-

nym of 'Heldé'. As some consolation for Bugatti, the T43 was the winner of the 3-litre class. A T44 which had been bored out to let it run in the over 3-litre class, driven by the Belgian Abel Blin d'Orimont, had run remarkably well. At 4am, half distance, it was leading its class ahead of sundry Chryslers and Delages, and it seemed that a class win was likely, but with three hours to go, the car stopped on the circuit at Burnenville and its race was over. A T37 driven by Evrard and Trasentier took the 1,500cc class, but it is likely that the failure of Chiron and Bouriat must have encouraged mutterings of 'I told you so' at Molsheim.

The GP d'Europe was the only race run in 1930 under the almost discredited fuel consumption formula and the competitors had to cover 40 laps of the 9.25-mile (14.9km) Spa circuit. The fuel supplied for the race by the RACB consisted of 70 per cent petrol and 30 per cent benzol. Three T35Cs were entered for Chiron, Bouriat and Divo, fitted with the bolster tanks, wide bodies, 150mm superchargers and the well-base wheels which had been tried at Monaco. Apart from a sole works 174S Peugeot driven by Henri Stoffel, the opposition was negligible, the only other factory entries being three Imperias which were virtually touring cars with racing bodies. For 12 laps, the three Bugattis led, with Chiron in front followed by Bouriat and Divo. The team order was spoiled when Divo burst a tyre and fell back, letting Stoffel up into third place, but on lap 19 Divo had regained his place. Chiron then stopped with oiled plugs, these were changed, but he was in again a lap later with the same problem. He was passed by Bouriat and Stoffel who had speeded up and retaken third place from Divo. The Bugatti performance was not going according to the script. On the last lap, Bouriat led from Stoffel with Chiron back in third place, but halfway round the lap, Stoffel ran out of fuel. Bouriat came up to the finish and stopped before the line waiting for Chiron.

Chiron appeared, took the flag as the winner and was followed across the line by Bouriat, while Divo was third. The result and the manner of the finish did not please the crowd which booed and jeered. Reinartz, whose T43 had failed in the 24-hour race, ran it in the Grand Prix stripped of road equipment and had the disappointment of running out of fuel on the last lap.

While the Bugatti team was being cat-called at Spa, almost all the Bugatti independents went to Dieppe for the local Grand Prix and made an all-Bugatti field. In the spirit expressed by *Motor Sport*, Marcel Lehoux must have felt it was about time he had a turn at winning a race and so it came about. He led from start to finish and although Etancelin and Dreyfus gave chase, they could not catch him. Etancelin dropped out and Dreyfus had obscure problems which dropped him back to fifth, so the places went to Fourny and de Pouget. Fourny had bought the T35C in which Bordino had crashed fatally at Alessandria in 1928; after the crash it had been rebuilt at Molsheim. While the French

A front view of a T45 engine.

drivers were enjoying their round of races, their Italian counterparts were doing much the same, but personality problems had arisen south of the Alps. Nuvolari and Varzi were not happy driving in the same Alfa Corse/Scuderia Ferrari team. Their antipathy was as strong as ever and when they raced their only desire was to beat the other. The outcome was usually two broken cars and success for neither driver. Varzi realised that the position was untenable and at the beginning of August he broke his Alfa Romeo contract and signed up with the Maserati brothers. The P2 Alfa Romeo, after the Targa Florio win, had been showing its years and the Tipo 26B Maserati had emerged as the fastest car in Italy and probably in grand prix racing. All it lacked was a front-rank driver so Varzi's arrival at Bologna was a godsend for Maserati.

Chiron had no racing commitments during August, so he was sent to Switzerland with the T45, where the car made its delayed competition debut. On 9th August, he ran in the 13.4-mile (21.5km) Klausen hill-climb and set a new course record in 16min 24.6sec. The Klausen meeting was followed by the inter-

national motor week at St Moritz, where some motorsport provided a backing to a hectic round of social engagements in which Chiron played a prominent part. On 20 August, there was a speed trial over a flying kilometre, on a road specially prepared by the Shell oil company, between the villages of Samaden and Pontresina. The T45 was going well and Chiron had little difficulty in setting the fastest speed at 119.54mph (192.5kmh). To round off a successful trip, Chiron set the best time in the Bernina hill-climb on Sunday, 24 August, watched by Ettore Bugatti who had come to St Moritz with his family.

To emphasise the Maserati superiority, Varzi led Arcangeli and Ernesto Maserati home in a 1-2-3 to win the Coppa Acerbo over the hard Pescara circuit on 17 August, so he was the favourite to win the Gran Premio di Monza on 7 September. No cars came from Molsheim, there was the valid excuse that the team was being prepared for the Grand Prix de l'ACF later in the month, but Costantini and Jean Bugatti knew the T35B and C were no longer fast enough to be competitive on the high-speed Monza track. The race was run on a shortened version of the track and road circuit and as in previous years, there were class-eliminating heats and a final. Etancelin ran his T35C in the 2-litre heat and after exchanging the lead with the T35C of Heinz-Joachim von Morgen, who had entered his car under the banner of 'Bugatti Team Germany', won by two seconds. Minozzi's T35C was third, and Giovanni Tabacchi, who had been Varzi's valiant fire-fighting mechanic in the Targa Florio, also drove a T35C but dropped out. In the next heat, Lehoux's T35B was not able to keep up with the Maseratis or the P2 Alfa Romeos, which had been bored-out to 2,002cc, and came seventh. Lehoux qualified to run in the *repêchage* for the fastest losers, he had found some extra speed and led the P2s of Campari and Nuvolari, which had not been able to match the Maseratis, but he spun off and retired. In the final, Varzi made an early

stop for plugs then fought his way through the field, beating his team-mate Arcangeli to the line by 0.2 seconds, cheered by a delighted crowd. Ernesto Maserati was third with the twin-engined V4, but Minozzi probably surprised himself by taking fourth place ahead of Fagioli's Maserati, while Etancelin was sixth, as the crowd invaded the track in traditional Monza style.

In 1922, the AC du Nord had instituted a somewhat bizarre race, the Circuit des Routes Pavées, which used an 8.25-mile (13.2km) circuit near Pont-à-Marcq, south of Lille. The roads were narrow with ill-laid pavée, loose flints and muddy verges and were still suffering from the neglect of the war years. The event was declared to be 'a test of suspension and holding-of-the-road'. As an added refinement, a 10in (250mm) artificial cobblestone ridge was laid across the road by the start line, followed by a crude level crossing with raised rails and a deep gully. The first race attracted 61 starters and had become a popular event throughout the 1920s. It had become suffi-ciently important that in 1928 and 1929 it attracted entries from Alfa Corse which probably considered that the roads near Lille were no worse than those encountered in the Mille Miglia and the Targa Florio. These entries were justified as a 6C-1500 won in 1928 and a 6C-1750 in 1929. In 1930, the race was held on 14 September, it was of six hours duration and attracted 33 starters divided into capacity classes with divisions for sports and racing cars. The main entry was a 6C-1750 Alfa Romeo driven by the 1929 winner, Goffredo Zehender. He was opposed by a T43, two T35Cs, a T37A and five T37s, together with a wide cross-section of French sports cars mostly in the 1,100c class. Zehender led in the early stages but retired with engine problems which left Count d'Arnoux (T35C) fending off challenges from Louis Joly, who had brought his T37 all the way from Tunisia for the race. Joly took the lead after three hours when d'Arnoux had two long pit stops. It was raining heavily and

9 August 1930: Chiron in the T45 breaking the course record at Klausen.

the course was covered in mud; attempting to catch Joly, d'Arnoux went off the road after the start and overturned, luckily he escaped with a shaking, but this let Brunet (T43) into second place. Joly held on to the lead but was being caught by Charles Montier with a Ford Model A special who had passed Brunet. With 40 minutes to go, Montier was only two minutes behind and when Joly stopped and worked on his engine, Montier took the lead. Joly left his pit as Montier went by and after a chase, regained the lead just as the six hours expired. As well as the outright victory, Joly won the 1,500cc racing class and Brunet who was third, won the 3-litre sports class.

The Automobile Club de France had intended to keep faith with the AIACR and run their grand prix to the fuel consumption formula. A date was fixed in July but the entries were minimal, so the date was changed to 21 September and the race became Formule Libre. It was held at Pau, not over the street circuit that became famil-iar in later years, but on a 9.9-mile (15.9km) triangular circuit on the outskirts of the

town, with the pits and main stands on the N117 road, near the junction with the D943 which formed the second leg. Bugatti had intended that the replacement for the T35, a benefit of the Miller purchase, would be ready but it still needed work so a T35B was entered for Bouriat and a T35C for 'Williams'. There were reports that the T45 would be entered, but the Swiss interlude had shown that it was likely to be unreli-able, as the gears linking the two crankshafts were fragile. Surprisingly, there was no car for Chiron who was nominated to share Bouriat's car. There were also entries for Divo and for Dreyfus who, despite his feel-ings that he was persona non grata at Molsheim, had been elevated to a works drive. For reasons that were not explained, the cars for Divo and Dreyfus did not turn up. Bugatti did not seem to have taken the race too seriously as the initial entries were for 'Pontet', 'Gaston' and 'Saintaud'. The field of 25 comprised mostly an army of independent Bugatti drivers. Prominent among the few non-Bugatti entries, partly for its size, was a supercharged 4½-litre

21 September 1930: Czaikowski (T35C) is chased by Birkin (Bentley). Czaikowski came fourth and Birkin passed him to finish second in the Grand Prix de l'ACF at Pau.

Bentley driven by Henry Birkin, which had its full four seat touring body. In his autobiography *Full Throttle*, Birkin said: '. . . among these greyhounds, my Bentley was like a large Sealyham. Its entry was regarded by the French as a sporting venture, and by their stern mechanics as a joke'.

The grid paces were allocated by ballot, Bouriat was on the second row, but 'Williams' was at the back. Bouriat was in the lead at the end of the first lap, and 'Williams' had come through to take second place, followed by Zanelli, Etancelin and Birkin. 'Williams' went to the front and Bouriat and Zanelli swapped places for several laps. On lap seven, 'Williams'

stopped to change a wheel, he restarted but his engine was off-colour and his race was run. Bouriat took the lead again but stopped on lap ten to hand over to Chiron, who was being followed by Etancelin and Birkin. The Bentley was faster than the Bugattis on the long straights, which made up for its slower cornering. Chiron stopped to change a tyre so Etancelin led and Chiron's car was in trouble with fluctuating oil pressure, he was caught by Zanelli and Birkin. When the Bentley came up to pass the Bugatti, Chiron was looking down into the cockpit and almost swerved into the Bentley's path. Birkin sounded the horn to warn Chiron of his presence. Birkin had an

eventful drive as 'Sabipa' overturned his T35C and was thrown out on to the road and Birkin had to take to the verge to avoid running over 'Sabipa'. On lap 19, Zanelli stopped for fuel and tyres so Birkin moved up to second place.

In the closing laps, Etancelin led, but his fuel was running low and he knew that a stop would let Birkin into the lead; worse still several of the retaining bolts in the clutch of Etancelin's car had sheared off. Birkin's position was not safe as Zanelli was gaining on him rapidly. Etancelin nursed his car to the finish; he had only a litre of fuel left and as he drove the car away after the finishing ceremonies, the last clutch bolt sheared. Birkin came second, 3min 26sec behind and only ten seconds in front of Zanelli. Phi-Phi Etancelin was one of the great characters of French racing in the 20th century. He was instantly recognisable in his soft blue cap with the peak worn at the back and his driving style was unique, as he sawed at the wheel constantly, even on the straights. His method of practising on a circuit was also unusual; he would start lapping at a slow touring pace, gradually speeding up, until after several laps he would be up to racing speed. He did this even on the second day of practice and when he knew the circuit well. With Etancelin's Pau victory, the T35 had won its last *grande épreuve* and had come to the end of its first line career after seven seasons of racing.

Among the drivers racing at Pau was a 22-year old Parisian, Jean-Pierre Wimille who was driving a T37A. He was the son of a journalist, and the car had been bought for him by Marguerite Mareuse, the driver of the T40 at Le Mans. This had been his first season and the Grand Prix de l'ACF was his first major event. He retired after two laps with supercharger problems, but he would soon make a much greater impression on the sport.

There had been no Italian entries at Pau, but the Scuderia Ferrari sent two P2 Alfa Romeos to Czechoslovakia on the same day for the Masarykuv Okruh, a Formule Libre grand prix on the Brno circuit. The P2s were driven by Nuvolari and Borzacchini and Nuvolari set off at his usual pace and retired after six laps with a burned out clutch. He took over Borzacchini's car and was in the lead on the last lap when the water pump burst and he had to slow down to a touring pace. He was caught by the two T35Bs of Bugatti Team Germany. The winner was Heinrich-Joachim von Morgen, whose own car had broken down with two laps of the 18-mile (29km) circuit left, but he took over the car of his team-mate Prince zu Leiningen. The Prince had connections with the British Royal family, being descended from the half-brother of Queen Victoria. The second place car was driven by Ernst Burggaller. The crippled P2 limped

home into third place. It is ironic that the T35 and the P2 had first raced at Lyon in 1924 and both ran their last race as first line racing cars on the same day. They had become obsolete at the same time and had dominated grand prix racing from their inception. The P2 Alfa Romeos never raced again, but the T35 still had a decade of racing ahead of it as the mount of countless amateurs.

There had only been one significant 1,500cc voiturette race during the season, this was at Brno, when Max Hardegg won a 17-lap, 307-mile (493km) curtain-raiser to the main event, with a T37A, otherwise the 1½-litre cars had run as a class with their bigger brothers, making up the numbers. Many Bugattis raced at Brooklands during the season. At the opening meeting on 23 March, Chris Staniland lapped at 118.30mph (190.22kmh) in his T37A to win a handicap, and Charles Brackenbury won another handicap with a T37. While gaining places in handicaps, P. W. Thorogood lapped at 124.20mph (199.7kmh) in a T35B and E. M. Thomas did an impressive 110.92mph (178.35kmh) in his T35. The JCC ran the Double-Twelve again on 9 and 10 May. Earl Howe and Malcolm Campbell shared a T43 which lost much time with a broken half shaft, but finished 23rd and won the 3-litre class. The BARC introduced a new and popular type of racing at the track during the 1930 season, over the Mountain circuit, which used the Finishing Straight and the Members' Banking. This gave a course with two corners and some semblance of road racing. P. B. Rogers scored the first Bugatti win in a Mountain handicap with his T37A at the Whitsun meeting on 2 June. Staniland startled the Brooklands regulars when he entered a 1,088cc Bugatti for the Bank Holiday meeting on 4th August. This was his T37A sleeved down to 58.8mm and using an Amal carburettor. The modification was effective as the car won a handicap lapping at 111.67mph (179.56kmh). At this meeting, Birkin drove a T35B, borrowed from W.

Y. Craig and won, only to be disqualified for contravening one of the many track regulations by crossing a forbidden line, despite lapping at 125.14mph (201.86kmh). Malcolm Campbell was more fortunate and won a Mountain handicap with his 2.3-litre -engined T36 monoposto. The T35 could still give a good account of itself in the Brooklands handicaps, and Clifton Penn-Hughes won a Mountain race at the closing meeting.

Brooklands saw some International class records broken during the season. George Eyston brought out his T35B and took the class D flying kilometre at 198.07kmh and the flying mile at 121.50mph and W. Y. Craig broke the class D standing start mile and kilometre records, the latter in 27.7 seconds. Craig also raised the class D one-hour record to 112.25mph (180.49kmh), but soon lost it to a 1924 GP Sunbeam. Staniland's 1,088cc T37A was reliable as well as quick, and he used it to take the class G 50-kilometre and 50-mile records at 104.73mph (168.40kmh), and the 100-kilometre record at 104.89mph (168.66kmh).

There are times in the history of motor racing when the course of the sport changes dramatically; a change of this kind had happened in 1924, and such was about to come in 1931. In the wider world, the post-war years were coming to an end and what turned out to be the pre-war years were beginning. The construction of a line of defences along the frontier with Germany had begun, supervised by the French war minister André Maginot. The depression was beginning to bite in France, the government had a fixation about maintaining the value of the franc and while the reserves of the Banque de France were growing continuously, exports had plunged, bringing a rapid rise in unemployment. The sales of the cheaper cars had plummeted and tourism, which had been a rapidly growing industry during the 1920s, had suffered greatly, with a steady closing of hotels along the Côte d'Azur.

Chapter 10

The going gets harder

At THE BEGINNING OF 1931, the AIACR capitulated to popular demand and abandoned the fuel consumption formula. It was replaced with a formula of stark simplicity: *grandes épreuves* would be of ten-hour duration and the only restriction on the cars was a requirement that these must have two seats. This ushered in one of the golden eras of grand prix racing, fiercely fought by three manufacturers and a clutch of leading drivers. It produced the closest motor racing that had yet been seen and also gave an opportunity for the best independent drivers to shine.

For Bugatti, the need for a new car was imperative. Alfa Romeo would be entering the lists with Jano's new 8C, and the Maserati brothers were improving their Tipo 26, already the fastest grand prix car, which would shortly become the 8C-2500. The answer was the T51, this was the direct result of analysing the two Millers and was largely the work of Jean Bugatti. The only feature that distinguished the T51 from the T35B was the engine. A new cylinder block was fitted to the T35 crankcase, keeping the dimensions of the T35B, 60mm x 100mm and the capacity of 2,262cc. It had an integral head with individual valve ports and two valves per cylinder at an included angle of 96°. The two camshafts operated the valves through inverted cups and were geared together through an idler gear and bevels, driven from the T35 vertical drive. The magneto was driven off the rear of the left camshaft. The supercharger drive was

speeded-up, instead of the 1:1 of the T35B and C, it became 1:1.2. The rest of the T35 engine was unchanged, but the inlet manifold was altered and the pressure release valve was lower, so the hole for this in the bonnet side was correspondingly lower than the T35B and C, giving a visual identification of the T51. When it was bench tested, one engine gave an output of 187bhp at 5,200rpm, although this was probably higher than most T51s, but the average engine was good for 170bhp at 5,500rpm. Inadequate cooling of the exhaust side in the first cylinder blocks resulted in the blocks cracking between the exhaust valve seat and the plug hole, but this was soon remedied by enlarging the water passages in the block.

Later in the T51's career, at least one block was cast in bronze. Apart from the engine, the rest of the car was identical to, and interchangeable with, the T35B and C, as it was reasoned that the earlier car was still as nimble and handled as well as any of the opposition. The only changes were the position of the magneto in the dashboard, the twin filler caps that been introduced for the factory team cars in 1930, and the well-based wheels with a fixed outer rim. These wheels had already made an appearance on the works T35Cs at Monaco and Spa in 1930. Some of the 1930 team cars were converted to T51 specification. The car was announced in the autumn of 1930 and was in the catalogue for the Paris Salon in October. It was offered for sale at

165,000FF, while the last T35Cs had been sold for 140,000FF. There were changes among the drivers. The age of the 'ace' had arrived. In the 1920s, some drivers had shown that they were faster than their rivals, but these were not particularly sought after for their virtuosity, a 'safe pair of hands' was equally highly regarded and the latter, frequently older drivers who had started in the sport before the war, could find drives in most teams. Now the racing circus was evolving and it was realised that there was a breed of drivers, such as Chiron, Nuvolari and Varzi who could get an outstanding performance from a car and secure results, even when the car was inferior to its rivals. This new generation of driver realised its value. The aces were becoming more widely known, marked out by their personalities and rivalries, the crowds wanted to see them in action, organisers knew that the presence of certain drivers boosted the attendances and the drivers themselves expected appropriate starting money and fees.

At the beginning of 1931, Achille Varzi agreed to drive for Bugatti. The reasons for his move from Maserati are not known, but he must have realised that the T51 was likely to be a faster car than the Maserati, there may also have been the allurement of a T51 for him to use in those races where the factory team was not competing, a luxury which the Maserati brothers probably could not afford. The immediate result of Varzi's departure from Bologna was the arrival there of René Dreyfus, who agreed to drive for Maserati in 1931; his results in 1930 had made him Champion of France, so he was a worthwhile prospect for Maserati. Varzi was joining Chiron at Molsheim. The contrast between the two men could not have been greater. W. F. Bradley gives a vivid portrait of Varzi: 'Varzi was ice. (His) piercing steely-blue eyes indicated grim determination, an iron nerve, steadiness, ruthlessness, and his well-knit body supplied the physical strength to back up his strong will-power. There was something so Nordic in his composition that he might have been mistaken for a Scandinavian. He was always self-controlled, usually grim and rarely displayed any of that exuberance we associate with the Latin character.'

Chiron was always known as 'Louis the Debonair'. He had an easy, suave charm which had been honed in the cosmopolitan atmosphere of Monte Carlo. He was friendly and approachable, but under the urbane veneer, there was a tough and ambitious man. Varzi and Chiron were joined in the 1931 team by 'Williams', Bouriat, Divo and Conelli. At the beginning of the year, there were four drivers who could lay claim to be at the top of the grand prix tree. Chiron had dominated the sport in 1928 and 1929 and was still at the top during 1930, but Varzi had arrived and was approaching Chiron in brilliance although he was perhaps still half a rung below him on the ladder. Caracciola was possibly Chiron's equal, but his grand prix appearances were spasmodic; Nuvolari was capable of extraordinary brilliance but he was erratic. His ultimate mastery was yet to come. For Bugatti, the prospects looked most promising, as he had two of the top four in his team.

The T43 had failed to give Bugatti the success in sports car racing that had been expected and it was abandoned at the end of 1930. There had been a proposal in 1929, that it should be fitted with the supercharged 2,986cc 16-cylinder T47 engine, thus becoming the T43A, but perhaps fortunately, nothing came of the idea. In the harsh economic climate, sports car racing victories could help to sell touring cars, so Jean Bugatti intended to try again but it would not be easy. Vittorio Jano's new 8C Alfa Romeo was designed to be a dual-purpose car. With a racing body it would be a grand prix machine, entered by Alfa Corse and the Scuderia Ferrari, but there were two sports car versions, the short racing chassis would carry a two-seat body for such events as the Mille Miglia, and a long chassis model took a four-seat body to comply with the regulations for Le Mans and the Tourist Trophy. With the experience gained in racing the 6C-1500 and 1750, the new Alfa Romeos were likely to be formidable opponents. It would have been possible to uprate the T43 by fitting the T51 engine, but if this was considered no car of this kind seems to have been built at Molsheim. The decision was made to build a team of T50s. Ettore Bugatti had misgivings about the prudence of the project but further misgivings about the financial burden were overcome. Bugatti had an agreement to race on Michelin tyres, so an approach was made, inviting Michelin to foot the bill for the building of three sports racing T50s.

It was suggested that it was time for France to be at the forefront of sports car racing; for too long it had been dominated by Italian and British cars. At Le Mans there was a particular need for a French victory as the race had been dominated by Bentley for four years. Michelin was persuaded by this argument and agreed to pay for the cars. The cars, which used the short 10ft 2in (3.1m) chassis, were sent to Van Vooren, the coach builders at Courbevoie, in the Paris suburbs, who fitted Weymann type fabric covered four-seat bodies, complying with the Le Mans regulations. The designer must have been influenced by the 1929/30 Le Mans Bentleys, as the bodies had many similarities and the large fuel tank at the rear, was protected by wooden slats like the Bentleys. The three cars were painted black, and not blue, which is surprising, considering the patriotic appeal made to Michelin.

The first T51 was completed in February 1931, it was a converted T35C which had been a team car in 1930 and had been the

29 March 1931: Varzi gives the new T51 a successful debut in the Grand Prix de Tunisie. The splash guard behind the front wheel is unusual.

winner of the GP d'Europe at Spa. It was retained at the factory and allocated to Varzi for his 'private' forays, and at his request it was painted red. The first complete T51 to be finished went to a customer and was sent to England for Earl Howe. As soon as it was ready, Varzi took the red car overseas to Carthage, for the GP de Tunisie on 29 March, over 37 laps of a new, 7.9-mile (12.7km) circuit. He faced the usual independents with T35Bs and Cs, led by Lehoux and Etancelin, but the main opposition came from three works Maseratis, the formidable V4 driven by Clemente Biondetti and two Tipo 26Bs, one for the new boy Dreyfus and the other for Luigi Fagioli, who had driven for Maserati in 1930 and had won the Coppa Ciano at Livorno. There were 28 starters and Varzi was drawn right at the back of the grid which lined up in rows of three on a narrow road. Mme Manceron, the wife of the Governor, dropped the flag and Fagioli went to the front. Varzi had to struggle past the

field, but by the end of the second lap, he had passed Fagioli and was in the lead. He pulled away easily while Fagioli was followed by Dreyfus, who stopped to mend a broken oil pipe and then went off the road soon after he restarted. Varzi seemed set for an impressive win but on lap 12 he burst a tyre and while he changed a wheel, Fagioli took the lead. Varzi regained the lead when Fagioli made a stop for plugs and the T51 went on to gain its first victory by almost two minutes. Fagioli was passed by Lehoux, but was back in second place before the finish and Biondetti followed Lehoux home to come fourth. The day before the Grand Prix, the circuit had been opened with a six-hour sports car race in which most of the field was road-equipped grand prix cars. A 2½-litre Maserati driven by Dreyfus and Count Castelbarco ran away with the race. They were pursued in vain by Joly (T37A) and Count Czaikowski (T43). During the fourth hour, Joly was disqualified as his exhaust pipe fell off and the fate

of Czaikowski's T43 was almost inevitable, as it caught fire.

Perhaps in the hope of redeeming the failure of the T43 in 1928, the team of three T50s was entered for the Mille Miglia on 12 April. For Varzi, the race had particular significance as he had been beaten into second place by Nuvolari in 1930 when both were driving 6C-1750 Alfa Romeos entered by Alfa Corse, and he wanted to gain revenge. Only one T50 was ready for the race and Varzi took the wheel. During final testing on the day before the race, the Michelin tyres had thrown treads, then the camshaft drive broke and the valves were damaged. Working with the mechanics, Varzi installed a new engine; he fell asleep in a cafe near the start and was woken just before the Bugatti was due to be flagged away. Two of the new 8C Alfa Romeos were making their debut and Caracciola was driving an SSKL Mercedes-Benz. Varzi was one of the last cars to be flagged away, the engine was reluctant to start and once it was going, his race only lasted for 12 miles (19km) as the water pump drive broke and all the water boiled away. For Alfa Romeo too, the race was a disaster, both 8Cs were slowed by tyre troubles, Arcangeli crashed and Nuvolari had a defective clutch, finishing ninth. The race was a remarkable victory for Caracciola, one of only two non-Italian drivers ever to win the race, the second being Stirling Moss in 1955, and both driving Mercedes-Benz.

Four T51s were entered by Bugatti for the GP de Monaco, the week after the Mille Miglia, and driven by Chiron, Varzi, Bouriat and Divo. These were backed up by Earl Howe driving his private T51 in his first *grande épreuve*; at the age of 47, he was graduating from sports cars to grand prix racing. The Scuderia Ferrari had entered three 8C Alfa Romeos but these did not appear in Monte Carlo. It was announced that the tyre problems were still being resolved with Pirelli, but it seems the reason was more prosaic; the cars were not ready. The Maserati team were there in force and

19 April 1931: Chiron takes his T51 thorough Tabac Corner on his way to victory in the Grand Prix de Monaco. (John Maitland Collection)

accompanied by all the Bugatti independents, including 'Williams' with a T35C. Caracciola despite his rejection the previous year had returned with an SSKL Mercedes-Benz. The race was over 100 laps of the street circuit as a ten-hour race would have been impossible. A mistral was blowing off the sea on race day and Dreyfus was on the front row of the balloted grid, so took the lead at the start followed by 'Williams', who passed Dreyfus after four laps, only to stop a lap later with a broken valve spring. This let Dreyfus into the lead again, followed by Lehoux and Varzi, but Varzi made a big effort on lap seven, and during that lap, passed both the cars ahead of him to take the lead. Chiron, who had been in the middle of the grid, was working hard, equalling the lap record and came up to third place behind Dreyfus on lap 10, when Lehoux dropped out with a broken gearbox. The order now settled down, but Chiron passed Dreyfus, so the T51s held first and second places and seemed even more secure when Dreyfus stopped with a broken oil pipe and lost eight minutes making a repair. On lap 27, Varzi had a puncture in the Tunnel, the car slid and broke a wheel on the kerb. He limped round to the pits on the remains of the wheel and was back to fifth when it had been changed.

Chiron now led from Bouriat and Caracciola with Varzi trying hard to catch up, but the Maserati cause was not lost as Fagioli had put on a huge spurt and moved up into second place behind Chiron. Caracciola dropped out with a slipping clutch and Howe's engine seized after an oil pipe broke when he was running sixth, and Bouriat who had been disputing second with Fagioli, stopped to change plugs. Chiron was easing away and by lap 80 was almost a lap in front of Fagioli who was looking over his shoulder at a rapidly gaining Varzi, both equalling the lap record in their efforts. Chiron cruised home to win completing the 100 laps nearly four minutes ahead of Fagioli who was only nine seconds in front of Varzi at the flag, while

19 April 1931: Chiron receives the victor's bouquet while his mechanic, Lucien Wurmser, looks on. (John Maitland Collection)

Bouriat was fourth. It had been quite a race, the T51 had shown it had the pace, but the Maseratis were quick too, and Alfa Romeo had yet to show its hand.

Ettore Bugatti had been slightly hurt when he fell asleep in a Royale driving back to Molsheim from Paris. Although he had handed the management of the racing team to Jean and Costantini, the final authority for race entries rested with him. He had been confined to bed after the accident and it was reported that it had not been possible to obtain his consent for entries in the Targa Florio on 10 May. Varzi must have realised the possibility of the entries being held up, so made his own entry with the red T51. Seven days after Monaco, he had won at Alessandria with the red car, seeing off a challenge from Nuvolari who was giving the 8C its first outing in racing form. Nuvolari had given chase for nine laps until the differential broke. Alfa Corse wanted a victory for the new car and to ensure a repeat of the 1930 Targa Florio win, so five cars were entered, two 8Cs and three 6C-

1750s, while Maserati had entered three cars. In March, a savage cyclone had caused part of the road to collapse in a landslide, so the race was run over four laps of the 92.5-mile (149km) Long Madonie circuit which had not been used since 1911. Just before the cars lined up for the start, clouds were gathering over the mountains so four of the Alfa Romeos were fitted with front mudguards. As an extra aid, the Alfa Corse depots in the mountains were equipped with two-way radios so vital information could be given to the drivers when they stopped. The cars started at five minute intervals and Varzi was the first to go.

The first lap took over two hours and Varzi had a three-minute lead from Borzacchini with one of the 8Cs, with Nuvolari's 8C in third place. During the second lap, the rain began to fall, the road turned into a quagmire of mud and all three Maseratis slid off the course. At the end of the lap, Varzi made a stop of 2min 7sec, while the car was replenished and the brake shoes were changed. The mudguards now began to pay dividends for the Alfa Romeos. At the end of the third lap, Varzi stopped, changed a plug, took some clean goggles and replaced his cloth helmet with a peaked cap, his stop taking 1min 50sec. He still led as he set off on the last lap, but Nuvolari was only two minutes behind; even more important, the radio link let Nuvolari know the problems Varzi was having and just how far ahead he was. In his biography *Ettore Bugatti*, W. F. Bradley gives a dramatic description of the last lap:

'With mud and stones flying in every direction, the brilliant red Bugatti soon became unrecognisable; its numbers disappeared. Goggles were useless and were thrown away. Varzi drove through seas of mud, he sat in mud, he swallowed mud, he was blinded by mud just when the utmost precision was needed to avoid disaster – but he hung on grimly . . . Varzi had finished first as he had started first. They lifted him out of his car; they stripped from him the once blue overalls; they sponged his face and placed a lighted cigarette between his lips but the Lone Wolf remained grim and silent. Only a dozen yards away, a muddy olive-skinned, exuber-ant Italian was clutching the black hair of two stalwarts who held him aloft and 'Victory' exuded from every pore of the vociferous Nuvolari.'

Nuvolari had won after over nine hours of racing. The mudguards had been crucial, Varzi had dropped seven minutes behind Nuvolari on the last lap and had even lost second place to Borzacchini. The unsung hero was Varzi's riding mechanic, the faithful Giovanni Tabacchi, known as 'Gianella', who had ridden with him in 1930, and was in the cockpit of the T51 for over nine hours and did not even have the protection of an aeroscreen. Bradley continues: 'That evening Vincenzo Florio met Nuvolari on the streets of Termini. "Where are you going?" he asked. "Oh, just a walk to get a

7 June 1931: The field lines up for the 1,500cc Grand Prix de Genève. No. 34 is Veyron's T37A and No. 52 is the T37A of Roux. The third car on the front row is the Delage of Sénéchal. This was Veyron's first major victory.

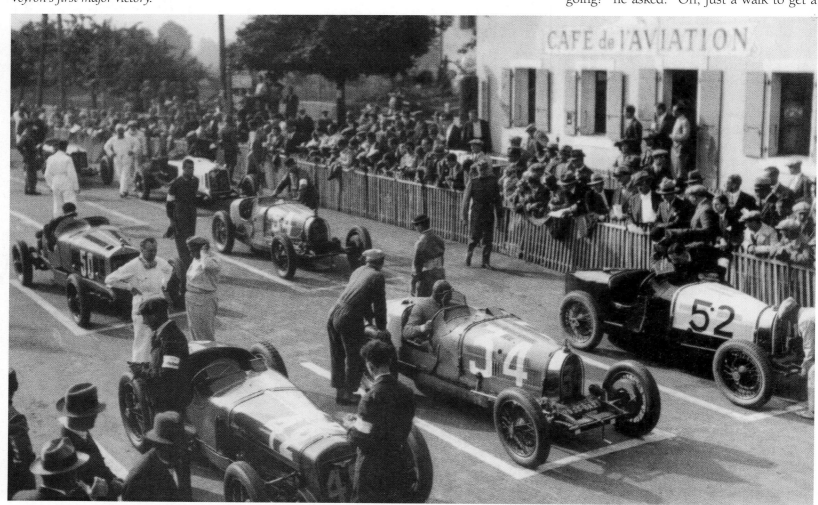

little fresh air." "Happy?" "Well, I'm glad I beat Varzi."'

Etancelin and Lehoux must have had season tickets on the Mediterranean ferry as they were back in North Africa on 17th May for the Grand Prix de Casablanca. This was run on a street circuit at Anfa in the outskirts of the city. The pair must have expected to have the race between them, but Count Czaikowski had taken delivery of a T51 and although Lehoux held a narrow lead for the opening laps, Czaikowski went through the race non-stop, so took the lead when Lehoux refuelled. Lehoux burst his engine trying to catch up and Etancelin followed the Count home, nearly four minutes behind. The burst engine cannot have troubled Lehoux too much as he had ordered a T51 which was ready for him at Monza on 24 May, for the Gran Premio d'Italia. This was a full ten-hour *grande épreuve*, the first to be run to the new formula. Bugatti entered two T51s, one to be shared by Varzi and Chiron and the other by Divo and Bouriat. Lehoux was sharing his new car with Etancelin and there was a fourth T51 which was shared by Jean-Pierre Wimille and Jean Gaupillat, and which seems to have been a joint purchase, possibly with some funds from Marguerite Mareuse. For Alfa Corse this was to be the first major test of the new 8C in racing trim. Two had been entered, one was for Minoia who had left Bugatti and was sharing the car with Borzacchini and the other was for Campari and Nuvolari. As an insurance premium, Alfa Corse had entered two additional cars. These had taken a leaf from the Maserati book and had two 6C-1750 engines and gearboxes geared together in a chassis somewhat similar to the 8C and carrying a single-seater body. The grand prix regulations stipulated two-seat bodies, but no one seemed to make a fuss about the two Alfa Romeos which were called the Tipo A. One Tipo A was entered for Arcangeli and the other for Nuvolari and Borzacchini, so the Alfa Romeo drivers were expected to dash between cars during the

7 June 1931: Nuvolari in the TN which retired in the second heat of the Premio Reale di Roma.

race. Unfortunately, Arcangeli overturned his Tipo A in practice the day before the race and was killed. Alfa Corse wanted to withdraw but received a stern reminder from their Fascist masters in Rome that they were racing for the glory of Italy and no withdrawal could be contemplated.

The race began at 8am and was started by Marshal Balbo the commander of the Regia Aeronautica, the Italian air force. Lehoux sprinted through from the second row of the grid to lead the race for a lap, but a lap later, Varzi went out at the front followed by Campari in the 8C and Lehoux. Divo had already fallen back as he had stopped to change plugs. Varzi put on the pace and pulled away for a while, but after an hour Campari had caught up and when Varzi stopped to refuel after two hours, Campari took the lead. The Alfa Romeo carried on for another nine laps before stopping for fuel which gave it a big advantage. Nuvolari

had already retired when the Tipo A ran its bearings, so he took over from Campari. Chiron managed to catch Nuvolari on lap 43 and went into the lead, but after a lap in front, he pulled into the pits as a bearing had broken in the differential, and the T51 was out. Lehoux and Etancelin continued to battle with the Alfa Romeos, but on lap 49 their T51 coasted into the pits as a valve had broken. The two 8C Alfa Romeos were left in charge of the race, Divo and Bouriat had lost more time when the near-side Michelin tyres kept throwing treads. Costantini decided the heavier tread tyres used in the Targa Florio should be fitted, which cured the problem, but they were too far behind. With only minutes to go, Borzacchini made a stop to inspect the damage caused when he hit a pheasant, but restarted.

When the race ended at 6pm, Campari and Nuvolari had covered 155 laps and had

13 June 1931: The start of the Le Mans 24-hour race. The three T50s, Nos 4, 5 and 6, are ahead of a Bentley and a Chrysler. The door of No. 5 is open.

a two-lap lead over the second 8C of Minoia and Borzacchini. Divo and Bouriat had chased hard in the closing stages and were a lap behind the second 8C, taking third place, while Wimille and Gaupillat had kept going steadily and were fourth with 138 laps to their credit. Perhaps if Divo and Bouriat had not made the additional stops, the result might have been different, but the Alfa Romeos seemed to have plenty in hand in the latter part of the race. *Motor Sport* commented that Wimille 'looks like becoming famous one day'. In recognition of the result, the racing 8C Alfa Romeo was thereafter called the 'Monza'.

Chiron should have been in Geneva on 7 June for the local grand prix, but his own T51 was damaged in an accident before the race which left the day to Lehoux, who had repaired the engine of his T51. He won his 16-lap heat on the 5.7-mile (9.1km) circuit and went on to take the final after Czaikowski crashed into the crowd, killing a spectator and injuring himself. The meeting began with a 1,100cc race and one of the single-seater T36s appeared, driven by Emilio Romano, taking second place, finishing two minutes behind the winning C6 Amilcar. On the same Sunday afternoon, Varzi was driving his red T51 in the Premio Reale di Roma, which had moved from the

Tre Fontana circuit to the Littorio airfield where an unusual track had been built with two banked turns, a fast corner and a hairpin. The Maserati team had scratched from the Monza race, but were now back in full strength. The race was run in capacity heats and a final. There were no Alfa Corse entries but amazingly, Nuvolari had entered his T35C, alias TN, which had now become a full monoposto instead of the off-set single-seater it had been before, in the 2-litre heat and he was also entered in the 3-litre heat with a T35B. He finished at the back of the 2-litre heat with ignition problems but took fifth place in the 3-litre heat and qualified. Varzi had an easy win in this heat, pacing himself to stay in front of the Maseratis of Fagioli and Dreyfus. He led the 60-lap, 149-mile (239km) final until he had a puncture on lap 15, and by the time he restarted, Ernesto Maserati, with the twin-engined V4, was in the lead, but Varzi carried on until ignition problems put him out after 30 laps. Nuvolari had stopped after five laps when the T35B broke a valve spring.

It was an indication of the strength of grand prix racing that there was a third event that day. The Eifelrennen meeting was held on the short, 4.8-mile (7.7km) southern loop of the Nürburgring. Caracciola had a win with his SSKL Mercedes-Benz after he had caught the T35B of Heinrich-Joachim von Morgen who held on to second place and staved off Manfred von Brauchitsch with another SSKL.

The failure in the Mille Miglia had been forgotten and three black T50s were at Le Mans for the 24-hour race on Saturday, 12 June. The drivers were Chiron/Varzi, Divo/Bouriat and Conelli/Rost. Maurice Rost was an experienced driver, who had competed against the T13s at Le Mans in 1920 with a Majola, and throughout the 1920s had driven a works-supported Georges-Irat in Formule Libre and sports car races. He had driven at Le Mans in 1924 and 1926, but the T50 was the most powerful car he had handled and it was his first competitive drive in a Bugatti. The long chassis 8C Alfa Romeos were likely to be the biggest threat, two of which had been entered by Alfa Corse while Lord Howe had a third car which had been prepared at the Portello factory of Alfa Romeo and was being shared with Sir Henry Birkin. Boris Ivanowski, a Russian emigre living in France, had entered the SSK Mercedes-Benz, now fitted with wings and lights, which he had taken into fifth place in the GP d'Italia at Monza. Slower, but still capable of being in the picture at the end of 24 hours, were two British Talbot 105s.

At the beginning of race week, Le Mans was full of rumours that Jean Bugatti had been told by his father to withdraw the entries and when the cars did not appear for the first practice session on the

Wednesday, the rumours intensified. During the Wednesday practice, the SSK was quicker than the 8C Alfa Romeos, so a decision was taken to raise the compression ratio of the 8C engines and run the cars on pure benzole. The three T50s arrived in Le Mans on the Thursday afternoon, just before the 4pm deadline for scrutineering and created a big impression, as they looked brutal but business-like. The cars were fitted with the heavy-tread Michelin tyres to a pattern apparently specified by Ettore Bugatti and when practice began on the Friday morning, the tyres threw treads. Alfa Corse was also in trouble, when the engine of the Campari/Minoia 8C was started after new pistons were fitted, one broke immediately and the engine was wrecked. The 8C was withdrawn from the race, leaving only two cars, and the prospects looked brighter for Bugatti.

Race day was hot and there was anxiety that the alloy wheels of the T50s would dissipate too much heat to the tyres, exacerbating the problems. The race began at the traditional time of 4pm and at the end of

13 June 1931: The wheel of Rost's crashed car, showing the thrown tread.

the first lap, Chiron led from the SSK Mercedes-Benz, then came Divo, Birkin's 8C, Rost and the T43 of Pierre-Louis Dreyfus, who had entered with his brother-in-law, Antoine Schumann under the pseudonyms of 'Ano' and Nyme', as their wives did not approve of their racing exploits. On lap three, Stoffel passed Chiron when the T50 overshot Mulsanne Corner. Marinoni

13 June 1931: Divo takes Pontlieu Corner.

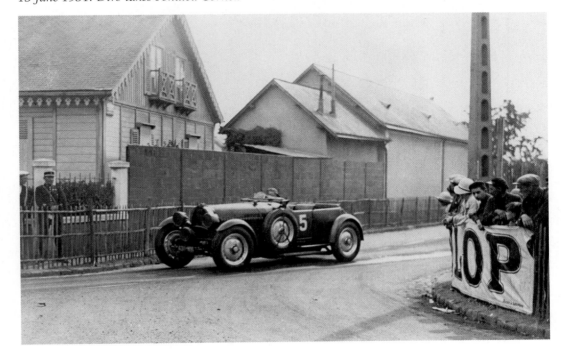

had been moving up with the second 8C and was in third place behind Chiron after an hour. Chiron went back into the lead when the SSK threw a tread but the T50 then had the same problem. He limped round to the pits and Marinoni took the lead, followed by Divo and Rost, while the T43 was in fourth place. Chiron pressed on trying to catch up and another tread failed. Jean Bugatti in the pits, put out a signal ordering the three drivers to slow. As an added disappointment, the T43 had stopped with a broken universal joint while holding fourth place, and later, the T40 of Mmes Mareuse and Siko, which had a chance of winning the biennial Rudge-Whitworth Cup, was disqualified for refuelling too early. Just after 6pm Rost was approaching the end of the Mulsanne Straight at about 115mph (185kmh) when a tread was thrown on the near-side rear tyre, it wrapped itself round the brake mechanism and the wheel seized, the tyre burst and the car skidded off the road. It leapt a ditch, broke down a fence and felled a tree before crashing into a group of spectators.

One was killed and three were seriously injured, Rost was thrown clear and suffered a broken collar bone and a lacerated scalp.

Divo had taken the lead when the 8C and the SSK stopped for fuel, then Chiron's T50 threw a tread in a similar manner to Rost's car. He held it on the road and toured round to the pits where he waited while Jean Bugatti spoke to his father on the telephone at Molsheim. Ettore Bugatti immediately ordered the team to be withdrawn from the race and Bouriat was signalled to come into the pits. It was announced to the crowd that the team had been withdrawn from the race and there was a chorus of boos and catcalls from disappointed spectators, as a long overdue French win was expected. The race was won by the 8C Alfa Romeo of Howe and Birkin; only six cars finished.

There was not too much sympathy for the Bugatti team, as the tyre problem had already emerged in the Mille Miglia and the tread throwing during practice should have been a sufficient warning. The T50 was a heavy car which put a lot of load on its tyres, but the legend that it was an ill-handling car is probably untrue. Rost's car went off the road because the wheel was locked by the tyre and the other drivers were not reported to have had difficulties. Those who drove a Le Mans T50 which came to England in the late 1930s, found that it handled well, but it was the end of a most unhappy chapter in Bugatti history. Ettore Bugatti said he would never enter cars for sports car races again, as he considered that the bodywork regulations made the cars inherently unsafe and Rost's accident would have been avoided if the rear wing had not prevented the tread flying clear. To reinforce his contentions about sports car racing, Bugatti withdrew the entries of the T50s from the Ulster Tourist Trophy and issued a challenge to other manufacturers to compete in a five-day race at Montlhéry for cars in racing trim, the cars being locked up overnight. He backed the challenge with a 300,000FF prize fund, but there were no takers. The reputation of the company had been seriously harmed by the accident which had come at the worst time with the growing economic crisis in France, but Ettore Bugatti's aversion to sports car racing would be short-lived. 'Might have been' speculation is pointless, but the performance of the Dreyfus/Schumann T43 showed the model was still not far off the pace, an uprated and properly prepared T43, with the T51 engine, could have been the equal of the 8C Alfa Romeo.

At Molsheim, there was little time to dwell on the accident as three T51s were being prepared for the Grand Prix de l'ACF at Montlhéry the following Sunday, and the cars were practising at the track on the Friday before the race. As it was a full ten-hour race the cars were shared, the driver pairings being Chiron/Varzi, Divo/Bouriat and 'Williams'/Conelli. As soon as practice began, the Michelin tyres on the T51s began to throw treads. With the Le Mans disaster in mind, the possibility of withdrawal was considered, but 'Williams' came to the rescue and produced a private haul

21 June 1931: Montlhéry. Chiron and Wurmser push out the T51 in the early sunshine for the start of the Grand Prix de l'ACF.

21 June 1931: A pit stop for the winning T51. Varzi refuels while Chiron waits on the pit counter.

of Dunlop tyres. In the circumstances, Michelin could raise little objection and the Dunlops were sufficient for practice, while Dunlop sent more tyres from England and Ireland before the race. The full, 7.7-mile (12.4km) circuit was used, with all the road course and half a lap of the banked track. A large crowd had already gathered when the cars were flagged away at 8am. Fagioli's Maserati led the pack followed by his teammate Dreyfus and the team T51s led by Chiron. The three Monza Alfa Romeos were well back, the team realising that ten hours was a long time. On the fourth lap, Chiron

took the lead, three laps later Fagioli was back in front, but was unable to pull away from Chiron and at the end of the first hour, his lead was about ten seconds. By 9.30am Chiron had retaken the lead and was not to relinquish it again. Dreyfus was in third place and Nuvolari had come through the field, passing the other T51s to take fourth place. Varzi had taken over the leading car, and as both Maseratis fell back, the Divo/Bouriat T51 moved up to second place.

As the Bugattis made their pit stops, Nuvolari, who was sharing his car with

Minozzi, held second place for a short time, but fell back behind the three T51s. At the fifth hour and half time, 1pm, Chiron/Varzi led by a lap from Divo/Bouriat, who were 1min 20sec ahead of the Dreyfus/Ghersi Maserati which had made a brief recovery. 'Williams'/Conelli were on the same lap as the Maserati and chasing hard. It had become an intensely hot day, the crowd had become slightly bored with the race and the correspondent of *The Motor* noted that over half the spectators in the main grandstand were asleep. The heat and Nuvolari's driving were having a most detrimental effect on the brakes of his Monza, which had several stops to change brake shoes and also to fit new brake drums. Maserati had the same problem and the front axle was removed from Fagioli's car which had retired and fitted to Dreyfus's car. Just before 2pm 'Williams' abandoned his T51 at the roadside as the gearbox had broken. This let Nuvolari up into third place, but another stop for brakes dropped him back, while at the front of the race Chiron and Varzi continued to reel off the laps, and at 4pm they were maintaining their one-lap lead over Divo/Bouriat, but Campari and Borzacchini, who were being kinder to the brakes of their Monza, had worked up to third place but were over four laps behind the second T51.

At the start of the last hour, a Bugatti 1-2 seemed almost certain, but with 40 minutes to go, Divo stopped out in the country as the engine mounting bolts had loosened and he had no spanners in the car to make a repair. Divo had to watch Campari and Borzacchini drive on to take a fortunate second place behind the victorious Chiron and Varzi, who had covered 786.64 miles (1,258.82km) in the ten hours. Varzi drove the last stint and as he crossed the line, was greeted by an exuberant Chiron who waved a plug spanner in salute. Divo and Bouriat were classified as seventh and Lord Howe, who had shared his T51 with Brian Lewis, was 12th and last, but still running at the end, having lost 90 minutes tracing a severe misfire to a chafed HT lead. After the defeats in the Targa Florio and at Monza, followed by the tragedy at Le Mans, the win did a lot to restore Bugatti morale and also the team's standing with the French public.

There was a lull of a fortnight before the next major events, which, following the intense activity in June, was probably welcome. The Spa 24-hour sports car race started at 4pm on Saturday, 4 July. There were capacity classes for sports cars and for 'dominant types', the latter being the model on which the manufacturer was concentrating. Most of the cars were driven by Belgian amateurs and three T43s were entered together with a 'dominant' T46. The race was a battle between the Le Mans-winning 8C Alfa Romeo of Birkin, who was sharing it with George Eyston, and the SSK Mercedes of Ivanowsky and Stoffel; both of which broke down, leaving the race to another SSK. Pierre-Louis Dreyfus, still racing as 'Ano' broke a wheel on his T43 in the early stages and then dropped out. Two Belgian T43s finished third and fourth in the over 2-litre sports class, the third-placed car was driven single-handedly by Joseph Zigrand for the whole distance, and the T46 was second in the 3-litre 'dominant' class, and sixth overall. As the Spa competitors were starting their last two hours at 2pm on the Sunday afternoon, 26 competitors were being flagged away at he start of the 50-lap GP de la Marne on the Reims circuit. The race had become of sufficient importance for Bugatti to make an official entry of Chiron's T51. He was racing against Dreyfus's Maserati and the usual independents including the T51s of Lehoux and Czaikowski, who had recovered from his Geneva injuries. Notably, Etancelin had abandoned Bugatti and arrived at Reims with a Monza Alfa Romeo, the first to be sold to a private customer.

Alfa Romeo had adopted the same policy as Bugatti and the semi-professional drivers could buy cars the equal (or nearly the equal!) of those used by the works drivers. Dreyfus led from the start, but at the end of the first lap Chiron took the lead in front of the stands. On the next lap Chiron came up to the pits still in the lead but coasted in with a silent engine – the prop shaft had broken. This let Dreyfus back into the lead but he was being hounded by Lehoux who went to the front a lap later. Dreyfus fought back and overtook Lehoux, staying in front

4 July 1931: The start of the Spa-Francorchamps 24-hour race. No. 7 is the T43 of Pierre-Louis Dreyfus, No. 8 is the T35B of Reinartz and André. At the bottom of the picture is the T43 of Zigrand, which finished third in the over 2-litre class.

12 July 1931: 'Williams' and Caberto Conelli wait beside their victorious T51 before the start of the Grand Prix de Belgique. (John Maitland Collection)

until lap 10. Lehoux must have become tired of playing games and went by again, this time he stayed in front, gradually pulling away to win by over two and a half minutes from Dreyfus. Czaikowski was third and beat Etancelin who was fourth. The local newspaper, *L'Eclaireur de l'Est*, held a champagne party in the pits at the end of the race, which each driver joined as he was flagged off. The voiturettes ran with the grand prix cars and T37As took the first three places in the class, led home by Philippe Auber. Speeds were rising at Reims and the circuit would soon be regarded as one of the fastest in Europe, Lehoux setting a new lap record at 92.24mph (148.32kmh).

The 24-hour race had ensured that the organisation was in full running order for the Grand Prix de Belgique, which was held at Spa a week later. This was run to the ten-hour formula and was the third and final round in the European Championship, the earlier rounds being at Monza and Montlhéry. The Maserati team had withdrawn so it was a straight fight between Bugatti and Alfa Romeo. The pairing of the drivers for the T51s was the same as at Montlhéry and once again the team used Dunlop tyres. At the 9am start Varzi took the lead, with Nuvolari only a few yards

behind. Varzi could not break away and on lap three the Monza Alfa Romeo was in front. The pair continued to pass and repass and at the end of the first hour, Nuvolari led Varzi by about 20 metres. 'Williams' was third, about 90 seconds behind, followed by Minoia's Monza, then came the T51 of Wimille who was going very well and keeping ahead of Divo. At the two-hour mark, Nuvolari still led, but the gap was the same and the Monza and the T51 pulled into the pits together for the first stops. Chiron took over from Varzi and immediately began to pull away from Borzacchini who had

12 July 1931: Divo (T51 No. 6) has taken the lead at the start from the T51 (No. 4) of 'Williams'. Minoia's 8C Alfa Romeo is beside 'Williams' while Chiron (No. 12) and Nuvolari (No. 10) are side-by-side. Further back is the T51 of Wimille (No. 18).

replaced Nuvolari in the Monza. More remarkable, Chiron was lapping steadily at two seconds a lap quicker than Varzi and Nuvolari, and his fastest lap at 6min 18.6sec was nearly six seconds better than Varzi's best lap, which may be a pointer to whom was the fastest driver at that time.

In four laps, the T51 had pulled out a lead of two minutes over the Monza. 'Williams'/Conelli were third, Minoia/Minozzi fourth, and Divo/Bouriat had managed to pass Wimille/Gaupillat, as the second driver of the latter pair lacked the burgeoning virtuosity of his partner. Chiron was swinging away happily in front, then at the end of the fifth hour when the lead was nearly four minutes, the T51 was overdue. Borzacchini came past the pits in the lead and Chiron was seen sprinting up the hill from Eau Rouge Corner on foot. The magneto drive had sheared so he gathered up some tools and ran back the car to make a repair. With the threat from Chiron gone, Nuvolari and Borzacchini eased off, as they

had a lead of over two-thirds of a lap from 'Williams' and Conelli, with Minoia and Minozzi back in third place. News reached the pits that Chiron's mechanical efforts had been in vain and the coupling was not repairable, but the Bugatti challenge was not finished, although the Divo/Bouriat car had dropped out with engine problems having done 51 laps. 'Williams' and Conelli were eating into the lead of the Alfa Romeo as they were making fewer stops and their pit work was noticeably quicker. Their three stops only took five minutes while the stops of the Alfa Romeo took nine minutes. At the last stop, all four wheels were changed and new brake shoes were fitted to the T51 in 2min 2sec. 'Williams' took over and began to motor with grim determination as the gap was less than two minutes. Borzacchini's lead shrank and to the delight of the team 'Williams' passed the Alfa Romeo and went into the lead. Borzacchini pulled into his pit complaining of fuel starvation, the car was worked on and Nuvolari

took over for the final stint, but 'Williams' had a lead of over a lap.

Nuvolari was in full flight and caught the T51, getting back on to the same lap, but it was still just ahead when the flag came out at 7pm and the race was over. Minoia had taken third place, supported by Minozzi and so became European Champion by virtue of steady, rather than rapid driving, while Wimille and Gaupillat took seventh place. Although since his marriage, 'Williams' had been driving infrequently, he had lost none of his flair, particularly as his fastest lap equalled that set by Varzi. For Bugatti, the win must have been most satisfying as the score against Alfa Romeo in the Championship rounds had finished two to one in Bugatti's favour. Alfa Romeo had expected that the Monza would give a marked superiority in grand prix racing; it was a highly competitive car but its performance had been equalled by the T51. Mussolini took a great interest in motor racing and had not been pleased with the results at Montlhéry and Spa; his displeasure was indicated to the Alfa Romeo directors at Portello with a strong hint that something had to be done.

The next major event in 1931 was only seven days later, and took place only a short distance from Spa, on the Nürburgring where the Grosser Preis von Deutschland was back in the calendar. Economic conditions in Germany had forced its cancellation in 1930. It was now being run as a race for proper grand prix cars instead of the previous sports car races and for the first time, the race was on the famous 14-mile (22km) northern loop of the circuit. The Germans were content to run a conventional distance race of 22 laps and were having no truck with a ten-hour endurance contest, and it attracted a strong entry. Bugatti sent Chiron, Varzi, 'Williams' and Bouriat, and were backed by independent T51s entered by Lehoux, Lord Howe and Wimille while the Bugatti Team Germany had put in the T35Bs of Burggaller and von Morgen. Against them were three works

Maseratis, but only one Scuderia Ferrari Monza Alfa Romeo for Nuvolari. To excite the local fans, Daimler Benz AG had entered three SSKL Mercedes-Benz and there were many more including a big voiturette contingent. Hopeful of a German victory a crowd estimated at 108,000 turned up to watch. The Mercedes-Benz team knew that if it was a dry day, the tyre wear on their heavy cars would put them out of contention, but a wet day could be their salvation. The team manager, Alfred Neubauer, made the drivers and mechanics practice until they could change four wheels in 30 seconds.

The 33 starters faced a wet day as it began to rain heavily just before the 9.30am start. Fagioli took his Maserati into the lead at the start followed by Caracciola's SSKL. Halfway round the first lap, the German car went to the front and at the end of the lap, Caracciola led from Fagioli and the T35B of von Morgen who was going remarkably quickly. Varzi came next, leading a string of cars with Chiron lying ninth. Caracciola, who had the advantage of being at the front and not driving behind the spray of others, was pulling away, and the heavy car was more stable in the wet. Nuvolari had speeded up and took von Morgen on lap three, then began disputing second place with Fagioli. Chiron too had quickened his pace as he became accustomed to the severe conditions.

After nine laps, he caught Fagioli, a lap later he went past Nuvolari and set off in pursuit of Caracciola who was two minutes in front. At half distance Caracciola made his pit stop, the pit crew refuelled the car and changed the rear wheels in 61 seconds and the white car was away before Chiron appeared. Chiron made his stop but the Bugatti mechanics were not so well drilled and it took 57 seconds just to refuel and top up the radiator. Chiron continued the chase 1min 47sec behind after the stops. 'Williams' had gone out after two laps with engine troubles and Lehoux had overturned into a ditch, escaping with a cut eye.

Probably much to Varzi's surprise von Morgen was ahead of him in third place having passed Nuvolari who had dropped back. With five laps to go the rain eased off, then stopped. This gave the Bugatti drivers the advantage they had needed. Chiron began to pull back 15–18 seconds a lap on Caracciola, but the German responded. Varzi speeded up and set a new lap record of 11min 48sec securing third place when von Morgen made a long pit stop. Caracciola held on and came home the winner by 1min 10sec, Chiron was second and Varzi was third in front of Nuvolari while Bouriat was seventh, Wimille eighth and Lord Howe was 11th. After all his efforts with a slower car, von Morgen had retired with one lap to go.

It rained again, at Dieppe on 26 July. Etancelin had come to terms with his new Monza Alfa Romeo and walked away with the four-hour race. He was chased by Lehoux, but the T51 was put into a ditch by Jacquin who had taken over from Lehoux after 17 laps. Wimille, who had taken over from Gaupillat at half distance and was holding second place, went off the road in St Aubin village and hit a house, the T51 caught fire, and to compound the damage, Max Fourny crashed his T35C into the wreck after the fire was extinguished. Czaikowski tried to catch Etancelin but his T51 was half a lap behind at the finish. In seventh place was a T35C driven by a lady driver, 'Hellé-Nice' who had started racing in 1928 and had been noticed when she won the Grand Prix Féminin at Montlhéry with an Omega-Six. She had been racing regularly with a T35 and had also raced a T35C owned by 'Philippe' but had driven mainly in hill-climbs. She bought her own T35C and in December 1929 took several short-distance national class records with this car at Montlhéry, with some support from Molsheim. Her real name was Helene Delangle, and she was a strip-tease dancer at the Casino de Paris and was the mistress of Marcel Lehoux. The pseudonym was a Gallic pun,

'elle est nice', with which the patrons of the casino probably concurred!

At the end of July, the Molsheim mechanics packed their bags and set off on an Italian tour. Chiron and Varzi had been entered for the Coppa Ciano at Livorno on 2 August and for the Coppa Acerbo at Pescara on the 16th. In both events they faced the full might of Alfa Romeo and Maserati. The Coppa Ciano was being run over ten laps of the 12.4-mile (19.9km) Montenero circuit on which the cars ran against the clock, as in the Targa Florio. The Scuderia Ferrari had entered two Monzas for Nuvolari and Borzacchini and had brought out the twin-engined Tipo A for Campari. In addition, there was a horde of 6C-1750s while Maserati had sent Fagioli and Biondetti.

At the end of the first lap, Varzi and Fagioli recorded the same time, with Chiron and Nuvolari a few seconds behind. On the second lap, Varzi had gained an advantage, while Nuvolari was up into second place, ahead of Chiron who lacked the circuit knowledge of his Italian rivals. Fagioli had fallen back as he was nursing a slipping clutch. On lap three, Varzi limped round to the pits with a puncture and had lost over five minutes before he set off again. This left Nuvolari to win from Chiron who was 44 seconds behind at the finish, with Varzi fifth. While the works T51s had been battling with the Italian opposition, von Morgen had been taking on the SSKL Mercedes-Benz team on the Avus track outside Berlin. His T35B went as well as it had done at the 'Ring and he was second behind Caracciola, but beat the SSKL of von Brauchitsch. A week earlier, von Morgen had been pipped by Caracciola for fastest time at the Freiburg-Schauinsland hill climb by 0.4 seconds.

There was a two-week interval between the Montenero and Pescara races so the Molsheim mechanics may have found time to enjoy the delights of the Adriatic holiday resorts. The entry for the Coppa Acerbo was smaller than that at Montenero, but the quality was there. Both Nuvolari and Campari had the twin-engine Tipo A Alfa Romeos and were supported by two Monzas, while Maserati had brought out the V-16 V4 and two 8C-2800s. The long, fast Pescara straights suited the Tipo As and after two laps Campari and Nuvolari were well ahead of Varzi and Chiron. Varzi put on the pace and caught Nuvolari and the two battled down the seaside straight side-by-side. Once again, Varzi had a puncture and lost time, but Nuvolari's car blew a head gasket which let Chiron up into second place where he finished behind Campari. Nuvolari limped into third place and might have been caught by Varzi, but he had been sent back into the race with an over-inflated tyre which upset the handling of the T51, so had to settle for fourth. On the weekend of 16 August, all the French independents were at Comminges for the local grand prix, attracted by a 90,000FF prize fund. The race also attracted the spectators of whom 15,000 were able to watch the race in comfort seated in a new concrete grandstand, 232 metres long and opposite the pits. Motor racing was becoming a serious spectator sport in Europe. The race was a three-cornered fight between Etancelin's Monza Alfa Romeo and the T51s of Lehoux and Czaikowski.

The Count led at the start from Lehoux and Etancelin. Lehoux took the lead after three laps while Etancelin waited for his chance which came when Czaikowski stopped with a puncture. The wheel was changed in 18 seconds but Czaikowski had lost touch. Etancelin passed Lehoux after nine laps, but Lehoux wrested the lead back again and stayed there until two laps before the end when he too had a puncture. This left the race to Etancelin and Czaikowski with Lehoux storming up behind, but unable to close the gap. The spectators probably felt they had received value for their money. Having seen off von Morgen at Freiburg, Caracciola gave the same treatment to Divo and Lehoux at

Mont Ventoux on 30 August. He did the climb in 15min 22sec with his SSKL, a new record. Divo with a T51, was second, but took 43 seconds longer, and Lehoux was third.

For some time, Ettore and Jean Bugatti had realised that the T51 lacked the speed to compete successfully on the faster circuits, such as Monza and the Avus, against the larger-engined and more powerful rivals, the Tipo A Alfa Romeo, the V4 Maserati and even the SSKL Mercedes-Benz. This problem was likely to become more acute in 1932, and much nearer home, as the AC de la Marne was submitting a tender to run the 1932 Grand Prix de l'ACF at Reims. The outcome of their concerns was a new car, the T54 which was more a clever combination of existing parts than a new design. If W. F. Bradley is correct it was 'designed, built and put on the road in 13 days'. *Motor Sport* said it took 14 days. The car was intended to race at Monza on 6 September so it is likely that work did not begin at Molsheim until the beginning of August. The T54 used the chassis of the abortive T47 which had a wheelbase of 9ft (2.75m) and a track of 4ft 1in (1.25m). Into this was installed a T50 engine, tuned to run on methanol, which gave an estimated 300bhp. It drove a three-speed gearbox in a casing that would later be used for the T55, one ratio being abandoned to provide space for heavier gears. The body was similar to the T35 and the car ran on the usual alloy wheels, it having the appearance of a heavier and stretched T35. Two T54s were built for the Monza meeting and were entered for Varzi and Chiron. Count Florio had adopted a similar format for the Gran Premio di Monza as in previous years, with three 14-lap heats and a 35-lap final on the short, 4.25-mile (6.8km) road and track circuit.

The 2-litre heat was a win for Ruggeri's Tipo 26 Maserati, while Czaikowski, who had preferred his T35C to his T51, ran second for several laps, but was passed by Biondetti's T35C near the end. The 3-litre

heat showed the superiority of the 8C-2800 Maseratis. Fagioli and Dreyfus gave a demonstration and pulled well clear of Minoia's Monza Alfa Romeo and Lehoux's T51. The third heat was the big one, where the T54s met the Tipo As of Nuvolari and Campari, and the V4 Maserati. Chiron led off the grid but Varzi was in front after a lap. Nuvolari took Chiron on lap two and closed on Varzi, the pair battling wheel-to-wheel for several laps, passing the stands at nearly 150mph (240kmh), then the Tipo A threw a tread and Nuvolari stopped to change the wheel. This left Varzi and Chiron to take first and second places while Nuvolari was third, ahead of Campari. Although only a heat, the T54 had won on its debut. A *repêchage* followed for the fastest non-qualifiers in the heats. Etancelin was one of these and he went off the course at the Lesmo bend on the tenth lap; some spectators were standing in front of the safety barrier and were hit by the Monza Alfa Romeo. Three were killed and ten injured, but Etancelin was unhurt.

The accident caused a long delay and the cars did not come out for the final until 5pm. Campari's Tipo A was absent as the gearbox had tightened up and there were no competitors from the first heat, as they had decided, or been told, they would not be fast enough and would get in the way. Fagioli beat the field away, followed by Chiron and Dreyfus with the second Maserati, but at the end of the first lap, Varzi was up into second place and chasing Fagioli, while Nuvolari had come up to pass Chiron and renew the battle with Varzi. For six laps the pair were wheel-to-wheel once more, then Nuvolari stopped with a broken piston. Despite Varzi's efforts, the 2.8-litre Maserati was uncatchable, making up for its deficit of power by much better roadholding, as the T54 was proving a difficult beast to tame; Chiron too could not shake off Dreyfus. On lap 13, Varzi came into the pits as the T54 had thrown a tread, and a lap later, Chiron had the same problem when

13 September 1931: 'Hellé-Nice' at speed in her T35C on the sands during the Grand Prix de La Baule. She finished in eighth place.

on one of the banked curves, but for him it had nasty overtones of Le Mans, as a brake cable was severed by the tread and he held the car with difficulty. The tyre troubles of the T54s left the two Maseratis with a comfortable lead, but it was then Fagioli's turn to throw a tread and Dreyfus stopped for a change of plugs. Varzi was not close enough to take advantage of their problems and when his car threw another tread he lost his third place to Borzacchini's Monza, which had being going steadily without the drama of the rivals in front. Dreyfus fell out with a broken piston which let Varzi regain his third place, but he was unable to catch Borzacchini. Fagioli came home as the winner followed by Borzacchini and Varzi, who was nearly four minutes behind the winning Maserati at the end. Chiron had

carried on, limping round and was seventh and last, having done 26 laps. At the end of the race, the crowd, excited by the heroic struggle it had seen, invaded the course, but fortunately there were no more accidents. Like the T50, the T54 was fast enough to beat the opposition, but there were inherent, and probably insoluble, problems.

A week after the titanic battle at Monza, there was a much more gentle race on the sands at La Baule, where the summer season was ending. 'Williams' had a T51, which although entered in his name was probably loaned from the factory and was up against a field of independents led by

Lehoux and Gaupillat, whose T51 had been mended since Dieppe. The course had two 3km straights with a hairpin at each end, and the sand was very bumpy. 'Williams' showed his class by leading all the way, followed by Gaupillat, who saw off a challenge from Lehoux. 'Hellé-Nice' would have been sixth, but lost two places when she stopped to change plugs on the last lap. The industrial north-east of France was much less appealing than the sands of La Baule, but 35 starters turned out for the Circuit des Routes Pavées on the same day. The competitors had practised in the wet, but race day was fine and the six-hour event became a battle between the 6C-1750 Alfa

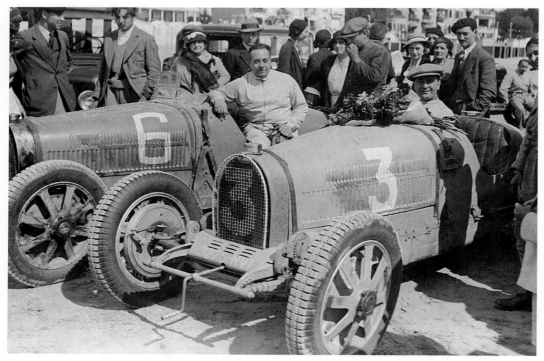

13 September 1931: 'Williams', the winner of the Grand Prix de La Baule, sits in his T51 and holds the bouquet, while Gaupillat, who was second, looks on. (John Maitland Collection)

29 September 1931: Varzi talks to Elizabeth Junek before the start of the Masarykuv Okruh at Brno. He retired when his T51 was damaged by the collapsing bridge.

Romeo of Goffredo Zehender and the T35Cs of Max Fourny and Roca. Zehender led for the whole race but was chased during the first hour by Fourny who overturned at La Capelle Corner during the second hour. The car caught fire but the driver was unhurt. Roca took up the chase, breaking the lap record several times, and when the pair had covered 26 laps, Zehender's lead was only 1.6 seconds, but Roca lost time with a slow refuelling stop. Roca started to reduce the gap again, but lost more time after a puncture and at the end of the six hours was 9km behind, although he won the 2-litre racing class. In the 1,500cc sports class, the T37 of Delommez was the winner and the T40 shared by Mmes Mareuse and Siko was second.

The last major race of the season was in Czechoslovakia at Brno, on 27 September. The full grand prix circus ran in the Masarykuv Okruh over 17 laps of the 18-mile (29km) circuit. There were full teams from Alfa Romeo, Maserati and Mercedes-Benz. Bugatti sent two T51s for Varzi and Chiron which were backed by Lehoux's T51 and the three T35s of the Bugatti Team Germany. There was also a T51 entered by the German driver Prince Georg-Christian Lobkowicz. Fagioli beat the field away, followed by Borzacchini, Varzi, Caracciola and Chiron, but as he completed his first lap, Fagioli ran wide on a bend and his Maserati clipped a foot-bridge spanning the course. The bridge, which was on a bend, collapsed and Borzacchini passed underneath as it fell. Varzi and Nuvolari who were following found the road blocked so both took to the sides of the road, one to a ditch, the other on to a bank. Nuvolari bent his rear axle and Varzi's car, although still driveable, was damaged. Forgetting their rivalry, Varzi gave Nuvolari a lift round to the pits where he found the car was too badly damaged to continue. Chiron was immediately behind Caracciola's SSKL and, unable to assess the whole scene, relied on Caracciola's judgment and followed him. The Mercedes-

Benz went into the ditch and came out on the other side of the debris with a broken shock absorber. Chiron bounced through the ditch unscathed, missing the SSKL and set off in pursuit of Borzacchini who was in the lead. Chiron soon caught him and took the lead, while Lehoux who had also avoided the debris passed Borzacchini and began to close on Chiron who, with a comfortable lead, was easing off. Lehoux tried too hard, ran wide on a corner and broke a wheel. He was able to fit the spare and continued, but had lost 19 minutes and retired shortly afterwards. Chiron was unchallenged and finished 14 minutes in front of Hans Stuck's SSKL which was second, von Morgen was third with his T35B, Lobkowicz was fourth and Prince zu Leiningen took fifth place with the German Team T35C. As the last major race, it was a most satisfactory note on which to finish the season for Bugatti. Maserati had not taken a car to Brno for Dreyfus so he was at a loose end that weekend. Count Czaikowski had entered for a small event, the Grand Prix de Brignoles organised by the AC du Var, and was using his T35C, so offered his T51 to Dreyfus. Scuderia Ferrari had entered a Monza Alfa Romeo for Minoia but this was a non-starter, so Dreyfus had and easy win, beating Lumachi with a T35B by nearly a minute, while his patron was third.

The 1931 season saw a resurgence of interest in voiturette racing which matched the vigorous grand prix scene. Many of the races had been curtain-raisers for the grands prix and the leading runners had been the survivors of the 1926/27 grand prix formula but overall the uncrowned champion had been José Scaron, the French driver with an 1,100cc monoposto C6 Amilcar. The bulk of the fields had been made up with T37s and T37As which were not as fast as the Amilcar or the 1927 Delages which made sporadic appearances. Production of the T37 and T37A had finished but there were still some cars at Molsheim and if a customer appeared, a new car would be built on request. The Geneva race on 7 June was won by a newcomer Pierre Veyron, with a T37A. Veyron, who came from the Lozere department in the Massif Central was 28 years old and was being supported by André Vagniez, an industrialist from Amiens who owned the car. He had already taken second place at Tunis in March. At Reims, T37As made a clean sweep with victory going to Philippe Auber. He was followed by Jean Delorme who had bought the last T37A to leave Molsheim, while in third place was a woman, Anne Rose-Itier, who had been competing since 1926, mainly in hill-climbs. She had bought her T37A at the beginning of the 1931 season. Delorme went on to take second place at Dieppe behind Lord Howe's Delage but both Delorme and Itier were out of luck at Comminges. Itier, who had been fourth at Grenoble, overturned her car but escaped unhurt and Veyron took another second place behind Louis Joly who had abandoned his T37A for a Maserati. The foreign customers had their successes as Hans Lewy won the 1,500cc class at the Avus, while at Brno, Florian Schmidt had avoided the debris from the fallen bridge and taken the voiturette class. The 1,500cc class would soon assume a much greater importance.

Amateur drivers continued to use their T35s and T37s at Brooklands. At the wet Easter meeting, Harold Purdy won a handicap with a T35 lapping the track at 105.97mph (170.39kmh) beating Selby's T35 by 0.4 seconds, A. N. Spottiswoode then won a handicap with his T35 which lapped at the excellent speed of 105.52mph (169.67kmh) and Charles Brackenbury scored a third handicap victory in his T37 with a fastest lap of 102.27mph (164.45kmh). Malcolm Campbell, who was driving his T39A in a Mountain handicap, had an alarming scare when the track rod broke as he was braking for the Fork Hairpin, but he was able to hold the car. Racing on the Mountain circuit posed a particular problem for Bugatti drivers. The surface of the track approaching the Fork Hairpin was very rough, and if a front wheel was pitched into the air by a bump as the driver applied the brakes, the wheel would be locked as it touched the ground and this sometimes caused the kingpin to break with unhappy consequences. The experienced Bugatti drivers fitted softer front brake linings and replaced kingpins after three or four Mountain races. Because of the rain, the faster races on the Outer circuit were postponed until the following Saturday when William Craig won the Founders' Gold Cup Race with a T37A, while Spottiswoode scored again with his T35. At the August Bank Holiday meeting, T35s won two handicaps, J. R. Jeffress's cream-painted car won on the Outer circuit and Thomas Fothringham scored in a Mountain race, but it was noticeable that wins for the T35 and T37s variants were becoming fewer. The age of the cars was beginning to tell and more modern machines were appearing.

Apart from the Le Mans disaster, the 1931 season had been reasonably successful for Bugatti. The initial fears that the 8C and Monza Alfa Romeos would dominate racing had been unfounded. The Italian cars were formidable, but the T51 had been able to match it and had gained some impressive victories. The going was to get much harder, politics were about to become a dominating influence in grand prix racing and would be so for the rest of the decade. Mussolini regarded motor racing success as one of the measures of the vigour and virility of a state; when Alfa Romeo competed, the prestige of a Fascist Italy was at stake. Mussolini expected Alfa Romeo 'according to the perfect Fascist style to race and win'. To comply with the edicts of the political masters, Vittorio Jano had completed a new and fundamentally different design for a grand prix car, which he showed to the Alfa Romeo directors in September 1931. The design was completed in the strictest secrecy, so it is possible that information about it had not reached Molsheim in the autumn of 1931, but it would make all existing grand prix cars obsolete.

Chapter 11

The monoposto scourge

REALISING THAT ALFA ROMEO had already cocked a snook at the grand prix formula by racing the Tipo A in 1931, the AIACR changed the rules during the winter of 1931/32. They stipulated that for *grandes épreuves* in 1932, no provision need be made for carrying a riding mechanic, or more simply, single seaters were now permitted in grand prix racing. There was an additional change as the length of *grandes épreuves* was reduced to five hours. Vittorio Jano had anticipated the change when he showed his design to the Alfa Romeo directors and received their approval to build six examples for the 1932 season. The new Alfa Romeo was a single seater, it had a 2.6-litre eight-cylinder engine boosted by twin superchargers which had been developed from the 8C and an unusual transmission with two prop shafts driven from a differential at the back of the gear box, each driving a back wheel via a bevel box. The car had a neat, slim body and the design immediately made all existing grand prix cars obsolescent. It had the factory title of Tipo B but became more commonly known as the P3.

Bugatti had little answer to the P3, the funds were not available to build new grand prix cars, the economic depression, partially delayed by the huge gold reserves of the Banque de France, was now biting hard in France, and trade was slow, not least at Molsheim where there were few orders for cars. The company was possibly saved from disaster in the most unlikely circumstances.

The T41 Royale had not sold to the crowned heads of Europe and the ultra-rich as Ettore Bugatti had hoped. To utilise the T41 engines lying in the Molsheim stores, Bugatti designed a railcar, although the detail work was done by Adolphe Nuss. The first drawings were dated 21 November 1931 and during the autumn of 1931 a number of patents concerning the design were filed in Jean Bugatti's name. Three types were produced, a twin-engined single car, a four-engined model which pulled a second car, and a four-engined version which pushed one car and pulled another. A new shed was built at Molsheim, much larger than the existing buildings, for railcar construction. The railcars had a maximum speed of 95mph (150kmh) and had an immediate appeal for the various railway companies, including the national organisation Etat, which was able to move right to the technical forefront of rail design. The orders for the first railcars were received in 1932 and the first prototype was handed over to Etat in the spring of 1933. There was no rail link between the factory and the railway at Molsheim and the prototype was pushed along the road to the rail connection by the factory staff, including Dreyfus, with sections of track being laid in front of it. For the production models, a rail link was made to the factory. The first railcar went into service on the Paris-Deauville Etat line in 1933. When production stopped in 1939, 76 had been sold to Etat, AL and PLM, which had been amalgamated into

SNCF in 1938. Driving a railcar, Jean Bugatti set a world record covering 70km at an average speed of 122mph (196kmh).

The advent of the railcars brought a significant change to the life of Ettore Bugatti. The offices of the railway companies which were interested in the railcars were in Paris and Bugatti realised he needed to be near the customers who were keeping the company alive. Substantial finance was also involved and the bankers were in Paris too. He opened a private office in Paris in the Avenue Montaigne, over the Bugatti showrooms, and took some draughtsmen with him, there he worked and lived. It is possible that Ettore Bugatti had lost some of his interest in the motor car, the firm would soon be committed to a one-model policy so perhaps he felt it was time to move into new fields. His inventive genius was unquenched and he was still feeding ideas to his small drawing office team in Paris. He was working actively on marine and aviation projects. Much of the day-to-day responsibility at Molsheim was handed over to Jean, but Ettore Bugatti had not relinquished control over important issues and he spent half his time at Molsheim where he continued to live the life of a mildly eccentric and autocratic country gentleman.

Even if funds had been abundant, the design staff at Molsheim were fully occupied at the beginning of 1932, not only with the unfamiliar technical demands of the railcars, but also with a new road car. This would become the T57, and was a new concept for Bugatti. The earlier luxury designs, the T46 and T50, were too large and perhaps too reminiscent of the racing siblings to have the broadest appeal to the luxury car market. The T57 was intended to be a *grand routier* in the true French tradition, a comfortable, luxurious and reliable touring car capable of covering great distances, quickly and in style. The concept of the T57 came from Jean Bugatti who realised that the economic depression would come to an end in France and a demand for luxury touring cars would follow. For the sporting driver, who was seeking a replacement for the T43, the T55 was announced at the beginning of 1932. It was only built in small numbers, with 38 being made before it was dropped in 1935, but it was an example of the praiseworthy economic principle that nothing should be wasted, as it used the T54 chassis with the T51 engine. Most were fitted with an elegant two-seater roadster body designed by Jean Bugatti.

A more revolutionary design emerged early in 1932. Bugatti had been having another look at the two Miller 91s and was fascinated by the front-wheel drive. The outcome was the T53 which seems to have been gestating at Molsheim for almost two years before being revealed to the world. This was a four-wheel-drive racing car, using the T50 engine, which had already been tried in the T54. The inspiration for four-wheel-drive may have come from the Spanish designer Wifredo Ricart y Medina, who had produced a design study for a four-wheel-drive competition car and had discussed it in correspondence with Bugatti. For the first and only time Bugatti had adopted independent front suspension, using two transverse leaf springs, with heavy duty friction dampers as additional suspension arms. A drive shaft passed forward from the four-speed, indirect drive gearbox, through the engine department to an off-set bevel box, from this unequal length drive-shafts drove the front wheels via normal universal joints. This was an

inherent weakness of the design as there was a need for constant velocity joints to prevent 'winding-up' at the front wheels. Another propshaft drove the conventional back axle with an off-set differential and was mounted on the customary reversed quarter-elliptic springs. Alloy wheels similar to those fitted to the T50, carried 28 x 5 tyres. The wheelbase was 8ft 6in (2.6m) and the track was 4ft 1in (1.24m). The body was wholly untypical, as there was a cowl with a mesh covering the radiator and a very large bolster fuel tank comprised the tail. Three cars were built. The transmission was the work of Guilio Cesare Cappa, who had a design consultancy in Turin and had already produced a front-wheel-drive design for Itala, a 1,500cc V-12, intended for the 1926 formula, but which never competed. Cappa had worked for Aquila-Italiana until 1914, so it is possible that he had received a recommendation from his old workmate, Meo Costantini. Cappa sent one of his engineers, Antonio Pichetto, to Molsheim to supervise the detail design work and construction of the T53. Pichetto arrived at Molsheim in November 1931, and it seems he liked the life in Alsace and stayed as a member of the Bugatti staff. The car was tested extensively around the roads at Molsheim by Chiron and Varzi, both forming the same view, that it was most difficult to drive. Dreyfus also drove it and commented some years later

'. . . it was a monster. It was huge, a terror to drive. I tested it frequently, finding it did have some advantages – stopping and starting on wet roads, it did beautifully, for example. But the car was impossible to drift; whatever direction you aimed it, that was the direction it went. Accuracy and a tendency not to hesitate were called for. I could handle that. The strength of Hercules was also called for. That I couldn't.'

According to an account given to Griff Borgeson by Roland Bugatti, the main purpose of the T53 was to explore the possibilities of four-wheel-drive for fast military off-road use. If this is correct it is a

further indication that Ettore Bugatti was looking for financial viability beyond the world of high-performance cars. After a decade of belief that another war was impossible, the fear of war was beginning to permeate France. In Britain, throughout the 1920s, military planners had abided by the 'Ten Year Rule', that there would be no armed conflict in Europe for another ten years. In 1930/31 the rule had been discreetly dropped, and much the same policy was followed in France. The National Socialist Party had won 107 seats in the German elections, making it the second largest party in the Reichstag elections, and Adolf Hitler was making belligerent noises about the injustices of the Versailles Treaty. In the autumn of 1931, Japan had invaded Manchuria and attacked Shanghai, so the opening of an international disarmament conference at Geneva on 2 February offered little comfort to the fearful French. In this climate, Bugatti knew that military contracts might be forthcoming.

Possibly to collect some bonuses or perhaps for the publicity, Divo took a T51 to Montlhéry on Thursday, 10 March and established new figures for the International class D short distance records. He put the one-mile record to 131.22mph, and the one-kilometre to 211.18kmh, he went on to set new figures for the five-kilometre, 50 kilometres and 50 miles, 100 kilometres and 100 miles, finishing with the 200 kilometres. The 200-kilometre record was set at 124.67mph (200.46kmh) and was also a world record for the distance. During the run, a class D one-hour record was established at 124.68mph (200.48kmh). On Saturday, 12 March, Chiron joined him and the T51 set off again. This time four world records were taken, the 200 miles at 118.00mph (189.89kmh), the 500km at 119.98mph (193.09kmh), the 500 miles at 119.24mph (191.89kmh) and the three-hours at 120.64mph (194.15kmh). It was a successful and profitable morning's work and the consistency of the figures was notable. Chiron had been at Montlhéry in

9 April 1932: The T35B of Cazzaniga and Rosa, which did not finish the Mille Miglia.

January with a T51, for the filming of a thriller, *Fantomas*, in which he had been one of a pack of drivers, jostling for places behind the hero, who was being towed in a T51 by the camera lorry on a steel tow bar, at about 20mph (30kmh)!

The Paris-Nice Rally took place at the end of March. The event ended with a hill-climb over the historic course at La Turbie on the outskirts of Nice, on Thursday, 24 March, which gave the competitors a chance to complete the rally in style and also catered for other runners. Wimille had bought a new T54 from Molsheim during March and ran this; storming up the hill he set a new course record. The first major race of the

season was the GP de Tunisie on 3 April. Varzi and Chiron entered T51s and were up against three T54s, as well as Wimille, cars had been sold to Lehoux and von Morgen during the spring. There was no sign of the P3 Alfa Romeo, but the Scuderia Ferrari sent a Monza for Eugenio Siena and there were works Maseratis for Dreyfus and Fagioli; it was an entry which would have graced many *grandes épreuves*. Varzi, whose T51 was painted red, walked away with the race after an initial challenge from Lehoux, who found the T54 was hard work and short of brakes, but came second three minutes behind the winner. Chiron and Dreyfus had been among the leaders but

both fell back after making stops to change plugs. After the race, Varzi must have travelled direct to Brescia, as the Mille Miglia was being held the following weekend. He had yet to gain a victory in this race and his defeat by Nuvolari in 1930 must still have rankled. He had entered a T55 which, in terms of specification and performance, would almost have been the equal of the 8C Alfa Romeo. As co-driver, Varzi had Count Luigi Castelbarco from Milan, who had finished third in the 1,500cc class at Tunis with a T37A, behind the T26 Maseratis of Joly and Veyron. At the end of the first stage to Bologna, Nuvolari's 8C led from the similar car of Caracciola with Varzi in third place, but so close was the racing that only five seconds covered this trio.

When the leaders reached Florence after 195 miles (312km). Caracciola led, as Nuvolari had gone off the road, but Varzi had dropped back to fourth and was eight minutes behind. Any satisfaction that Varzi might have had at Nuvolari's mistake was short-lived, as the T55 stopped between Florence and Siena with a split fuel tank.

The P3s were still not ready for Monaco on 17 April, so the four T51s, driven by Chiron, Varzi, Divo and Bouriat, faced the three Alfa Corse-entered Monzas of Nuvolari, Campari and Borzacchini. There was a fourth works-supported Monza for Caracciola, who had been forced to go to Italy for a drive as the depression had put Mercedes-Benz out of racing. It would only

be a short absence. The T53 was taken to Monaco and given to Divo as the strongest driver in the team physically. He tried it in practice, but it was too heavy for the driver, overheated and lacked adequate brakes for the circuit and to race it for 100 laps would have been an impossible task. One report described him as 'cornering gingerly as if he expected it to turn over'. The starting grid was balloted and Chiron was on the second row, and at the start he went to the front leading 'Williams' and Lehoux, both with T51s. Chiron began to extend his lead, but Nuvolari, who had started from the fourth

row, came up to second place after ten laps, followed by Varzi. Nuvolari was putting on the pressure and after 30 laps was only three seconds behind. On the 30th lap, Chiron came up to lap Czaikowski's T51 at the Station Hairpin. The Count would not give way and in trying to stay in front, he spun at the chicane. Chiron tried to pass the spinning T51, but clipped a sandbag and the car rolled three times, throwing Chiron out. Chiron escaped with minor cuts and a shaking and was taken across the harbour on the ambulance boat. This left Nuvolari leading Varzi by six seconds, and

16 April 1932: Divo drives the T53 away from the pits during practice for the Grand Prix de Monaco, with Wurmser in the passenger's seat, while Jean Bugatti looks on.

17 April 1932: 'Williams' shares the front row of the Monaco grid with the Alfa Romeo of Etancelin and the Maserati of Ruggeri. On the next row are Chiron (No. 12) and Czaikowski (No. 18). (Fiat Auto Arese)

gradually pulling away, but on lap 57 Varzi coasted in with a broken back axle. Bouriat had hit the sandbags at the Station Hairpin and broken a wheel. He restarted but neither he nor Divo had been in the running, so it was left to Lord Howe to uphold Bugatti honour by taking fourth place with his T51, behind the Monzas of Nuvolari and Caracciola, and Fagioli's Maserati.

Varzi took his red T51 to the Littorio track outside Rome, a week after Monaco

for the Premio Reale, which was run in capacity class heats with the fastest cars going into the final. Varzi led his heat, then dropped behind the T35B of von Morgen and the Maserati of Dreyfus but speeded up again, passed them both and won the heat. In the final, Fagioli with a new and even fiercer twin-engined Maserati, the 5-litre

V5, led all the way, Varzi staying with him until two wheels broke up. He limped to his pit and started off again with new wheels, but had to settle for fourth place behind von Morgen. On the same afternoon, Wimille scored his first important victory when he won the GP d'Oranie in Algeria. For this race he abandoned his new

T54 and returned to his trusty T51. He led all the way although he had to fight off a challenge from a 22-year-old newcomer, Guy Moll who lived in Algeria, and was being encouraged by Marcel Lehoux, and was driving Lehoux's old T35C. Mme Mareuse, Wimille's former sponsor, crashed her T37A when a wheel broke up, breaking her ribs and cutting her face. Wimille visited her in hospital after the race and presented her with his victor's bouquet.

After Varzi's single entry in 1931, Bugatti returned to the Targa Florio in greater strength on 8 May. The landslide which had forced the use of the old long circuit in 1931 was not repairable, so a new circuit had been devised, the 44.73-mile (71.9km) short Madonie circuit which used part of the old circuit with a new link road, the costs being met from Fascist government funds. This circuit remained in use until the race was abandoned in 1974. Another Italian win was expected and Scuderia Ferrari had entered five cars to oppose the T51s of Varzi and Chiron. In 1932, the drivers raced alone, there were no riding mechanics. Nuvolari led from the start of the eight-lap race and at the end of the first lap his Monza had a two-minute lead from Borzacchini with another Monza, who was tied on time with Chiron. Varzi, racing in a black beret instead of the usual cloth wind-cap, had been in fourth place, but dropped out at the end of the opening lap with a broken gearbox. Nuvolari and Borzacchini began to pull away from Chiron, who was having problems with the intense heat of the day and also with erratic brakes. Oil was leaking into the drums and Chiron had been pressing so hard on the pedal, that he had worn a hole in his shoe. After four laps Varzi took over the car but was unable to make any impression on the Alfa Romeos in front of him and finished third, 20 minutes behind the victorious Nuvolari. The season had begun badly for Bugatti; in both serious confrontations with Alfa Romeo, the T51 had been beaten, and the P3 was imminent.

All the French independents went to Nimes on 16 May where the local club had organised a 'round the houses' race meeting with a multitude of classes. The 1.8-mile (2.9km) circuit was rather unimaginative, using two parallel lanes of the Avenue Jean Jaurès in the centre of the town, linked by a hairpin at each end and several straw bale chicanes. After various short races for motorcycles and the smaller capacity cars, the 30-lap 1,500cc race saw a small piece of motor racing history being made, as Mme Anne Rose-Itier led all the way in her T37A to beat a field of male rivals and become the first woman to win a voiturette race. In the 35-lap, 2-litre race, a newcomer, Louis Trintignant, fought with Czaikowski all the way, both with T35Cs, only to spin on the very last corner and lose the race by five seconds. The big race of the day, the GP de Nimes, was over 70 laps and had attracted Chiron. His main rival, Etancelin with his Monza, lost three laps at the start when he collided with Canin's T35B whose brakes had jammed, so Chiron seemed to have the race in his pocket, but an oil pipe broke. This left an amateur, Benoit Falchetto, with a T35B in the lead being chased by Dreyfus. The Maserati was unable to catch the T35B and Falchetto won a good race, which left Dreyfus wondering if he should part company with Maserati, if he could not catch an amateur in an elderly car.

A dissatisfied Dreyfus went to the Avus on 22 May where he drove the V5 Maserati and should have faced the T54s of Varzi and Chiron, but neither appeared. The factory was represented by Divo's T54 and Bouriat's T51, while 'Williams' also had a T54 which seems to have had very strong factory connections, although entered in his name. A third T54 was driven by the Czech, Prince Lobkowitz, which he had bought through Bucar, the Bugatti agent in Zurich, the previous month. Dreyfus was not the only dissatisfied driver at the Avus, as Caracciola, having been told the company was withdrawing from racing,

found he was competing with his Monza Alfa Romeo against two works-entered SSKL Mercedes-Benz. 'Williams' led from the start and almost immediately there was a fatal accident when Prince Lobkowicz overturned his T54 at the South Bend while attempting to overtake another car. 'Williams' dropped back and retired, leaving Fagioli with an 8C-2800 Maserati in front, but he too fell out and Divo took the lead, but after five laps the T54 expired, which left the race as a fight between the SSKLs and Caracciola. Lehoux had taken his T54 to Casablanca and had better luck that afternoon. For half the race, Wimille led with his T51 but then fell out with engine problems, which left Lehoux to win comfortably from a hard battle for second place in which Etancelin's Monza got the better of Czaikowski's T51.

After the Avus race, Dreyfus agreed with Ernesto Maserati that their ways should part. Chiron offered Dreyfus the use of the T51 that he had been using as an independent when the factory cars were not running. Although the car had been funded partly by Freddy Hoffmann and Nerka, it seems that it had become Chiron's property and it was agreed that any prize money won by Dreyfus would be shared between them. Dreyfus's first race with the T51 was at the Nürburgring for the Eifelrennen, on 29 May. During practice on the day before the race, von Morgen had an unexplained accident when he went off the road on the main straight and was killed when his T51 overturned. Caracciola had his revenge and led all the way in his Monza, easily outpacing the two works SSKL Mercedes-Benz. Dreyfus could not catch Caracciola, but hung on to him all the way and was only 22 seconds behind at the end of the 14 laps. The two SSKLs were third and fourth, while Chiron had to be satisfied with fifth, though he had the consolation of half the second place prize money.

Perhaps the P3 had not been ready for the earlier races, or perhaps Alfa Corse, with an eye to 'the perfect Fascist style',

27 May 1932: During practice for the Eifelrennen at the Nürburgring, Dreyfus stands behind the T51 which he has hired from Chiron.

had kept it back for the big occasion, but two of the new cars appeared for the Gran Premio d'Italia at Monza on 5th June. This was the first five-hour *grande épreuve* under the new rules, the P3s were entrusted to Nuvolari and Campari, and were backed by a phalanx of Monzas. Bugatti realised the need for a maximum effort and entered T54s for Chiron and Varzi, accompanied by a T51 for Divo. These were supported by Wimille's T54 and the T51s of Lehoux and Dreyfus. Fagioli's V5 Maserati offered a strong threat to both teams. The race attracted a disappointing crowd, but there were rival attractions in Milan, as the Italian Cup Final was being played and the Tour of Italy cycle race was passing through the city. The race, run

on the full 6.2-mile (10km) combined track and road circuit, was started by Achille Starace, the Secretary-General of the Fascist Party. Nuvolari and Chiron, who started from the second row, went straight to the front and were side by side at the end of the first lap, the pair battled together for several laps and Fagioli came up to join them, each holding the lead in turn. Chiron realised that five hours was a long time and eased up, leaving the two Italians to battle on, while Varzi tucked in behind Chiron. *Motor Sport*'s correspondent noted that the P3 seemed to handle better than the T54, but the Bugatti had the advantage in sheer speed. After 100km, Fagioli led Nuvolari by one second, while Chiron and Varzi were together, eight seconds behind.

The two T54s gradually began to drop back, it was evident that the cars were tiring the drivers who could not maintain the pace.

The Alfa Corse mechanics were much better drilled at pitwork than their Maserati rivals and as the stops began, Nuvolari secured an advantage of almost two minutes over Fagioli. After 260km, Varzi retired with a malfunctioning gearbox, so he took over Chiron's car. He set a new lap record but the car had a fuel feed blockage, resulting in a weak mixture, and within a few laps a piston seized and the second T54 was out. Dreyfus was driving a splendid race and had been up into third place as the faster cars made more stops. Divo had kept going steadily and was relieved by Bouriat as the race continued, who then handed the car over to Chiron in the closing laps. At the end of the five hours, Nuvolari brought the P3 home to a memorable first victory. Fagioli, delayed by his pitwork was second, a lap behind, and just ahead of Borzacchini's Monza and Campari's P3. Dreyfus was fifth, but was on the same lap as the three cars in front of him and only 35m behind Campari. The trio sharing the other T51 was sixth. Bugatti may have regretted the decision to run T54s for Chiron and Varzi instead of T51s.

Ettore Bugatti's decision that he would never enter for sports car races again, following the 1931 Le Mans disaster, lasted less than 12 months. When the entry list for the 1932 Le Mans 24-hour race was published, there were two supercharged 2,300cc Bugattis entered. Although these had not been entered by Usines Bugatti, it was common knowledge that the cars had been built at Molsheim. The drivers were Chiron and Bouriat for the first car, with Czaikowski and Friderich for the second. Friderich, who had prepared cars for Dreyfus, had taken on the preparation of cars for the Count in his Nice workshop, and after a break of eight years, had decided to return to the wheel. It is possible that some of the expenses of the second car were met by Czaikowski. A T55 had already been raced in the Mille Miglia and was an ideal car for Le Mans, but the race regulations required cars over 1,500cc to have four-seat bodies, which in the past, had necessitated the use of long chassis. Two T55 chassis were fitted with Weymann four-seat bodies which were close-coupled so the rear seats were over or behind the rear axle. When the cars were presented for scrutineering at Le Mans, the Bugatti team found that their cunning had been matched; among the opposition, there was a short-chassis 8C Alfa Romeo, entered by Raymond Sommer which had a close coupled four-seat body with the rear seats behind the rear axle line. The short-chassis 8C and the T55 shared a wheelbase of 2.75m, so both had followed the same logic. There were two T40s entered in the 1,500cc class; the Druck/Verlouvet car was a standard Grand Sport, but the Sebilleau/Delaroche car was supercharged.

Czaikowski and Friderich made their headquarters at the Pavilion de St Hubert, a country house about ten miles (16km) from Mulsanne. During practice, the two Bugattis showed they were the equal of the Alfa Romeos in lap times. Race day was intensely hot and before the start there was a one-minute silence to honour the memory of André Boillot, the Peugeot driver who had been killed in the Côte d'Ars hill-climb at La Châtre on 5th June. He was driving the 201X, which had an engine design commissioned from Bugatti by Peugeot and given the Molsheim number T48. It had a 996cc engine which was in effect, one half of a T35. From the start the 8C Alfa Romeos battled for the lead, and Bouriat who had taken the first driving stint, watched in fifth place. The second T55 was well back, Friderich had said before the start: 'I will only push forward in the last six hours of the race'. Sadly, after two hours, Bouriat pulled into the pits and retired, the car was out of fuel and had not covered the minimum distance

18 June 1932: The T55 shared by Chiron and Bouriat before the start of the Le Mans 24-hour race.

18 June 1932: Friderich and a mechanic adjust the windscreen of the T55 while Czaikowski stands on the pit counter.

before refuelling was permitted. A stone had lodged between the rear axle casing and the fuel tank and had chafed a hole through which the fuel leaked away. By 10pm, the leading Alfa Romeos had battled so fiercely only three cars were left, but these held the first three places. The Czaikowski/Friderich T55 was fourth, while the Sebilleau/Delaroche T40 was in fifth place. At 4am, the halfway point, only two 8Cs were left and both were having serious problems with broken wing stays, head-lamp brackets, exhausts and windscreens. There was a slight setback to Bugatti hopes at 7am when Druck, whose brakes had been deteriorating, overshot Mulsanne and struck the barriers; the T40 was too badly damaged to continue. The T55 was seven laps behind the leader, in third place at 8am

and began to put on the pace. At midday, four laps of the deficit had been pulled back and the crowd realised a French victory might be possible. The T55 was still closing the gap and the excitement of the crowd was rising, but at 1pm it was all over, an oil pipe broke and Friderich came to a stop at Mulsanne with a seized piston. Molsheim records seem to show that after the race, this car was sold to King Leopold of the Belgians. The two 8Cs limped on to take first and second places and the British Talbot 105, which had been struggling on five cylinders, was third. Sebilleau and Delaroche who had fallen back with various problems were sixth and a lap behind the Aston Martin which won the 1,500cc class. Once again, Bugatti had failed at Le Mans, but French enthusiasts hoped national

fortunes would be restored in the Grand Prix de l'ACF at Reims.

Jean Bugatti's great and frustrated desire was to race a Bugatti. This had been forbidden by his father although his performances while testing cars had shown he was a driver of competence whose ability might have gained him a place in the factory team. European hill-climbs were harsh Alpine events covering many kilometres in which the grand prix aces showed their virtuosity. In England there was only one significant hill-climb, Shelsley Walsh, over a mere 1,000 yards (915m), up a wooded country lane. Jean Bugatti had persuaded his father that this was an event in which he could come to no harm – in Continental terms it was not a hill-climb at all, although it had been a round of the European hill-climb Championship. In 1930, Hans Stuck had discomfited the British hill-climb experts by setting a new course record of 42.8 seconds in his Austro-Daimler, a record which still stood in June 1932.

When the 24-hour race was over, Jean Bugatti travelled on to England as he had entered a T53 for the summer meeting at Shelsley Walsh the following Saturday. This was the car's competition debut and perhaps it was considered that this should be at a relatively low-key event, away from the racing mainstream. Jean Bugatti was a great Anglophile, he visited the country frequently and had many British friends, and it was the best foreign market for Bugatti where the cars had established a great following among sporting enthusiasts. The Bugatti Owners Club had been flourishing in Britain since 1929. On the day before the meeting, Bugatti seems to have done only one practice run in the T53. The climb was disastrous, the T53 slid at Kennel Bend, a slight left-hand bend after the start and hit the bank, severely damaging the front suspension and transmission, though the driver was unhurt. For many years there have been rumours that he did two climbs recording 43.00 seconds on the first run, but the story of the two runs seems to be

24 June 1932: Lord Howe and Jean Bugatti talk while the T53 is made ready for its disastrous practice run at Shelsley Walsh. (John Maitland Collection)

unlikely. There is no official confirmation of it and practice times were not then recorded by the Midland Automobile Club, the Shelsley Walsh organisers. Raymond Mays, who had been standing by the start-line and hand-timing cars over the first 200 metres of the course, said in later years that the Bugatti was a second faster over the distance than any car he had timed previously. René Dreyfus tells a story which may be apocryphal.

'The night before practice he (Jean Bugatti) had met a pretty English girl and he promised her that if she would be at a specified corner with a rose pinned to her coat, he'd wave to her as he went by. This was scarcely the car for such a flirtatious gesture. When he arrived at the curve, and began looking for the rose, he forgot that the Type 53 was not a machine to forget, even for a moment.'

Lord Howe who was Jean Bugatti's host during the visit, suggested that his father should be told about the accident. Eventually Jean was persuaded to telephone Molsheim and the bystanders witnessed a frantic conversation which became more and more agitated, with increasingly over-dramatic gestures. Afterwards he said 'I broke it very fast'! The event was run in heavy rain, conditions in which the T53 would have had a great advantage, Lord Howe rose to the occasion and set fastest time with his T51, while Jean Bugatti salvaged some pride by winning the 3-litre sports car class with a T55, borrowed from Colonel W. L. Sorel the British importer.

The Grand Prix de l'ACF at Reims was the second round of the European Drivers' Championship and was also the second five-hour *grande épreuve*. After the Monza result, the Alfa Corse P3s were hot favourites. Three were entered, for Nuvolari, Borzacchini and Caracciola who had become a full member of the team. On the Reims circuit, maximum speed was essential, so Bugatti brought out two T54s, and perhaps with memories of Monza, there was a T51. Lehoux and Lord Howe had

entered T54s and there were several independent T51s, including 'Williams' and Dreyfus. Wimille had abandoned his T51 for a new Monza Alfa Romeo and had already gained his first win with the car the previous weekend at Nancy, beating the T51s of Lehoux and Czaikowski. No Maseratis were running, a new 8C-3000 was being built, but Alfieri Maserati had died on 3 March, and his death had left the firm bereft and disorganised. For several days Reims was the centre of the motor racing world. T. G. Moore, the *Motor Sport* correspondent described it:

'Brilliantly lit cafes down the length of the street, crowded tables and the bustle of waiters; an endless procession of dusty, travel-stained cars, Bugattis and Delages from distant parts of France, Lancias and Alfa Romeos from Italy, cut-outs open and engines revving – and swarms of Citroëns, Renaults and Peugeots; fireworks and crackers thrown into the road; the continuous peal of 'musical horns', from church chimes to theme-songs; noise, laughter, excitement and gaiety!'

The circuit had been transformed for the race, permanent concrete pits and a control tower had been built on one side of the main straight, opposite a new concrete grandstand for 20,000 spectators. The Bugatti team was based in Gueux village and when the cars were brought to the start it was seen that Varzi and Divo had the T54s and Chiron was in the T51. When the 16 starters were flagged away, Caracciola took the lead, followed by Varzi and Nuvolari. For five laps the T54 harried the P3, but then Varzi slowed and was out of the race after 12 laps with a broken gearbox. With Varzi gone, the three P3s took over the race, Chiron was hanging on, still on the same lap after an hour and briefly moved up to third as the P3s made their stops. 'Williams' whose green T51 had been up with Chiron, slowed with a thrown tyre tread. It was noted that on the very fast curve after the pits, the P3 was noticeably quicker than the T54, but the T51, with its eight-year old chassis

design, was as fast as the Alfa Romeos. The T54s were having a bad day, Lehoux fell out after 22 laps with a broken gearbox, the fuel tank of Divo's car split and he stopped at Thillois on lap 52, while Lord Howe was slowed by a cracked brake shoe and the loss of first and second gears. He handed the car over to Hugh Hamilton and there was great drama when a wheel broke up as the car was passing the pits, several officials were peppered with pieces of flying rim. Chiron had no chance of challenging the P3s but hung on desperately, still on the same lap followed by 'Williams' and Dreyfus. During the last hour, Chiron was lapped by Nuvolari. and as the five hours came to a close, Vittorio Jano signalled the three Alfa Romeo drivers to close up and make a triumphant finish. Nuvolari would not comply, not trusting his team-mates who might have snatched victory on the line and spoiled his chances of the Championship. Chiron was fourth, a lap behind, while Dreyfus and 'Williams' were fifth and sixth, two laps behind the winner. For Bugatti, the results were grim reading, the T51 was no longer competitive and although the ill-handling T54 had the speed, the transmission was not up to the task.

The final round of the European Championship was two weeks later at the Nürburgring on Sunday, 17 July, where the Automobilclub von Deutschland had decided the Grosser Preis would be over 25 laps of the 'Ring. It was assumed that the cars would take more than five hours to cover the distance, so the race duration would comply with the Championship regulations. It was evident that Bugatti was demoralised by the Reims result. T51s were entered for Chiron, Varzi and Bouriat, but only Chiron appeared at the race. Varzi had been struck in the eye by a stone at Reims and the wound had not healed, and Bouriat was absent. Chiron was accompanied by Lehoux, and by Dreyfus whose T51 was now receiving works encouragement, although not elevated to the status of a full team car. The race attracted a crowd of

150,000 which was not deterred by grey skies and showers; to provide additional interest, there were classes for 1,500cc and 1,100cc cars. It was a repeat of Reims, the three P3s went into the lead at the start, Chiron, whose T51 had a extra fuel tank in the cockpit, perhaps in the hope of a non-stop run, hung on and managed to get past Borzacchini, but after four laps he came into the pits where he was stationary for eight minutes while an ignition fault was traced. He restarted, but his goggles had broken and he received a squirt of oil in the eye when a pipe broke, so there was another stop for medical attention and repairs to the pipe. Chiron set off again, but on lap six the rear axle broke and he was out of the race. A broken axle had eliminated Lehoux on lap three, so it was left to Dreyfus to continue the fruitless chase. The German Bugatti Team of von Morgen had been replaced by the Pilesi Rennteam and Paul Pietsch of the team had stopped his T35B after a lap with a burst radiator, so he took over the T51 of his team-mate Hans Lewy. Pietsch was up to fifth place by lap five, then he tried too hard at the South Bend past the stands, struck the bank and overturned. He crawled out from under the car unhurt, and walked back to the pits.

Dreyfus had made no impression on the three Alfa Romeos which ran on to win, but contrary to expectations, completed the course in 4hr 47min. Caracciola was first and Nuvolari was second, the time the race had taken was conveniently forgotten and no one raised a protest, so Nuvolari took the Championship in which Borzacchini was second and Caracciola was third. Dreyfus, by reason of his fifth places at Monza and Reims and his fourth place in Germany, was fourth in the Championship, so took a modest share of the 150,000FF prize fund presumably sharing it with Chiron. There was a secondary championship for entrants. Alfa Romeo took the first prize of 75,000FF, but remarkably Dreyfus took the second prize of 30,000FF. Bugatti took fourth place behind Maserati

so winning 15,000F and Lehoux as the fifth placed entrant took 7,500FF. Despite the frustrations of chasing the P3s, the Championship had been reasonably profitable for Chiron!

It must have felt like a return to old times when the Bugatti regulars arrived at Dieppe for the four-hour Grand Prix on 24 July and found there were no P3s. Chiron and Bouriat had Molsheim-entered T51s and 'Williams' had his private green car. Gaupillat led for a lap, then Chiron went to the front. After three laps it began to rain and Chiron overshot the downhill Val Gosset corner after the pits. This let 'Williams' into the lead followed by Wimille's Monza Alfa Romeo. Wimille also made an exaggeration at Val Gosset, while Chiron was working hard making up the lost ground. After an hour 'Williams' led Chiron by 30 seconds and both had lapped the rest of the field. Chiron hit the bank in his efforts and made a slow pitstop which increased 'Williams's' lead, but Chiron kept to his task and after three hours had caught up, while Bouriat who had lost his bonnet was in third place. Chiron tried to outwit 'Williams', when both were lapping Howe on the hairpin before the pits, but 'Williams' held on and Chiron did not get by until the next corner. 'Williams' did not give up and repassed Chiron and it took another three laps before Chiron got by and began to establish a lead. There was a long gap before 'Williams' appeared with a mud-spattered car, he too had been caught out by the slippery conditions and had gone off the road into a ditch. The race finished with no more drama and Chiron won by three laps from 'Williams', with Bouriat in third place.

On the last day of July, the grand prix world split, the Italian connection including the three Alfa Romeo P3s were at Montenero for the Coppa Ciano, accompanied by Varzi's works-entered T51, while the French had gone to Nice for a grand prix on the sea front, akin to the Monaco event, over a two-mile (3.2km) circuit. The Riviera was now the height of fashion

during the summer holiday season and all the principal Bugatti drivers were there with their T51s, led by Chiron, Dreyfus and Czaikowski. It was a race intended to entertain, there were three capacity heats and a 15-lap final. The 2-litre heat over ten laps, went to Louis Trintignant (T35C) by a margin of 18 seconds. He beat Czaikowski who was driving his old T35C, which had been converted by the factory to T51 specification, thus becoming the only recorded 2-litre T51. In the 15-lap unlimited heat, Dreyfus beat Chiron by a second, but in the final, Chiron was standing no nonsense and won by 3.6 seconds from Sommer's Monza Alfa Romeo, with Dreyfus back in third place. It was a much sterner affair at Montenero. The race was started by Mussolini's son-in-law, Count Ciano, the Minister for Communications and the cars were released in groups of three at one-minute intervals. Varzi started in the first group, but at the end of the first lap, Nuvolari was in front, followed by Borzacchini while Varzi was back in third place. He was not getting good pit signals on each 12.4-mile (20km) lap, so did not realise he was being caught by Campari until it was too late, so he finished fourth, nearly three minutes behind Nuvolari and 14 seconds behind Campari.

Chiron and Varzi joined forces a week later in Switzerland for the Klausen hill-climb, both driving T53s. Run over 13.3 miles (21.5km) of the Klausen pass and rising 4,170ft (1,273m), the contrast with Shelsley Walsh could not be greater. A crowd of 60,000 watched the two-day event and as each car tackled the course it left a plume of white dust. Victory in the 2-litre racing class went to Trintignant's T35C, but in the 3-litre class, Caracciola brought out a P3 Alfa Romeo and the Bugatti drivers must have had an inevitable sense of déjà vu. Caracciola's time was 15min 50sec, Chiron was next with 16min 27.8sec and Varzi was third, recording 16min 45.4sec. The T53s took first and second places in the unlimited class but both drivers probably reflected that if they had driven T51s, the result would have been the same.

Having been bested by a P3 in the Swiss mountains, Chiron and Varzi cannot have gone on to Pescara for the Coppa Acerbo on 15 August with any expectation of a different result. They were only racing for the prize money, as a burglar had stolen the Coppa a week before the race. Only two P3s appeared, for Nuvolari and Caracciola, Campari was absent as his relationship with Alfa Corse was becoming strained, but it made little difference to the result and they took first and second places. Varzi dropped out with no oil pressure after five laps and Chiron chased very hard, but when he closed up the pair of P3s eased away from him and he was two minutes behind at the end. While Varzi and Chiron were having a frustrating afternoon, the French independents were in south west France at Comminges, where 36 starters battled in the local grand prix. Bugatti had entered 'Williams' in a T51 and he led the pack at the start, but was out after a lap with a fuel blockage, which left Dreyfus chasing Lehoux. Dreyfus went by and the two battled for several laps until Lehoux stopped for tyres. Dreyfus was well ahead of the Monza Alfa Romeos of Wimille and Zehender and all remained unchanged until the start of the last lap when there was a short shower of rain. Dreyfus encountered the wet road and slid, hitting a tree and badly damaging the T51, but escaped with bad cuts. Wimille found the same wet patch with the same effect and ended up in hospital in the next bed to Dreyfus, which left Zehender an unexpected win followed home by Lehoux and Sommer (Monza).

'Williams', Zehender and Wimille left Comminges as soon as the race was over, as, with several other drivers, they had a date at La Baule, three days later on Wednesday, 17th, for the GP de La Baule, run on the sands of the fashionable seaside resort in the mouth of the Loire. The

7 August 1932: Chiron in the T53 taking second place at Klausen.

course, on the firm sand, had two straights, three kilometres long, linked by a hairpin at each end. Recognising that 'Williams' was on home ground, Molsheim sent a T54 and, in front of a huge crowd, he ran away with the race, the power being a telling factor. Lehoux and Bouriat gave chase and at the end of the 25 laps, Bouriat (T51) was second and Falchetto (T35B) was third. While 'Williams' was playing on the sand, Chiron and Varzi were travelling from Pescara to southern Germany where, the following Sunday, they performed with the two T53s at the Freiburg-Schauinsland hill-climb. This was an eight-mile (12km) course, with 140 corners, which must have been hard work in the T53s. Once again, Caracciola was there with a P3 to spoil their chances, and set a new course record in 8min 35.8sec, Varzi was second, five seconds slower and Chiron was third.

Chiron and Varzi had a break before they

went to Czechoslovakia for the Masarykuv Okruh on the tough 18.1-mile (29.1km) Brno circuit on 4 September. Here they met a new rival; the Maserati brothers had recovered and produced a new car, the 8C-3000, it was a two seater and not a monoposto as expected, but a single-seater was promised for 1933. The main Alfa Romeo effort was being reserved for the Gran Premio di Monza the following week, so only one P3 was sent to Brno, which surprisingly, was given to Borzacchini while Nuvolari had a Monza. The race was run in miserable conditions with heavy rain and a strong wind. Borzacchini led at the start, but soon stopped with a broken differential, this left Chiron with an unchallenged lead, as Nuvolari was in and out of the pits with ignition problems, probably caused by the conditions. Varzi stopped, apparently still troubled by the eye injury he received at Reims and Bouriat went off the road.

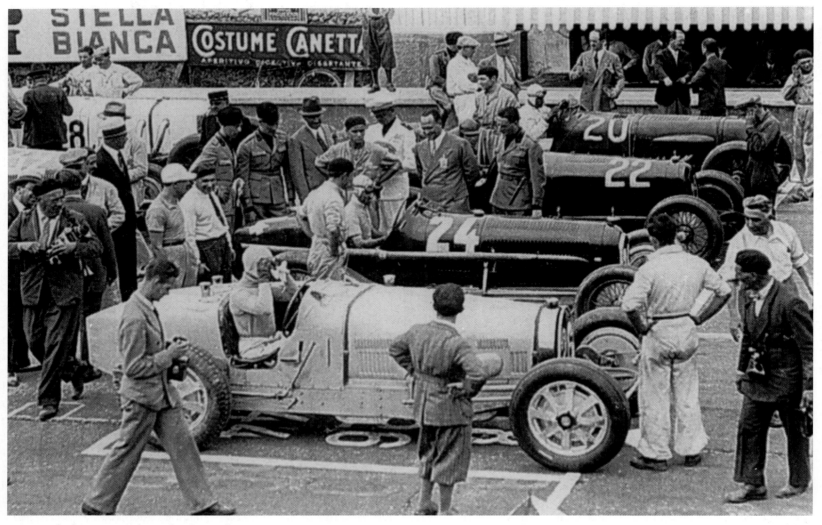

11 September 1932: Chiron sits in his T54 and adjusts his goggles as he waits for the start of the second heat of the Gran Premio di Monza.

None of this seemed to bother Chiron who carried on to win with a margin of nearly five minutes over the new Maserati, driven by Fagioli. Nuvolari was third, 29 minutes behind the T51. Albert Divo had a different task on 4 September. He was sent to Mont Ventoux with a T53, which was another round of the European Hill-climb Championship with a prize fund of 60,000FF and as an additional incentive, there was a 6,000FF bonus for the driver who broke the course record. Unfortunately for Divo, Caracciola was there with a P3. Divo broke the course record with a time of 15min 21sec, but Caracciola broke it too, and was nine seconds quicker.

As in previous years, the Gran Premio di Monza was run in ten-lap heats and a 20-lap final on the combined course. Paul Sheldon comments in *A Record of Grand Prix and Voiturette Racing*, 'The entry was absolutely magnificent – far better than any of the grands prix'. Alfa Corse entered four P3s while Maserati brought out the V5 for Fagioli, and there was the pick of the independents. Chiron and Varzi had the T54s and were supported by the T51s of Bouriat and Lehoux. A huge crowd had assembled when racing began at 10.30am and the meeting was honoured with the

presence of Crown Prince Umberto. Varzi ran in the first heat, and knowing that third place would get him into the final, held back, letting Caracciola's P3 win, followed by the works Maserati 26M of Minozzi. The second heat was much tougher. From the start, Nuvolari and Fagioli battled for the lead, Nuvolari clipped a kerb and buckled a wheel, alleging that Fagioli had 'closed the door' on him. Chiron made an untypical error and ran on to the verge, breaking a wheel rim. Both he and Nuvolari stopped to change wheels and Chiron just managed to qualify for the final, finishing fourth. Before the final, there was high drama, as the Alfa Corse team declared it would not run unless Fagioli was disqualified for the alleged incident with Nuvolari. An official protest was lodged and Fagioli said he had merely held the correct racing line and Nuvolari had tried to pass without enough room; circumstances all too familiar in 21st century World Championship racing. The Bugatti team waited, doubtless hoping that Alfa Corse would storm out in a huff, but the Fascist political masters intervened and insisted that the P3s should race, so the cars were pushed out to the grid cheered by the crowd. At the start, Varzi was slow away as he had engaged second gear in error and was still lowering his goggles as the flag fell. The three P3s took the lead followed by Fagioli, who was able to take second place behind Caracciola when Nuvolari and Borzacchini made brief stops. Varzi and Chiron finished fifth and sixth, but the T54s were not up to the pace.

The Monza race was the end of the grand prix season apart from the GP de Marseille. This was run on 25 September over the Miramas oval and Chiron and Varzi with T51s were up against Nuvolari's P3. Varzi chased Nuvolari for the opening laps but both T51s dropped out and Nuvolari was beaten by Raymond Sommer with a Monza after the Alfa Corse pit had made an error in their lap charts.

In the 1,500cc voiturette class, the T37As in the hands of private owners, had scored victories in the lesser events, but in the major races had been well beaten by several rivals. The most consistent had been the Tipo 26 Maserati of Pierre Veyron who was the uncrowned class champion, but the T37A had also offered no challenge to the 1927 GP Delage driven by Earl Howe, although this car had appeared infrequently. In the spring of 1932 a 1,493cc version of the T51, the T51A, had been announced. This had a stroke of 66mm but was otherwise identical to the T51, but few had reached customers during the season. The first racing appearance for the T51A was in the 1,500cc class of the Grosser Preis von Deutschland at the Nürburgring. It was driven by the German, Ernst Burggaller but he retired after four laps. Burggaller took his T51A to Brno on 4 September where he raced against Veyron's Maserati in the wind and the rain. To back up Chiron's win in the main event, he beat Veyron by 15 minutes to win the 1,500cc class and also beat Ernesto Maserati with a new 4CM Maserati, which in the seasons to come, would be a formidable voiturette. If the outlook in grands prix was poor, the T51A offered a glimmer of hope.

In England, private owners had raced their Bugattis at Brooklands during the season. At the Easter meeting, a Mountain handicap was won by a highly tuned and improved T22 driven by J. A. Robinson and Charles Brackenbury won an outer circuit handicap with a T37, lapping the track at 103.11mph (165.80kmh). At the Whitsun meeting, Lord Howe ran his T51 and beat the American millionaire Whitney Straight with a Tipo 26M Maserati in a Mountain handicap by 0.4 seconds, equalling the lap record during the race. Howe also ran his T54 in the Gold Star handicap on the outer circuit and lapped at 128.69mph (206.93kmh). Brackenbury scored again at the August Bank Holiday meeting, winning an outer circuit handicap and lapping at 105.52mph (169.67kmh) with his T37, while there was another T37 win at the closing BARC meeting in September, when Lindsay Eccles won a mountain handicap. Since 1929, the British season had closed with the British Racing Drivers' Club 500-mile race, a class handicap on the Brooklands outer circuit. There had been much excitement at reports that Chiron would be driving a T54 in the race on 24 September, but no entry appeared. Count Czaikowski drove his 2-litre T51 but found that continuous flat-out running took its toll, after trying to maintain an average of 118mph (190kmh), Lord Howe also fell out when the tank of his T51 split.

For Bugatti, the 1932 season had been most depressing. The T51 was not fast enough to match the P3 Alfa Romeo and had only beaten it once. The new 8C-3000 Maserati was fast and would be even quicker when it was reduced to one seat. The design of the new grand prix car was proceeding slowly at Molsheim, much of the design was a work of Jean Bugatti and the car, the T59, showed a common ancestry with the T57. Priority was still being given to the railcars and to the T57, so it seemed unlikely that the T59 would be ready for the beginning of the 1933 season. For Ettore Bugatti, there were some personal consolations for the disappointments of the 1932 season; in August he had been appointed an Officer of the Legion d'Honneur in recognition of his services to the French nation. Henceforth he would be entitled to wear the buttonhole insignia known and respected by all Frenchmen. On 16 December, accompanied by Jean, he visited London, where he was the guest of honour at the Bugatti Owners Club dinner in the Grosvenor House Hotel and received a rapturous reception. Although his achievements had been formally recognised, events were about to unfold in motor racing and also in the wider world, that would have a great and lasting impact upon Bugatti and upon many others.

Chapter 12

A downwards turn

IN NOVEMBER 1932, the AIACR met to discuss a change to the grand prix formula. There had been concern that racing cars were getting too fast, especially the T54 and the V5 Maserati. It was noted that the fastest cars were the heaviest, so in a wholly logical decision, it was agreed that there should be a new formula which would begin on 1 January 1934. This would limit the weight of grand prix cars to 750kg without fuel, oil, water and tyres. There was a minimum body width of 850mm. The new formula would have caused little anxiety for Jean Bugatti as the T59 would be within the weight limit, and as it was being designed with a two-seat body, the secondary limitation was expected to be immaterial.

There were notable changes among the drivers for the 1933 season. For some time, relations with Louis Chiron had been clouded. The lack of success during 1932 had affected the morale of the team and had rankled with Chiron who felt that he deserved a better car to match his talents. Matters had come to a head at Monza in September when Costantini had booked the team into a small hotel there, but Chiron said he preferred to stay at the Hotel Principe di Savoia in Milan. Costantini said if Chiron did not stay with the team, he would not drive for Bugatti in 1933, and was true to his word, as he had been with Nuvolari in 1928. There was another underlying cause of tension. The Hoffmann marriage had broken down, there was a divorce in 1932 and Baby Hoffmann was living with Chiron, but Costantini had been flirting with Baby during the 1932 season to Chiron's great annoyance. Freddy Hoffmann had become a great friend of Jean and Ettore Bugatti who had tended to side with him in the matrimonial dispute. Chiron was not offered a contract for 1933 and decided to become an independent.

At the time, when Chiron's dispute with Bugatti was coming to a head, Alfa Corse announced that it would not be racing in 1933. Alfa Romeo was making a loss, as the P3s had dominated grand prix racing in 1932, little additional publicity would be gained by continuing to race and substantial savings could be made. Enzo Ferrari expected to be offered the P3s to run under the banner of his Scuderia and was disappointed and humiliated when he was told the P3s would not be made available to him, but would remain stored at the Portello factory. If Ferrari wanted to race in grands prix in 1933 he would have to make do with Monzas.

The withdrawal of Alfa Corse placed the drivers on the market. Nuvolari and Borzacchini decided to join Ferrari while Caracciola, with some covert sponsorship from Mercedes-Benz, suggested to Chiron that they should buy a pair of Monza Alfa Romeos and form a private team, the

The prototype T59 at Molsheim in the spring of 1933. The chassis frame is undrilled. The oil cooler is below the exhaust pipe.

3 April 1933: In the Grand Prix de Monaco, Varzi's T51 shares the front row with the Monza Alfa Romeos of Chiron and Borzacchini. (John Maitland Collection)

Scuderia CC. The withdrawal of Alfa Romeo must have delighted Bugatti, without the P3s, it was almost a level playing field again and it ensured that Varzi's services would be available. Varzi cannot have been happy with the 1932 results, but he had little alternative but to sign with Bugatti again. Nuvolari had closed the Ferrari door on him and the only other possibility was Maserati, where Fagioli was well established. As well as Varzi, 'Williams' and Divo remained and Dreyfus was invited to join the team. Bouriat who had suffered from appendicitis during the autumn and had made a slower recovery than expected, was to run a separate car with support, and was working at Molsheim as a member of the staff. Pierre Veyron had made a good impression with his performance in André Vagniez's Tipo 26 Maserati. He was engaged as a Molsheim test driver and was retained to drive a T51A in voiturette races. Dreyfus received a salary of 1,500FF a month, a proportion of prize money and free board at the Hôtel Heim, the Bugatti-owned hotel in Molsheim. Prize money was not retained by the individual drivers, but was pooled and shared among the team.

On 30 January 1933, Adolf Hitler became Reichschancellor. Apart from the international repercussions, this was to have a great and lasting effect on motor racing and would change the face of the sport completely and irrevocably. Like Mussolini, Hitler believed that motor racing success was one of the means by which the strength and virility of an industrial society could be measured. He issued immediate directives that German companies were to enter grand prix racing and win.

Rumours abounded about the T59, Ettore Bugatti said at the Bugatti Owners Club dinner, that the first car would be ready for testing in January. In reality, the cars were still in the earliest stages of construction and would not be tested until mid-summer, so the team had to rely on the T51 again. The season began early with the

3 April 1933: Nuvolari leads Varzi at the Gasometer Hairpin during their titanic duel. The crowd was enthralled. (Fiat Auto Arese)

GP de Pau on 19 February. This was on a new 1.76-mile (2.83km) 'round the houses' circuit in the middle of the town. The organisers had anticipated reasonable weather in the milder climate of the Pyrenean foothills, so were disconcerted when it began to snow the night before the race and was still doing so when the race was due to start. It was decided that the drivers were sufficiently competent to race, so salt was sprayed on to the course and the race began. Dreyfus had been entered in a solitary factory T51 and the field comprised the usual Bugatti/Alfa Romeo independents. Guy Moll led for the opening laps with his T51, while Lehoux who had been near the back of the grid, worked his way through the field. Etancelin who had been following Moll, stopped to remove snow from the plugs of his Monza which let Czaikowski into second place. The snow turned to rain and on lap 32, Lehoux took

the lead, while Moll dropped behind Czaikowski. The count stopped with a broken rear axle, so Moll retook second place but could not catch Lehoux who drove an excellent race in extraordinary conditions. Etancelin was third and Dreyfus, whose eyes had been affected by the salt was fourth in front of Bouriat with his privately entered T51.

The first encounter of the major rivals was in Tunis on 29th March. Bugatti sent Varzi with a T51, while Nuvolari and Borzacchini had Ferrari-entered Monza Alfa Romeos and Fagioli and Zehender had works Maseratis. Nuvolari and Borzacchini ran away with the race, Varzi gave chase but stopped when the back axle broke after nine laps. It was not an auspicious start for Bugatti, while Enzo Ferrari must have felt

more confident even without the P3s.

The first *grande épreuve* was at Monaco on 3 April. Two of the Ferrari Monza Alfa Romeos had been fitted with uprated engines enlarged to 2,556cc and two of these engines were supplied to the Scuderia CC which was making its debut. Maserati had completed two of the new monoposto 8CMs, although surprisingly these were driven by Sommer and Zehender as independents, while Fagioli as the factory driver had an older 8C-3000 two seater. Bugatti entered three T51s for Varzi, Dreyfus and 'Williams'. During practice, Caracciola crashed his CC Monza at the chicane, wrecking the car and breaking his femur. It was a warm day with a slight sea breeze, as the cars were pushed out on to the starting grid, which was based on practice times.

Varzi was on pole position having equalled the lap record, and with him on the front row were Chiron and Borzacchini, while behind Varzi on the second row was Nuvolari with a 2,556cc Monza. Varzi leapt into the lead as the flag fell and at the end of the first lap, Nuvolari was fourth behind Borzacchini's Monza and Lehoux's T51. He forged past the pair and on lap four was on Varzi's tail, passing him during the lap. Nuvolari held the lead for three laps, then lost it for two. Varzi took the lead on lap 13, was passed on lap 17 and went in front again on lap 19. Borzzachini, Lehoux and Etancelin (Monza) were not far behind and watching how the remarkable duel ahead of them was developing. Nuvolari took the lead again on lap 23, lost it on lap 29 and was back in front again on lap 33. On lap 39 Varzi led again, but a lap later, Nuvolari had passed him. For ten laps, Nuvolari was in front, then Varzi was back there on lap 50.

The crowd was enthralled, appreciating that a legend was being made before them. Etancelin was still giving chase but lost time when he hit the sandbags in the chicane. He was able to make up the time as Varzi and Nuvolari were probably slowing each other down during their duel, so on lap 65 Nuvolari led Varzi, but Etancelin was only a few lengths behind. Etancelin's hopes went when a half shaft broke and Borzacchini, who was third, dropped back as his engine lost its tune. On lap 81 Varzi was in front again, but two laps later, Nuvolari went by. He began to pull away and by lap 90 had a four second lead. Varzi was not done, perhaps he had been conserving his energy for one last effort, as he started to close the gap and on lap 98, pulled up level with Nuvolari as the pair took the Gasworks Hairpin and came up to the line to start the 99th lap. As the cars went up the hill to the Casino, Varzi risked everything and took the T51 engine up to 7,500rpm, edging past Nuvolari into the lead. Nuvolari responded by making similar demands of his engine, but as the cars came out of the tunnel, a cloud of smoke showed a piston had broken in the Alfa Romeo engine and Nuvolari coasted to a stop. Varzi did not ease off, but broke the lap record during the 100th lap and crossed the line to the acclaim of the crowd. He had won one of the greatest motor racing duels of all time. For Nuvolari, there was nothing, as a mechanic helped him to push the car to the line and disqualification resulted. Borzacchini was second, nearly a lap behind and Dreyfus was third. Varzi had led for 34 laps and Nuvolari for 66; throughout the 100 laps, their cars had not touched and both had always made room for their rival to pass. The motor racing world waited impatiently for a renewal of the duel at Alessandria on 30 April, but Varzi, had delayed his entry so it was not accepted by the RACI. Attention moved to the Gran Premio di Tripoli on 7 May, this had become a major race and was combined with an Italian national sweepstake. The object was to stimulate interest in the Italian colony of Libya, of which Tripoli was the capital, with the aim of increasing immigration to it and also to increase government funds. The counterfoils of the tickets were sent to Tripoli and 30 tickets were drawn by Marshal Badoglio, the Governor of the colony on the day of the Alessandria race.

A driver was allocated to each ticket, so a week before the race, the ticket holders knew which driver carried their hopes and chances. During that week, there was frantic activity, much of it encouraged by Nuvolari. There was allegedly, a meeting in Rome between Nuvolari, Varzi and Borzacchini, which was attended by the ticket holders who had drawn those drivers, accompanied by their lawyers. It was agreed that the three drivers would race to win, but would have a cut of the lottery prize and share the race prize money, while the three ticket holders would share the lottery winnings. It was assumed that one of the three drivers would

6 May 1933, Avus: Stanislas Czaikowski is acclaimed after taking the World's Hour Record in his T54. The record had previously been held by George Eyston.

be the winner, but to avoid any problems, Campari may have been brought into the plot. All would be well unless a driver outside the plot won the race. The sums involved were large, the winning ticket was worth 1½ million lire, which in the values of nearly 70 years later was £1.2 million.

Varzi's T51 was entered by the factory and an extra fuel tank was fitted in the passenger's seat so he could go through the race non-stop. Marshal Badoglio dropped the flag and upsetting the carefully laid plans, Birkin took the lead with his 8C-3000 Maserati, followed by Nuvolari, Campari and Varzi. Birkin stayed in front for four laps, then Campari who had already passed Nuvolari, took the lead. When Campari stopped for fuel, Nuvolari went back to the front and at half distance, 15 laps, Nuvolari led from Birkin and Varzi. When Birkin stopped for fuel on lap 16, the Maserati team mechanic who should have been in his pit had disappeared so he had to refuel the car himself. He burned his arm while doing so, and the burn may have contributed to the the blood poisoning from which he died six weeks later. At 20 laps, Nuvolari still led, but Varzi was only a length behind. Three laps later, Nuvolari made a quick stop for fuel and restarted 20 seconds behind Varzi. During the remaining seven laps Nuvolari closed the gap and at the start of the last lap was on Varzi's tail. The engine of the T51 stammered from fuel starvation and Varzi switched over to the reserve tank, but the hesitation let Nuvolari through. Varzi hung on and on the last corner, out-braked Nuvolari and beat him to the line, winning by 0.2 seconds. It had been a fast race, the average was 104.69mph (168.59kmh), both the driver and the ticket holders must have been happy, but Birkin who was third, must have wondered what had happened to his mechanic. It has been suggested that the result may have been rigged between Varzi and Nuvolari, but remembering their rivalry and Nuvolari's defeat at Monaco, this seems most unlikely.

21 May 1933: The Avusrennen 1,500cc race is about to start. The grand prix cars wait their turn. The T54s of Varzi and 'Williams' stand beside the SSKL Mercedes-Benz of von Brauchitsch (No. 21). (John Maitland Collection)

Two days before the Tripoli race, on Friday, 5 May, Count Czaikowski was at the Avus track, outside Berlin with his T54. His aim was the World Hour Record. The car had been prepared in Friderich's workshop in Nice and was being tended by Jean Georgenthum, his personal mechanic. Czaikowski had been testing and practising for two days and after some warming-up laps he set off on his record attempt. The Hour record was held by George Eyston with a Panhard at 130.87mph (210.43kmh) on the Montlhéry banked track in a flat-out run and Czaikowski had the handicap that he had to slow for the 80mph (130kmh) hairpins at each end of the six-mile (10km) Avus straights. The Count set himself a target of 133mph (215kmh) and timed by his anxious-looking wife in the pits who signalled his time to him on each lap, he tackled the task with vigour. The first record to fall was the World 100 kilometres at 212.06kmh, followed by the 100 miles at 132.90mph (213.70kmh), the 200 kilometres at 213.62kmh and finally the Hour at 132.87mph (213.65kmh). The T54 had run on Dunlop tyres and used Castrol oil. The Automobilclub von Deutschland held a dinner in Czaikowski's honour after the run and he was presented with the club's gold medal by the Duke of Mecklenburg, a signal honour as the only previous recipient had been Caracciola. In March, Eyston and Kaye Don had taken Don's T54 to Montlhéry and broken the international class C hour record at 123.01mph (197.80kmh) and the 200-mile record at 122.36mph (196.75kmh). The car had been modified as the engine was moved back in the frame and Lockheed hydraulic brakes had been fitted. The speeds achieved in this attempt may have prompted Czaikowski to go to the Avus.

It is not known if Czaikowski left his T54 at the Avus after the record run, or took it back to Nice to be serviced, but the car was back at the track 15 days later for the Avusrennnen on 21 May. Czaikowski was joined by two factory T54s entered for Varzi and 'Williams', they were opposed by the Monza Alfa Romeos of Nuvolari, Borzacchini and Chiron and two SSKL Mercedes-Benz, ostensibly private entries but with the aura of factory support. One of the SSKLs driven by Otto Merz, crashed in practice, killing the driver. The meeting was attended by Adolf Hitler with the full panoply of Nazi ceremonial and began with a ten-lap, 1,500cc race which was a T51A benefit. Ernst Burggaller, who had converted his car to a single-seater during the winter with a neat body, took the lead, followed by Pierre Veyron with his factory-entered car and after a lap Veyron went to the front. He stayed there, but was unable to shake Burggaller off and at the finish was only 0.4 seconds in front. Both pulled out a big lead from Howe's Delage. In the 15-lap main race, the Monza Alfa Romeos made a more nimble start and took the lead, but by the end of the first straight the superior speed of the T54s told and Czaikowski went into the lead followed by Varzi. 'Williams' stopped when his car caught fire, but Czaikowski carried on in front for 13 laps, then Varzi put on a spurt at the start of the last lap and took the lead going into the North bend, in front of the main grandstands. Czaikowski fought back, but Varzi held on to his lead and at the line was a mere 0.2 seconds in front. Nuvolari and Borzacchini tied for third place, over five minutes behind. After the race, Varzi was presented with the Hindenburg Cup by Hitler, who cannot have been pleased with the result as von Brauchitsch's SSKL was sixth.

During the afternoon that the T54s were battling at Avus, the minor Grand Prix de Picardie was held on a narrow circuit outside Peronne in the heart of the 1914–18 battlefields. In practice, the day before the race, Louis-Aimé Trintignant, a vineyard owner from Chateauneuf-du-Pape, who was showing considerable promise, swerved to avoid a gendarme who stepped on to the course, hit a kilometre stone and was fatally injured when he was thrown out of his T51.

In the race, Bouriat with his works-supported T51 was fighting for the lead with Etancelin's Monza Alfa Romeo. On the ninth lap, they came up to lap Villars's Alfa Romeo which moved over to let Etancelin through, and went into Bouriat's path. The cars touched and Bouriat went off the road, hitting a tree, the car burst into flames and Bouriat was killed instantly. Guy, Comte Bouriat-Quintart was 31 years old. He had been a most reliable third string driver for Bugatti, although he had never scored a major win, he had gained many places and he was the moral winner of the 1930 GP d'Europe at Spa. During the first half of the 1933 season, he had set the best time at five hill-climbs with his T51. He was an enthusiastic and popular member of the Bugatti team and his death was a great shock. The Automobile Club Picardie-Artois subsequently erected a substantial memorial to both drivers near the startline of the circuit.

Bouriat's death may have been an influence, but from the end of May, the Bugatti racing programme fell into disarray. No cars were entered for the Targa Florio or the Eifelrennen and it was left to the independents to carry the flag at Nimes against the Scuderia Ferrari on 4 June. The 2-litre race for the Trophée de Provence was won by Marcel Jacob with a T35C and in the main Grand Prix de Nimes, Lehoux with his T51, led the Monza Alfa Romeos of Nuvolari, Etancelin and Moll until the engine overheated and he dropped out. Worse was to come, it had been hoped the T59 would be ready for the Grand Prix de l'ACF at Montlhéry on 11 June. All the resources at Molsheim had been devoted to building the railcars and work on the T59s had slipped behind schedule. A T59 was entered for Varzi and T51s for 'Williams', Dreyfus and Divo. The first two days of practice passed with no factory Bugattis appearing. 'Williams' and Divo were at the track and made evasive excuses for the cars' absence. Early on the Friday evening, Jean Bugatti told the ACF that the T59 had been finished and after a short road test at

Molsheim, it would be sent to Montlhéry for Varzi to drive. Soon afterwards, Divo said the cars were on their way and asked for the deadline for scrutineering to be extended. Later in the evening, Jean Bugatti admitted that the T59 had been driven on the road round Molsheim for about 100km during the afternoon and was unfit to race, so the entry was scratched. It was also admitted that no work had been done on the three T51s since Monaco, the cars had been put on one side and ignored.

There was no alternative but to cancel the factory entries for the race, a decision which was very badly received by the French press and public. The Vicomte de Rohan, the President of the ACF was particularly critical of Ettore Bugatti, whom he felt had deceived the ACF. It was left to the T54 of Czaikowski and the T51s of Lehoux, Gaupillat and Howe to represent Bugatti in the major French event of the year. Gaupillat and Lehoux went out on the first lap, Czaikowski stopped with the inevitable T54 gearbox problems after eight laps and Howe was forced out when a stone hit his eye. The race was won by Campari with an 8C-3000 Maserati and should have presented a comfortable win for the factory T51s.

At Le Mans a week later, two Bugattis started the race, a T50 with a body identical to the ill-fated 1931 cars, was entered by Mme Desprez with Tarante as her co-driver, and Czaikowski ran his 2-litre T51 with road equipment, accompanied by Jean Gaupillat. The T51 was in ninth place at 10pm when a flat battery finished its chances. The T50 kept going steadily, not fast enough to challenge the 8C Alfa Romeos for the lead, but in fifth place at 10pm. It held this place throughout the night but at 8am on the Sunday morning the water pump broke, ending its run.

Throughout June, Lehoux seemed to be the only driver still racing his T51 with enthusiasm, a broken con rod had stopped him at Montlhéry, but the car was repaired and he took it to Barcelona for the Gran Premio de Pena Rhin on 25 June, where despite several stops with gearbox and ignition problems, he came third and had the satisfaction of finishing in front of Nuvolari. He went on to Reims on 2 July, leading the field until slowed by several pit stops to investigate noises in the gearbox, and eventually retiring. Count Czaikowski must have liked high speed runs with his T54, as he took the car to Brooklands on Saturday, 1 July for the British Empire Trophy. He had factory support for the race as Costantini came with him. It was an unusual event for Brooklands, as it was a scratch race over 45 laps of the Outer Circuit, 125 miles (200km). Czaikowski's main opposition came from Kaye Don's modified T54 which led at the start, Czaikowski followed Don closely and on lap 10, when they came up to lap Oliver Bertram's 10-litre Delage, which had held the Land Speed Record in 1923, Czaikowski dived inside Don and Bertram, taking the lead. Don eased off as he had falling oil pressure and Czaikowski, informed of his progress from his pit by his wife, went on to win from Don by over a minute, at an average speed of 123.58mph (198.71kmh).

Ettore and Jean Bugatti were not the only patrons with problems in the summer of 1933. Enzo Ferrari was confronted by an increasingly unhappy and disaffected Nuvolari. The Monza Alfa Romeos of the Scuderia Ferrari had broken under him with great regularity, so he insisted that Ferrari should persuade the Alfa Romeo directors to release the stored P3s. Ferrari had been begging Alfa Romeo for the cars since the beginning of the season but had met with a stony refusal. Exasperated, Nuvolari had entered into a secret deal with Maserati and had bought an 8CM. At the beginning of July he came into the open about his purchase and arranged to drive an 8CM in

17/18 June 1933: Czaikowski in the T51A he shared with Gaupillat. The car retired from the Le Mans 24-Hour race in the early evening when the lights failed.

the Grand Prix de Belgique at Spa on 9 July; the car had been prepared for Campari who was unfit, having injured an eye at Reims. Probably to keep the trade suppliers happy, the car was entered at Spa under the Scuderia Ferrari banner. Campari had moved from the Scuderia Ferrari at the beginning of the season as he felt that Nuvolari was being favoured at his expense. With the high drama always associated with Italian racing, Campari, when he knew Nuvolari would be joining Maserati, walked out and went back to Ferrari and was joined shortly afterwards by Fagioli, who felt that he had been demoted at Maserati when Nuvolari arrived. All these manoeuvres must have been watched by Varzi with interest, tinged with frustration.

As in previous years, the Belgian promoters ran their 24-hour sports car race at Spa a week before the *grande épreuve* to ensure that the organisation was functioning smoothly. The 8C Alfa Romeos were the hot favourites, but as the event was run in capacity classes with no outright winner it gave encouragement to a pair of Bugattis running in the 4-litre class. One was entered by Jean Desvignes, who shared the car with Marcel Mongin, an experienced driver who had raced a T30 at Boulogne in 1925 and had come second at Le Mans in 1926, driving a Lorraine. The other was driven by Orban and Collon. It seems that the Orban car was a genuine T49, but that of Desvignes was a low-mileage 1929 T44, and he had persuaded the organisers that it had been bored out to over 3-litres, thus taking it out of the Alfa Romeo-dominated class. Both cars had been fitted with lightweight four-seat bodies, Desvignes's was somewhat crude, with slab-sides and sheet alloy wings, the spare wheel was recessed into the side behind the cockpit. The race began at the traditional time of 4pm and in the early stages, the 4-litre class was led by a Hotchkiss. After six hours racing, both Bugattis had passed the Hotchkiss and the Desvignes/Mongin T44 led its rival by just over a lap. Both kept going steadily, unable to offer any challenge to the 8C Alfa Romeos which were battling fiercely among themselves. At the end of the 24-hours, Desvignes and Mongin came home to a comfortable class win, the T44 having covered 1,509 miles (2,431km) and finishing 40 miles (60km) in front of the Orban/Collon T49. Desvignes and Mongin covered the fourth greatest distance in the 24-hours after the three surviving 8C Alfa Romeos.

In an attempt to redeem lost prestige, the three T51s had been overhauled and were entered for the Grand Prix de Belgique on 9 July, to be driven by Varzi, 'Williams' and Dreyfus, and were backed by Lehoux's hard worked car. To show the world that the T59 existed, the car appeared in the paddock for the second day of practice, Varzi did a few slow laps and the car was then put away as it was clearly not raceworthy. Harold Nockolds, the correspondent of the normally reliable *Motor Sport* cannot have been at the circuit for the Saturday practice as he poured scorn on the rumours that the T59 would appear and said: 'More cautious observers remembering the proverbial uncertainty of the Molsheim manufacturer's plans, decided to reserve their judgment, and they were right'! As well as Nuvolari's Maserati, there was a clutch of Monza Alfa Romeos from Ferrari, supported by the cars of Chiron, Sommer and Moll. The fastest drivers in practice were Chiron and Nuvolari, who were over ten seconds a lap faster than Lehoux who was the best of the T51 drivers. It was a tough race, 40 laps of the 9.2-mile (14.8km) circuit. The grid was by ballot and Nuvolari was on the back row, but at the end of the first lap he was in the lead, having passed the whole field. He was pursued by Borzacchini and Chiron, with the T51s further back; 'Williams' stopped for plugs. Nuvolari continued to pull away and Varzi, who was fourth, gradually fell behind the pair of Monzas.

When the cars made refuelling stops, Chiron led the race but when he stopped, Nuvolari was back in front. At half distance, Chiron pulled off with a broken differential and two laps later Borzacchini was out with a broken con rod. This left Nuvolari with a lead of over two minutes from Varzi, who was followed by Lehoux and Dreyfus, while 'Williams' who had made several plug changes was in sixth place. Varzi lost more time when he stopped to change a wheel, although his mechanics did the job in 14 seconds, while in the closing laps, Lehoux lost third gear and was passed by Dreyfus. At the finish, Nuvolari had a lead of over three minutes from Varzi, Dreyfus was third, Lehoux was fourth and 'Williams' sixth. During the season, Ferrari had been improving the 2.6-litre Monza and it was now appreciably faster than the T51; the 8CM Maserati was probably flattered by Nuvolari's driving, but it too was in a different class to the T51. For Bugatti, the need to make the T59 raceworthy was pressing, while for Ferrari, who had lost his ace driver, the need for the P3 was equally great.

The Bugatti team must have been relieved that neither the Scuderia Ferrari nor Nuvolari were at Dieppe the following Saturday, 15 July, but their relief must have been tinged with sadness. The previous day, Bastille Day, Count Trossi, one of the sponsors of the Scuderia Ferrari, had been driving through the Bois de Boulogne in Paris during the evening, accompanied by Pierre de Vizcaya. Trossi had a collision with another car, he was unhurt, but de Vizcaya was seriously injured and died in hospital a few hours later. His death was a great loss to the Bugatti family, as well as being a team driver, he had been a great friend of the family and the Vizcaya backing had been vital for Bugatti in the earlier years. The Dieppe race was of three hours duration and 'Williams' and Dreyfus with T51s were matched against a big field of independents led by Lehoux and Czaikowski, who was running his T51 in 2-litre form, while Veyron had a works T51A. The day before the race, there had been a concours d'élégance which had been won by Countess Czaikowski with a T55 coupé. The

27 August 1933: Dreyfus stands beside his T54 and talks to Antony Nòghes before the Grand Prix de Marseille at Miramas. The car lost a wheel during the race.

numbers on the factory cars were painted in silver, edged with yellow. When the field of 20 was released, Lehoux showed his class by leading the race from start to finish. He was pursued by Dreyfus and 'Williams' who battled together until 'Williams' went off the road in St Aubin village and jammed his car into the straw bales, where he was unable to free it. Dreyfus closed the gap with Lehoux, but was 26 seconds behind at the finish, while Czaikowski was third, three laps behind.

That weekend also saw a British road race, the Mannin Moar which was held for grand prix cars on a circuit through the streets of Douglas in the Isle of Man. A 50-lap, 230-mile (370km) event it attracted a wholly British entry and an archaic regulation required the carrying of riding mechanics. At the start, Brackenbury led, driving the T51 which had been crashed by Chiron at Monaco the previous year, but he was passed by Brian Lewis with a Monza Alfa Romeo who stayed in front for the rest of the race, although chased hard by Tim Rose-Richards with a T51, who only dropped back in the closing laps when he lost third gear. Brackenbury handed his T51 over to the owner, Richard Shuttleworth, who crashed the car through the pit counter when stopping to refuel, while Mathieson with another T51, went through a shop window when his brakes failed.

Even the faithful Lehoux was having doubts; at the beginning of August, he took delivery of a new Monza Alfa Romeo. He drove it during practice for the Grand Prix de Nice on 6 August, but raced his T51, supporting Varzi and Dreyfus with their factory T51s. There was drama before the race when the crowd jammed a footbridge over the course which nearly collapsed and several spectators were hurt in the crush. Nuvolari took the lead with his new 8CM Maserati, chased by Etancelin, Lehoux and Varzi. Varzi did not last long as he had inadvertently emptied the auxiliary oil tank into the engine and had to make many stops to change oiled plugs. Etancelin and Nuvolari exchanged the lead several times, then on lap 20 Nuvolari stopped to adjust his brakes which let Lehoux into second place, but he was also having brake difficulties and spun, letting Nuvolari pass him. Lehoux fell back and Etancelin retired when the brakes of his Monza expired so Nuvolari won and a steady Dreyfus was second, while Lehoux was fifth.

After the Nice race, Varzi and Dreyfus travelled to Italy, journeying to Pescara for the Coppa Acerbo. Here they encountered an elated Scuderia Ferrari, as Alfa Romeo had relented and had released two P3s, which were being driven by Fagioli and Campari. The 8CM Maserati had been impossible to beat, but the P3 was even quicker and in the race, Varzi could only watch the faster cars in front. Fagioli won from Nuvolari with Taruffi in Nuvolari's own 8CM in third place, Varzi was fourth, four and a half minutes behind the winner. It was more like old times on the sands of La Baule that afternoon, a mainly Bugatti field battling in front of the holiday crowds, Lehoux had entered his new Monza, but probably fearing that sand might spoil the works, ran his T51 instead. He tried very hard to keep up with 'Williams' who had a T54, but the extra power told on the two one-mile straights which comprised the course and 'Williams' won from Lehoux by 32 seconds, with Falchetto's T35B in third place. Czaikowski ran his T51 in the 2-litre class and had an easy win, finishing fifth overall.

Chiron had been having a dismal season. After Caracciola's accident he had been the sole representative of Scuderia CC, but his results had been negligible. The nadir came in Sweden when his Monza was wrecked in a multiple accident in the Sveriges Sommar Grand Prix. His fortunes were transformed when Enzo Ferrari offered him a P3 Alfa

Romeo for the Grand Prix de Marseilles at Miramas on 27 August. For such a fast track, Bugatti entered Dreyfus with a T54. The car had been prepared at the last minute and there was insufficient time to transport it in the usual Chevrolet covered lorry from Molsheim to Miramas, so Dreyfus drove it to the track followed by the factory T40 truck with tools and spares. The organisers offered a prize for the leader of the race on every fifth lap. The race was a three-cornered fight between Nuvolari with an 8CM Maserati, Chiron and Dreyfus. Chiron led at the start and Dreyfus was in front on lap four, but was passed by Nuvolari on the fifth and profitable lap. Dreyfus fell back leaving Chiron to cope with Nuvolari, who seemed to summon an extra effort to take the lead every fifth lap. Dreyfus held third place until lap 55, when the car spun wildly and uncontrollably on one of the curves. A rear hub had broken, the wheel came off and was thrown into a car park damaging a spectator's car. Dreyfus was shaken but unhurt; in his autobiography, he comments that the pounding that car received on the minor roads he covered during the 400-mile (650km) drive to the track, may have cracked the hub. Nuvolari continued to take the five-lap prize money until his rear axle broke, leaving victory to Chiron.

In the hope of bringing in a larger crowd, the Gran Premio d'Italia had been put back until 10 September and was part of a festival of motor racing, with the *grande épreuve* being run in the morning and the short Gran Premio di Monza, with three heats and a final, in the afternoon. Both races were on the combined road circuit and banked track. Once again, there were unfounded rumours that the T59 would be ready, but as the T51 would have been outclassed, there were no entries from Molsheim. The Gran Premio d'Italia was a full 500km race and Gaupillat, Brunet and Lord Howe were the only Bugatti runners, their T51s providing a supporting cast for the inevitable Alfa Romeo/Maserati battle.

Gaupillat had made extensive modifications to the engine of his car. It had a one-piece crankshaft giving a different firing order from the standard T51, the main bearings had split casings and the big ends were also split and ran on needle rollers. The supercharger was larger and had two lobes instead of the standard three. On a course made slippery by a drizzle before the start, Gaupillat, despite the more powerful engine, dropped out, and at the end, Brunet was tenth and Howe 12th, both many laps behind the winning P3 of Fagioli.

Several of the runners who had done 500km in the morning came out again after lunch for a race which was seen as entertainment for the crowd. It was still raining intermittently and *Motor Sport*'s correspondent complained: 'And mud! Mud everywhere – nasty, sticky yellow-brown mud'. The Fascist banners and national flags hung limply, but the crowd cheered the drivers as they paraded with their cars before the start of the first heat and Crown Prince Umberto watched from the stands. Czaikowski, who had scratched from the Gran Premio in the morning ran his T54, which was up against a 4½-litre Duesenberg entered by the Scuderia Ferrari and driven by Count Trossi. Premoli led from the start with his BMP, a T35 with a Maserati engine, but Trossi and Czaikowski soon went to the front and after three laps they were abreast as they passed the stands. Czaikowski took the lead and after seven laps, the Duesenberg stopped when a con rod broke as it took the South Curve of the banked track. Czaikowski eased off for the rest of the 14 laps and won by ten seconds from Moll's Monza Alfa Romeo. At the start of the second heat, Campari had a huge ovation from the crowd as he had announced he was retiring from the sport and it would be his last race. History has always recorded that the Duesenberg left an oil slick when the con rod broke, but Giovanni Canestrini, the Italian journalist said in later years that when he looked at the engine, the crankcase and sump were intact. The start

of the heat was delayed while officials swept the curve, but it is possible that the Duesenberg was not guilty and the oil slick came from a car running in the morning's Gran Premio. At the start of the heat, Campari passed Borzacchini going into the South Curve and slid, a wheel mounting the retaining wall, the P3 ran along the wall for 100 metres then plunged over the top and overturned. Borzacchini braked hard to avoid a collision and his Maserati also mounted the wall, went over the top and overturned. Campari was killed instantly and Borzacchini died a few minutes later. Lehoux had driven his Monza in the morning, finishing fourth in the Gran Premio, but he handed this over to 'Hellé-Nice' for the afternoon and brought out his T51 for the third heat. Some drivers in the third heat refused to race, there was a meeting between the drivers and the organisers and the start was delayed for two hours, meanwhile the crowd bayed and jeered. Five drivers agreed to start and Lehoux led throughout the 14 laps, Pietro Ghersi was second with his T35B and Howe was fifth and last in his T51.

Eleven sad and reluctant drivers came out for the 22-lap final. Whitney Straight led from the start with his 8C-3000 Maserati, but after a lap, Czaikowski was in front, followed closely by Lehoux. They stayed together for eight laps, then Czaikowski slid on the South Curve at the same place where the earlier accident had occurred. The T54 went over the retaining wall and overturned, the fuel tank split and the car burst into flames. Czaikowski was trapped underneath and was dead when he was pulled clear. Lehoux lifted his foot and avoided a collision with the T54; he came round to the pits, slowed and shouted that there had been a crash, then went on to win a race which had little meaning to anyone and had been shortened to 14 laps. In these sad circumstances, the T51 had gained its last major victory.

Stanislas Czaikowski was a popular and much-loved man, a member of a rich Polish

24 September 1933: The T59 makes its debut in the Gran Premio de Espana at San Sebastian. The three cars stand in front of the pits during practice. The car driven by 'Williams' was damaged in a practice accident.

The engine of the T59. The inlet manifold which caused many problems can be seen.

émigré family, he was born in 1899 at La Haye (Pays-Bas), served in the French Army during the First World War and started racing with a T37A in hill-climbs in 1929. A *bon viveur* with a particular enthusiasm for pernod, his epitaph was written by Dreyfus, 'He was a completely likeable man always – and a fine driver'. The news of his death reached Molsheim in a radio report of the race and he was deeply mourned by the Bugatti family and in the factory. A brave man whose skill and experience had often been shown during the five seasons in which he raced, he had matured rapidly as a driver during the 1933 season. Although never officially a team driver, with the rumoured financial backing that he gave to Bugatti, he was a highly favoured customer receiving much support and his cars were often transported in the works lorries. He was buried at Houville-la-Branche, near Chartres.

A subdued racing circus went to Brno a week after the Monza disaster, Bugatti made a token gesture by sending Dreyfus with a T51 and he was joined by Lehoux. In the race, run in most unpleasant conditions, the P3s were unbeatable and Dreyfus could only manage fourth place, while Lehoux stopped after a lap with a broken gearbox. This was the last event in which Bugatti entered a T51, as on 24 September, the T59 made its long-overdue racing debut in the Gran Premio de Espana at San Sebastian. Costantini had given the car its first test run on the eve of the Grand Prix de l'ACF, it had made a brief appearance in Belgium, and thereafter Dreyfus had carried on the testing with the other team drivers. The T59 has been considered by many as the most beautiful grand prix car of all time, although some of the design has been credited to Jean, there were many features which were pure Ettore Bugatti. The eight-cylinder engine had dimensions of 67mm x 100mm giving a capacity of 2,820cc. The cylinder and block were integral and there were two valves per cylinder at a 90° angle. As a complete breakaway from previous practice, there were plain bearings throughout. The crankshaft design had similarities to the T57, running in five main bearings and the two overhead camshafts, operating the valves via fingers, were driven by a gear train from the rear of the engine; the supercharger, mounted on the off-side, was driven from this train and drew from two downdraught Zeniths. The inlet manifold was a long pipe running the length of the block with short stubs leading to the ports. A single eight-branch manifold emerged from the side of the bonnet, similar to the T54, and the tailpipe ran down the nearside of the car. The nearside camshaft drove a scuttle-mounted Scintilla magneto. The centre line of the crankshaft was below chassis level, so no starting handle could be fitted at the front and there was a side-mounted handle on the near-side driving the rear gear train through bevels.

In its early form the output of the engine was probably about 230bhp. The engine drove a separate four-speed gearbox, operated by an outside lever through the usual multi-plate clutch, and the low transmission line necessitated a reduction gear on the back axle which was located by a torque arm. Drawings were found at Molsheim in later years, which indicated that consideration was given to fitting the T59 engine into a T51 chassis, presumably to get the benefits of the more powerful engine at an earlier date, but it seems the idea went no further than the drawing board. It is puzzling that the engine was initially of 2.8 litres capacity when the impending production T57 model, which had much in common with the T59, was to be of 3.3 litres.

The extremely low-built chassis, was similar in design to the T35 and T51. The semi-elliptic front springs passed through the axle which was tubular. It is possible that Jean Bugatti wanted to use independent suspension and the front axle was a clever compromise as it was divided in the middle, permitting a slight rotational movement which prevented the vertical movement of one wheel having too much effect on the other. The rear axle was mounted on parallel reversed quarter-elliptic springs and De Ram shock absorbers were fitted at the front and the rear. These were very expensive and complex, combining friction and hydraulic operation. The wheelbase was 8ft 6in (2.6m) and the track was 4ft 1in (1.25m). The brakes, which were much larger than those of the T51, were mechanically operated by cable and chain. The chassis frame, which was evolved from the T47, was a very deep channel section, 9in (230mm) at its greatest depth and an oil cooler was mounted on the near side. Unusually, and to some extent retrograde, there was a two-seater body in which the driver sat beside the transmission. It had beautiful proportions with a 30-gallon (135-litre) tank in the tail, which had a distinctive Jean Bugatti trademark, with an external riveted joint running along the centre line. The crowning glory of the design was the wheels. The splined hub was attached to the rim by straight piano wire spokes. The brake drum was attached to the hub and there was a circumferential flange which drove the rim through gear teeth. All torque and drive passed through these teeth and not through the spokes. The wheels carried 5.50 x 19 tyres at the front and 6.00 x 19 at the rear. The visual effect of these wheels in light alloy was remarkable, but it has to be questioned if the complexity and expense of manufacture gave any great benefit over the normal Rudge-Whitworth wheel. Each wheel was stamped with an individual number. The historian Robert Jarraud has concluded that at least 117 of these wheels were made, so the cost must have been an appreciable drain on Bugatti's resources, as they were only fitted to the factory competition cars and never appeared on a production model.

The drivers were not wholly enamoured of the T59. Dreyfus said: 'None of us cared for the car much in the beginning'. They disliked the low seating position, were critical of the handling and worried by the audible chattering of the teeth on the wheel

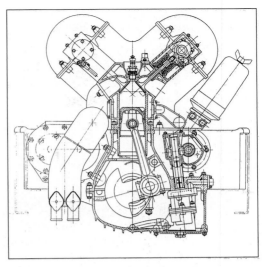

A front view drawing of the T59 engine.

rims. These criticisms were gradually resolved, and tests soon showed that the car cornered faster than the T51. Fundamentally, the drivers were disappointed, they had waited over a year for the car to appear and had expected great things of it. When they started to practise at San Sebastian, they found that the cars lacked power and they seemed to be no better off than they would have been with the T51s. The cars were entered for 'Williams', Dreyfus and Varzi, they were up against the P3s and the 8CM Maseratis. 'Williams' damaged his car in a practice accident so did not start and the race was a disaster for Varzi and Dreyfus. Throughout the 30 laps, they made continuous stops, one of the major problems was loose carburettors. The race was an easy win for the P3s of Chiron and Fagioli, once Nuvolari had eliminated himself in a crash. Lehoux was third with his T51, Varzi was fourth, but 24 minutes behind the winner and Dreyfus was sixth. It was an unhappy team that returned to Molsheim, aware that a lot of work was needed if the car was to be made competitive.

If the grand prix outlook seemed gloomy, the season had been much happier in the voiturette class. Veyron had been most successful with his factory-entered T51A.

After the Avus victory, there had been a slight setback at the Eifelrennen on 28 May when he and Burggaller were beaten by Lord Howe with his 1927 GP Delage. The two T51A drivers then made a long journey to Lwow in Poland for the Grosser Preis von Lemburg on 11 June, where Veyron led Burggaller home in an easy win. Veyron was at Albi on 27 August in the heat of south-west France, where he ran away with the 1,500cc race in the first Grand Prix d'Albi meeting. He finished the season at Brno where the voiturettes ran with the grand prix cars on the Masaryk circuit, the race was run in heavy wind and rain and Veyron led the class, but went off the road after three laps and was slightly hurt. This gave Burggaller his chance and he went on to win followed by another T51A driven by the Czech driver Bruno Sojka. Several T51As had been sold during the season, Mme Anne Rose-Itier was one of the customers and at the sad GP de Picardie meeting, when Bouriat and Trintignant were killed, she won the supporting 1,500cc race. At the end of the season, the T51A had made its mark and was regarded as the dominant car in the rapidly growing 1,500cc class, which would soon assume a much greater significance.

Veyron made a quick recovery from his Brno injuries and took the T51A to Montlhéry on 28 October to attempt international class F records. He had a successful day as he established new figures for the 500 kilometres (109.18mph/175.56kmh), the 500 miles (107.71mph/173.19kmh), the 1,000 kilometres (107.60mph/173.02kmh), the three hours (109.16mph/175.52kmh) and the six hours (107.52mph/172.89kmh). Having recovered from his efforts, he went out again on 4 November and took the 200 miles at 116.49mph (187.31kmh). The T51A seemed to be going faster at each attempt and a week later Veyron took the 100 miles (119.01mph/191.36kmh), the 200 kilometres (118.88 mph/191.15kmh)

and the one hour (119.01mph/191.36kmh). In May, the little-known amateur Cohas, who also ran under the pseudonym of 'Trebuh', had taken his T35B to Montlhéry and with a most impressive start, took the class D standing start kilometre at 129.97kmh (27.7 seconds). Trebuh's record did not stand for long: in August, the Hungarian driver Lazlo Hartmann used a T35B on a long stretch of local road at Tat, outside Budapest to take the class D standing start kilometre record at 132.61kmh (27.1 seconds) and the standing mile at 92.18mph.

There had been a big and significant change in British motor racing during 1933. A road circuit, the first in the country, had been opened at Donington Park, near Derby. The 2.25-mile (3.6km) circuit ran through undulating parkland and gave most British drivers their first experience of road racing. There were three meetings during the season, at first, most entrants drove stripped and modified sports cars, but at the closing meeting on 7 October, there was a close fight between the T51s of Lord Howe and Lindsay Eccles and the T35C of T. A. S. O. Mathieson in the 20-lap Donington Park Trophy, which was won by Howe. At Brooklands, the only important scratch race was the stirring British Empire Trophy won by Czaikowski. There were the usual handicaps at the BARC meetings, relieved by the long-distance handicap races for the JCC International Trophy and the BRDC 500-miles. At the opening BARC meeting on 11 March, Bobby Bowes won a Mountain handicap with his T35B and took second place in another Mountain race, just beating Don's T54. Mathieson won an outer circuit handicap with his T35C at the Easter meeting, his best lap at 120.59mph (193.90kmh). At the Whitsun meeting, the BARC finally relaxed a rule which had stood since the track had opened in 1907 and permitted lady drivers to race at BARC meetings on equal terms with the men,

instead of being restricted to their own races. Eileen Ellison, was the first woman to gain a place, and driving a T37 was just beaten to the line in an outer circuit handicap by Aubrey Esson-Scott's T35. Later in the day, Charles Brackenbury won the seven-lap Gold Star Handicap and a prize of £100 with his T37, lapping at 106.42mph (171.12kmh). There was only one Bugatti victory at the August Bank Holiday meeting when T. P. Cholmondley-Tapper, driving the T37 which he shared with Eileen Ellison won a Mountain handicap. The main event at the closing meeting on 21 October, was the Mountain Championship, a ten-lap scratch race over the Mountain circuit. Lord Howe who was unwell, invited Nuvolari to drive his T51 in the race. Nuvolari came to Brooklands and practised on the Thursday before the race, but decided to return to Italy, so the car was taken over by Piero Taruffi. Taruffi led the race from the start only to be passed by Straight's Maserati when he slowed to avoid a spinning car, then when he was about to retake the lead, he was baulked by another spinning car and came second, two seconds behind Straight.

For Bugatti, 1933 had been a bad year, the T59 had been 'too little, too late'. If it had appeared in 1932, the story might have been different, but it was already obsolete when it made its debut and instead of putting Bugatti ahead of his rivals, had merely brought him up to their shoulders. There was not enough money available to make a truly modern grand prix car, the depression was still biting hard in France, cars were not selling well and all the resources at Molsheim were needed to get the T57 into production and to build the profitable railcars. Even a modern grand prix car would soon have been irrelevant, the grand prix world was about to change in a dramatic and revolutionary manner and there would be little chance for Bugatti in it.

Chapter 13

The shadows fall

THROUGHOUT THE WINTER of 1933/34, the motoring press was full of speculation about the forthcoming 750kg formula. Most of the speculation centred upon the German cars which were being built, and gradually facts emerged. Mercedes-Benz was re-entering grand prix racing and would be joined by a new car, the Auto Union, which was being built by a consortium of four manufacturers, Horch, Audi, Wanderer and DKW. Both Mercedes-Benz and Auto Union were breaking wholly new ground with their designs. Both cars had front and rear independent suspension, both had streamlined, faired bodies and the Auto Union, designed by Ferdinand Porsche, whose previous work had included the SSKL Mercedes-Benz, was even more revolutionary as the engine was behind the driver. The German cars made all the existing grand prix cars obsolete.

Varzi must have been waiting for the T59 and when it made such a disappointing debut at San Sebastian, his mind was made up. He told Bugatti he would not be available for 1934 and went to discuss a contract with his old employer Enzo Ferrari, where the door was wide open as Nuvolari had gone. Chiron was happy to continue the arrangement which he had begun with Ferrari in 1933 and the pair were joined by Marcel Lehoux, whose evident ability had been recognised by Ferrari. A luncheon was held in Paris in January, organised by six French motor clubs, at which Lehoux was presented with a gold medal in recognition of his efforts during the previous seasons. Bugatti still had the services of Dreyfus, and was joined by the promising Jean-Pierre Wimille, and it was a term of their contracts, that both Dreyfus and Wimille should reside at Molsheim during the season, living in the Hôtel Heim. Dreyfus was required to demonstrate the new T57 to prospective customers. The third member of the team was more surprising; Bugatti had signed up the 1927 World Champion, Robert Benoist. Benoist had not raced since he drove for Bugatti at San Sebastian in 1928, since then he had been managing a garage in Paris; the rewards for becoming World Champion have improved in the ensuing 70 years.

Benoist, whose contract began on 1 March, was employed not only as a driver, but also to work within the Molsheim factory, so he had little choice where he lived. Pierre Veyron was still working at Molsheim and was to continue racing in the voiturette class. There seemed to be a desperate need to engage drivers as the Marchese Antonio Brivio was also given a contract. Brivio who was 28 years old, had been a member of the Scuderia Ferrari in 1932 and 1933. He probably made a contribution towards the cost of his Scuderia drives but had gained a number of successes, including the 1932 Spa 24-hour race and the 1933 Targa Florio. Ettore Bugatti liked aristocrats so it is unlikely that Brivio's contract included a term that he should reside at the Hôtel Heim and he continued to live in his castle at Vercelli, near Milan.

While Bugatti signed up drivers, the political scene in France was becoming increasingly turbulent. In the elections held in May 1932, the Radicals had gained power with a narrow margin of seats over the Socialists in the Chamber of Deputies. The Socialists refused to join a coalition, but agreed to support the Radical government, although neither could agree on the remedies needed to stop the economic slowdown and the rise of unemployment. Several right-wing groups and factions had formed during 1933, many connected with ex-servicemen's organisations and all expressing discontent with the government and its remedies for the economic difficulties. Matters came to a head on 8 January 1934, when the financier Alexander Stavisky shot himself. Stavisky had been awaiting trial on fraud charges and several members of the government were alleged to have been involved in his schemes. During January, the right-wing groups began to riot in the Paris streets and these riots came to a head on 6 February when there was an attempt to storm the Chamber of Deputies. There was a pitched battle between the police and the rioters in the Place de la Concorde during the evening, which resulted in 15 dead and 1,500 injured. The following day, the government resigned and was replaced by a 'national unity' ministry under the former President, Gaston Domergue, which appeased the

2 April 1934: The old rivals, Varzi and Nuvolari, stand in front of Nuvolari's T59 before the Grand Prix de Monaco.

political unrest, but did little to cure the economic ills.

In these unpropitious times, the T57 was announced. This was a radical departure from previous Bugatti touring cars as it was a refined high-performance car which would be able to match the *grands routiers* which were appearing from Delahaye, Talbot-Darracq and Hotchkiss, giving fast, reliable and elegant road transport. It was also a car which would appeal to foreign buyers and with the falling value of the franc could be sold at a competitive price abroad. The T57 brought a radical change to Bugatti production and marketing. There would henceforth be a one-model policy. Production of the T49 and T50 stopped and the T46 was tailed-off, although it was still available to special order. The T57 engine had the dimensions of the T49, 72mm x 100mm giving a capacity of 3,257cc. Like the T59, the eight-cylinder engine was of monobloc construction and

had a crankshaft running in five plain bearings, with plain big ends. There were two valves per cylinder set at 90° and operated by the two overhead camshafts through fingers, fed by a double choke UUR2 Stromberg carburettor. The camshafts were driven by a gear train at the rear of the engine. The four-speed gearbox was in unit with the engine and driven through a single-plate clutch. The chassis was conventional Bugatti. It has been suggested that Jean Bugatti wanted to fit independent front suspension as had the main rivals and two prototype T57s were seen with double transverse leaf suspension similar to that fitted to the T53. Ettore's will prevailed though and the car had the standard front axle with semi-elliptic springs passing through it. The large brakes were mechanically operated. Much of the chassis design work was done by Pichetto. Initially, the T57 was marketed as a pure touring car, but sporting versions would follow.

At the beginning of 1934, the team drivers were kept occupied in the testing of the early T57s and Veyron was the first to engage in sporting action. The class F records he had broken in October and November had been taken by a Riley, so on 30 January, he took his T51A to Montlhéry, and despite flurries of snow, he recaptured the 200 miles, 500 kilometres, three hours, 500 miles, 1,000 kilometres and six hours. The fastest speed was for the 200 miles at 116.51mph (187.434kmh) and the speed for the six hours was 112.72mph (181.25kmh). On 6 February, George Eyston broke Czaikowski's World Hour Record with a Panhard at Montlhéry. That afternoon, he drove to Houville and placed a wreath on Czaikowski's grave.

Benoist had realised he was short of racing experience and at the beginning of March, he took a T51 to Montlhéry and spent some time lapping the circuit, working up to a lap time which would have been competitive in the 1933 Grand Prix de l'ACF. The first important race of the season was the Grand Prix de Monaco on Easter Monday, 2 April. The previous Thursday, 29 March, Dreyfus had been at La Turbie, the hill-climb on the outskirts of Nice. The event had been arranged to coincide with the finish of the Paris-Nice Rally and a number of rally competitors tried their hand at the hill-climb. The T53 had been dusted down and brought out for Dreyfus who summoned up all his skill and strength for 3min 45.4sec, which gave him the best time of the day and took 6.6 seconds off the previous record held by Wimille. The result was gratifying as the T53 beat the P3 Alfa Romeo of Count Trossi.

Greatly to Dreyfus's relief, he did not have to drive the T53 at Monaco as he was driving one of four T59s entered for the race. The cars had been fitted with new chassis frames during the winter, which were extensively drilled to save weight. The sensation was that one of the T59s was being driven by Nuvolari and painted red in his honour. The previous October he had been approached by Costantini and offered a place in the team for the 1934 season. A few days later he received an offer from Mercedes-Benz, but declined this having already agreed to accept the Bugatti offer. It was arranged that he would run as a private entrant for the 1934 season and would negotiate a drive for each race, with his own 8CM Maserati as a stand-by. The disagreement of 1928 had been forgotten and the T59 was loaned to him and entered in his name, although it was prepared by the Molsheim mechanics and formed part of the team. The other T59s were entered for Dreyfus, Wimille and Benoist, a T51 was brought for Veyron although it was entered in his name. The opposition came from the full team of Scuderia Ferrari P3s and several 8CM Maseratis. Neither German team was ready to race so little had changed since 1933. During the Saturday practice, Benoist spun at Ste Devote and bent the back axle of his T59 which could not be repaired in time for the race. At the weighing-in the T59s passed without problems, being under the 750kg limit, but the chassis frame was only 800mm wide, so to comply with the body width regulation, vertical metal strips 25mm wide and 300mm long were screwed to the sides of the frame in front of the rear wheels. With the weight problems the team had later in the season, the Monaco scales may have been operated sympathetically.

Trossi (P3) was fastest in practice with 1min 58sec and shared the front row with Etancelin (Maserati) and Dreyfus who both recorded 1min 59 sec. Race day began with heavy rain, but this cleared and the race was started in bright sunshine. As the flag fell Chiron brought his P3 through from the second row to lead Dreyfus, who was followed by Etancelin and Varzi. Chiron stayed in front and was content to keep ahead of Dreyfus, so at 20 laps the lead was only five seconds. Nuvolari was in fifth place behind Etancelin and Moll (P3) but seemed unable to close the gap. Wimille had already dropped out when the rivets sheared on a rear brake shoe and the wheel

2 April 1934: Nuvolari takes Tabac Corner in his red-painted T59 on his way to fifth place.

2 April 1934: Dreyfus (T59) leads Moll (Alfa Romeo P3) at the Station Hairpin. Moll went on to win and Dreyfus was third. (Fiat Auto Arese)

locked up as he took the Gasworks Hairpin. Chiron was pulling away and Etancelin caught Dreyfus on lap 30 and started to close on Chiron, but hit the sandbags at the Hotel de Paris and retired. Dreyfus was being slowed by a slipping clutch and stopped for adjustments which let Moll up to second, while Nuvolari had speeded up and also passed Dreyfus into third place only to drop back when he stopped to adjust the brakes. It seemed that Chiron would win, but with two laps to go, he spun and hit the sandbags at the Station Hairpin which let Moll go on to win, Chiron restarted before Dreyfus could take second place, so the T59 was third, a lap behind the winner while Nuvolari brought his car into fifth place, two laps down but perhaps comforted that he was three seconds ahead of Varzi at the flag.

The Monaco result should not have been too discouraging, Dreyfus and Nuvolari had lapped in practice only a second slower than Trossi and a second faster than Chiron. Dreyfus had been in front of Moll,

the winner, until the stop for clutch adjustment. On 15 April, Dreyfus took a saloon T57 to the Côte Chauvigny hill-climb at Nancy and won his class. This was the competition debut of the T57; the competing car had been road tested by *Motor Sport* in the early spring. The team's next engagement was in Tripoli, on 6 May, Nuvolari had entered his Maserati but was not running as he had broken a leg when he crashed at Alessandria on 22 April so three T59s were entered for Dreyfus, Wimille and Brivio. Despite the second place at Monaco, the morale of the drivers was low. The T59s were unhappy cars. They were difficult to start, condensed fuel accumulated in the manifold under the supercharger and the manifold was inclined to flood under heavy braking, so the pick-up could be poor out of slow corners and the engine sometimes died completely.

During practice on the very fast Mellaha circuit another problem emerged as the cars would jump out of gear, which on such a fast circuit, could not only be disconcerting,

but also dangerous. During practice, Brivio's engine blew up extensively with a broken con rod and at the end of the session, Dreyfus was asked by Costantini to drive round the circuit in his T59 and tow Brivio back to the team's headquarters. Dreyfus connected the two cars with a tow rope and was starting to cross the circuit to the exit road when Varzi's P3 came round the adjacent corner flat-out. He braked and hit the bank just avoiding a collision. A heated argument between Dreyfus and Varzi followed, Dreyfus rightly pointing out that the session had finished and Varzi should not have been travelling at racing speed! Brivio's car could not be repaired before the race, Wimille dropped out with a broken oil pipe after 25 laps and Dreyfus completed the 40-lap race in sixth place, but 13 minutes behind the winner, having made several stops with various problems, so the team retreated to Molsheim to lick its wounds.

There was an interval of nearly two months before the T59s raced again. The Auto Unions raced for the first time at the Avusrennen on 27 May and slowed by teething troubles were beaten by Moll's Alfa Romeo. A week later, both Auto Union and Mercedes-Benz ran in the Eifelrennen at the Nürburgring. The Mercedes-Benz of von Brauchitsch won and the Auto Union of Stuck was second. The P3 Alfa Romeos struggled to keep up and it was evident that a new era of motor racing had begun. The T51 had become an also-ran, even in the lesser events. The sole British contribution to grand prix racing, the Mannin Moar, was held in the Isle of Man on 1 June and was won by Brian Lewis with a P3 borrowed from the Scuderia Ferrari. Rose-Richards chased Lewis with his T51 until the water pump broke and three other T51s dropped out. Veyron was sent to Montreux on 3 June with one of the 1933 team cars, although it was entered in his name and could only manage seventh place behind the P3 Alfa Romeos and 8CM Maseratis.

14 June 1934: The standard-bodied T55 of Fourny and Decaroli at scrutineering before the Le Mans 24-hour race. It was disqualified for refuelling before covering the permitted distance.

16/17 June 1934: The T44 of Desvignes and Mahé before the start at Le Mans. The tyres are being kept cool; it finished ninth.

On 16 June, Veyron was at Le Mans with a T50, identical to the 1931 cars but painted pale blue. Under the new paint, it was the 1931 car which had been driven then by Divo and Bouriat. Manifestly it was a factory entry, although the nominal entrant was Ecurie Veyron. Veyron's co-driver was Roger Labric who had driven in previous 24-hour races in elderly Cabans and Lorraines. Robert Brunet had entered a T55 which he was sharing with Goffredo Zehender, modified with a long sloping tail to accommodate the compulsory rear seats and another T55 was driven by Max Fourny and Louis Decaroli, who raced a T37A in voiturette races. Jean Desvignes entered his T44, still with its crude body and had

engaged a Breton garage owner, Norbert Mahé, as his co-driver. There was also a T37 which had been sleeved down to 1,350cc, in the hope of gaining some advantage in the Index of Performance. From the start it was the usual 8C Alfa Romeo battle, but Labric and Brunet held fifth and sixth places after the first hour. The two Bugattis kept going steadily and at 10pm Veyron and Labric were third, five laps behind the leading 8C, while Brunet and Zehender were fifth, two laps further back. The leading 8C lost its lights, so at 11pm the T50 was in second place but it only stayed there

for an hour, as at midnight, it was out with a run big end. Shortly afterwards, Brunet's run finished when he spun into the ditch at White House trying to avoid an MG and a Tracta which had collided. The ill-fortune continued as just before dawn, the second T55 was disqualified for refuelling before completing the permitted laps and the diminished T37 also retired. In the midst of these misfortunes, the T44 continued to motor without drama and at the end of the 24-hours was in ninth place having covered 1,604 miles (2,584km).

16/17 June 1934: The T50 driven by Veyron and Labric being refuelled; it ran a big end when in second place at midnight. This car had been one of the 1931 team.

At Molsheim, it was realised that the honour of France was at stake and it was essential that the T59s were at Montlhéry for the Grand Prix de l'ACF on 1 July. Three cars were entered for Benoist, Dreyfus and for Nuvolari who was driving, although probably not fully fit, and had become a full team member with a blue car. Since Tripoli, two engines had been bored out to 72mm giving a capacity of 3,257cc, and these were

fitted to the cars of Nuvolari and Dreyfus, but Benoist had to manage with the 2.8-litre engine. The opposition was strong, there were full teams from Auto Union, Mercedes-Benz and Alfa Romeo. In practice Benoist was the fastest of the T59 drivers, lapping in 5min 13.8sec, which compared rather badly with the fastest lap by von Brauchitsch, whose Mercedes-Benz went round the 7.8-mile (12.5km) circuit in

5min 5.6sec. Dreyfus's car was being attended by Jean Georgenthum, who had joined the Molsheim team following Czaikowski's death. The cars were weighed on the Saturday afternoon after the end of practice. The Bugatti team was in trouble; eventually, after the tyres had been removed and all the fluids had been drained from the cars, Nuvolari and Benoist's cars weighed 747kg, while Dreyfus's just scraped in at 749.5kg. There was an additional anxiety, if the cars could not reach the weight limit, the entry fee of 30,000FF for each car would be forfeited. It has been suggested that with understandable French chauvinism, the scales were 'adjusted'; in later years, a T59 was stripped of tyres and fluids as the cars had been at Montlhéry, and when it was weighed, it recorded 822kg, 158lb over the limit. Fortunately, as the T59s were certified as being within the weight limit at Montlhéry, the team was spared the embarrassment of being weighed for the rest of the season.

Race day was intensely hot and a huge crowd arrived. As the cars left the balloted grid, it was clear the T59s were not going to make any impact on the race which was a three-cornered fight between the two German teams and Alfa Romeo. Chiron in a P3 put up a tremendous struggle and his efforts were rewarded, the pace was too much for the German cars and all dropped out. The T59s ran at the back of the field. Nuvolari stopped several times for plugs in the opening laps and handed the car over to Wimille after eight laps. Reporting the race for *Motor Sport*, Harold Nockolds commented: 'The Bugattis were not distinguishing themselves. All the cars seemed to be suffering from their old fault, a choking when getting away from the corners, which did not clear itself for 100 yards'. On lap 16, Dreyfus stopped for a change of plugs, the engine would not restart, the plugs were changed again and after much more fruitless winding of the side mounted starting handle, the car was pushed away to the dead car park alongside the pits. Wimille stopped, the same ritual was enacted and the car was pushed into the dead car park, although it was later reported that his car had gearbox problems too. The race was a triumph for the Scuderia Ferrari P3s which were running in the first three places as the opposition faded away. Benoist was still going but the engine begin to misfire, he stopped and the plugs were changed, there was handle-winding for two minutes before the engine fired. He came in again for more plugs and restarted with difficulty. At the end the three Alfa Romeos finished 1-2-3,

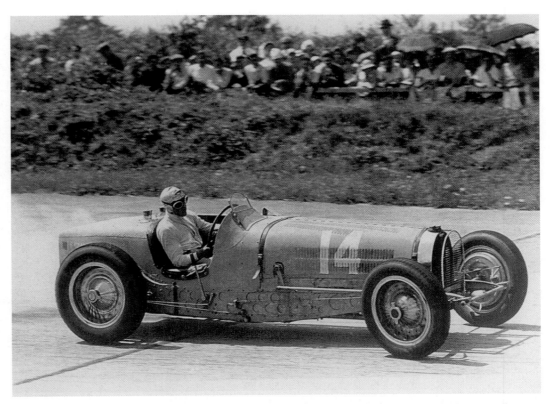

1 July 1934: Nuvolari in the T59 he shared with Wimille in the Grand Prix de l'ACF at Montlhéry. It retired on lap 17 with a broken gearbox. The metal strip to comply with the bodywork regulations can be seen below the cockpit.

led home by Chiron, Benoist's T59 was the only other car still running, although misfiring badly, and he was flagged off in fourth place having done 36 laps.

A demoralised team returned to Molsheim, no entries were made for the GP de la Marne at Reims on 8th July, although Lord Howe ran his T51 and managed to take fifth place behind the P3 Alfa Romeos. A week later the Grosser Preis von Deutschland at the Nürburgring was also ignored, but on the same day, Dreyfus was sent with a solitary 2.8-litre T59 to the Grand Prix de Vichy where he found two Scuderia Ferrari P3s and a host of 8CM Maseratis. The race was run in two 30-lap heats and a 60-lap final on a fiddly, 1.46 mile (2.35km) circuit. Dreyfus ran in the second heat and finished nearly a minute behind the Maserati of Straight and the P3 of Lehoux who fought for the lead all the

way. The final began with a bitter fight between Etancelin (Maserati), Trossi (P3) and Straight, with Dreyfus in fourth place. Dreyfus then quickened the pace and moved up to second, but Trossi fought back and repassed the T59. Straight did the same thing and at the end Dreyfus was fourth, he just failed to catch Etancelin who had fallen back as his brakes gave out.

The Dieppe race on 22 July was another happy hunting ground which was ignored. Several private entrants ran T51s, Staniland who had gone so quickly in a T37A at Brooklands drove a T51 in the first heat and was third, while another British driver, Lindsay Eccles, escaped with minor injures when he rolled his car. In the second heat, Jean Gaupillat was in fourth place with his modified T51, and desperately hanging on to the leaders. He rolled the car at Val Gosset Corner on lap 3 and was killed when he was thrown out. The Maseratis and Alfa Romeos dominated the final and the best T51 was driven into fourth place by Tim Rose-Richards. Gaupillat had been racing the T51 which he had shared with Wimille in 1931, he was a popular and well-liked competitor, and was one of the keenest Bugatti independents. He had started racing in 1928 with a BNC then moved on to a T37A, although never a leading driver, he had gained a number of successes. Many drivers attended his funeral at Bellevue, in the Paris suburbs, and an impressive memorial was subsequently erected at the place where he crashed.

Once again, the RAC de Belgique organised a sports car race on the Spa-Francorchamps circuit, a week before the Grand Prix. There had been major changes in the regulations and format of the race. Instead of 24-hours, it was limited to ten hours so there would be no night driving. The race was restricted to production models and any car which was suspected of being 'super sports' or a disguised racer was excluded. To reinforce this ban, no cars with two overhead camshafts were acceptable. The production model rule did not exclude 'out of production' models, so Desvignes entered his T44 with Mahé as his co-driver. It seemed likely that the winner would be one of a team of three Lancia Asturas with Castagna saloon bodies. One of these, driven by Carlo Pintacuda, who drove for the Scuderia Ferrari, had already won the over 3-litre class in the Mille Miglia and followed this up with outright victory in the Giro d'Italia, a remarkable 3,530-mile (5,680km) road race around Italy between 26 May and 2 June. There was also a works Hotchkiss and some quick independents, including two Aston Martins and a Bentley. The T44 kept going steadily at a good pace and as the Lancias had trouble, moved up the order. At the end of the ten hours, the T44 was the winner, finishing four miles (6km) in front of the Hotchkiss, while Pintacuda with the surviving Lancia

was third, 36 miles (59km) behind. After the fruitless efforts made with the T43, T50 and T55, it was ironic that the first success for a touring model Bugatti in a sports car race should come with the humble T44, which was never envisaged as a competition car. To round off a good day, the 2-litre class was won by a T35 driven by the Belgians du Roy and Blicquy.

A full team of T59s was entered for the Grand Prix de Belgique, a week later, on 29 July. Presumably, the news of the T44 win at Spa, reached Molsheim before the teams set out for Belgium, but much more heartening news came when the team reached Spa and heard that both German team had scratched from the race. The excuse was given that there had not been time to prepare the cars after the Nürburgring race. A more likely reason was the demand made by Belgian customs for a large payment of duty on the fuel being brought into Belgium by the teams. It was understandable that the German teams wanted to bring their fuel with them as this ensured quality control, which could be dubious if local supplies were used. Without Auto Union and Mercedes-Benz, the field was rather thin, comprising the three T59s driven by Dreyfus, Brivio and Benoist, two Ferrari P3s with Chiron and Varzi, Sommer's 8CM Maserati and the unusual Montier Ford special. Some contemporary reports suggested that the T59s had been bored out to 3.5 litres, but the factory notes do not show this and the cars ran with the 3.3-litre engines.

There was a slight drizzle as the seven cars lined up on the grid. The Spa circuit had been modified and several corners had been eased and made quicker, thus beginning the process of speeding-up the circuit in rivalry with Reims which would continue until the late 1960s. The eased and faster corners were ideal for the T59 as it left only one slow corner, La Source Hairpin, where heavy braking could induce the disastrous 'choking'. Despite this, Brivio was in the pits after one lap, for a plug change and on

the second lap, Benoist stopped for the same purpose, followed a lap later by Dreyfus. This left the two Alfa Romeos swinging along, followed by Sommer, and the outcome seemed certain. Brivio and Dreyfus stopped three times and Benoist stopped twice. At 20 laps, half distance, Benoist's car was running better and he had caught Sommer, but the two P3s had a ten-minute lead when they stopped to refuel. Chiron set off in the lead after his stop, he had intended to adjust the shock absorbers but this was not done and a few hundred metres after he had restarted, he went off the road and on to the verge at the Eau Rouge corner, the P3 struck a concealed rock and overturned. Chiron escaped unhurt but this left Varzi with a commanding lead. Chiron had set a new lap record and this irked Varzi who set about taking the record himself. He pressed on, and on lap 25, the Alfa Romeo hopes disappeared in a plume of blue smoke as a piston broke. Astonishingly, the race was being led by Dreyfus, followed by Brivio and Benoist. Benoist had to make a ten-minute stop to mend a broken throttle pedal which let Sommer up into third place.

Brivio meanwhile, had speeded up and was vying with Dreyfus for the lead. Fortunately sanity prevailed and he eased up when signalled by Costantini from the pit, but while chasing Dreyfus, he set a new lap record which must have irked Varzi even more. For once fortune smiled on Bugatti, as Benoist approached the 110mph (170kmh) Burneville Corner, he found the road was wet from a local shower, the T59 spun and went backwards towards the side of the road, at that point the road was lined by a ditch and high bank, but providentially there was a short section of smooth verge and a gap in the bank through which the T59 went. After some energetic winding with the side starting handle, Benoist restarted the engine and motored back to the pits to change a buckled wheel. Dreyfus had pulled away from Brivio and after 4hr 15min 3.8sec racing, he completed the 40 laps and was flagged off as the winner. Brivio was second nearly two minutes behind, Sommer was third and Benoist was fourth, having done 37 laps. According to Dreyfus, the team had a celebration lunch in Spa the next day. Jean Bugatti toasted the drivers then threw his glass over his shoulder, the glass flew through an open window behind him and hit a man who was walking past!

Sadly, a great era had ended, never again would a Bugatti racing car win a *grande épreuve*. The problems of continuing in grand prix racing at the highest level must have been appreciated at Molsheim, Spa was a fine victory, but in reality it was a second division event. Auto Union and Mercedes-Benz had taken the technical standards of racing on to a wholly new level, to match these teams would need technical and financial resources which Bugatti could only dream about. Maserati was in the same situation as Bugatti, and even Alfa Romeo, with its wider commercial and industrial background, would find the pace could not be maintained and would gradually fall away during the racing seasons to come.

The German teams were back in action for the Pescara meeting, with the Coppa Acerbo as the main event on Wednesday, 15 August. The 24-hour Targa Abruzzo was run over the circuit on the 13th and 14th and attracted a field of 45 sports cars. The heavy metal in the field came with the Scuderia Ferrari 8C Alfa Romeos backed by several private entries. The Scuderia had also entered a team of the new unsupercharged 6C-2300 Alfa Romeos which were fitted with stylish saloon bodies while Pintacuda had returned with his Lancia Astura. Matched against these was the faithful T44 of Desvignes and Mahé. In the 1,500cc class there was a T39A entered by Count Luigi Castelbarco, with Count Giovanni ('Johnny') Lurani as his co-driver. Castelbarco who had been Varzi's co-driver in the 1932 Mille Miglia, was very experienced and Lurani was a successful driver

with sports cars and voiturettes, driving Alfa Romeo, Maserati and MG. The red-painted T39A was fitted with rudimentary road equipment and lighting. To aid reliability, the supercharger was removed and replaced with two Solex carburettors, but the low compression of the supercharged engine remained, so the performance was not sparkling. The race began at midday and in great heat, Marshal Balbo flagged the cars away. The 8Cs battled among themselves and fell apart and the Lancia broke a piston after two hours. As the faster cars fell out, the new 6C-2300s moved up and took the first three places, setting a pace which the T44 could not match. The T39A made a bad start and was plagued with carburation problems which were solved by tuning the carburettors in the pits as the race progressed. The car ran through the night with only one working headlight and the front wing stays broke, but despite these problems, it gradually worked its way up the field. During the closing hours the battery was almost flat and the starter was reluctant to engage after pit stops, but Castelbarco and Lurani kept going and were rewarded with sixth place, and victory in the 1,500cc class. The T44 also ran steadily and finished, having done 58 hours reliable racing in eight weeks.

The Coppa Acerbo, which was run on the Ferragosto public holiday, had an entry that would have flattered a *grande épreuve*, and a solitary T59 painted red, was entered for Brivio. Perhaps inspired by racing on home ground, the Scuderia Ferrari rose to the occasion and battled with the Germans on almost level terms. The pace of the race caused several retirements among the German teams and at half distance, Moll's P3 led the race, he lost the lead to Fagioli's Mercedes-Benz when he refuelled, but set off determined to regain the lead. His car was caught by a gust of wind on the long straight beside the sea and went off the road, hitting a house. Moll was killed instantly. Fagioli went on to win, followed by Nuvolari, while Brivo was third having

picked up places as others dropped out. The T59 had not been running well and been troubled throughout the race by the usual carburation and misfiring problems. Moll was deeply mourned, he was 24 years old and had only been racing for two years, but even in his early races with Lehoux's T35B, he was noted as a driver with an extraordinary talent. During the race, cars were timed over a kilometre along the seaside straight, Brivio's T59 recorded 159.3mph (256.1kmh), which was comparable with the P3 Alfa Romeos whose speeds ranged from 168.7mph (271.2kmh) to 156.9 mph (252.29kmh), but could not match the 179.6mph (288.8kmh) of Caracciola's Mercedes-Benz.

Four days later the circus was in Nice for the holiday season Grand Prix, and once again, a solitary T59 was entered, this time for Dreyfus, while Veyron had his nominally private T51. Dreyfus was third fastest in practice and was on the front row of the grid, alongside Varzi and Nuvolari, who was in his 8CM Maserati again. At the start, Chiron nipped through from the back to take the lead from Varzi and Nuvolari, with Dreyfus in fourth place. Dreyfus went past Nuvolari and moved up to second place when Chiron made an error on lap seven. Nuvolari kept harrying Dreyfus and he succumbed to the pressure, spinning at the Gambetta Corner on the Promenade des Anglais. The engine stalled and despite winding away at the side handle until he collapsed exhausted, Dreyfus was unable to restart it, so his race was over. Veyron had kept going steadily and at the end was sixth, one place in front of Lord Howe's T51. They had stayed together for most of the race.

The burgeoning interest in grand prix racing throughout Europe, had encouraged the Swiss to hold a *grande épreuve* and their first event was held on Sunday, 26 August on a new circuit in the Bremgarten, a park in the western outskirts of Berne. It was a fast, difficult 4.5-mile (7.27km) circuit, running mostly through woodland and suited the T59 as it comprised mostly fast bends, with only one slow corner to provoke 'choking'. Auto Union, Mercedes-Benz and Ferrari sent full teams, there was a works Maserati and numerous independents, including Nuvolari. One T59 was entered for Dreyfus. Both Dreyfus and the car were going well and in practice, he was faster than the P3s of Varzi and Chiron, and it was evident that some work had been done at Molsheim to remedy the carburation problems. A crowd of 50,000 turned up to watch the race and from the start, Hans Stuck took the lead with his Auto Union and stayed there for the whole race distance of 70 laps. It was a bad day for Mercedes-Benz and the three cars were slowed by fuel pump and braking problems. Nuvolari held second place from Chiron in the early laps with Dreyfus going well in fourth place. At half distance, Dreyfus had passed Chiron into third place, then moved up to second when Nuvolari fell out with a bad misfire.

A second place seemed certain, but with a few laps to go, the T59 began to overheat and Dreyfus had to stop for the radiator to be topped up. He was passed by Momberger's Auto Union while in the pits and did not have sufficient time to catch up, so he finished third, a lap behind the victorious Stuck. It was raining in the latter part of the race and the course became very slippery. The conditions caught out the British driver, Hugh Hamilton who was driving one of Whitney Straight's Maseratis, he skidded off the road on the last lap and was killed when the car hit a tree. On the same day, Wimille had taken a T59 to Comminges where he raced against the faster amateurs and the Ferrari P3s of Lehoux and Comotti. A stop to change tyres after three laps put him out of the running and he finished the race in fifth place, two laps behind.

On 2 September, a minor grand prix was held at Biella, north of Turin and the home town of Count Trossi. The event attracted an all-Italian field, including every leading driver. Brivio entered a T51 which must have been one of the 1933 team cars. Castelbarco entered his mechanic Ernesto Bianchi in the hard-working T39A, presumably with the supercharger replaced. The race, on a very tight circuit in the middle of the town, was run in three heats and a final. Brivio ran in the third heat and came second behind Varzi's P3 Alfa Romeo and the T39A came sixth. In the final, Trossi was the fitting winner in a Ferrari P3 followed by Varzi. A promising newcomer, Giuseppe Farina, was third with a 1,500cc 4CM Maserati, and Brivio had to settle for fourth, the T51 lacking the speed to keep up. A week later, the German teams joined the Italian aces for the Gran Premio d'Italia at Monza. Once again, Bugatti entered only one car, this time it was Brivio's turn, he was back in a T59 and was on the front row of the balloted grid, but the car had an off-day and stripped supercharger gears put him out at the end of the first lap. Lord Howe ran his T51 and came ninth and last, 12 laps behind the winning Mercedes-Benz.

At Monza, Nuvolari had driven a new Maserati, the 6C-34 which had a 3.7-litre engine. It was a quicker car than the 8CM but surprisingly, when the teams gathered at San Sebastian for the Gran Premio de Espana on 23 September, he was back in a T59. Although painted red, it was a works entry and there were three more cars for Wimille, Dreyfus and Brivio. Factory records and subsequent historical research seem to show that Nuvolari used the same car throughout the season and this was the car also raced by Brivio; San Sebastian was the only race where both were in the team so Brivio drove another car. Mercedes-Benz had sent Caracciola and Fagioli and there were two Auto Unions for Stuck and von Leiningen, while Varzi and Chiron represented Alfa Romeo; with Nuvolari's return to Bugatti, Maseratis were only entered by some independent drivers. The improvement shown at Berne was maintained, on the second day of practice, Dreyfus was fastest with 6min 27sec and Wimille did

6min 32sec. Caracciola's best time was 6min 38sec and Stuck's was 6min 39sec. Nuvolari was preoccupied as his son Giorgio was seriously ill with typhoid, but despite his concerns, he equalled Dreyfus's time during the Saturday practice session. On the first day of practice he had completed several laps in an Auto Union giving rise to much speculation about his intentions for the 1935 season. On the morning of the race, Nuvolari received better news about his son and his whole demeanour changed.

Stuck jumped the start, while Nuvolari stalled and at the end of the first lap, Stuck led from Caracciola with Wimille in third place. Nuvolari was working hard to make up the lost ground and was up into fourth place at the end of the second lap ahead of Dreyfus, while the Scuderia Ferrari P3s could not stay with the pace. Brivio had fallen to the back of the field, making the first of many pit stops. Stuck dropped out on the third lap, with a broken oil pipe, leaving Caracciola in the lead, followed by Wimille; Fagioli had speeded up and had passed Nuvolari into third place, but on lap nine the T59 was back in front of the Mercedes-Benz. At ten laps, Caracciola only had a lead of 17 seconds from Wimille, but Fagioli was pulling away from Nuvolari who was running in company with Dreyfus. At half distance, Fagioli was into second place and had caught up with Caracciola. When the refuelling stops came, there was a disaster for Wimille as the engine would not restart and he lost over a minute before he was away again. He was still in second place, but on lap 23, he stopped as a carburettor union had broken and five minutes were lost while it was repaired. Nuvolari moved into third place but Bugatti hopes had a further setback when Dreyfus also stopped with a carburettor fault.

Nuvolari was driving on the limit and showed that the T59 could almost match the Mercedes-Benz performance, he was catching Caracciola, setting a new lap record at 6min 20sec, and winning a 2,000 peseta prize and a cup presented by the Omnia Assurance Company, but the effort came too late and he was still 24 seconds behind at the finish. His third place was the best T59 performance of the season and gives rise to speculation as to what he might have done with the car if he had been fully fit throughout the season. Wimille and Dreyfus were fifth and sixth, a lap behind and Brivio was 11th and last, two laps behind. *Motor Sport* summed up its report of the race by declaring enthusiastically: 'The finest Bugatti performance for some time and proving the Molsheim factory to be a dangerous competitor for the German cars next year'. There was an enormous affection and respect for Bugatti in the sport and an intense desire for the marque to regain the former glories, which clouded reality.

A week later, Wimille and Benoist were in Czechoslovakia for the Masarykuv Okruh, the Czech GP on the Brno circuit. Any hopes they might have had after the Spanish race were dashed as both T59s were outclassed and ran at the back of the field. Wimille only lasted six laps and Benoist was out, two laps later. As a final effort in a frustrating season, Bugatti sent Wimille to North Africa on 28 October for the Grand Prix d'Algérie. His solitary T59 was up against all the better independents and two Scuderia Ferrari P3s, one was driven by Chiron and the other by Brivio who had been released from his contract with Bugatti and had returned to Ferrari for the last two races of the season, at Naples and in Algeria. The race was on a tough, winding five-mile (8km) circuit. During practice, Wimille changed the axle ratio of his car, then reduced his lap time by 17 seconds, setting fastest time. The race was run in two 15-lap heats with the times aggregated to find the result. Chiron led from the start of the first heat, but after two laps, Wimille was in front and he stayed there to the finish. Chiron stopped to adjust his brakes and Brivio took second place. Chiron took over Brivio's car for the

second heat and led for ten laps but could not break away from Wimille. He took the lead when Chiron stopped to investigate a broken shock absorber and went on to win. As the winner of both heats, Wimille was the outright winner. It was a rewarding end to the season and was additionally satisfying as the Scuderia Ferrari P3s had been beaten.

As well as his outings with the obsolete T51, Veyron had been busy with the factory-entered T51A in the voiturette class which was becoming increasingly active, attracting impressive entries and regarded as the nursery class for those drivers who had ambitions in the higher spheres of the sport. Veyron's first voiturette event was at the Avus on 27 May, once again he was confronted with Burggaller's single-seat T51A, but he managed to pull away and although the German closed the gap on lap four, he went on to win the ten-lap race by over half a minute. On the same day, Louis Decaroli won the 1,500cc supporting race at the Grand Prix de Picardie with a T37A which had also been converted to a single-seater. The Eifelrennen meeting was held at the Nürburgring a week after Avus. Veyron gave this a miss, but Castelbarco showed that the 4CM Maserati was becoming a powerful competitor by beating the T51As of Florian Schmidt and Burggaller. The 1,500cc, 1,100cc and 750cc classes started with the grand prix cars so 40 cars were released together. In the mêlée of the start, the Austrian driver, Emil Frankl clipped another car and an alloy wheel on his T37A was broken, the car overturned and Frankl was killed.

There was a seven-week lull in the voiturette season before the next event, the Grand Prix d'Albi on 22 July. The start of the race was delayed and several cars overheated on the grid including Veyron's T51A. He took the lead at the start but had to stop after a lap to change plugs. This let the Spanish driver Genaro Léoz into the lead with a T37A, but the plug change had the desired effect and Veyron chased Léoz, took the lead and went on to win the 18-

lap, 100-mile (160km) race by 17 seconds from Leoz, while Henri Durand with another T37A was third.

The Swiss attracted an impressive entry of 22 cars for the Prix de Berne, a voiturette race which preceded the Grosser Preis von Schweiz on the new Bremgarten circuit. At the start, the lead was taken by Romano Malaguti with a 4CS Maserati, he was followed by Veyron and Burggaller. The British driver, Dick Seaman, had started from the back of the balloted grid with an K3 MG and he came through the field, taking both Burggaller and Veyron and went into the lead as Malaguti dropped out. Veyron had been caught napping and speeded up, but could not catch Seaman who won by 22 seconds, while Burggaller was third and the T51A of the Czech, Bruno Sojka was fourth. Seaman was already showing himself as a driver of exceptional ability. During 1933, he had started racing with a T35 at Brooklands and Donington.

The last important voiturette race was a preliminary event at Brno on 30 September. Here, another rising star, Giuseppe Farina with a 4CM Maserati, led all the way. He was chased hard by Burggaller and Sojka who could make no impression and were nearly three minutes behind at the end of the 15-lap race. The going was getting difficult for Bugatti, even in the 1,500cc class as the 4CM Maserati and the K3 MG had shown they had the pace of the T51A. A new and promising British car, the ERA, had appeared during the season and in its first races had shown it was likely to be the fastest voiturette yet. In the rather less competitive atmosphere of British racing, Bugattis were still gaining successes. At the opening Brooklands meeting on 3 March, Mountain handicaps were won by Lindsay Eccles with a T51, Shapley's T35B and Jack Robinson with a much-modified Brescia. Eccles had a good day at the Easter meeting winning the Ripley Junior Short Handicap on the Outer circuit with his T37, then taking a Mountain race with his T51, while Shapley won another Mountain handicap with his T35B. On 28 April the JCC ran the International Trophy, a 250-mile race where the performances of the different capacity cars were levelled by constructing three chicanes of increasing severity at the Fork, the widest part of the Brooklands track. The largest cars went through the sharpest corner and the smallest had an almost straight run. The race became a battle between the Maseratis of Straight and Brian Lewis and the T51 of Tim Rose-Richards and they finished in that order with Howe's T51 in fifth place.

The Whitsun meeting was a good day out for Bugattis, Mrs Kay Petre, lapping the track at 106.42mph (171.12kmh) in a T35 won the Merrow Senior Short Handicap, while the seven-lap Gold Star Handicap saw a fierce battle between the T51s of Staniland, Eccles and Howe, who were chased by Don's T54. Don lapped at 129.03mph (207.48kmh) but threw a tyre tread and the race went to Howe, who lapped at 129.70mph (208.55kmh). Lindsay Eccles won the Senior Long Handicap with his T51, then on the Mountain circuit, Nicholas Embiricos won a handicap with his T55, running without wings. On the 23rd, the British Empire Trophy, a 100-lap handicap, saw Eccles take third place with his T51. Unfortunately, John Houldsworth suffered fatal injuries when his T35 hit a straw bale and over-turned on one of the artificial corners. At the August Bank Holiday meeting, run on a very hot day, there were two wins, Thomas Fothringham lapped at 123.28mph (198.23kmh) in his ex-Campbell T35B to win the Esher Lightning Long Handicap and Aubrey Esson-Scott won a Mountain handicap with the ex-Czaikowski 2-litre T51. The Brooklands season closed on Saturday, 13 October and there was only one Bugatti victory when E. K. Rayson won a Mountain handicap with his T35C.

The Donington Park circuit had been extended before the start of the 1934 season and in the five meetings that were held, there was a mixture of scratch races and handicaps. The most successful drivers were Eccles and Staniland with their T51s, but at the closing meeting on 6 October, the 20-lap, 50-mile (80km) Donington Park Trophy was held for grand prix cars. It was won by Straight's 8CM Maserati but he was chased hard by Staniland and Howe with their T51s. Staniland retired with a misfire and Howe was passed by Penn-Hughes's Monza Alfa Romeo, but came third, followed home by the T51 of Richard Shuttleworth and the T35B of Charles Martin. Richard Shuttleworth, a rich land-owner was building up a collection of veteran cars and early aircraft when this was regarded as an eccentric fad. With his T51, he had established fastest time at the Brighton Speed Trials on 1st September, beating Martin's T35B. This was held along the seafront of the holiday resort and was one of the few British events, apart from those at Brooklands or Donington.

The season had ended for Bugatti some-what better than it had begun. The Belgian victory may have been slightly hollow, but it was a victory and from then on, the fortunes had improved in a somewhat patchy manner. By the end of the season, the T59s were still not as fast as the German cars, but the performance had been improved to a point where, in Spain, at least Mercedes-Benz had to work for the win. After the humiliation of Montlhéry, it must have been gratifying that Alfa Romeo had followed Bugatti home in Spain and Algeria. While the positive aspects of the T59's performance must have given some comfort, Ettore and Jean Bugatti knew that the future in grand prix racing was bleak. The German teams had only just begun and had enormous potential for development; Vittorio Jano was working on a new V-12 Alfa Romeo with all-independent suspen-sion. At Molsheim, the T59 had already reached the end of the road, in design terms it was firmly placed in the 1920s and little or nothing, apart from enlarging the engine could be done to make it more competitive. The development of a new design, capable of taking on the opposition was beyond the resources of the company and even if the money had been found, by the time a new car had been produced, the opposition would have moved on. Although nothing was said in public, and the less-perceptive elements of the press still talked of the likelihood of victory in 1935, it was probably tacitly accepted at Molsheim, that Bugatti was finished in grand prix racing.

René Dreyfus realised what the future held and prompted by Chiron, went to Enzo Ferrari to discuss terms. Ferrari was keen to secure Dreyfus's services and when Bugatti heard that he would be leaving, there was no animosity, a dinner was held in his honour and he was presented with a horseshoe-shaped Bugatti wristwatch, designed by Ettore and made for him by Mido in Switzerland. These watches of which only about 50 were made, were given rarely, and only as a mark of special favour. Brivio had already gone, so Wimille and Benoist were left, supported by Veyron. The Italian magazine L'Auto Italiana published a table of drivers' winnings during the season and credited Dreyfus with 125,000FF. With due allowance for inflation, at the rates of 2000, this would have been approximately £67,000, although the pooling arrange-ments which Dreyfus had accepted when he joined the team in 1933 were probably still in force.

The decline of French influence in grand prix racing was a matter of national concern and at a meeting in Paris on 6 November, the FNCAF (Fédération Nationale de Clubs Automobiles de France) resolved to start a fund to support a national team. The clubs contributed generously and the fund grew quickly, but already within the inner sanc-tums of the ACF an idea was gestating that would change the whole face of French racing, and also provide Bugatti with a wholly new sporting outlet.

Chapter 14

Into the shadows

AT THE BEGINNING OF 1935, the economic situation in France showed little signs of improvement. The Popular Front government that had come into power after the riots in February 1934 had taken few measures that had had any significant effect. Industrial output was still dropping and was receiving no stimulus from the over-valued franc and unemployment had remained unchanged. For France, the international scene was also disturbing. The Treaty of Versailles had placed the Saar, the German territory adjoining Alsace and Luxembourg, under the control of the League of Nations; it was an area rich in coal mines which France was allowed to exploit as a war reparation. In January 1935, a plebiscite was held by the League of Nations and 90 per cent of the Saar residents voted to rejoin Germany, only 0.4 per cent wanted to be French. Emboldened by this, on 6 March, Hitler declared that the limits imposed on the German Army by the Versailles Treaty would be ignored. He went further, on 11 March, Hermann Goering announced that Germany was creating an air force. The reaction of the French government was immediate; on 15 March it extended the period of compulsory military service to two years. Italy too was making war-like noises and had ambitions to annexe Abyssinia, troops and aircraft were massing in the adjoining Italian colonies of Eritrea and Somalia, using a frontier incident the previous December as a pretext.

For Bugatti, the problems of a future in grand prix racing were compounded at the close of 1934 when Meo Costantini decided that he wanted a rest, that ten years at Molsheim were enough and he would be returning to Italy. Costantini knew that the great days seemed to be over and with the limitations of a racing programme with the T59, there would be little need for his talents. His last act before going was to recruit Piero Taruffi for the team. His services were secured under rather unusual terms; he would run a factory-prepared T59 for the early part of the season as an independent, but would become a full works driver for the later races. The 28-year-old Taruffi had been a most successful motorcycle racer and had driven for the Scuderia Ferrari and for Maserati. He was not an 'ace', but was certainly a top second-string driver and was also an experienced test driver, who would be able to help with any technical development.

It has been suggested that enough parts were made in 1933/34 to assemble 12 T59s and according to remarks made by Jean Bugatti, when he attended the Bugatti Owners' Club dinner in London during December, by the end of the 1934 season, nine cars had been built. In December, four T59s were sold to British drivers, in *The French Sports Car Revolution*, Anthony Blight hints that Lord Howe, who had become a personal friend of the Bugatti family, played a part in facilitating the sales, although he had been sufficiently impressed to take one

car himself. The other buyers were Lindsay Eccles, Charles Martin and Noel Rees, a motor dealer who bought the car for the Hon Brian Lewis to drive. Howe and Rees arranged for their cars to be maintained at Molsheim. Martin collected his car at Molsheim and drove it back to England in early April. He had an arduous journey mostly in heavy rain and with no protection as the car was in racing trim. The mixture was too rich and the plugs kept cutting out, but this was cured by the desperate measure of adding ordinary petrol to the racing mixture. It is very difficult to establish the identity of cars within a factory team as identities are lost when components are changed within the cars of the team. It seems possible that Martin received the Nuvolari/Brivio car and the GP de Belgique victor went to Eccles.

There were many rumours about a new grand prix car, and it was reported that Ettore Bugatti had said this was costing eight times as much to build as a T59 and would be ready in mid-summer and would attack the short distance international records held by Auto Union and Mercedes-Benz. For the record attempt, a *route nationale* would be used to demonstrate the stability of the car at 200mph (320kmh).

The efforts of the FNCAF to raise funds for French participation in grand prix racing had been taken over by a government-sponsored committee, the *Comité de la Souscription Nationale pour les Fonds des Course*, which became generally known as the *Fonds des Course*. In February, it held a National Day to collect funds with the sale of buttonholes and car badges. One British journalist commented that with a fee of 5 francs for a car badge, the collection of an adequate fund to finance French motor racing manufacturers would take a long time! While the collecting boxes were being rattled, the first important event of the 1935 season was held at Pau on 24 February. Marcel Lehoux had left Ferrari at the end of 1934, as he had been tempted by the offer of the SEFAC, an under-funded grand prix contender which was being sponsored by *Fonds des Course*. This was not ready for Pau, so Lehoux entered a T51, and was joined by Veyron with his obsolete works car. Nuvolari had returned to the Scuderia Ferrari in January 1935 and was running at Pau accompanied by Dreyfus. At the start, Lehoux went into the lead and it took several laps for Nuvolari and Dreyfus to pass him, he hung on, battling for third place with Etancelin's Maserati but had to retire after 32 laps with engine problems. Veyron had an unhappy race and was in the pits several times before abandoning the race with an overheating engine.

A T51A was taken to Montlhéry on 1 April, driven by Veyron, Roger Labric and Louis Villeneuve, it had De Ram shock absorbers to smooth out the bumps and took the class F 2,000-mile record at 92.12mph (148.12kmh), the 3,000-kilometre record at 93.22mph (149.89kmh), then went on to take the 24-hour record at 92.73mph (149.10kmh). The car was fitted with headlights for the night running. In April, the T53 was taken out and dusted

1 April 1935, Montlhéry: Labric is in the cockpit of the T51A and Villeneuve stands beside it at a refuelling stop during the successful class F 24-hour record attempt.

5 May 1935: Wimille shares the front row at the start of the Grand Prix de Tunisie with Varzi (Auto Union No. 34) and Nuvolari (Alfa Romeo No. 4). Varzi won and Wimille was second. (John Maitland Collection)

down and Benoist took it to two small hill-climbs. On a one-kilometre course at Chauvigny, near Nancy, he broke the record. The second event was at Château Thierry, over a course on the Soissons road, where there was an odd feature as cars had to stop at the finishing line. Benoist set fastest time and a new record on his first run, on the second runs, Jean Cattaneo with a T51A, braked hard as he approached the line, the car spun and went into the crowd, it spun again and went across the road into the crowd on the other side. Cattaneo was unhurt, but six spectators were killed and

two died of their injuries later, while many more were injured. An official inquiry was subsequently held, which exonerated Cattaneo but held the organiser, Victor Breyer, the editor of the magazine L'Echo des Sports to blame, fined him and directed very large payments to the families of the dead and to those who had been hurt.

Molsheim ignored the first grande épreuve of the season, the Grand Prix de Monaco on

22 April, but Wimille drove a T54, a surprising choice at La Turbie on 18 April and made the fastest time, beating Dreyfus's P3 Alfa Romeo. The only Bugatti representative at Monaco was Lord Howe with his T59. He ran at the back of the field until lap 34 when a brake locked at the chicane and the car hit the straw bales. The first outing for a factory T59 came a week after Monaco when Wimille was sent with a single car to

16 June 1935: Taruffi's T59 is pushed out for the start of the Eifelrennen by NSKK troopers.

Carthage for the Grand Prix de Tunisie. The return of Nuvolari had prompted Varzi to leave Ferrari and join Auto Union, he was also at Carthage with a single car and regarded as the odds-on favourite for the race. The Scuderia Ferrari was represented by two P3s driven by Nuvolari and Comotti who were joined by the best of the Maserati independents. Wimille was third fastest in practice and on the front row of the grid. Varzi went straight into the lead and was never headed. Nuvolari held second place in front of Wimille for five laps until an oil pipe broke and he was out, which left Wimille in a secure second place. When Varzi made his fuel stop he had such command of the race that he was able to smoke a cigarette before restarting. This let Wimille close the gap to 11 seconds but he too stopped for fuel and Varzi went on to win by nearly five minutes from the T59.

Bugatti ignored the Tripoli race and the Avusrennen knowing that the T59 would be completely outclassed on such fast circuits and against such new cars as the Alfa Romeo Bimotore. At the Avus, the British driver Dudley Froy arrived with the Kaye Don T54, but he was lapped in a five-lap heat. While Froy was watching titanic battles from the back of the field, on the same day, Benoist was sent with a T59 to Peronne in Northern France for the Grand Prix de Picardie. In the past, minor grands prix of this kind had been regarded as the playground of the amateurs, so the appearance of a full works entry must have been rather dispiriting for some of the competitors. Benoist's T59 was matched against Howe's similar car and the pair walked away with the race. Benoist led for 18 laps until he stopped to adjust the brakes, which let Howe into the lead, but he then made two brake adjusting stops; his mechanics had difficulty in restarting the engine, so Benoist went to the front again and won by a lap from Howe.

At the end of the following week, on Friday, 31 May, the Mannin Moar was run again in the Isle of Man. Howe's T59 was still on its way home from Peronne, but the other three British T59s were there. Initially the race was led by Shuttleworth who had replaced his T51 with a P3 Alfa Romeo, but he stopped with a broken gearbox after 13 laps which left Lewis's T59 in the lead followed by Martin. Eccles was holding his T59 in third place and was fending off Raymond Mays with a new ERA. Eccles's efforts finished on lap 31 when a universal joint broke, but Lewis and Martin ran on steadily to take first and second places. It seemed that Bugatti was seeking out the easier races as on 9th June, Veyron was entered by Molsheim with a T51A in the Grand Prix des Frontières, a minor event held on a most rural circuit, just inside the Belgian border. Veyron found he was meeting an old adversary, the white single-seat T51A previously raced by Burggaller, and now owned by another German, Rudolf Steinweg. In the opening laps, Seaman ran way from the field with a new ERA then went off the road, while Veyron had a long pit stop which left Steinweg in the lead. Veyron worked his way up the field and at the end was second, but two minutes behind Steinweg. Anne Rose-Itier was third with her T51A.

The weekend of 15/16 June was very busy. Once again, the hopes of Molsheim were pinned on the veteran 1931 T50 at Le Mans. The car was entered by Ecurie Veyron, but as it was being attended by two senior mechanics from the factory, Robert Aumaitre and Lucien Wurmser, the nature of the entry was evident to all. The drivers were Veyron and Roger Labric. It was the biggest field yet for the race with 58 starters and the T50 was one of seven Bugatti entries, there were two four-seat T55s, a T44, a T43 running with a 2-litre engine, an unsupercharged T51A and a T57, making its first important race debut. There should have been another T50, but its driver, Valence, put it off the road during practice, the day before the race. From the start, Veyron and Labric were up with the leaders and holding the 8C Alfa Romeos and 4½-litre Lagondas. At 10pm, after six hours

23 June 1935: A famous photograph showing Benoist catching the errant bonnet of the T59 during the Grand Prix de l'ACF, at Montlhéry. The old T50 engine was revealed to the world. (Guy Griffiths Collection)

racing, the T50 was in fourth place, two laps behind the leading 8C and at 4am, the halfway point, it was up to second place, on the same lap as Lord Howe's leading 8C and only two minutes behind. Unfortunately, shortly afterwards, Veyron pulled into the pits and retired as the rear axle had broken. The other Bugatti entries played little part in the race, the T57 dropped out after 29 laps with a broken gearbox and at the end, all bar one had been eliminated. The survivor was the T51A of Villeneuve and Vagniez, which finished in 14th place and eighth in the 1,500cc class.

While the 24-hours were ticking away on the Sarthe circuit, another endurance event was taking place in Czechoslovakia. This was a 1,000-mile road race, over roads which were guarded, but not closed; there were four stages, with major check points at Prague and Bratislava. The start was fear-

some with the field of 55, lined up in a single column and starting simultaneously. Victory in the over 2-litre class went to the Czech, Jan Kubicek who was driving what some reports describe as a T55, but may have been his T35B, running with road equipment. That Sunday, Taruffi was having a first outing with his T59 in the Eifelrennen, at the Nürburgring. It was an unhappy event; the engine broke in practice putting a lot of oil on the circuit, a new engine was fitted for the race and on the eighth lap, a universal joint at the front of the propshaft broke while Taruffi was flat out on the straight. The flailing propshaft bent the radius rod and moved the rear axle, jamming the brakes and locking the rear wheels. The car went off the road and through the boundary hedge, fortunately, it did not overturn, Taruffi was thrown out but escaped unhurt, although badly shocked.

Great things were expected of Bugatti for the Grand Prix de l'ACF at Montlhéry on 23 June, which was restricted to manufacturers, the independents were turned away. It was expected that the promised new car would appear and would redress the balance with the German teams, but only one car had been entered with Benoist as the driver. In practice, Benoist appeared with a T59 in 1934 trim and assurances were made that the new car would be at the circuit in time for the race. The entrants submitted their cars for scrutineering and for the weighing ceremony on the Saturday afternoon before the race. There was the usual farce as parts were stripped from Zehender's Maserati before it made the mandatory weight, but the evening drew on and the Bugatti did not appear. The regulations stipulated that cars had to be submitted for inspection before midnight and with minutes to spare, the car was produced, inspected, weighed and declared eligible to race. Apart from the race officials and the Bugatti team no one else was present and it seems that the car was merely declared as being within the 750kg limit!

Sadly, the rumours had merely been rumours and Bugatti had been indulging in wishful thinking, it was not a new car, it was merely a T59 fitted with a 4.9-litre T50 engine, and a cowled radiator, which was moved forward to make space for the larger engine and a large oil cooler projecting from the scuttle in front of the driver. The engine had come from the ill-fated T54 driven by Czaikowski at Monza. This had been a works-development engine and had subsequently been fitted with a larger supercharger and a modified sump. The enlarged engine bay had been fitted with a rather flimsy one-piece bonnet. Part of the top flange of the chassis frame had been cut away to accommodate the larger supercharger. The T59 already had obesity problems, so with the cast-iron block and extra size of the T50 engine, the weight of the car must have strained the scales and the credulity of the officials. The darkness prob-

ably made it difficult to read the scales, so perhaps the car was given a chauvinistic benefit of the doubt! Great secrecy surrounded the car, the bonnet was not opened when the cars assembled for the start, and Benoist did two warming-up laps. The car still had the T59 gearbox which had to cope with the extra power of the T50 engine, and Benoist was given instructions not to exceed 2,500rpm in the intermediate gears, but to rely on the power of the engine in top gear.

During the opening laps, Benoist managed to pass the works Maseratis of Sommer and Zehender, but even to get near the tail of the three-cornered battle for the lead between Mercedes-Benz, Auto Union and Alfa Romeo was an impossibility. On the fourth lap, as the T59 passed the grandstands, the bonnet flew off and dropped on to the head of the driver who caught it with considerable skill, while controlling a massive slide. The T50 engine was exposed for all to see and Benoist drove slowly round to the pits where the mechanics tried to beat the bonnet into shape and refit it to the car. The task was impossible and the T59 went back into the race without it. Benoist struggled on until lap 34, making many stops, then retired with multiple mechanical bothers. French hopes had been further dashed as the SEFAC had been brought to Montlhéry, but was wholly unfit to race and was evidently grossly overweight. It had been taken away without being presented to the scrutineers.

The failure of Bugatti to produce a new car, the disappointing performance of the T59 and the fiasco of the SEFAC forced the hand of the ACF. During the week after the Grand Prix, it reached a decision that had been gestating since the beginning of the year. It decided that in 1936, the race would be held for sports cars as there was little point in organising a race which provided a shop window and a lucrative prize fund for the German teams. The activities of the French motor industry had provided the incentive. During 1935, new

sports cars had been introduced by Delahaye and Talbot, Delage had also indicated that a sports car was imminent and Bugatti had the T57, which had sporting potential. It was anticipated that the sports car formula would produce a reasonable field, and would result in a French victory which would give a boost to the French motor industry. The proposal received a mixed reception; it was denounced in the press, the influential Charles Faroux complained that the race would be reduced to the level of the many sports car races already held, perhaps forgetting that the racing car GP de l'ACF was already on the level of the other *grandes épreuves* and had long since lost its pre-eminence. *Motor Sport* said: 'A change of this sort will be lamented by most enthusiasts', but qualified the observation by noting that the race had been held for sports cars in 1928. The drivers also expressed views, and Wimille said: 'This is not elegant on the part of the ACF'.

While the French motoring world was digesting this sweeping change, equally sweeping changes were happening in the national life of France. At the beginning of June, the national government formed after the riots of the previous year, had fallen and a new right-wing ministry had been formed under Pierre Laval, the leader of the Moderates. Laval realised that there was a desperate need to deal with the economic malaise, and as soon as he came to power, the Chamber of Deputies gave him authority to govern by decree. He acted immediately, cutting the wages and salaries of all public workers by 10 per cent and also cutting the price of bread and the price of all public services. He lacked the courage to take the crucial step of devaluing the franc, so his measures had no great effect on the economic decline and he merely enraged the left wing which showed its opposition by serious riots.

Amidst the turmoil, motor racing continued and Wimille was sent with a T59 to Nancy on 30 June for the Grand Prix de

Lorraine which was the major event of a large meeting. The race was of three hours duration on the 3.42-mile (5.5km) Seischamps circuit. Wimille took the lead at the start and stayed there for four laps until he was passed by Chiron's Scuderia Ferrari P3, he hung on but lost a lot of time when he spun and hit a straw bale chicane. After 27 laps, Wimille stopped to change brake shoes which dropped him to third behind Comotti in the second Ferrari P3. Wimille now began to motor and passed Comotti setting a new lap record, but was still a lap behind Chiron at the end of the three hours. Before the main event there was a 90-minute sports car race, the Criterium de Tourisme, restricted to types that had been exhibited at the Paris Salon in 1933 and 1934. This became a fierce battle between a T57 with a sports body, driven by Gaston Descollas and a group of 3.6-litre Delahayes. The T57, which had been prepared at Molsheim, had already run in the Paris-Nice Rally which was held between 13 and 15 April and had been beaten into second place by a Hotchkiss driven by Jean Trevoux. At Nancy, a Delahaye driven by Laury Schell took the lead and at half-time was ahead by 20 seconds, but Descollas speeded up and caught the Delahaye. The pair battled for the rest of the race and the cars were never more than a few lengths apart. Schell held on to the lead on the last lap to win by two lengths.

The effort at Nancy must have been too much for the T59; Wimille was entered for the GP de la Marne, a week later but the car did not appear. The race was strongly supported by the British T59 contingent, with Howe, Martin and Lewis attending to battle against the Scuderia Ferrari Alfa Romeos of Chiron and Dreyfus, although Howe was a non-starter as the cylinder head cracked in practice. Martin had gearbox problems and rushed the car to Molsheim for repairs before the race. The race was run in two 15-lap heats and a final of one hour duration. In the first heat, Dreyfus was an

7 September 1935: Brian Lewis with a T57T leads Howe's similar car and the Bentley of Hall in the early laps of the Ulster Tourist Trophy.

easy winner, Lewis finished third behind Etancelin's V8R1 Maserati, which was a new car but proved to be as uncompetitive in grand prix racing as the T59. Martin repeated the performance, taking third place in the second heat. In the final, the two Ferrari P3s made a demonstration run while the independents fought for third place. Lewis seemed likely to take it but stopped to change a plug just before the end and dropped back to fifth, while Martin was sixth. Between the heats and the final there was a 28-lap, 121-mile (195km) sports car race, the GP de Tourisme, which had three capacity classes and three T44s ran in the 3-litre class. The fastest was driven by Jean Trevoux who had a considerable reputation gained driving a Hotchkiss and had won the 1933 Monte Carlo Rally. Trevoux battled with the Delahayes running in the 5-litre

class and held on to the leader Perrot, for some time. He dropped back in the closing stages but took second place overall behind Perrot but finished in front of three more Delahayes. Second and third places in the 3-litre class were taken by the T44s of Norbert Mahé and Jean Desvignes. There was a sad sequel, Jean Desvignes left Reims to drive back to Paris in his T44. At Jonchery-sur-Vesle, about five miles (8 km) from the circuit on the Soissons road, he had to swerve to avoid an oncoming car. The T44 hit a tree and rebounded into a wall, Desvignes was killed instantly and his mechanic, Botazo was seriously injured. Desvignes was 32 years old, and by careful preparation and good driving, he had gained some very good results with his elderly car.

On the same day as the Reims race, Taruffi was in Turin with a T59 for the Gran

7 September 1935: Howe's T57T which finished third. (John Maitland Collection)

Premio del Valentino, which was held on a tight, 2.54-mile (4km) circuit in the Valentino Park, beside the River Po. He was up against five Scuderia Ferrari P3s led by Nuvolari. The race was held in three 20-lap heats with a 30-lap final. Taruffi ran in the first heat and chased the P3 of Tadini and the 6C-34 Maserati of Farina, finishing third, but nearly a minute behind Tadini. Taruffi made a splendid start in the final

and led the field for the first lap, but was then passed by four of the Ferrari P3s. He hung on but stopped after eight laps with a broken gearbox.

Perhaps the results of the previous year had raised hopes of success in the Grand Prix de Belgique at Spa on 14 July. Three T59s were entered for Wimille, Taruffi and

Benoist, accompanied by a reserve car, but the opposition was tough, there were three Mercedes-Benz and two Scuderia Ferrari P3s. Race day was intensely hot, and several drivers jumped the start which was chaotic. At the end of the first lap, Wimille was in second place behind Caracciola's Mercedes-Benz, but lost his place to von Brauchitsch as the cars passed the pits to start the second lap. Wimille held third place for three laps then came into the pits to change plugs, and Taruffi came in at the same time. Wimille restarted at the rear of the field but Taruffi lost over a lap before he rejoined the race. Wimille lasted for three more laps then he stopped and the T59 was pushed to the back of the pits. Benoist and Taruffi kept going and were still running when Caracciola was flagged off as the winner; Benoist was fifth and Taruffi was sixth, but both were three laps behind.

Despite the setback at Spa, Molsheim entered two T59s for Wimille and Benoist at the Grand Prix de Dieppe a week later, where they were supported by the four British-based T59s entered by Howe, Eccles, Martin and Lewis. The favourites for the race were the two Scuderia Ferrari Alfa Romeos of Chiron and Dreyfus. There was no sign of the factory T59s during practice and the two drivers waited patiently. Misfortune struck the British contingent, Lewis was slightly hurt when a brake locked and the car went off the road at Val Gosset Corner, while Martin had a terminal engine disaster. He was keen to race so made an immediate purchase of Lehoux's old T35C and arranged with the organisers to substitute this for the T59. Lehoux was still waiting patiently for the SEFAC and had entered an 8CM Maserati for Dieppe. Many British drivers and enthusiasts attended the race and Lehoux had brought the T35C with him, shrewdly realising that there was a good chance of making a sale to one of the visiting Britons. The obsolete T35C had very little value in France, but could still be raced actively at Brooklands and in other British and Irish events. The day before the Grand Prix, there was a voiturette race, while the field was assembling for this, the two T59s appeared from Molsheim. The road was closed, but Wimille and Benoist did two untimed practice laps before being warned off the circuit by outraged officials. Both the T59s started from the back of the grid and the two Ferrari cars went into the lead at once. Wimille worked his way through the field and chased the leaders. The T59 had lost the edge from its exhaust note, but when Chiron and Dreyfus stopped to refuel, it took the lead and held it for a few laps until passed by Dreyfus. When Wimille made his stop the plugs were changed, the car sounded fitter and went back into second place when Chiron stopped to adjust his brakes. Wimille slowed as a piston had cracked but was able to keep going and finished third. Benoist had dropped out after three laps when the supercharger drive sheared. Eccles had stopped after five laps with snatching brakes and Howe finished tenth, having suffered both braking and engine problems. Martin's purchase had availed him little, a piston broke on his third lap.

Grands Prix without the German teams had become second division events, but the full might of the grand prix world was at the Nürburgring for the Grosser Preis von Deutschland on 28 July. This race has become a motor racing legend as it saw Nuvolari, against all the odds, show an almost unbelievable brilliance to beat both German teams with an obsolete P3 Alfa Romeo. Bugatti sent one T59 for Taruffi, who held ninth place for two laps then went off the road, but did not hurt himself. Bugattis were notable for their absence even in the minor races during the holiday month of August. T59s were entered for Wimille and Benoist at Comminges and Nice but the cars did not appear. At Comminges, Wimille arrived and waited in vain for his car to arrive which seemed to indicate that with the departure of Costantini, communications between the factory and the drivers had deteriorated. Martin ran his T59 at Nice but never rose from the back of the field and gave up with a defective clutch after 29 laps. Lord Howe ran the only Bugatti in the Grosser Preis von Schweiz at Berne and finished tenth, ten laps behind the winner. At the end of August, there was a personal sadness for Ettore Bugatti. On the 29th, his friend, King Leopold of the Belgians had been touring in Switzerland with his T57. He went off the road and hit a tree, his wife, Queen Astrid was thrown out of the car and killed, although the King escaped with broken ribs.

Despite the disappointments of the T59, the British customers still remained loyal and Bugatti was asked to build two T57s for the Ulster Tourist Trophy which was being held on the Ards circuit on Saturday, 7 September as a class handicap, over 35 laps of the 13.6-mile (21.9km) course. The cars had the standard 10ft 9in (3.3m) wheelbase chassis, fitted with De Ram shock absorbers, but the compression ratio was raised to 8:1 and a back axle ratio of 3.9:1 was fitted. The engine developed 148bhp. The lightweight two-seat bodies were made of duralumin and had an extended decking behind the cockpit. The cars which were known initially as the T57TT later becoming the T57T, were bought jointly by Lord Howe and Noel Rees and were entered in the race for Howe and Brian Lewis. *Motor Sport* said the two T57Ts were works cars, which was probably an accurate description, although the customers had paid for them. This description was endorsed by the Bas-Rhin Department registration numbers which were carried by both cars. A third T57 with a locally built body was entered by an Irish driver, Philip Dwyer, with Hugh McFerran as the co-driver. The Bugattis were running in the unlimited class, and were up against two Lagondas, similar to the Le Mans winner and a Rolls-Royce-built Bentley, which had substantial factory support.

Before the race, Howe tested his car on the five-mile (8km) undulating and bumpy straight of the Clady circuit where the Ulster Grand Prix motorcycle race was held as he was anxious to adjust the De Rams. The 35-lap race began at 11am and at the end of the first lap, Lewis led the unlimited class from the Bentley driven by Eddie Hall and the Lagonda of Hindmarsh. Lewis maintained his lead and at the end of the third lap, Howe had passed the Bentley and

Lagonda to take second place in the class. Howe was speeding up and broke the lap record for unsupercharged cars in 10min 1sec, taking the lead from Lewis. So close was the battle that after six laps less than 100 metres covered the two Bugattis, the Bentley and the two Lagondas on the road; Lewis had taken the lead with a lap in 9min 56sec and was in second place on handicap behind Freddie Dixon's 1½-litre Riley.

At ten laps, Howe led the class then stopped to change the rear wheels, but Lewis had slowed and stopped at his pit as the clutch was slipping. A fire extinguisher was squirted on to the clutch and it was adjusted, Lewis set off after a five-minute stop but the malady was incurable and after another stop, he retired. Howe's stop had dropped him behind the Bentley and the Lagondas, and he also had signs of clutch slip so was unable to maintain the pace of the earlier laps, but he passed both Lagondas when they stopped to change wheels and refuel. Hindmarsh's stop was extended while a broken fuel pipe was repaired. Hall had only made one stop which made his lead over Howe impregnable, but he was unable to catch Dixon who was flagged off as the winner after over six hours of racing. Hall was second on handicap, winning the unlimited class and Howe was third on handicap, finishing 2min 53sec behind the Bentley and taking second place in the class in front of the Lagondas. McFerran had stopped on lap 10 when he drove his T57 into the sandbags protecting Newtownards Town Hall. For Bugatti, the result must have given some welcome encouragement after the humiliations of the grand prix world. If an almost standard T57 could put up such a competitive performance, the prospects for a season of sports car racing in 1936 looked brighter.

The day after the Tourist Trophy, the Gran Premio d'Italia was held at Monza. To the great excitement of the Italian crowd, a new Alfa Romeo appeared, the 8C-35, which had independent suspension all round and was expected to challenge the German teams. Bugatti sent two T59s, for Wimille and Taruffi. In the early laps, Wimille stayed on the heels of the front runners, he had probably been pushing the car beyond its limits trying to keep up, but he began to drop back, then on lap 27, a con rod broke as he was going down the main straight and bits of crankcase were scattered across the track. Taruffi made several stops as a carburettor jet was blocked, and he kept running and moved up the field as the hot pace at the front took its toll. At the finish he was flagged off in fifth place, but was 15 laps behind the winner Hans Stuck, whose Auto Union gained a narrow win from the new Alfa Romeo.

A fortnight later, on 22 September, there was a slight flicker of revival at San Sebastian where the Gran Premio de Espana was being run over 30 laps of the Lasarte circuit. Molsheim sent Wimille and Benoist with T59s, the opposition was tough with full teams from Mercedes-Benz and Auto Union as well as the new 8C-35 Alfa Romeo. Wimille was at the top of his form and at the end of the first lap was in fifth place in front of Varzi's Auto Union, Nuvolari's 8C-35 and von Brauchitsch's Mercedes-Benz. To general surprise, the T59 did not expire but maintained its pace, and at half-distance had risen to third place, as the Auto Unions of Stuck and Rosemeyer had run into problems and dropped back after unexpected stops. The race was being led by the Mercedes-Benz of Caracciola and Fagioli; Neubauer, the Mercedes-Benz team manager, wanted a 1-2-3 so ordered von Brauchitsch, who had been driving a rather lack-lustre race, to speed up. He did so and caught Wimille two laps before the end. Wimille was fourth, 40 seconds behind von Brauchitsch, while Benoist who had kept going steadily, was sixth. As soon as the Spanish race was over, the grand prix circus packed up and moved on to Brno where the Masarykuv Okruh was being held the following Sunday. Mercedes-Benz rested on its Spanish laurels and withdrew from the race, while Auto Union probably sent newly prepared cars, only one T59 was entered for Wimille, so he too may have had a fresh car. In the race, he held fifth place for five of the 18-mile (29km) laps then dropped out with engine problems.

The Czech race was the last major Continental event of the season, but Donington Park had grown sufficiently in stature that the Derby & District Motor Club, which promoted most of the events at the circuit, had decided to run the first 750kg Grand Prix in England. This was a 306-mile (492km) race, over 120 laps of the circuit and was held on Saturday, 5 October. There had been suggestions that Auto Union and Mercedes-Benz would send cars but these hopes evaporated and apart from a V8R1 Maserati and Sommer's P3 Alfa Romeo, the field was made up of British drivers. Prominent among these were Howe, Martin and Eccles with their T59s. The race was run on a wet, dismal day and Giuseppe Farina took the lead from the start with the V8R1, followed by Sommer. Howe and Martin ran in fifth and sixth places during the early laps. Farina retired shortly before half distance which left Sommer in the lead followed by Martin, 1min 40sec behind, with Howe in third place. When Sommer stopped for fuel on lap 59, Martin took the lead, Sommer was about to catch him when he was called into the pits by the stewards to repair a broken bonnet strap, a compulsory British fitment that was only a voluntary requirement in Continental events. This angered Sommer who began to press his car too hard and after 70 laps his back axle broke. Martin was left with a comfortable lead which he held when he stopped to refuel on lap 104. A lap later he spun and stalled his engine, and by the time he had restarted, he had been overtaken by Shuttleworth's P3 and by Howe's T59. Shuttleworth held the lead to the end, followed home by Howe and a frustrated Martin, while Eccles was sixth. After a disappointing season the British T59s had found reliability at last.

In the voiturette world, the fortunes of Bugatti had fallen as sharply as in grands prix. The threat of ERA at the end of 1934 had come to fruition throughout the 1935 season. The ERA was lighter, more powerful and had a chassis design that was ten years younger than the T51A. The 4CM Maserati had matured into a full 1,500cc car and that too, was more than a match for the Bugatti. Veyron continued to work at Molsheim and the works T51A was entered for him during the season. He missed the first major event at the Nürburgring during the Eifelrennen meeting, but T51As were entered by the Czech, Bruno Sojka but by Steinweg who changed the engine size of his single-seater to suit the event. The pace of the ERA was too fast, and these cars won the race and took four of the first five places, Sojka was sixth and Steinweg retired with a split fuel tank. Veyron's first outing was at Nancy where he ran in the 1,500cc class of the three-hour GP de Lorraine on 30 June. He was somewhat discomfited when he was led for 2½ hours by a very competent British amateur, 'George' Cholmondley-Tapper with a T37A, and Veyron only took the class lead when the T37A spun with a locking brake. Veyron went on from Nancy to Albi for the local grand prix on 14 July. The field ran in two 20-lap heats on the 5.5-mile (8.9km) circuit, and the times were aggregated to get the final result. In the first heat, Veyron chased the 4CM Maserati of Ferdinando Barbieri and finished in second place over a minute behind. In the second heat, Barbieri took the lead again, but Veyron held on and went past the Maserati after two laps. Barbieri was in trouble and dropped back, then retired, which left Veyron to carry on to win by nearly three minutes from Howe's 1,500cc GP Delage. Veyron had shown remarkable consistency as his time in the first heat was 1hr 17min 34.2sec and in the second heat was 1hr 17min 35.8sec. Sadly, this was to be the last voiturette race of any significance to be won by a Bugatti, and yet another era had come to an end.

The voiturette race which preceded the Grand Prix de Dieppe was a major event and all the ERAs were there as well as the fastest 4CM Maserati. It was a race of two hours duration, Veyron chased the ERAs very hard, although fast they could be brittle, two dropped out and after 16 laps he was in second place behind Fairfield's ERA. Veyron was being followed by another ERA driven by Prince Birabongse of Siam, 'B. Bira'. Bira closed the gap and two laps before the end the ERA passed the Bugatti, so Veyron was third. Steinweg took his monoposto T51 to Pescara for the Coppa Acerbo Junior on 15 August, this was the principal Italian voiturette race of the season, but he was confounded by Richard Seaman who ran away with the race in an ERA and Steinweg had to settle for third place behind the 4CM Maserati of Ettore Bianco.

All the top drivers in the class assembled at Berne for the Prix de Berne which was the curtain-raiser for the Grosser Preis von Schweiz. Once again, it was an ERA benefit, Steinweg managed to secure eighth place, and the T37A of Cholmondley-Tapper was tenth, but Sojka fell out with a slipping clutch and Veyron, who had held fifth place for a while, stopped on lap 17 of the 20-lap race as a fuel pipe was blocked.

On 29 September, Veyron accompanied Wimille to Brno as the T51A was running in the 15-lap, 271-mile (435km) voiturette race which preceded the main grand prix race. Veyron led for the first lap from Sojka, but then Seaman took his ERA into the lead and went on to win. Veyron got the better of a battle with Hans Ruesch's 4CS Maserati and took second place, but was 3min 26sec behind Seaman at the finish, and Sojka was third. Sadly, in October, Steinweg was killed when he crashed his monoposto T51A while practising for the Mount Gugger hill-climb, near Budapest. A café owner from Munich, he was 47 years old.

At Brooklands, the obsolete T35s and T51s continued to gain successes during the 1935 season and were joined by the T59s. The season opened on 16 March and

Charles Martin, using his T51 instead of his T59, won a Mountain handicap. The first appearance of a T59 at the track was during the Easter Monday meeting when Eccles ran his car on the Outer circuit. He lapped at a relatively slow speed of 122.67mph (197.25kmh) and was unplaced, although later in the meeting, he took second place in the final of the British Mountain Handicap. Mrs Kay Petre won the Junior Long Handicap in Shuttleworth's T51, lapping at 125.48mph (201.77kmh). The JCC ran its International Trophy with the unusual handicap channels, on Monday, 6 May, the day marking the Silver Jubilee of King George V. Three T59s ran, driven by Eccles, Martin and Lewis; Lewis broke a con rod, and Martin struggled with a misfire, then stopped with a broken gearbox. Eccles's retirement was more spectacular. He had an experience akin to that of Taruffi in the Eifelrennen, as the torque arm broke, locking up the rear axle, the car slid wildly on the Byfleet banking, but came to a stop safely. Martin had more misfortune at the Whitsun meeting on 26 May. He drove the T59 in a Mountain handicap and the propshaft broke, this flailed around, splitting the fuel tank. There was a slight consolation for him as he lent his T51 to Charles Brackenbury who won the Gold Star Handicap, lapping at 130.72mph (210.19kmh). Staniland retired from this race in his T51 with a thrown tyre tread, but as he had lapped at 133.16mph (214.12kmh), perhaps this was not surprising. Rayson won the last race of the meeting, a Mountain handicap, with his T35C.

At the August Bank Holiday meeting, Eccles returned to his T51 and starting from scratch, won the second August Mountain handicap. An event of some significance occurred on 21 September in the BRDC 500-mile race. Lord Howe and Brian Lewis shared a T59, which was not one of their imported cars, but a factory car sent from Molsheim. The supercharger had been removed and it ran with a single Zenith carburettor, contemporary press reports saying it had a T57 engine, but later research seems to indicate that it was a full T59 engine. In the best Molsheim tradition, Howe and Lewis waited impatiently for the car, which did not arrive at Brooklands until 6pm in the evening before the race. The race, a handicap, began at noon with the smallest capacity class released first, and it was not until 12.24pm that the 24-litre Napier-Railton, the scratch car shared by its owner John Cobb and Tim Rose-Richards, was flagged away. The Napier-Railton had taken every world record from 50km to 24-hours at the Bonneville Salt Flats in the previous July and was strongly fancied to win. Cobb was lapping the track at 125mph (200kmh) and soon moved into the lead on handicap, while Howe, who took the first stint with the T59, was in third place and averaging 115mph (185kmh). A team of 2-litre Rileys were improving on their handicap and posed the greatest threat to the larger cars, but at 2.15pm, Howe was running in second place at an average of 118.4mph (190.4kmh) when he came in to refuel and hand over to Lewis. Four wheels were changed and 20 gallons (90 litres) of fuel were taken on board in 1min 40sec, so second place was held, but 15 minutes later, Lewis made two brief stops as the engine was misfiring. The trouble righted itself but he came into the pits again, the plugs were changed and it was discovered that the engine-driven air pump was over-pressurising the fuel tank and causing the carburettor to flood and wet the plugs. Lewis, who was unfamiliar with the car, did not know how to release the pressure. The T59 had dropped to third place behind the fastest Riley which it pursued for the remainder of the race. At 4pm the deficit was one minute and when Cobb was flagged off as the winner, the gap between the Riley and the T59 was only 200 metres, but the Riley held on and led the T59 across the line by eight seconds. Had it not been for the stop to change the plugs, the

T59 would probably have won the race, but it was a most creditable result and was carefully noted at Molsheim.

In October, Bugatti announced that six new grand prix cars would be built for the 1936 season with 4½-litre engines and new gearboxes, but utilising the T59 chassis. On the strength of this announcement and with the promise that a sports Bugatti would race in 1936, Bugatti persuaded the *Fonds de Course* to give him a grant of 100,000FF. It was also announced that Wimille, despite blandishments from Ferrari, would stay at Molsheim as would Benoist and Veyron. Perhaps to show that the promise of participation in sports car racing was genuine, a new version of the T57 was introduced and exhibited at the Paris Salon, the T57S which had much in common with the cars that ran in the Tourist Trophy. The wheelbase was reduced to 9ft 9in (2.98m), and the frame was new with deep side members; the rear axle passed through slots in the frame, which tapered at the rear to support a 29-gallon (130-litre) fuel tank. The suspension was damped by De Ram shock absorbers and the front axle was split and joined by a rotating collar in a similar manner to the T59. The body was panelled with elektron and had a cover over the minimal rear seats required by international sports car regulations. A feature that was already becoming a Jean Bugatti trademark was the external butted and riveted central joint on the body panels. The compression ratio was raised to 8.5:1, the lubrication system was converted to dry sump, ignition was provided by a Scintilla magneto driven from the left-hand camshaft, and the engine drove through a double-plate clutch. Although apparently a sports racing car for the customer, the T57S was in reality, a high-performance grand tourer; Bugatti had much more exciting plans for sports car racing and in particular, the Grand Prix de l'ACF.

While the French proposals to go sports car racing in 1936 had caused a turmoil

within motor racing, events in the outside world of international power politics were causing an equal stir and great anxiety for the European nations. Italian nationalism had been building up throughout 1935, centred on the Abyssinia dispute and greatly fanned by the Fascist Party. It had reached a level in September that made Dreyfus feel uncomfortable as a Frenchman driving for Scuderia Ferrari and he agreed with Enzo Ferrari that he would leave the team after the Gran Premio d'Italia. On Wednesday, 2 October, Italy invaded Abyssinia, arguing that it was a pre-emptive strike to protect the Italian colonies of Somalia and Eritrea from an Abyssinian invasion. The League of Nations, meeting in Geneva, voted to impose economic sanctions against Italy which took effect on 18 November. The sanctions did not include oil, so were largely ineffective, but had the effect of enraging Mussolini, who felt that Italy was unfairly ostracised by the other European nations. Britain and France had been assiduously fostering relations with Italy in the hope of forming a united power block to frustrate Nazi ambitions in Germany. This hope was dashed and Italy began to look at Germany, previously treated with suspicion, as a likely ally.

Among the Italian reactions to the sanctions, was a decree that no Italian drivers or teams would race in France during the 1936 season. The prospect that there would be no Italian participation in the Grand Prix de l'ACF, or in any other grands prix in France, gave an additional impetus to the sports car racing proposals. If it was held as a 750kg formula race, the *grande épreuve* would be even more of a German demonstration and without the appearance of the Scuderia Ferrari and the lesser Italian scuderia, the lesser races would only attract French and British amateurs with obsolete cars. With renewed vigour, French race organisers began to plan sports car races, or the substitution of voiturette races for the previous minor grands prix.

Chapter 15

A sporting revival

THE 1936 SEASON BEGAN at the very earliest moment for Bugatti as a factory car raced on New Year's Day. This was in the South African Grand Prix on the 11.0-mile (17.7km) Prince George circuit outside East London. Wimille was sent with a T59 in full race supercharged trim. The car travelled first from Molsheim to Southampton, late in November 1936, accompanied by Robert Aumaitre who was now the chief racing mechanic. At Southampton it was loaded on to the *Warwick Castle*, for the sea voyage to Cape Town, accompanied by some British-based cars which were also competing in the race. Wimille elected to fly himself to Cape Town in an elderly Farman biplane, accompanied by two companions, one of which was François Sommer, the brother of Raymond Sommer. The race was an 18-lap handicap, with the handicaps set by A. V. Ebblewhite, the Brooklands handicapper and it attracted a crowd of 100,000 spectators. Wimille was on scratch, together with the P3 Alfa Romeo of Shuttleworth. The T59 ran well and Wimille worked his way through the field of 25, which included many locally built specials; at the finish he was in second place behind the T35B of an Italian expatriate, Dr Mario Mazzacurati, a cousin of Nuvolari, whose car was alleged to have been owned by Nuvolari in the 1920s.

France, at the beginning of 1936 was preparing for national elections in April and May. Laval's government had not delivered the economic reforms that were essential and it was becoming accepted that devaluation of the franc was the measure that would have the greatest benefit, although there were many elements which opposed this move. When Paul Reynaud, who was subsequently prime minister during the defeat of France in 1940, suggested the benefits of devaluation, he was denounced by *Action Française*, the right-wing magazine as: 'vermin with the mind and morals of a termite'. A Popular Front was formed in January, with some of the Radicals, the Socialists and elements of the Communist Party, which, as well as proposing a 40-hour working week and holidays with pay, had the aim of fighting the elections on the platform of making the necessary economic reforms and blocking the fascist-inclined elements of the right wing. One benefit had come to the French motor racing world from the Laval administration. In December 1935, the ACF had successfully lobbied the government to increase the annual fee for a driving licence from 50FF to 60FF, half of the increase going to the *Fonds de Course* which was expected to benefit annually by over FF1.2 million. Unfortunately, in January there was a governmental change of heart and it was decided that the grant would be restricted to FF1 million only, with the government keeping the excess.

During the latter half of 1935, much work had been done at Molsheim on the T50 engine as it was realised that in its existing form, the engine was too heavy to go motor racing. A new cylinder block had been made in light alloy, and many of the other castings had been reworked in elektron. The need for steel cylinder liners in the block reduced the bore to 84mm and the capacity to 4,739cc. This engine became known as the T50 B1 and developed 402bhp at 5,300rpm; ten were built. Probably to justify the grant from the *Fonds de Course*, which was made on the understanding that Bugatti would continue in grand prix racing in 1936, a T59 chassis was modified and converted to a monoposto with central steering. This was fitted with a single-seater body which had a slightly ungainly appearance as it had the full-width T59 tail and fuel tank. The radiator was covered with a cowl which had the Jean Bugatti riveted centre join and there was a wire-mesh grille. Tommy Wisdom, writing in *Speed* in June 1936, suggested that Bugatti had hoped for an additional grant from *Fonds de Course*, but this had been withheld for political reasons as Ettore Bugatti still retained his Italian nationality. Despite the political tensions, this seems most improbable.

The first race of the season was at Pau, on 1 March and the entry was substantially reduced in both quality and quantity when the Scuderia Ferrari entries were stopped by guards and custom officials on the Italian side of the French frontier and told to go home. The Italian government had decreed they should not race. This left a race for amateur drivers with only Wimille bringing a factory entry. He produced a 3.3-litre T59

April 1936: The debut of the T59/50B monoposto at the Grand Prix de Monaco. Wimille drove it in practice but it did not run in the race.

and set fastest time in practice, two seconds better than the best of the opposition, but was lapping seven seconds slower than the record established by Nuvolari's P3 Alfa Romeo in 1935. In the race, Wimille went to the front on the first lap and pulled away from the field, he seemed set for an easy win but on lap 30 he stopped at his pit and retired as some of the braking mechanism had broken away. This left Etancelin leading with his V8R1 Maserati, but he was being hotly pursued by Sommer's P3 Alfa Romeo and Lehoux with the T51 which Varzi had driven during the Monaco duel with Nuvolari in 1933. Lehoux seemed capable of winning the race, but he was hit in the face by a stone thrown up by one of Sommer's wheels and the T51 struck a

kerb, bursting a tyre. He stopped to change the wheel and lost a lap, but finished third.

At the beginning of April, the whole motorsporting world was on the French Riviera, first for the Paris-Nice Rally and then for the Monaco Grand Prix. The La Turbie Hill-climb was held at the end of the rally on Thursday, 9 April. Wimille, who had the course record to defend, took a T59 running with a 3.3-litre engine with the standard body. He was up against Hans Stuck with a short chassis C-type Auto Union and the extra power of this carried the day. Stuck climbed in 3min 39.8sec and the best Wimille could do on a slightly

damp road, was 3min 43.4sec, which gave him second place, although there was the slight consolation of winning the 3-litre to 5-litre class. For the Grand Prix on Easter Monday, 13 April, Wimille was entered on a T59 and he was joined by an unexpected team-mate, 'Williams' with a second car. The single-seater T59/50B came with the team and was tried by Wimille in practice, but was discarded for the race. Wimille did a very good practice lap in the standard T59 and managed to beat the Mercedes-Benz of Fagioli and von Brauchitsch with a time of 1min 56.6sec. 'Williams' was slower with 2min 5sec, a time bettered in practice by

Lord Howe's ERA, which was running in the preliminary voiturette race. It was raining heavily on race day, Caracciola led Nuvolari from the start and during the first lap, Tadini was creeping round slowly as his Alfa Romeo had fractured an oil pipe. The oil was spread generously all round the circuit by the time Tadini had arrived at the pits, and when the field reached the chicane on the second lap there was chaos. Nuvolari and Caracciola got through but there was a multiple accident which eliminated five cars. Soon afterwards, Fagioli's Mercedes-Benz and Rosemeyer's Auto Union had separate accidents and dropped out which left Wimille in fifth place behind the Auto Unions of Stuck and Varzi. He was not fast enough to offer any challenge, but held his place without incident until the closing laps when he was passed by the 8C-35 Alfa Romeo of Farina, and he finished sixth, three laps behind the victorious Caracciola. 'Williams' had an unhappy race, not liking the conditions, but finished in ninth and last place having completed 84 laps.

Bugatti missed the ultra-high speed Gran Premio di Tripoli, but Wimille was sent to Carthage with a standard 3.3-litre supercharged T59, the week after the Tripoli race for the GP de Tunisie, where he encountered some of the Tripoli competitors who were taking in the race before returning home. It was a bad day for Auto Union, Varzi had a spectacular crash, Rosemeyer's car caught fire and was burnt out and Stuck burst his engine. Chiron, who had joined Mercedes-Benz for the 1936 season, retired and the race was won by Caracciola. Wimille profited from the attrition to finish third behind Pintacuda's 8C-35 Alfa Romeo and three laps behind the winner. The flat, featureless track at Miramas saw the first sports car race of the new era in French racing. It was of three hours duration and was held on 24 May and saw the debut of the new T150C Talbot and the T135CS Delahaye. Two Talbots ran, one driven by René Dreyfus who had returned to the rela-

April 1936: Wimille's T59 is weighed before the Grand Prix de Monaco.

tive tranquillity of a home team after the political stress of Ferrari. There were 11 Delahayes, and no T57 Bugattis, but the day before the race, Bugatti announced that no factory cars would be at Miramas as all the efforts of Molsheim were being applied to the building of a team to participate in the GP de l'ACF. Bugatti's honour at Miramas was upheld by three T44s running with the customary lightweight bodies and competing in the 3-litre class, but with little hope of an outright win. Both Talbots retired with blown head gaskets and the Delahayes took the first six places, but in seventh place and winning its class was the T44 of Gaston Descollas which beat a Tipo 26M Grand Prix Maserati, driven by Raymond Chambost which ran with wings and without a supercharger. Norbert Mahé's T44 took third place in the class.

In the first round of the national elections held in April, the Popular Front had not established a mandate, but in the second ballot, on 2 May, it was the clear leader, winning 376 seats in the National Assembly, a majority of 154 over the right-wing parties. The largest single group in the Front was the Socialist Party led by Leon Blum, so he claimed the leadership of the Front, but the ability of the Front to form a government depended on the 116 Radicals who had been elected and they were not wholly behind the aims of the Front. Blum set about forming an administration but indicated that he had doubts if, without an overall Socialist majority, he had a mandate to bring in the essential economic reforms that had been promised in the election campaign. Blum's reluctance brought a sense of disillusion among the French electorate. A wave of strikes began throughout France on the Tuesday after the Miramas race, these spread rapidly and by the end of that week, the country was almost paralysed. Blum announced the formation of a government on 4 June, but by then over 2 million workers were on strike and there was talk of a second French Revolution.

The railcar projects had brought a number of more politically motivated workers into the Molsheim factory who had less regard for the family atmosphere engendered by 'Le Patron'. Molsheim was not immune from the mood which had enveloped France, all work stopped and a strike committee took charge of the factory. Ettore Bugatti was summoned from Paris and was horrified to find that his word was no longer law in his own business. The paternal manner in which affairs had been conducted was no longer acceptable to the workers and the committee made clear to Bugatti that any

reforms which were introduced by the new government would apply as much to Molsheim as to any other enterprise. Ettore Bugatti's reaction was immediate and typical of the man. If the workers did not want his style of management, they would lose him with it. He declared that he wanted no more involvement with the running of the factory, he would withdraw to Paris and all the responsibility of Molsheim would fall upon Jean; whereupon he turned his back on the enterprise which had been his life for over 25 years and drove back to Paris, a sad and deeply wounded man. The family atmosphere in the factory had gone for ever.

Married factory workers had received an addition to their pay of 60FF a month and had received another monthly allowance of 50FF for their first child. When the CGT demanded collective pay bargaining, these allowances were abolished. Jean Bugatti was also deeply affected by the strike. He had always addressed the workers with the intimate and familiar 'tu'. After the strike, he only used the more formal 'vous'.

Although the strike had closed the factory, it seems that the activities of the racing department were still being conducted with some semblance of normality. The strike committee may have been

June 1936: The T57Gs are tested before the Grand Prix de l'ACF, at Montlhéry. Veyron stands in the foreground while his car receives attention.

persuaded that the honour of France was at stake. On Sunday, 7 June, Wimille was in Barcelona for the Gran Premio de Pena Rhin with a T59. He was running against full German and Italian opposition and the car only lasted for eight laps, then stopped with a broken gearbox. It was a matter of surprise that the race was held, as Spain was in a political turmoil and five weeks later, the Civil War began. The Le Mans 24-hour race was an immediate victim of the strike and the AC de l'Ouest announced that the race, which should have been run on 13/14 June was postponed, and subsequently it was cancelled. There were fears that the Grand Prix de l'ACF which was to be held on Sunday, 28 June, would also be cancelled, but despite this possibility, and the problems of the strike, preparation of three cars for the race continued at Molsheim.

As an indication that Bugatti was taking the Grand Prix seriously, the Montlhéry track was booked for 7 and 8 June so the first of the new cars could be tested. The car did not disappoint those who went to watch the tests. The car was nominally a T57S, so Bugatti could argue that it was within the race regulations which stipulated that at least 20 similar cars must have been manufactured between 1 January and 1 June 1936. If the regulation had been strictly enforced, there could have been difficulties, as factory records show that only one T57S was invoiced to a customer before 1 June. A study of the car showed that Bugatti subscribed to the view that the race began as soon as the regulations were received. Even to a casual observer, it was evident that a substantial number of T59 parts had been incorporated in it, so much so, that it had been given the factory designation of T57GP, but soon abbreviated to T57G. The engine was an unsupercharged 3.3-litre unit, which probably owed more to that which had run in the BRDC 500-mile race the previous September, than to the production T57S. An extra pinion in the camshaft gears drove a magneto which

protruded into the cockpit and the valve timing had been modified. A single double-choke updraught Zenith carburettor fed a long inlet manifold.

The chassis frame had side members of similar dimensions to the T57S but were of lighter gauge steel and were punched with many lightening holes in the same manner as the T59. The chassis cross members were fabricated from duralumin instead of steel, while the wheels and brakes were the unique design of the T59, with 28 x 5.50 tyres at the front and 28 x 6.00 at the rear. The front axle was damped by De Ram shock absorbers, with the operating arms acting as brake torque rods as in the T57S and the T59. The accumulators were mounted on the off-side of the frame, balancing the spare wheel and dry-sump oil tank which were on the near side. The bodywork was a full-width magnesium alloy shell, with a horseshoe-shaped air intake for the radiator between two vertical cooling slots for the brakes. The headlights were faired into the base of the front panel and the narrow cockpit had two seats and the scuttle was humped in front of the driver. The rear wheels were enclosed by spats which were hinged at the top and there were front and rear jacking points which extended outside the body shell.

The rear of the body covered a 30-gallon (130-litre) fuel tank with twin fillers. This car was not beautiful, but had a purposeful look and was immediately christened the 'Tank', although a much more aesthetically pleasing car than the T32. The bodywork was painted in two-tone blue. The complete car was heavy despite the attempts to reduce weight, and when weighed before the GP de la Marne, the three cars recorded 1,265kg, 1,245kg and 1,225kg respectively – over 200kg heavier than the Delahaye and Talbot rivals. The bodywork of the T57G set new standards in sports car racing and *Motor Sport* commented rhetorically 'A model for future sports cars?'. The car would not have looked outmoded at Le Mans 15 years later.

The Montlhéry trials were conducted by Veyron, 'Williams', Benoist and Philippe de Rothschild. During the two days of the trials, the drivers drove the car for 1,000km, the distance of the Grand Prix, at racing speeds, while fuel and tyre consumption was checked, and drove an extra 50km as an additional check. The car gave no trouble during the run and the fastest lap was at 83.41mph (134.33kmh). To the French racing world, the message was clear, Bugatti was back in business and was a favourite to win the Grand Prix de l'ACF.

Three T57Gs were built and entered for the race, and it has been suggested that a fourth car was built, but there is no conclusive evidence about this car and historians are divided on the matter. The trial drivers were paired as Veyron/'Williams' and Benoist/ Rothschild. The leading car of the team was driven by Wimille, who had Raymond Sommer as his co-driver. In the ten seasons in which he raced before the Second World War, this was the only time that Sommer drove a Bugatti; he been expected to co-drive a Talbot in the Grand Prix with Dreyfus and the change of car seems to have been a last-minute decision. There were no Italian entries and the German entries were restricted to three of the new 328 BMWs, ten British cars were entered and in all 37 cars came to the line, 24 of these were French, despite the difficulties caused by the strikes. The ACF must have felt that the size and quality of the entry had more than justified the fundamental change in the format of the race, but unfortunately, the French public thought otherwise and only a small crowd attended the race. It clashed with a big horse race meeting at Auteil, which may have been an alternative attraction for some.

The day was already hot when the cars lined up in echelon in front of the Montlhéry pits in readiness for a Le Mans 'run-and-jump' start. The race was expected to lie between the cars in the Group II 2-litre to 4-litre class, where the three Bugattis faced nine T135CS Delahayes and four

28 June 1936: Wimille leaps into his T57G at the start of the Grand Prix de l'ACF, but Léoz, the driver of the Lagonda has been a quicker runner. The cooling holes and jacking points on the T57G can be seen.

T150C Talbots. When the flag fell at 10am, Dreyfus took the lead with his Talbot and was still in front as the cars swept off the banked track to enter the road circuit and begin the second lap. Benoist was close behind and went to the front during the second lap and began to pull away; on the third lap he had a 15-second lead, while Wimille and Veyron had moved up to third and fifth. Benoist's effort may have been too much, as on the next lap he came into the pits for a plug change which let Dreyfus into the lead again, but only for a lap, as Wimille speeded up and went past the Talbot. Dreyfus dropped back with a number of problems as did the other Talbots while Wimille consolidated his lead,

at ten laps he was 30 seconds in front of Brunet's Delahaye while Veyron held on to third place.

The Delahayes had smaller tanks than the Bugattis and needed to refuel more frequently, so when they began their stops, the T57Gs moved up into the first three places and were still there at the 300km mark. Unfortunately, the Bugattis made slow stops, the lack of cooling within the wheel spats had overheated the rear brakes and the shoes needed changing. Wimille was stationary for four minutes and as *Motor Sport* commented: 'The Bugatti pit work was however, far from clever', although in fairness to the mechanics, the wheels were very difficult to remove from

the hubs. There was also another problem, Jean Bugatti had been taken to hospital the previous Tuesday with acute appendicitis and the pit management may have been less effective. By lap 32 all the advantage had been lost and Delahayes held the first four places. Sommer took over from Wimille, and demonstrating the quality he showed throughout his career, the ability to turn in astonishing laps when needed, he went by three of the Delahayes and on lap 50, passed the Brunet/Zehender Delahaye to take the T57G into the lead again. On lap 52, the lap record was broken by Benoist who was pressing on at the back of the field in 13th place after losing more time with plug changes. Two laps later, Sommer took 0.2 seonds off the new record with 5min 38.0sec, but on lap 55, the leading Bugatti stopped for tyres, fuel and brakes again and was in the pit for 4min

41sec, so almost a lap was lost. Wimille set off in third place and chased the Delahayes in front of him, and on lap 68 he went past Brunet and took the lead again. Wimille began to ease away from the Delahayes by about two seconds a lap and halfway round the 80th and last lap, it was announced that he had covered the 1,000km distance and was the winner, he pulled off the banking and received a huge acclamation as he took the chequered flag. The Delahaye of Michel Paris and Marcel Mongin was second, 50.3 seconds behind and the Brunet/Zehender Delahaye was third. Veyron and 'Williams' were sixth, having done 78 laps and Benoist/Rothschild were 13th with 73 laps.

For Bugatti, the victory was a sweet triumph, four years of disappointment had been forgotten and in the brave new era of French motor racing, Molsheim was setting the standards. After the Grand Prix, the three T57Gs were kept at Montlhéry overnight and the following morning were brought out again. After some routine maintenance, Benoist took his car out on to the banked track and proceeded to lap steadily at over 130mph (210kmh), he kept going and took the class C 100km record at 210.45kmh (130.88mph), carrying on to cover 135kms before pulling into the pits. He went out again and did three laps, the fastest at 138.94mph (223.74kmh). Veyron then took his car out and did nine laps, the best at 136.41mph (219.66kmh). The last to go was Sommer with the winning car, but he was forced to stop by a rainstorm before he could get into his full stride. This exercise had a dual purpose, not only did it rub salt into the wounds of the opposition, but it was also a useful check on the cars before they were taken to Reims for the Grand Prix de la Marne the following Sunday. A cynic could have suggested that the speed demonstration might have been fatal for their reliability at Reims!

The Reims race saw another encounter between the Bugattis, Talbots and Delahayes. The three T57Gs, driven by Wimille, Benoist and Veyron, faced three Talbots, ten Delahayes and a Lagonda, all running in the 3-litre to 5-litre class. There was a subsidiary 2-litre to 3-litre class, in which a new marque, the SS Jaguar, was making its international debut, the start of a remarkable racing story. The race was over 51 laps of the circuit, a distance of 248 miles (400km). In practice, the Talbots

29 June 1936, Montlhéry. The morning after. The team of T57Gs line up before their high speed demonstration. In their cars (from left) are Veyron, Sommer and Benoist, while Wurmser and Aumaitre stand behind.

6 July 1936: At the start of the Grand Prix de la Marne, Wimille is between the Talbots of Dreyfus and Morel, while Veyron and Benoist are hot on their heels.

showed they were the faster cars on the circuit, the T57Gs had a higher maximum speed, but the Talbots were more nimble and faster out of the corners. Wimille was in the centre of the front row of the grid between the Talbots of Dreyfus and Morel. Race day started dull, but the sun was shining as the circuit was closed by Ettore Bugatti driving a Royale. Etancelin was the honorary starter and when he dropped the flag for the 22 starters, Dreyfus streaked away and was leading Wimille by eight seconds at the end of the first lap, with Benoist in third place. At ten laps the gap had opened to 26 seconds and Veyron was up into fifth place behind 'Heldé''s Talbot, so it had become a Talbot/Bugatti battle with the Delahayes out-paced. Dreyfus seemed to be uncatchable and at 20 laps he was 45 seconds in front, but on lap 25, when his lead was 50 seconds, he coasted to a stop 200 metres after the pits with a broken crankshaft. He ran back to the pits and took over the Talbot of 'Heldé', otherwise Pierre-Louis Dreyfus, but by the time

he was in the race again, Wimille and Benoist had a lead of over a lap. The clouds had gathered and it began to rain heavily as Wimille completed his 35th lap, but despite the conditions he reeled off the remaining laps and won by 63 seconds from Benoist. Dreyfus was third in the shared Talbot and to complete Bugatti's satisfaction, Veyron was fourth, nearly three minutes behind the winner. Although it was evident that the Talbot was the faster car, Bugatti had gained the results which was all that mattered.

The Abyssinian war had ended on 9 May when the victorious Italian Army entered Addis Ababa. Britain and France realised that to continue the economic sanctions against Italy was futile and these were withdrawn on 19 June. The new French government had been active; wage increases averaging 12 per cent were accepted, collective wage bargaining was introduced, as well as a 40-hour working week and two weeks paid holidays for workers. The government still held back from the one

measure that was essential, a devaluation of the franc. With the removal of the sanctions, Dreyfus was invited back by Ferrari and it was agreed he would drive on a race-to-race basis. Ferrari also invited Wimille to join him, but the offer was declined. Wimille must have realised that the decline of Alfa Romeo was unlikely to be arrested and he was better off staying with Bugatti and winning sports car races. He would drive for Alfa Romeo in the future, but it would be in very different circumstances.

The sports car circus moved on to Spa-Francorchamps for the 24-hour race on 11/12 July. With the cancellation of Le Mans this assumed a much greater importance, but the T57Gs were not entered and it was left to two private entrants to uphold Bugatti honour. Yves Giraud-Cabantous entered a T57T, apparently the car driven by Brian Lewis in the 1935 Tourist Trophy, sharing it with Roger Labric; although nominally a private entry it is possible that this car still belonged to the works. A T44 was also entered by Trasenter, but both cars went off the road after four hours racing and were too badly damaged to continue. A week after the Spa race, the Bugatti team turned up in force at Deauville where a grand prix race had been organised to amuse the fashionable holiday crowds. The 1.64-mile (2.63km) circuit was narrow and ran along the promenade, with a return road running through the town. Apart from the Pau race in the spring, this was the only 750kg formula race to be run in mainland France in 1936 and two 3.3-litre T59s were entered for Wimille and Benoist, while freed from the sanctions, Ferrari had entered two 8C-35 Alfa Romeos for Farina and Dreyfus. Marcel Lehoux, who had been driving for the ERA team in voiturette races, was entered with a 2-litre ERA. The rest of the entrants were independents and included Etancelin with a T51. Certainly with a view to encouraging sales among the better class of customer, Ettore Bugatti attended the race with his Royale and drove it round to close the course. Farina jumped into the lead followed by Wimille and Lehoux. Benoist hit the sandbags lining a corner and retired and Dreyfus stopped with a broken gearbox. When Farina stopped to refuel, Wimille took the lead and Lehoux moved up into second place. Farina gave chase and when he caught Lehoux on the bend before the grandstand straight the cars collided, the ERA overturned and burst into flames. Lehoux was thrown out and killed instantly, Farina's car also overturned, but he escaped with severe cuts. There was another fatal accident during the race when Chambost overturned his 8CM Maserati and died of his injuries soon afterwards. Wimille continued and was flagged off as the winner but it was a meaningless victory. Lehoux was 48 years old and was deeply mourned, a likeable and popular man with the ability to battle on equal terms with the best of his contemporaries, it is surprising that he was never offered a factory drive by Bugatti, although his ability was recognised by Enzo Ferrari. It is ironic that the week before Lehoux's accident at Deauville, 'Hellé-Nice' was driving a Monza Alfa Romeo in the Gran Premio de Sao Paolo in Brazil. She had a terrible accident when the car crashed into spectators who ran on to the course. Seven were killed and she was seriously hurt. She was told of her lover's death while she was in hospital.

The AC du Midi, which organised the Grand Prix du Comminges had realised that their event would have little impact if it was run as a 750kg formula race, so decided that the 1936 event should be a sports car race, but to be different, the race regulations provided that the cars could run stripped of road equipment. The race, which was held on 9 August, brought in a good entry led by two Bugattis in the names of Wimille and Benoist. The rest of the field in the 2-litre to 4-litre class comprising the usual Talbots and Delahayes. The 3-litre class was wholly Bugatti, with the T44s of Kippeurt and Delorme facing a T51 entered by Chaude,

who had Lehoux's former car running unsupercharged and two T35Ts. The trouble began when the Bugatti team arrived and the other competitors found that two full 3.3-litre T59s had been entered, fitted with engines from the T57Gs. As a small sop to the regulations a passenger's seat had been fitted over the oil tank on the near side of the cockpit. Bugatti had complied with the letter of the regulations but not the spirit. There was talk of a competitors' boycott of the race if the T59s were allowed to run. Practice showed the unsupercharged cars were lapping the circuit faster than the 750kg formula cars had been in 1934 and the critics were slightly mollified when Dreyfus set the fastest lap in his Talbot, although it was suggested the two Bugatti drivers were not trying too hard, for obvious reasons.

The race was run in two heats of 20 laps on the 6.83-mile (11km) circuit, the final result being found from the aggregated times of the heats. 'Heldé' and Dreyfus took their Talbots into the lead at the start, but at the end of the first lap, Wimille was in front, Benoist made a slow start but closed up behind the Talbots and went into second place after another lap. The two T59s pulled away steadily, at the flag, Wimille had a lead of 1min 27sec. Benoist had kept station behind his team-mate but towards the end, his car was evidently off-colour and Dreyfus caught up, finishing only four seconds behind. The order was the two Bugattis, followed by four Talbots, then came four Delahayes. During the half-hour interval between the heats, Benoist's car was worked on intently and seemed to be cured when the second heat started. Wimille took the lead again, followed by Benoist with Dreyfus trailing behind, but the work on Benoist's car had been ineffective and it began to leave a thin trail of smoke. Dreyfus closed up, but as he was about to pass and take second place, the Talbot slid to a stop with a broken stub axle. Benoist held on to second place for two more laps then stopped with a cracked

piston, which let 'Heldé' and Raph up into second and third places, but neither could make any impression on the flying Wimille who reeled off the laps to win by 1min 13sec. The pace set by Wimille had caused problems for the pursuers and several dropped out, which let Chaude's T51 into sixth place and Kippeurt's T44 into seventh, so the 3-litre class went to Chaude.

Any euphoria engendered in Wimille by his four successive victories would have been swept away by harsh reality at Berne on 23 August. Since its brief appearance in practice at Monaco, the T59/50B monoposto had been lying unused at Molsheim, but it was a surprise entry for the Grosser Preis von Schweiz. Jean Bugatti must have known that it was a forlorn hope and its entry was merely a symbolic gesture. It is possible that the *Fonds de Course* had pointed out that its grant was intended to assist Bugatti to race at the highest level and not to play in minor events at Deauville and Comminges. It was an indication that the race was not being taken seriously when the car only arrived in time for the last practice session, and Wimille recorded 2min 52.8sec, one of the slowest times. In 1934, this would have been the second fastest practice time at Berne, but even then the car would have been obsolescent. In appearance and design it would have been a worthy opponent for the P3 Alfa Romeo and 8CM Maserati in 1933. In the race, the car lasted for three laps then stopped, as the gear lever had come adrift and could not be repaired, although some reports suggest that the torque of the larger engine had been too much for the rear axle.

Although the T57Gs had put Bugatti right back at the forefront of the sports car racing world, the private customers who raced the catalogue T57S were having a much harder time. The T57S was not as quick as the Talbots and Delahayes and could only play a supporting role. On Saturday, 5 September, the RAC promoted the Tourist Trophy over the Ards circuit, which was the usual class handicap and, despite the need to promote sales of the T57 in Britain, no interest was shown by Jean Bugatti and there was not even a press rumour that the T57Gs would be entered. It was left to the Anglo-Greek shipping heir, Nicholas Embiricos, who had previously raced a T55 at Brooklands, to enter a T57S. This was fitted with an elegant body made by the London coachbuilder Corsica, which was only completed four days before the race. The race began in heavy rain, and halfway round the second lap, Mongin, who had made a slow start with his Delahaye, tried to pass the T57S. He made the attempt on the fastest part of the course, the straight between Newtonards and Comber, where there was a slight curve with a bump on the apex. Possibly affected by the bump, the cars touched; both left the course and were too badly damaged to continue, although the drivers escaped with minor injuries. In the closing stages of the race, a Riley crashed into the crowd and eight spectators were killed, so the circuit was not used again.

On 22 September, the International Sporting Commission of the AIACR announced that the 750kg grand prix formula would be continued for the 1937 season, but there were heated discussions on the details of the formula that would replace it in 1938. The extension of the 750kg formula for another year enabled the ACF to announce that the Grand Prix would be a sports car race for a second year and also gave the minor French clubs the incentive to promote their events for sports cars. Much of the discussion about the terms of the new formula had hinged upon the French insistence that it had to provide for unsupercharged cars to race on level terms with supercharged cars. It was hoped that the renaissance in French racing brought about by the new generation of unsupercharged sports cars could be carried through into the grand prix world. The French proposals had been accepted in principle by the Commission,

but the ratio between the capacities of the supercharged and unsupercharged engines took another month to agree. The result of the deliberations was a formula which in broad terms provided for 3-litre supercharged and 4½-litre unsupercharged cars. There was a complex table of minimum weights which was intended to put supercharged cars from 1,500cc to 3-litres on equal terms, but this was impracticable and was ignored.

For Bugatti, the new formula was largely of academic interest. The resources at Molsheim were capable of preparing fully competitive sports cars for the 1937 season, but there were neither the facilities, nor the funds available to build a modern grand prix car which could offer any challenge to the German teams. On 1 October, the Popular Front government had finally bowed to the inevitable and devalued the franc by 30 per cent. This made a dramatic reduction in the price of the T57 for foreign buyers and sales began to improve, so all the efforts of the factory were directed to satisfying these orders, giving an essential boost to the precarious Bugatti finances, as the railcar orders had dwindled. The racing department had not been wholly inactive during the autumn. On Saturday, 26 September, Benoist took one of the T57Gs to Montlhéry and, lapping the banked track without any bother, set new class C records for the 100km and 100 miles, then took the one-hour at 135.42mph (217.75kmh) and finished off the morning's work with the 200km record. Two weeks later, on Saturday, 10 October, the T57G was back at Montlhéry and Benoist was joined by Veyron. The car ran steadily and at the end of the day, new class C records had been set for 200 miles and 500 miles, 500km and 1,000km, and for three hours and six hours. The six-hour record was set at 126.90mph (204.05kmh) and the fastest speed was recorded during the 200 miles at 127.73mph (205.38kmh).

While Benoist and Veyron had been rushing around Montlhéry, Wimille was cross-

ing the Atlantic Ocean in the liner *Ile de France*. He had embarked at Cherbourg with the T59/50B and with a T59 and was on his way to New York for the George Vanderbilt Cup on Monday, 12 October. This was run on a new track built at Westbury, on Long Island, about 40 miles (60km) east of New York. It was a tortuous, artificial road circuit, which had been built on the site of Roosevelt Airfield where Charles Lindbergh began his historic flight to Paris in 1927. The race attracted a large entry from Europe including three 8C-35 Alfa Romeos from the Scuderia Ferrari, all lured by the impressive prize fund. There was also a large contingent from the American track-racing community. Entry was restricted to supercharged and unsupercharged cars under 6-litres and the number of permitted starters was 44, so the field was thinned out by qualifying trials during practice. These trials were unusual as the drivers had to set their best time over a five-lap distance. The race should have been over 100 laps of the four-mile (6.4km) circuit, but the newly laid surface broke up during practice, and the distance was reduced to 75 laps. Wimille qualified easily, but only set the 14th fastest time, and even Nuvolari with his Alfa could only take eighth place on the grid, although Brivio set the fastest time with his 8C-35. Much further back on the grid were two local drivers, David Evans with a T51 and Overton Phillips with a T35. The American driver, Louis Meyer, had blown up the engine of his Miller-Stevens early in the qualifying trials, so Wimille lent him the T59, but Meyer put this over the guard rails beside the track and the car was too badly damaged to race.

At the start of the race, the American Billy Winn, took the lead with his Miller, followed by Nuvolari and Brivio. The two Alfa Romeos soon moved into the first two places, but Winn hung on, Wimille moved up to fourth place behind Winn, when Farina's 8C-35 stopped with broken steering, but he was unable to pass the Miller

12 October 1936: Wimille is pushed out in the T59/50B for the Vanderbilt Cup. He finished second.

and only moved up into third place when Winn dropped out after 64 laps with a broken back axle. Brivio had problems with a broken fuel line and then had to stop again as his bonnet was not properly fastened and his delays let Wimille move up to second place which he held until the finish, although he was over eight minutes behind the victorious Nuvolari. Evans took 14th place with his T51, but Phillips retired with a broken con rod.

On his return to France, Wimille had another commitment as he joined Veyron and 'Williams' for a further attack on class C records with a T57G, which seems to have been the Montlhéry and Reims-winning car. The trio went to Montlhéry on

Saturday 19th November, and began the run at noon. At 3.30pm, the car pulled off the track with a broken fuel pump which took the factory mechanics almost four hours to repair, supervised by Jean Viel, one of the Molsheim engineers. The run began again at 8pm and the car ran faultlessly for 24-hours, completing the run as it had started, in darkness. The car took the 1,000-mile and 2,000-mile records, the 2,000km, 3,000km and 4,000km records and those for 12 hours and 24 hours. The highest speed recorded was for the 4,000km at 124.58mph (200.32kmh), while the 24-hour figure was 123.93mph

(199.27kmh). For an unsupercharged sports car to average virtually 200kmh for the full 24-hours was a remarkable feat and equally meritorious was the fuel consumption of 13.4mpg (21 litres per 100km). It was an indication to the motoring world of the likely result at Le Mans if the race had taken place.

In the voiturette world, ERA and Maserati had looked forward to sharing the honours during the 1936 season, but their expectations had been spoilt by an elderly interloper. Dick Seaman, believing that his ERA would not be fast enough to beat the improved works cars, had bought the 1927

GP Delage from Earl Howe. He entrusted the car to Giulio Ramponi, who had previously worked for Alfa Romeo, Enzo Ferrari and Whitney Straight. Ramponi, who recognised the undeveloped potential in the design, rebuilt and reworked the car so it became virtually unbeatable during the season. Just as the T39A had chased the Delage in vain in 1926 and 1927, so ERA and Maserati had the same thankless task ten years later. Sadly, there was no undiscovered magic lurking in the T51A to give it a new lease of life, and it was realised at Molsheim that for Veyron to race it against the new and superior opposition was a waste of time and resources. The motoring press published a stream of rumours about a new 1,500cc Bugatti which had been tested, had an engine which was giving an impressive output and was always about to make its debut. The rumours came to a head at Albi on 12 July when it was confidently announced that the new car was to race, a rumour reinforced when a factory entry was made for Veyron, but he appeared with the faithful T51A on an ancient trailer and an excuse was made that the factory strikes in May had delayed the new car.

The race was run in two 20-lap heats with the times aggregated to find the winner. The first heat was dominated by the ERAs of Bira, Lehoux and Fairfield. Veyron was fifth behind Ettore Bianco's 4CM Maserati and was lapped by the winner, Bira just before the end. Lehoux's supercharger had seized as he finished the first heat, so he was unable to start in the second heat. Bira went into the lead again, followed by Fairfield, but his gearbox broke after four laps and Bianco also dropped out when the Maserati caught fire. This left Veyron in second place, but with no hope of catching Bira, he was lapped again but held his place to the end and by sheer survival was placed second overall on aggregate times. This was the last time a Bugatti would be placed in an international voiturette race. During the

season, Louis Villeneuve and Anne Rose-Itier made some 'starting money' forays with their T51As, but nothing was achieved. The new 1,500cc car was never seen and no factory drawings, or even preliminary studies, have been discovered, so it is likely that it was a pure flight of fancy and takes its place with the 200mph grand prix car as one of the great Molsheim might-have-beens.

In 1946, Ettore Bugatti announced that he intended to build a new supercharged 1,500cc racing car, the T73, but it was a design which would have been obsolete in 1936. The drawings for this were made during the war, so the non-existent voiturette cannot have been the embryo T73.

In Britain, amateur drivers still competed with Bugattis, but at Brooklands, a rule had been introduced which banned cars more than ten years old, so the earlier T35s were not acceptable. Safety was paramount at Brooklands and Hugh McConnell, the BARC scrutineer kept a dossier on each car, and for those Bugattis which raced on the alloy wheels, he had individual notes on each wheel. At the BARC opening meeting on 14 March, the T37s had a good day. A. C. Kelway won a Long Handicap on the Outer circuit, while on the Mountain, Andrew Leitch won a handicap with his T37 as did Arthur Baron with a T37A. At the Bank Holiday meeting on 3 August, Kelway won a Long Handicap with his T37 and was followed home by Leitch's similar car, but these were the only Bugatti victories at Brooklands during the season. The T59s had been a great disappointment to their British owners. At the end of the 1935 season, Noel Rees had sold his car through a dealer to an inexperienced amateur and Charles Martin had abandoned his, preferring to rely on an ex-Scuderia Ferrari P3 Alfa Romeo for the 1936 season. Lindsay Eccles ran his car in the JCC International Trophy on 2 May, but soon dropped out with ignition problems. Lord Howe had bought an ERA and had

been incorporated into the works team so there was little use for his T59, but he ran it at the Whitsun meeting on 1st June. In a Long Handicap on the Outer circuit, he lapped at 138.34mph (222.45kmh), the highest speed recorded by a Bugatti at Brooklands, this effort gave him third place in the race. The T59 was brought out again for the main event of the day, the Gold Star Handicap. In this Howe started from scratch and lapped at 137.96mph (221.83kmh), but had to retire with a thrown tyre tread. Charles Martin had sold his T59 to the Duke of Grafton during the early summer. The Duke was an inexperienced driver who had only competed in a few races with an 8C Alfa Romeo sports car. He took the T59 to Ireland for the Limerick Grand Prix, a handicap race run on a circuit in the streets of the town on August Bank Holiday Monday. On the first lap, the T59 hit a bump on the road on the apex of the tricky Roborough Road corner and spun, it hit a post and burst into flames. The Duke was trapped in the car and was badly burned before he could be released. Sadly, he died of his injuries a few hours later.

Before the Second World War, it was noticeable that British enthusiasts rarely referred to racing Bugattis by their type numbers. The T35 was the 'unblown 2-litre', the T35C, the 'blown 2-litre', the T35B the 'blown two-three', the T37 and T37A were the 'unblown and blown one and a half' and the T51 was the 'blown twin-cam two-three'; the T59 was the 'three-three'. The trade dealers such as Jack Lemon Burton and Jack Bartlett relied on this nomenclature and rarely used type numbers in their advertisements in the motoring press. The only car which was always referred to by its type number was the T57. Even in the early post-war years, type numbers were rarely used and it was only in later years as the cars became highly sought after, that type numbers came into common usage.

Chapter 16

Just like old times

THROUGHOUT 1936, the *Fonds de Course* had been accumulating the cash received from the French Government, accruing from the levy on the driving licence fees of all French motorists. The government had not expected the managing committee of the *Fonds* to sit on the money and do nothing, as it had been provided to put France back into the forefront of grand prix racing and the committee was under considerable pressure to use it for that purpose. The committee evolved a scheme for spending the money and on 1 January 1937, this was announced to the press by M Bedouce, the Minister of Public Works. There would be a competition among French manufacturers and the winner would be given a grant, comprising most of the accrued fund, to assist in building a new car for the 1938 grand prix formula. One million francs would go to the manufacturer of a car complying with the new formula which exceeded, by the greatest margin, an average speed of 146.508kmh (90.98mph) over a distance of 200km at Montlhéry before 31 August 1937.

The target speed seemed arbitrary but it was established by adding 2 per cent to the fastest race speed ever recorded on the combined road and track at Montlhéry. This was recorded by Chiron's winning P3 Alfa Romeo in the 1934 Grand Prix de l'ACF. It was conveniently forgotten that the German teams were still finding their way in 1934, that the P3 was a car of the same generation as the T59 and its speed had

been reduced by refuelling stops in a race of 312 miles (500km). Perhaps most significant of all, the committee seemed to have ignored the embarrassing fact that there had been enormous steps in grand prix performance in the intervening three years. As far as the committee was concerned, the announcement of the competition satisfied the government and stopped the asking of awkward questions. Among the French manufacturers, there were only two serious competitors, Bugatti and Delahaye. Much to the disappointment of the government, the SEFAC was still hopelessly uncompetitive, while Talbot and Delage only had their sports cars which would not be fast enough to make a worthwhile attempt. Delahaye was building a 4½-litre V-12 engine which was intended primarily for the French sports car racing series, but had the potential to compete in the new GP formula. For Bugatti it was more difficult, there was no spare money in the coffers to build a new car for the competition. Even if the prize could be won, it was appreciated that one million francs would only be a fraction of the money needed to build a team of cars which could challenge the German teams.

Despite Jean's responsibility for the racing programme, it was Ettore Bugatti who approached the *Fonds* committee and explained that the company wanted to take part in the competition but needed cash to build a car. His plea swayed the committee which also held an additional 480,000FF contributed partly by public subscriptions

and partly by French industry. It was announced there would be a subsidiary competition with a prize of 400,000FF and a closing date of 31 March. The speed and distance would be the same, but with typical Gallic cynicism, a competitor would be permitted to run with an engine up to 10 per cent larger than the 3/4½-litre limits of the 1938 formula. If the prize was won with an oversize engine, 20 per cent of the prize would be withheld and only paid over when the winner brought a new car to the start-line of the first Grand Prix de l'ACF to be run under the new formula. It was evident that the rules had been made to enable Bugatti to run a supercharged 3.3-litre T59 and take the prize, as Delahaye would not be ready by 31 March. The announcement of the rules of the subsidiary competition brought forth surprisingly little outcry in France, as it was realised that it was a means of giving Bugatti a grant, something he had earned with his efforts in grand prix racing over the previous 15 years.

Apart from the two *Fonds de Course* competitions, Jean Bugatti was making plans for an active racing season. The GP de l'ACF was to be held for sports cars again at Montlhéry on 4 July and the regulations remained unaltered from 1936, apart from the requirement that a minimum of 20 cars of the type being raced had to have been built or under construction before 1 June. This posed no problem as the T57G would still be eligible under the slightly flexible operation of the rules. The Automobile Club

21 February 1937: Wimille goes out to the start of the Grand Prix de Pau in the sports T59.

de l'Ouest, after a fallow strike-ridden year was preparing for the Le Mans 24-hour race again and had changed the regulations, dropping the requirement that the larger cars should have four-seat bodies. This brought the race into line with the GP de l'ACF, so the T57G had become eligible to run at Le Mans too. Apart from these two principal events, several French clubs were proposing to promote sports car races similar to those run successfully in 1936. A regulation was introduced that refuelling would not be allowed in a race of under 300km. The controversial victory at Comminges had encouraged Jean Bugatti to look again at the T59 as a sports car. The car raced by Benoist at Comminges was stripped and rebuilt. The engine was the unsupercharged T57G unit, reported to be developing 170bhp with a 9:1 compression ratio.

The T59 gearbox was replaced with a new four-speed all-synchromesh box, with twin-pump, dry-sump lubrication and a central change, designed by Edouard Bertrand from a sketch made by Ettore Bugatti. The rear axle was fitted with two radius arms which extended forward along the sides of the frame and were located by the front edge of the cockpit. The car was fitted with a new body; the T59 radiator was retained and two small headlights were mounted on the front of the dumbirons, the bonnet was similar to the T59 but there was a T57G exhaust manifold which swept downwards and the tail pipe was concealed under panels which extended over the sides of the frame. The scuttle was retained and fitted with a full-width wooden dash, and the cockpit had two small doors, but the oil tank was in the cockpit under a shallow passenger's seat. A new 85-litre rectangular fuel tank was covered by a short rounded tail to the body, with the exposed spare wheel recessed into the top. It weighed 2,112lb (960kg). This small and dramatic sports car, which had begun life as the T59 driven by Dreyfus in the 1934 GP de Monaco, was stretching the regulations, much as it had done at Comminges, and even with the new body, the T59 origin was apparent. In an attempt to cover the car with a cloak of respectability and to persuade the opposition that it was a derivation of the T57, it was given the chassis number 57248 and road registered 344 NV 3. To the mechanics at Molsheim, it was affectionately known as *Grand-Mère*.

Only three drivers were on the Molsheim payroll at the beginning of 1937. Wimille, whose abilities would have been appreciated by many teams, had stayed, while Benoist and Veyron were working in the factory and were available to drive if needed. The racing season began with the South African series of races; the first was the South African Grand Prix on New Year's Day, held on the East London circuit. Probably hoping to encourage the sale of DKW cars in South Africa, two Auto Unions were entered for Rosemeyer and von Delius and Lord Howe ran his T59. The race was a handicap and Howe finished fifth behind Rosemeyer. Howe had arranged to drive a works-supported ERA in voiturette races during the 1937 season. He would have little opportunity to race the T59 and also realised that it was unlikely to gain success in British races, so he sold the car in South Africa before he returned.

The first important European race was held at Pau on Sunday, 21 February. The AC de Basco-Bernais had abandoned the 750kg grand prix run in previous years and followed the fashion by promoting an 80-lap sports car race. This attracted a powerful entry; there was a pair of works T150C Talbots, three works T135CS Delahayes backed by seven private T135CSs and a T57S with a lightweight body, driven by Raymond de Saugé. This was the field opposing the sports T59 which was making its debut driven by Wimille, who was recovering from influenza. In the first practice session, Wimille was fastest, lapping at 1min 56sec, two seconds faster than Sommer's Talbot and in the second session, on the Saturday afternoon, Wimille lowered his time to 1min 53sec. Pau was pleasantly warm, a change from some previous races, but race day began wet and there was persistent drizzle. The 14 starters were lined up on a two-by-two grid with Dreyfus (Delahaye) sharing the front row with Wimille. When the flag fell Wimille took the lead immediately and pulled steadily away from the field. Behind him, Dreyfus and Sommer began a battle for second place, but neither had the pace to offer any challenge to the T59, which after 20 laps was 1min 34sec ahead. By lap 27, Wimille had come up to lap the second-place battle, and did so, two laps later. He then eased his pace back to that of Sommer and Dreyfus and reeled off the laps to come home the winner by a lap and a half. While Wimille had been dominating the front of the race, de Saugé had been bringing up the rear and almost changed the result when he just avoided a collision with Dreyfus and Divo (Talbot) while being lapped. He finished in 11th and last place, 11 laps behind Wimille.

As soon as the race was over, the T59 was taken back to Molsheim so it could be prepared for the 400,000FF prize attempt. The sports body was removed and replaced with a standard grand prix body and a standard supercharged T59 engine was installed. The new gearbox and the radius arms to the rear axle were retained. It is puzzling that the other T59, the car used by Wimille at Comminges the previous year, was not prepared for the attempt, but it seems likely that all the stretched financial resources of the company were being used for the preparation of cars for Le Mans and the GP de L'ACF and funds could not be spared for the rebuilding of a second T59. On Tuesday, 23 March, the T59 was taken to Montlhéry for the attempt, various problems prevented the run that day, so the car was brought out the following day, and Wimille started off but he could only lap the course at an average of 144kmh which was not sufficient to take the prize. Two days of rain prevented an attempt, but on Saturday, 27th, the weather cleared and Wimille tried again. This time he was able to lap at an average of 149kmh, but after a few laps, the fuel tank pressure pump failed and the car came to a halt. Night fell before

the pump could be repaired, so the car came out again the following morning. Wimille set off once more, but the car had only done a few laps when it stopped with a broken final drive. There was no spare axle at Montlhéry so the car was taken back to Molsheim and was still being repaired when the deadline of midnight on 31 March was reached.

For Bugatti it was a disaster, even when the rules had been rigged to assist, the car had been inadequate. Ettore Bugatti spoke to Augustin Perouse, the President of the Sporting Committee of the ACF and the guiding hand behind the *Fonds de Course*. Perouse was most sympathetic, for if Bugatti failed, and no prize was awarded, the prestige of the *Fonds* would be damaged, particularly in the eyes of the government. Perouse approached Antony Lago of Talbot and Charles Weiffenbach of Delahaye and explained the dilemma. He persuaded them that Bugatti should be granted an extension time to make another attempt; Lago suggested, perhaps cynically that Bugatti should be given the 400,000FF without the need for another run at Montlhéry. After some face-saving deliberations, the ACF announced that the time

would be extended until Sunday, 18 April. Wimille was back at Montlhéry on Monday, 12 April with the repaired T59. To ensure success and allow a margin for the slower first standing lap, Wimille could not afford to lap in a time more than 5min 3sec. He set off on the 16-lap run and after four laps, his average was 146.807kmh (91.224mph), so he was inside the time margin, but he was having to drive on the limit and those watching realised it was going to be a close thing. He was trying to build up a cushion of time so he could relax in the later laps, by lap 10, he was 19 seconds ahead of the set time, but then he began to ease off and his lap times dropped to 5min 8sec, the time in hand began to diminish. On lap 15, his time dropped to 5min 11.2sec as the brakes were wearing down and the waiting team, led by Jean Bugatti, feared it would all be in vain. The lap speed on the 16th and last lap was only 5min 15sec and the T59 came into the pits to be greeted by a delighted team, having taken the prize by the desperately narrow margin of 4.9 seconds, or a distance on the road of about 200 metres. His average speed was 91.072mph (146.654kmh). A cheque for 320,000FF

12 April 1937, Montlhéry: Wimille in the sports T59, back in racing trim for the 400,000FF prize attempt. The rear radius arms are evident with the sports body removed.

18 April 1937. At the Gran Premio del Valentino, in Turin, Wurmser and Aumaitre push out Wimille in the T59/50B. The car retired with an oil leak. (Guy Griffiths Collection)

was handed over, but as Ettore Bugatti ruefully pointed out, a substantial part of it had already been spent in the costs of making the attempt.

The T59 returned to Molsheim and was put back into sports trim again, but Wimille had another commitment. As soon as he had finished the run at Montlhéry, he set off to Italy where he met a party from Molsheim with the monoposto T59/50B. The car was entered for the Gran Premio del Valentino on Sunday, 18 April. This was a 60-lap, 109-mile (175km) race on a twisting circuit in the Valentino Park

in Turin, beside the River Po. It was a full 750kg formula race, but the organisers had been unable to attract cars from either of the German teams and wanted some opposition to the four 12C/36 Alfa Romeos, entered by the Scuderia Ferrari. Having regard to the financial stringencies at Molsheim, it seems likely that the attraction of taking the car to Turin was the prospect of some very good starting money. This was

likely to have been increased by the bargaining counter that the appearance of the T59/50B would give the race an international element, and without it, the race would have been a local Italian event. The car had been modified since it ran in the United States and had been fitted with a flowing tail with a headrest. In practice, Wimille could not match the times of the four 12C/36s, but had the doubtful satisfaction of being quicker than the four independents who made up the field. In the race, he held fourth place ahead of Pintacuda's Alfa Romeo for the first lap, then pulled into the pits; he set off again, three laps behind the field, did three slow laps then retired with a broken oil pipe.

At the beginning of May, the sports T59 was shipped across the Mediterranean to Tunisia for the Grand Prix de Tunisie on the 16th. This race had attracted all the leading sports car racers, probably drawn by a prize fund of 78,000FF. It was held on the 7.8-mile (12.6km) circuit near the ancient city of Carthage and to increase the spectator interest, it was run in three eight-lap heats of 100.8km. There was a 45-minute break between heats, and as the total distance was only 2.4km more than the stipulated 300km, no refuelling was allowed. Practice showed that the T59 was undergeared, so a rear axle with a higher ratio was flown from France to the local El Aouina airfield. The heats began with a Le Mans-type start and in the first race, Sommer's T150C Talbot led from Wimille at the end of the first lap. Wimille then speeded up and passed the Talbot on the third lap, establishing the fastest lap of the day, and began to pull away from the field as he had done at Pau. As Wimille came up to the finish his lead was 35 seconds, but he was puzzled to be greeted by a waved black flag instead of the usual chequered flag. Concluding he had miscounted the laps, he completed another lap before stopping.

In the second heat, Wimille repeated the performance but the winning margin over the Talbot had increased to a minute. Wimille again dominated the third heat and at the start of the last lap, his lead was 56 seconds. With the finishing line almost in sight, the T59 spluttered to a halt, out of fuel and Sommer swept past to win. On his lap of honour, Sommer stopped beside the T59 to commiserate with Wimille and tell him he had been the moral victor. It had been calculated that the fuel would just be sufficient for 300km, but the extra lap in

the first heat had been Wimille's undoing. The failure indicated that the fuel consumption of the sports T59, if the tank was full at the start, was approximately ten miles per gallon (27 litres per 100km). The tank had only one filler and it is possible that it had not been filled to the brim.

After his unexpected win, Sommer returned to France, but the remaining competitors travelled 120 miles (190km)

westwards from Tunis, into the French province of Algeria. The destination was the seaport of Bone (subsequently renamed Annaba), where a sports car grand prix was being held the following Sunday, 23 May. During the week between the races, Robert Aumaitre and Lucien Wurmser, who were tending the T59, checked the whole car carefully to prevent another embarrassing failure, and removed the lights and wings

16 May 1937: Before the Grand Prix de Tunisie, Wurmser stands behind the sports T59 which has the modified tail and recessed spare wheel.

which the race regulations decreed were unnecessary. The rear axle ratio was changed, as the circuit on the quayside and through part of the old town was only 1.18 miles (1.89km), parts of it were surfaced with *pavée*. Wimille's main rival was Dreyfus whose Delahaye T135CS set the fastest practice lap. The race was run in two 50-lap heats and in the first heat Wimille ran away from the field and won by over a lap from Dreyfus. In the second heat, Wimille led again but stopped to change plugs. The engine had a suspect piston and a plug had oiled up. Dreyfus had dropped out and the heat was won by Carrière's T150S Talbot, but Wimille had restarted and carried on gently. He let Carrière set the pace and went fast enough to avoid being lapped. Wimille finished second and the aggregate times of the heats gave him victory.

The sports T59 went back to Molsheim immediately it returned from North Africa. An additional filler was added to the fuel tank, and the passenger's side of the cockpit was partially cowled. On its previous appearances, the car had been painted the usual Bugatti pale blue, but while at Molsheim it was repainted a darker blue. In its new paint, it was taken to Miramas for the Grand Prix de Marseille on 6 June. This was the next major race in the French sports car series and brought out all the main contenders. The T150C Talbots had been improved with larger brakes and aluminium cylinder heads and were expected to set the pace. The race was unusual, as it was run in three heats of one hour, with the times aggregated to find the winner. For the first heat, two chicanes were built on the straights of the featureless 3.1-mile (5km) circuit. For the second heat, one chicane was removed and for the third heat there were no chicanes, so the cars had an almost flat-out race. No refuelling was permitted between the heats but fuel could

6 June 1937: Waiting for the start of the Grand Prix de Marseille, at Miramas, Wimille settles into the cockpit of the sports T59 while his main rival Sommer, sits in his Talbot and adjusts his goggles. The T59 now has a radiator cowling.

20 June 1937: The victorious Wimille pulls into the pits in the T57G during the Le Mans 24-hour race. Bugatti's result was regarded as a national triumph.

be added at pit stops during the races. In practice, Sommer's Talbot was fastest, but Wimille was only two seconds slower. Race day began with rain, but it had cleared and it was a superb Provençal day when the 25 cars came to the line for the first heat. Wimille knew that the T59 would not have the speed to match the Talbots in the second and third heats, so had to build up a lead in the first heat. Sommer led at the start and the Talbot was much faster on the straights, but the Bugatti caught up in the chicanes. Wimille held on and after two laps took the lead, he began to pull away by about a second a lap and at the end of the hour was 25 seconds ahead of Sommer.

Wimille had to make a fuel stop in the second heat so must have felt that fate was on his side when Sommer's Talbot refused to fire at the start of the second heat and had lost 29 seconds before joining the race. Comotti, with the second Talbot soon passed Wimille then Sommer stormed through the field and caught the T59, Wimille was back in third place and after the fuel stop, finished 1min 19sec behind Sommer. In the flat-out pace of the third heat, Wimille could not keep up with the Talbots and fell back. At the half-hour mark,

an oil pipe cracked and he retired without oil pressure, leaving Sommer and Comotti with an easy win.

The failure at Miramas was a disappointment, but the Bugatti sights were set upon a much more important target, the Le Mans 24-hour race, which raises one of the major puzzles of the later Bugatti racing history. Bugatti entered two cars for the race, which was held on 19 and 20 June. These were declared to have a capacity of 4½-litres and as the largest engined cars which had been entered, were given the race numbers

1 and 2. It seems great efforts had been made to prepare two cars which were fitted with the 84mm x 100mm, 4,431cc alloy T50B engine and became known as the T57S45. When it became evident that the two cars would not be ready in time, two 1936 T57Gs were substituted, but the mystery of the two T57S45s had only begun. Minor changes were made to the T57Gs, a door was fitted to the near side of the cockpit, the spare wheel was mounted in a recess on top of the tail, an extra head-light was mounted in the middle of the radiator aperture and an angled light was recessed into the off-side of the body, ahead of the cockpit, to help the driver to pick up the line of the right-hand corners in the dark. The drivers were Veyron and Labric with the first car, and Wimille and Benoist with the second, which seems to have been the car which won at Montlhéry and Reims in 1936. One historian has suggested that a T57S45 arrived at Le Mans for practice and did several laps of the circuit, but this is unsubstantiated and there is no reference to it in the records of the AC de l'Ouest.

Joining the T57Gs was the T57S of de Saugé, his co-driver was the Spaniard Genaro Léoz, who had raced a T51 in 1934 and 1935. The T57S aroused some curiosity, as there were six separate small diameter tail pipes emerging under the rear of the car. An elderly T44 was entered by the French driver René Kippeurt, who was sharing the car with Poulain. The greatest rival to the T57Gs, apart from the inevitable Talbots and Delahayes, was a 2900B Alfa Romeo which was driven by Raymond Sommer and Giovanni Guidotti, the principal Alfa Romeo test driver. It was a works entry but was painted black as there was a slight coyness about the company involvement. The Alfa Romeo pit was managed by Meo Costantini who had joined Alfa Romeo at the beginning of 1937 as a technical inspector, working with Vittorio Jano, the Alfa Romeo designer. Much was expected of the Alfa Romeo, as a sister car had already won the Mille Miglia.

Practice was uneventful for the T57Gs which were at the head of the field as the 49 competing cars lined up for the 4pm

start. The course had been closed by a Lagonda, driven by the former holder of the World 24-hour record, John Cobb. Cobb was also given the honour of dropping the flag and there was some confusion, as he was told to drop it by the chief timekeeper, while the race commentator was also counting down the seconds to 4.00pm. The commentator reached the vital moment about a second before the timekeeper, and some drivers were already sprinting to their cars when Cobb dropped the flag. Wimille was one of those who waited for the flag. Sommer led for the opening laps while Wimille worked his way up from fifth place on the first lap until he caught Sommer on lap five. The Bugatti began to pull away and by the eighth lap had an 18-second lead. The leaders were starting their tenth lap, as Kippeurt who was already two laps behind, slid wide taking White House Corner, the T44 hit the bank and rolled, throwing the driver out on to the road. He was probably killed instantly. The T44 was about to be lapped by two 328 BMWs driven by Hans Roth and Pat Fairfield. Roth swerved to avoid Kippeurt's body and crashed through the hedge and Fairfield also swerved, striking the overturned T44. A Delahaye driven by Jean Tremoulet hit Fairfield's BMW and cannoned it into the field beside the track, while the Delahaye itself was struck by Raph's Talbot. Fairfield was severely injured and died during Sunday night, while Roth, Tremoulet and Raph all received serious injuries. Wimille arrived at the crash and managed to avoid hitting any of the stricken cars, Sommer also avoided a collision, but in the frenzy of the moment, over-revved the Alfa Romeo engine. He limped to the pits and after another lap the car was withdrawn from the race.

With the retirement of the Alfa Romeo, Wimille dominated the race, by 6.30pm he had a lead of over a lap. Benoist took over the wheel and continued to build up the lead. At about 8pm there was a heavy storm and Benoist, who had set a lap record at 96.42mph (155.04kmh) had to slow until

Le Mans 24-hour race: The Bugatti mechanics, with Aumaitre on the right, stand behind the Veyron/Labric T57G, which retired with clutch slip. The angled spotlight is mounted in front of the cockpit.

July 1937: The T57S45 at the pits during practice for the Grand Prix de l'ACF.

he was lapping at no more than 80mph (130kmh), but he speeded up as the circuit dried. By midnight, Wimille and Benoist had covered 84 laps and had a three-lap lead over the T135CS Delahaye of Laury Schell and René Carrière. The second T57G was in third place a lap behind the Delahaye, but was suffering from intermittent clutch slip. Gradually, Veyron and Labric dropped back, being passed by two Delahayes and at 5am, the slipping clutch gripped no more and the T57G retired. The Bugatti pit announced that the retirement was caused by a leaking fuel tank. At this time, the T57S also stopped with a broken gearbox. The leading T57G continued to increase its lead and at 8am was seven laps ahead of the Schell/Carrière Delahaye; it

seemed to be running on to a certain victory, but the brakes were wearing.

At noon, with four hours to go, Benoist was passing another competitor as he came up to Arnage Corner and over-estimated the power of the weakening brakes. The T57G slid off the road and across the grass until it came to rest against a bank. It was over ten minutes before it was pushed clear by marshals and rejoined the course. It had received outside assistance which contravened the race regulations, but these also permitted assistance to be given if the car was in a dangerous place and needed moving for the safety of other competitors. No one disputed that it had been in a

dangerous place and to the relief of the Bugatti team, the race officials permitted it to continue and none of the other competitors made a protest. A check in the pits showed that apart from slight damage to a front hub the car was unharmed, so Wimille and Benoist, their lead secure, toured round for the remaining four hours and were unconcerned that the pursuing Delahayes pulled back several laps. The pair were greeted with acclamation when the T57G came to the finish at 4pm. It had covered a record distance of 2,041 miles (3,287km) and finished seven laps ahead of the second-placed Delahaye of Joseph Paul and Marcel Mongin.

July 1937: Jean Bugatti sits in the second T57S45 at Molsheim just before his abortive drive to Montlhéry.

Victory at Le Mans was the one major success that had eluded Bugatti and the result was regarded as a national triumph. It had been 11 years since a French car had won the 24-hour race and France had watched an unbroken series of British and Italian victories in one of the most prestigious races of all. A French car winning at Le Mans went a long way to compensate for the humiliation in grands prix at the hands of the Germans and Italians. For Bugatti, the victory had additional importance, the winning car was a T57 and the result could only help to boost sales among discerning customers.

Attention now moved to the Grand Prix de l'ACF which was held at Montlhéry two weeks later, on Sunday, 4 July. A French victory was certain, there were no foreign cars entered, but the race promised to be a fierce battle between the rival marques. The V-12 Delahaye, the T145, was finished and was to make its debut, as was a new V-12 Delage. The rule that 20 cars should have been built or be under construction seemed to have been conveniently forgotten. Bugatti had entered two T57S45s, but the specification of these cars is not fully

known. It seems that the chassis was similar to the T57G, while the engine was the alloy T50B in 4½-litre form with the synchromesh gearbox already used in the sports T59. It has been suggested that one of the cars was based on the third T57G, which had not been used since the 1936 season. A second T57S45 was built which has given rise to much subsequent speculation. This may have been based on the alleged fourth T57G which many experts consider did not exist, it could have been built from scratch or, probably unlikely, it was based on one of the Le Mans T57Gs and was created in a mere 13 days. The T57S45 body was slimmer than the 'tank' bodies of the T57Gs, there was a valley between the bonnet and front wings and a pronounced dip between the front and rear wings. In appearance, it was a more handsome car than the T57G.

There was a preliminary practice session on the Thursday before the race and the official sessions, together with the scrutineering were on the Friday and Saturday. There was no sign of the T57S45 on the Thursday or Friday. Wimille and Benoist waited at the circuit and after telephone calls to Molsheim, were told that Wimille's

car would be arriving at the circuit on Saturday morning. Benoist's car was still being built and would be driven to Montlhéry by Jean Bugatti when it was finished, but it was indicated to Benoist that there was a possibility it would not be completed in time. The new V-12 Delage had a coupé body and was being displayed to the world at Montlhéry as the ultimate grand tourer. It occurred to Benoist, that if his T57S45 was unready, he could substitute a T57 Atalante coupé which was a demonstrator at the Paris showroom. He would get a drive in the Grand Prix and the Atalante would possibly show up the pretensions of the new Delage. Benoist approached the race organisers and believed he had been given permission to substitute the Atalante for the T57S45 if it was not ready, so took the Atalante on to the circuit for practice. The organisers had a different view and Benoist was informed that he was disqualified from the race for practising with an unauthorised car. When the news of the disqualification reached Ettore Bugatti in Paris, he said that both T57S45s would be withdrawn from the race, but was persuaded by Benoist and Jean Bugatti that his decision was premature and he should wait until the first car had reached Montlhéry and its performance on the circuit had been assessed.

The first T57S45 arrived at Montlhéry after the practice session had begun on Saturday. Wimille took it on to the circuit and to the consternation of the rival teams, set the fastest practice time. Meanwhile, the second car had been finished at Molsheim and while probably not fully race prepared, set off for Montlhéry, driven by Jean Bugatti. The organisers agreed, with the consent of Antony Lago and Charles Weiffenbach, that the deadline for scrutineering the car would be extended until midnight. The drive from Molsheim showed that the car was unfit to race and the problems were compounded when it was involved in a minor accident. Benoist's disqualification had been lifted and a fine of

1,000FF was substituted, but it still rankled with Ettore Bugatti and when he heard that the second car would not be able to race, he announced that both cars would be withdrawn from the race, making an apology that with the effort devoted to winning at Le Mans, it had not been possible to prepare the cars in the time available. It has been suggested that practice showed the T57S45 was handling badly, but the times belie this, and a more likely reason for the withdrawal was signs of incipient engine problems. The two T57S45s went back to Molsheim and were never seen again. Presumably they were dismantled and the parts went back into the stores for use in the other competition cars.

The Montlhéry fiasco was soon forgotten as two weeks later the French sports car circus was engaged at Reims for the Grand Prix de la Marne. Bugatti sent Wimille with the sports T59, now repainted in the usual pale blue, and he was matched against two of the new V-12 T145 Delahayes, seven T135Cs Delahayes and five T150C Talbots. One of the Talbots was being driven by Louis Chiron, who had announced his retirement from the sport after an abortive and unhappy grand prix season with Mercedes-Benz in 1936. Anthony Lago had lured him back to the wheel and after an

unsuccessful outing at Le Mans, when his Talbot's radiator had been punctured by debris from the Kippeurt crash, he had shown that he had lost none of his skill and flair by winning the GP de l'ACF at Montlhéry. Practice on the Friday before the race was wet, but the following day it was dry and Wimille showed that despite the Miramas defeat, the T59 was still a car to be reckoned with, by setting the fastest time, beating Dreyfus's T145 Delahaye and Sommer's Talbot, although he used a tactic prevalent in 21st century Formula 1 and ran with an almost empty tank. Despite the fast

18 July 1937: Wimille passes the grandstands during his winning run in the Grand Prix de la Marne with the sports T59 Grand-Mère.

practice lap, Wimille was not the favourite, it was evident that the T145 Delahayes were faster cars. Wimille was facing an additional handicap; it was a 63-lap race, a distance of 305 miles (492km), so the T59 would need to refuel, whereas the main rivals would go through the race non-stop.

Race day had the glorious weather always associated with the Reims-Gueux circuit and a large crowd came to watch. At the start, Wimille left the field behind, but after a lap he was only just ahead of Dreyfus who was sitting on the T59's tail. Dreyfus stayed a few lengths behind Wimille until the third lap, but as the cars ran down to La Garenne Corner, before the start of the fast poplar-lined Thillois Straight, a front tyre burst on the Delahaye and the car spun off the road. Dreyfus came to a halt with a cut wrist and his race was run. The second T145 Delahaye, driven by Carrière, had not practised so had started from the back of the grid, but had come through the field to second place and began to pursue Wimille. On lap 22, Carrière suffered the same fate as Dreyfus, the Goodrich-Colombes tyres fitted to the Delahayes were not equal to the weight of the cars, the speed and heat of the day. Carrière limped into the pits, changed the wheel and restarted in fourth place, but nine laps later another tyre burst so he retired from the race. After 30 laps, Wimille had a lead of 70 seconds over Sommer; although the Talbots had outrun the T59 at Miramas, they did not have the pace to hold it at Reims. There were dark but unproved suggestions that the T59 was running on a fuel mixture which was more exotic than the *ternaire* stipulated in the regulations and this had permitted a substantial increase in the compression ratio. On lap 32, Wimille pulled into the pits and the car was refuelled; his lead over Sommer was still 31 seconds when he rejoined the race.

Chiron had passed Sommer and taken up the pursuit of the T59, but the pace it was setting was too fast and on lap 45 he had to retire with a blown head gasket, while Sommer also began to drop back as his Talbot was misfiring. On lap 52, with a lead of over two minutes, Wimille came into the pits again for fuel and a tyre check. The second stop gave rise to more grumblings about illegal fuel and high consumption, but the stop was probably a precaution after the Carthage mistake. In the closing laps, Wimille eased off, Sommer had slowed and dropped to fourth place, he was lapped by the T59 in the closing laps, as was Le Bègue's Talbot in third place. 'Toto' Roche, the race director, flagged off Wimille with an enormous chequered flag; he finished 2min 49.8sec ahead of Divo's Talbot which was in second place. This was the last race for a Molsheim-entered T59 and the model left the front-line racing world in a blaze of glory. As a grand prix car its career had been uneasy, but as a sports racer it had been superb. The critics who dismissed it as a thinly disguised grand prix car overlooked the great advances in development that had happened since the French sports car race series had started at the beginning of 1936. The T145 Delahaye was an out-and-out racing car and the works-entered T150C Talbots were far removed from their production siblings. The gallant and triumphant *Grand-Mère* had served its purpose, it raced no more and fitted with a more elegant radiator cowl, it was sold to one of Ettore Bugatti's most favoured customers, King Leopold of the Belgians.

The sports T59 had been entered for the Grand Prix du Comminges, on 1 August, but this was cancelled as there was a shortage of entries. Freed from this distraction, Bugatti was able to concentrate on a much more important aim, to win the Million Franc prize. Only six weeks remained to the deadline of 31st August. The T59 monoposto had been fitted with the unsupercharged alloy 4½-litre T50B engine, probably one taken from a T57S45, so it was eligible for the forthcoming grand prix formula and complied with the prize regulations. Montlhéry was booked for a preliminary test on Sunday, 15 August, with the intention of making an attempt for the prize the next day. On Saturday, Wimille left his home at Beaulieu on the Riviera and set off for Paris in his T57 Ventoux coupé, accompanied by Raph who had been convalescing there since his Le Mans accident. Running along the N7 outside the town of Trets, about 12 miles (20km) east of Aix-en-Provence, the T57 collided with a tanker lorry that was crossing the main road. The T57 was wrecked while both occupants received facial injuries and were severely bruised. They were taken to hospital in Aix, then moved to a clinic in Marseille.

The accident was a severe setback to Bugatti; Wimille would not be discharged from the clinic for a week, and there was a possibility that he would not be fit to drive before 31 August, and if he was fit, might still be below his best form. Jean Bugatti tested the T59/50B at Montlhéry and decided to postpone the attempt until Monday, 23 August, he was anxious as a spell of bad weather or a major mechanical disaster could wreck the chances of winning the prize.

Benoist was told he would drive the car if Wimille was not fit. Benoist was reluctant, as he felt he no longer had the ability to produce the necessary performance and Wimille's effort in April had shown it would not be an easy task. Benoist practised with the car during the week and was unable to achieve the target speed. There was some comfort for Bugatti; when the rival Delahaye team arrived at Montlhéry with the T145, the gearbox broke after Dreyfus had covered a few practice laps and the car was taken back to the factory for repairs. At the end of the week, Jean Bugatti was told that although Wimille's doctors would be discharging him from the clinic on the 23rd, they had decreed he would not be fit to drive before Friday, 27th. Benoist was told that the attempt would be made on the 23rd and Jean Bugatti decided the run would be made in the late afternoon when the temperature was cooler. Donning his dark leather jacket and light overall trousers, Benoist set off on the attempt. He made a disappointly slow start and his standing lap time was 5min 26sec, over eight seconds slower than Wimille's first lap in April, and although in the next eight laps he was achieving the target time of 5min 7sec, he was unable to go faster and clear off the deficit of the first lap. Frantic signals came from the pit, in response Benoist recorded 5min 3.7sec on lap 11 and the deficit began to diminish. He continued to lap at 5min 5sec but it was too late, the T59/50B finished the 16 laps and was 9.5 seconds outside the time limit. The slow first lap had been the decisive factor.

Benoist knew he could go no faster, so the Bugatti team waited at Montlhéry hoping that Wimille would be fit enough to make an attempt before the deadline. On the 27th, Dreyfus brought out the T145 Delahaye and began his run at 10am. He too made a poor start and lost time on the standing lap, but unlike Benoist he was able to make up time and was lapping steadily in 5min 5sec, he was still behind the target speed, but in the closing laps he drove right on the limit, the off-side rear tyre was down to the canvas, but he did not ease off and finished the 200km inside the target by a mere 4.9 seconds. His average speed was exactly the same as that recorded by Wimille in April, 91.072mph (146.654kmh). He was greeted by a delighted Delahaye team, the prize was in sight for them, and they could sit back and wait for the Bugatti to set a higher speed.

Wimille arrived at Montlhéry on Friday afternoon, having flown from Nice; he was pale and his face was scarred by the injuries. On Monday morning, he and Benoist took the T59/50B out for practice but the oil pressure was dropping and the tests came to a halt when a shaft broke in the gearbox. The car was taken back to the Bugatti depot in Paris where the engine was changed and the gearbox was repaired. The Delahaye team waited and the Bugatti did not reappear at Montlhéry until 4pm the

31 August 1937, Montlhéry. Wimille is about to start his abortive attempt to win the Million Franc prize in the T59/50B. His face is bruised and swollen from the road accident.

following afternoon, with only eight hours left in hand. A large contingent of the French press waited expectantly, aware of the unfolding drama. For Bugatti it was now or never, but there was the tactical advantage that if the Delahaye time was beaten in the late afternoon or early evening, there would be insufficient time for Dreyfus to make another attempt. At 5pm Wimille began a warming-up lap, but to the dismay of the Bugatti team, he returned to the pits with a broken half shaft. Eight mechanics, led by Aumaitre attacked the T59/50B and by 6.30pm the axle had been changed and the car reassembled. The Delahaye team had decided that Dreyfus would go out and make another attempt as soon as Wimille started his run, thus ensuring that if the Bugatti set a better time, there was still a chance to win back the prize.

Wimille did a warming-up lap then came to the line and at 6.42pm began the attempt for the prize, two minutes later, Dreyfus set off with the Delahaye. Wimille did his first lap in 5min 20sec, a time which was bettered by Dreyfus, but after two laps, the Bugatti pulled into the pits as it was

misfiring. It was stationary for six minutes while the plugs were changed then it went to the line to start another attempt. The time was 7.2pm and Wimille protested to Jean Bugatti that it was too late, darkness would have fallen before he could finish the run, but Bugatti brushed away the protests and told him to start. Dreyfus was still reeling off the laps and Wimille set off again, but the engine of the T59/50B was smoking, Dreyfus said he could smell the smoke as he started his fifth lap and realised that Wimille was in trouble. As Dreyfus completed the lap, he saw the Bugatti in the pits, a piston had picked up and broken a ring. The attempt to win the Million Franc prize was over and a distraught Jean Bugatti conceded victory to the Delahaye.

Although the prize had been lost, Jean Bugatti was unwilling to admit defeat, he nursed the hope that a repaired T59/50B would be able to beat the time set by the Delahaye and prove that the Bugatti was the faster car. The team made several visits to Montlhéry during September and on Sunday, 19th, Wimille made another attempt on the Delahaye's figures, but the run was abandoned almost as soon as it started. Jean Bugatti decided it was essential that the run should be made during the Paris Salon as this would ensure the greatest publicity. The Salon closed on Sunday, 17 October and on the preceding Thursday, Wimille was at Montlhéry making an apparent final test before the run. Once more there was trouble and Wimille was back at the track on Monday 18th for further testing. Jean Bugatti realised that the efforts were fruitless and the publicity of the failures was harming the reputation of Bugatti, and probably equally important, precious funds were being wasted, so on 25 October he finally admitted defeat. There was a sad sequel; Jean Viel, the engineer who had supervised the preparation of the T59/50B was made the scapegoat and was dismissed.

The T57 was finding some buyers in Britain, but most of the customers wanted a fast touring car and were less interested in the sporting aspects of the marque. The Bugatti was being sold in an increasingly competitive market, sales were being affected by a rejuvenated Lagonda which had been redesigned by W. O. Bentley, by an improved Rolls-Royce-built 4¼-litre Bentley and by a newcomer, the Railton, built to high standards with components from the American Hudson and offering remarkable value. The change in the character of the road-going models and the lack of a modern competition car meant that Bugatti was playing a diminishing part in British motor racing. The T59s had disappeared, being unable to offer a challenge to the ERAs which now dominated British racing and only a few Bugattis still raced at Brooklands. At the Easter meeting on Monday, 29 March, Charles Mervyn White, driving the T51 formerly owned by Earl Howe, won the First Easter Handicap, lapping the track at 126.23mph (202.97kmh) then followed this by taking third place in another handicap and improved his lap speed to 126.41mph (203.26kmh). Mervyn White

took the T51 to Ireland on 22 May where he ran in the Cork Grand Prix, a handicap race on a very fast circuit. He lost control on the winding back leg of the circuit and died of the injuries he received when he was thrown out of the car. It was a coincidence that he had raced the T51 at Cork in 1936 and had crashed at the same place, but escaped with cuts and bruises. At the Whitsun meeting, held on Monday, 10 May, two days before the Coronation of King George VI, Stephen Mond with a T37 won the first heat of the Coronation Mountain Trophy, a handicap held in heats and a final. It was a strong indication of changing times that Mervyn White and Mond were the only Bugatti drivers to gain success at Brooklands during the season.

With the victory at Le Mans and the successes gained by the sports T59, it had been a good year for Bugatti, although some of the glory had been taken away by the fiasco of the withdrawal from the Grand Prix de l'ACF and much more prestige had been lost by the failure in the Million Franc prize competition. The successes that were gained probably owed as much to the skills of Wimille as to the qualities of the cars. The subsequent attempts to equal the Delahaye's speed at Montlhéry had done nothing but harm. If Jean Bugatti had accepted defeat at the time, the failure could have been attributed to Wimille's lack of fitness after his accident, but the subsequent abortive efforts had revealed all too much of the decline at Molsheim. In the autumn, the press discussed the prospects for the new grand prix formula in 1938 and it was reported that Bugatti would be building two unsupercharged 4½-litre cars.

In the wider world, the economic situation of France was still poor. The devaluation of the franc in the autumn of 1936 had been too little, too late; the economy was still in the doldrums and the sale of manufactured goods, including cars was sluggish. The luxury car market was particularly

badly affected, and for Bugatti, there was the problem that Delahaye and Delage were selling *Grands Routiers* which were as effective as the T57 and were cheaper. The greatest hope for the stimulation of the economy lay in rearmament to meet the rapidly-growing German threat. In Britain, rearmament had begun in 1935 and the economic benefits were beginning to dispel the effects of the depression. In France the political parties had been so involved with vicious in-fighting that the German threat had been ignored until February 1937 when the Chamber of Deputies approved a budget for building up the French armed forces to match those of Germany, which had become formidable.

The Luftwaffe was the largest air force in Europe, the German navy was being equipped with new, powerful ships and a large submarine fleet, tanks were being mass-produced and the length of compulsory military service had been doubled from 12 months to two years. War was already too close to France for comfort, the Civil War was raging in Spain; Germany and Italy had agreed with France and Britain that there would be no international intervention in Spain, but in May 1937 this agreement was abandoned by Germany and Italy. Their pretext was the active support of the Republican cause by Soviet Russia and their fear that Communism would spread throughout Europe if the Republicans were victorious. The Condor Legion or German Volunteer Force began to play an active part in the war and provided a massive boost to the Nationalist forces. An air of cynical resignation was growing in France that another war was likely. It was accepted that rearmament was necessary, but any wider benefits from it would take at least a year to spread through the depressed economy. For Bugatti, there must have been the hope that arms contracts would be a lifeline, as there were no more orders for railcars in sight once a batch for the newly created SNCF had been completed.

Chapter 17

Tribulation, triumph and tragedy

THE NEW GRAND PRIX formula came into force on 1 January 1938, Mercedes-Benz was already testing the new W154 and it was known that Auto Union was working on the 3-litre D-type. With the aim of making Alfa Romeo more competitive, the company had bought a majority holding in the Scuderia Ferrari in March 1937 and the cars were entered by Alfa Corse during the 1937 season. On 1 January, coinciding with the new formula, it was announced that the Scuderia's workshops at Modena were being closed and the competition activities of the company would be conducted from the Milan factory at Portello, where Vittorio Jano was busy working on three designs for the new formula, the Tipo 308, the Tipo 312 and the Tipo 316. It seemed likely that with such divided effort, success would probably elude Alfa Romeo, but there was great determination to restore the company to its former glory. Even the Maserati brothers, who had sold the control of their company to a rich industrialist, Adolfo Orsi, were rumoured to be working on a new 3-litre car. In France, partly funded by the Million prize, Delahaye was building a monoposto around the V-12 engine.

This activity must have been a source of envy and frustration at Molsheim where there was no money available to build a new car. The financial situation had deteriorated to a point where one of the company's four bankers had sent a team of consultants and inspectors to the factory to supervise expenditure and enforce economies. The unsold stock of T57s was vested in the bank to secure the company's credit and a ban had been imposed on racing. It seems the ban was lifted sufficiently to permit the preparation of a car which offered the semblance of a new design and could appear at the GP de l'ACF in July to collect the balance of the 400,000FF prize. The T50B engine design, which was almost three years old, was revised and a new version was built with a bore and stroke of 78mm, giving a capacity of 2,980cc. The square dimensions indicated a realisation of the direction that engine design was about to take.

It seems that the detailed work was done by Antonio Pichetto, but in addition to the revision of the earlier engine, he also produced a development of the T50B that was virtually a new design. Before he began, Pichetto must have studied earlier Mercedes-Benz designs and also glanced at the work of Jano. In principle, the upper part of a T50B block was cut away, leaving the base which carried the crankshaft. For this engine, a new base was made on which eight separate steel cylinder liners were mounted. Screwed to the top of each liner was an individual cylinder head, cast in bronze, with the same combustion chamber and port dimensions as the T50B. The whole structure was covered in a superbly made duralumin water jacket, built up in several pieces and retained with screws. So well was this made, that it was difficult to see where the plates joined. As an indication that the T50B design was being abandoned, the pattern for the camshaft gear housing of the T50B was used but was cut and joined, as the height of the new engine was 17mm less. In using separate cast heads and a fitted sheet alloy water jacket, Pichetto had followed the design of the W25 and W125 Mercedes-Benz. A new supercharger layout was used. There were two superchargers driven by a common shaft from the front of the engine and mounted on the off side. Each supercharger fed four cylinders and in appearance there were similarities to the 8C Alfa Romeo engines of Jano. The output of this engine is not known, but it was probably similar to the 3-litre T50B which developed 275bhp at 6,000rpm. This could offer no challenge to the German teams, as the prototype W154 was showing 430bhp in early bench testing, but was comparable with Alfa Romeo which had produced 295bhp from the Tipo 308 and 320bhp from the Tipo 312.

The advantages of this engine, which has subsequently become known as the 'compound' engine, over the 3-litre T50B are questionable. It had a lower centre of gravity when installed in a car and the separate heads would have reduced the cost of subsequent modified head designs, but it is unlikely that there would have been an appreciable weight saving and the concept of the twin superchargers was already obsolete as the German teams were adopting

23 April 1938: In the early laps of the Cork Grand Prix, Wimille comes out of Victoria Cross Corner in the 3-litre-engined T59/50B. Louis Gerard slides his Delage in pursuit.

two-stage supercharging. Although the straight-eight engine was still accruing glory, the V-engine designs were coming to the fore. This engine represented a rather sad end of a great line, as it was the last racing engine to come from Molsheim before the Second World War. The 1938 racing programme, such as it was, centred around the supercharged 3-litre engine. No attention seems to have been given to the possibility of running a car with the unsu-

percharged 4½-litre T50B unit. Perhaps it was felt that after the failures at Montlhéry, there was no purpose in continuing with its development.

The French diversion with sports car racing had ended, the GP de l'ACF was to be a proper formula grand prix again, as was the Grand Prix de Pau. Other organis-

ers had abandoned their sports car races so Le Mans would reign once more as the supreme sports car event of the French season. There was no Bugatti entry for Le Mans, although the T57Gs remained at Molsheim and would have been fully competitive. It is suggested that Jean Bugatti wanted to run the T57Gs, but his father forbade it, saying there was insufficient opposition to justify the entry. It is more likely that the bankers would not sanction the expenditure, as to run at Le Mans and to fail would be more damaging to their fragile investment than not to take part, perhaps also, Ettore Bugatti had admitted to them that a well-prepared T145 Delahaye might be too fast for the T57G, and the Talbots had also been improved.

The GP de Pau was the first race to be run under the new formula rules on Sunday, 10 April. Two T154 Mercedes-Benz were entered, opposed by two Tipo 308 Alfa Romeos, one driven by Nuvolari and two stripped sports T145 Delahayes. There were no Auto Unions; their racing programme was in disarray as Bernd Rosemeyer had been killed on 28 January during a record attempt on the Frankfurt-Darmstadt autobahn. Wimille was entered with the T59/50B, but the car did not appear at the meeting. During practice, Nuvolari crashed when his car caught fire and he escaped with slight burns and announced that he was retiring from racing. The race had a sensational result. From the start, Dreyfus's T145 Delahaye held onto Caracciola's W154 and took the lead on lap seven. He ran through the race non-stop and pulled out a two-minute lead when the W154 stopped to refuel. The gap remained and Dreyfus won to huge acclamation. For France, this was the long-awaited renaissance in grand prix racing, the unsupercharged engines seemed to be the equal of the supercharged, and the Million Franc prize had produced all that had been expected of it.

The next grand prix was in Ireland on Saturday, 23 April, over the very fast 6.1-mile (9.8km) Carrigrohane circuit, outside Cork. The circuit had a 2.7-mile (4.35km) main straight which had been used for a successful attempt on the World motorcycle speed record in 1930. The organisers had hoped to attract the German teams, but after the result at Pau, the entry of Dreyfus was almost as prestigious. It must

have been pointed out to the bankers that if a car was to take the balance of the prize at Reims, it would need a preliminary canter, as Wimille was entered with a T59/50B, the unsuccessful Million Franc prize car, fitted with a new attractive radiator cowling, an exhaust pipe running under the side of the car and other minor modifications. It is not certain whether the compound engine or the T50B was fitted, it seems more likely that it was the latter, but the matter has never been resolved. The car arrived late and had a number of minor troubles and Wimille was only able to do three slow practice laps. During scrutineering, the car was weighed at 2,044lb (929kg), 84lb (38kg) heavier than the Delahaye. Wimille started the 33-lap, 200-mile (321km) race from the back of the grid and began slowly, unfamiliar with the difficult circuit. The race was led initially by Bira with an elderly 8CM Maserati, but Dreyfus took the lead on the second lap, while Wimille came through the field to pass Comotti with the second T145 Delahaye and move into third place, 42 seconds behind Bira who was pulling away. It was noticeable that the Delahayes were faster on the narrow, bumpy back leg of the course, although the Bugatti was timed at 147.25mph (236.77kmh) on the straight, the fastest speed recorded in the race. The T59/50B was misfiring, and Wimille lost 55 seconds when he refuelled and was then lapped by Dreyfus. On lap 21, the Bugatti stopped at the Poulavone Hairpin, halfway round the circuit with either a broken valve or broken valve springs, although one report said a piston had failed, and Wimille walked back to the pits. Dreyfus went on to win his second grand prix of the season, confirming French views that they had returned to grand prix glory.

The levy from the driving licence fees had continued to be paid over to the *Fonds de Course* and by the spring of 1938 another FF1 million was waiting to be distributed. The committee of the *Fonds* realised that although the Million Franc competition had

produced a satisfactory result, the competition itself had been difficult to conduct, so it was decided that the next award would be made to the company which produced evidence that it was working on a new design for a grand prix car. Delahaye, with victories at Pau and Cork and with the new monoposto T155 half-built, expected to be the lucky recipient, but Antony Lago instructed his designer Walter Becchia, to make some detailed drawings of a proposed supercharged 3-litre V-16 Talbot which they had discussed in general terms. The plans were shown to the Committee and an announcement was made at the end of April that Lago would receive an award of 600,000FF to assist in the building of the new car. There were bitter recriminations between Delahaye and the committee which ended in an announcement that Delahaye would boycott the Grand Prix de l'ACF in July. It was an indication of how Bugatti's standing had fallen that the company was not given any consideration when the grant was made, nor was any enquiry made at Molsheim about the possibility of new designs emerging. It may have been realised by the *Fonds* committee that any grant would probably be used to reduce the company's debt and would not be directed towards a new car.

Wimille had been entered with the T59/50B for the Gran Premio di Tripoli on 15 May, but the car stayed at Molsheim. The Delahaye team raced but harsh reality shattered French hopes and added to Delahaye's misery, when Dreyfus could only take seventh place behind two Maserati voiturettes and the race was dominated by Mercedes-Benz. Despite the attractions of the new formula, there was a paucity of grand prix races in 1938 and almost eight weeks elapsed before the next event. At Le Mans, a T135 Delahaye was victorious after the V-12 T145s had retired, but the winning car covered 67 miles (108km) less than the T57G in 1937. The Grand Prix de l'ACF at Reims on 3 July, was the major French race of the season and had been restored to its full glory. To the satisfaction of the organisers, the race saw the first appearance of Auto Union in 1938 and the team produced four cars, but these were an interim design and were poorly prepared. The loss of Rosemeyer was still affecting the team which lacked a front-line driver. The race was expected to be another demonstration of Mercedes-Benz superiority; the Delahaye team had stayed away and French hopes rested on three stripped sports T150C Talbots and the promised Bugatti.

There was no sign of the car during the practice sessions on the Friday before the race. The T59/50B did not arrive at Reims until 4.45pm on Saturday afternoon, after practice had finished. Little had been done to it since the Cork race and it is not known which version of the 3-litre engine was being used. The race day was superb and the T59/50B was pushed out on to the back row of the grid behind the Talbots and Auto Unions, the latter team having been reduced to two cars when Hermann Müller crashed in practice and slightly damaged himself as well as the car. When the flag fell, Wimille made a superb start and driving alongside the pit wall, swept past the three Talbots and drew level with the two Auto Unions. The three W154 Mercedes-Benzs led the field as the cars came down the long straight to the Thillois Hairpin, but Wimille was still on the tail of Hasse's Auto Union and well ahead of the second car, driven by Kautz, which had clipped a wall on the first corner in Gueux village. As the cars rounded Thillois, Hasse spun, it is uncertain if the Bugatti collided with the Auto Union or Wimille went off the road to avoid a collision, but the Auto Union and the Bugatti came slowly up the pits straight and pulled into the pits. The T59/50B had a broken oil pipe and retired, and it is unlikely that there were many regrets in the Bugatti pit, the car cannot have been prepared to last a 300-mile (500km) race, and the 80,000FF balance of the Prize had been secured.

After the Reims race, Wimille was released from his contract with Bugatti and went to Milan to sign up with Alfa Corse for the rest of the season. With the ban on racing, it would have been unreasonable to have kept him at Molsheim kicking his heels and his departure, even if temporary, meant that the wages bill was relieved of one expensive item. His release was a most dramatic signal to the world of the decline of Bugatti as a racing power and 'Auslander' the Continental correspondent of *Motor Sport* commented: '. . . it does look as if we have seen the last of Bugatti in racing under the present Grand Prix system'.

The minor grands prix in which amateur-driven Bugattis had raced in the 1920s and the early 1930s, had disappeared. Some, such as Albi and Peronne had become voiturette races, but the circus of minor grands prix, run to the grand prix formula had gone. The two-year break while France raced sports cars along with the new formula had killed off the lesser grand prix races in France, many of the Italian organisers had also adopted voiturette racing, being unwilling to provide a stage for examples of German supremacy. One of the few minor grand prix races which had survived was the small, rural event at Chimay, the Grand Prix des Frontières. This was held on 7 June, and was won by a 20-year-old driver, Maurice Trintignant, driving the T51 in which his elder brother had been killed at Peronne in 1933. It was the start of a distinguished career and in the future Trintignant would race another Bugatti in very different circumstances. The British amateur, Taso Mathieson, finished third at Chimay in a stripped T57S. At Brooklands there were only two Bugatti victories during the season. At the Whitsun meeting on Monday, 6 June, Charles Brackenbury, driving a T35C, won the Whitsun Short Handicap lapping the track at 123.28mph (198.23kmh), then at the closing meeting on Saturday, 15 October, Martin Soames, in a T37 owned by Cleveland Harmer, a London dealer in second-hand Bugattis,

won a handicap on the Campbell circuit. Soames was later killed in action, flying a Wellington bomber, in 1941.

The world had little real enthusiasm for motor racing in 1938 as the threat of war had been growing since the beginning of the year. Germany had been attempting to annexe Austria since 1934, but had been resisted by Italy. The sanctions against Italy following the invasion of Abyssinia had persuaded Italy to form the Axis alliance with Germany and with the making of this alliance, Italian opposition to the Austrian annexation had diminished. Emboldened by this and by the apparent lack of opposition from Britain and France, civil unrest was provoked in Austria by Nazi agitators and with this pretext for intervention, the *Anschluss*, or annexation of Austria, took place on 12 March. German forces occupied Austria in a bloodless invasion and the country was incorporated as part of the Greater Reich. There was reluctance in Britain to become involved in Central European politics, while in France, there was domestic political chaos, the government of Leon Blum had fallen in January, having been replaced by a government led by Camille Chautemps, which had itself been replaced by another Blum ministry in April. Blum had failed to have his budget ratified by the Chamber of Deputies, and resigned, and a new ministry was formed by Edouard Daladier on 8 April. Germany then claimed its right to annexe the Sudetenland, a province of Czechoslovakia which adjoined the German border, on the pretext that the German-speaking inhabitants were being persecuted by the Czechs. On 29 April, Daladier signed an agreement with the British prime minister Neville Chamberlain, promising to defend Czechslovakia against German aggression.

The Anglo-French agreement did nothing to stop German claims, Hitler declared German troops would march into the Sudetenland if his demands were not met. In France and Britain, desperate attempts were made to speed up rearmament, and on 5 September, the Maginot Line, the defence system on the Franco-German frontier was fully manned, all leave was stopped for the French Army and mobilisation of the army reserves began. At a meeting with Hitler, Chamberlain and Daladier agreed the they would try to persuade the Czechs to accept the German occupation, but the Czechs refused. On 26 September, the British fleet was mobilised and two days later, Hitler announced that German occupation of the Sudetenland was imminent. Chamberlain and Daladier returned to Munich and on 30 September, an agreement was signed conceding the German claims, despite Czech opposition. The threat of war seemed to have been averted and Britain and France had gained time to continue rearmament. In reality, neither had been fit to go to war, the French Army, although nominally the largest in Europe had out-of-date equipment and the aircraft of both countries were largely obsolete.

A commission from the War Ministry visited Molsheim and inspected the factory, and after some delay it produced a report in February 1939 which confirmed the suitability of the company to undertake aero-engine sub-contracts. The prospect of a government contract must have given relief to a hard-pressed Jean Bugatti. The T57 was still being produced but was not selling in sufficient numbers to make a significant difference to the parlous finances. A supercharger had been fitted to the T57 which became the T57C, the output of the engine was increased to 160bhp giving a remarkable performance for a full-bodied touring car and deliveries to customers began at the end of 1938. The chassis was also uprated. Lockheed hydraulic brakes were finally adopted with twin master cylinders and the expensive De Ram shock absorbers were replaced by telescopic Alliquants.

Perhaps the prospect of an influx of government moneys softened the hearts of the bankers, or perhaps Jean Bugatti decided to go racing anyway, but plans were made for a limited racing programme in

1939. A new monoposto was built, using a T59 frame fitted with hydraulic brakes and with a supercharged 4.7-litre T50B engine, it was fitted with a rather fuller body than the 1938 3-litre car. Wimille had returned to Molsheim as Alfa Corse had dispensed with his services. Italy was claiming that France should cede Tunis, Nice and Corsica, relations between France and Italy were tense and Mussolini had decreed that no foreign drivers should be engaged by Italian teams. Wimille was free to drive whatever car Bugatti could prepare for him. His first drive was at La Turbie on Thursday, 13 April, where the hill-climb coincided with the end of the Paris-Nice Rally. Unfortunately for Bugatti hopes, Hans Stuck was entered with a short chassis 6-litre C-type Auto Union and this was too quick for the new T59/50B, which was taken to the event almost untested. Stuck broke the course record, climbing in 3min 30.2sec and Wimille was four seconds slower, although there was the minor satisfaction of setting a time eight seconds better than Sommer with a Tipo 308 Alfa Romeo, which although nominally a private entry, had all the marks of full Alfa Corse support.

The Olazur oil company sponsored the Coupe de Paris meeting at Montlhéry on Sunday, 7 May which was little more than a club event. There was a programme of races over the 2.1-mile (3.3km) short circuit which used part of the banked track and the first section of the road course. The main race was a 30-lap Formule Libre event and Wimille was entered with the 4.7-litre T59/50B, the opposition coming from Sommer with the Tipo 308 Alfa Romeo, two new 4½-litre off-set monoposto Talbots driven by Le Bègue and Carrière, and several stripped T135 Delahayes. Before the race, Sommer took the Tipo 308 on to the banked track and set a new outright record at 148.44mph (238.69kmh). This was a record easily within the capabilities of the Bugatti and it is surprising that Wimille did not reply. In the race, Wimille took the lead

from the start, pursued by Sommer; at 15 laps he held a two-second lead, but in the latter part of the race he began to pull away and at the end, won by nine seconds from Sommer, Le Begue and Carrière.

Another raid had been made upon the collection of T59 components which remained at Molsheim. Evidently inspired by *Grand-Mère*, a car was built up with a sports two-seat body which in appearance had much in common with the new monoposto. This was fitted with an unsupercharged 4½-litreT50B engine, and a central change T57S45 gearbox, with the starter motor mounted on it. The car was entered for the Grand Prix du Centenaire, a 50-lap race run over a 2.8-mile (4.5km) circuit outside the city of Luxembourg on Sunday, 4 June, celebrating the centenary of the foundation of the Duchy. It was a major event which attracted three Alfa Corse entries. Two of the Alfa Romeos were Tipo 412s, built for the 1939 season and comprising a 2900B chassis fitted with a 4½-litre V-12 engine taken from the 1937 12C-37 grand prix car and running unsupercharged; these were driven by Giuseppe Farina and Clemente Biondetti and had come from a 1-2 victory in the Antwerp Grand Prix on 22 May. The third Alfa Romeo was a 2900B similar to the winner of the Mille Miglia and the Spa 24-hour race in 1938 and driven by Emilio Villoresi. At the start, Farina took the lead with Wimille on his heels, the Alfa Romeo held a narrow lead until lap 20 when Farina pulled into the pits to refuel. He was stationary for 2min 5sec and Wimille took the lead, only to pull in for fuel himself a lap later. His pit work was good and the Bugatti was away in less than a minute. On lap 22, Farina stopped again while his mechanics fiddled with the engine, he lost nearly seven minutes and retired after another slow lap. Wimille had a lead of 2min 17sec over Biondetti and he eased off to win and to receive the Coupe from the Princess Louis of Bourbon-Parma, the sister-in-law of the Grand Duchess

13 April 1939: Wimille in the new T59/50B takes second place at La Turbie.

4 June 1939: Wimille in the T59/50B sports car beating the Alfa Romeos in the Grand Prix de Luxembourg.

Charlotte. The local Luxembourg driver, Joseph Zigrand, was seventh in his light-weight-bodied T44.

Bugatti returned to Le Mans for the 24-hour race a fortnight later, on 17 June. The car was driven by Wimille and the faithful Veyron, who was still employed at Molsheim. It was based on a T57C, a chassis frame had been requisitioned from the factory stores and selected by Robert Aumaitre in January 1939. The supercharged engine was virtually in standard trim, although the carburation had been modified and there had been careful detailed tuning; it was reported to have developed 200bhp. It was fitted with a T57S45 gearbox, a higher axle ratio and T59 wheels. The body was a 'tank' and a development of the 1936 style, but with a cleaner line; a spotlight was recessed into the off-side of the body pointing into the kerb. The opposition came from three works 4½-litre T150C Talbots, three private Talbots, a variety of Delahayes and Delages, while the unknown quantities were two new V-12 4½-litre Lagondas, which had been designed by W. O. Bentley. Sommer had been expected to drive a 2900B Alfa Romeo, but was entered by Alfa Corse with a 6C-2500 coupé. In a typical Bugatti manner, the T57C was presented for scrutineering only 15 minutes before the closing deadline on the Wednesday before the race. Race day was fine with a clear sky and at the start, Chinetti with a Talbot took the lead. Wimille was not drawn into a battle for the lead and after an hour was running in fourth place. Chinetti, who was sharing the Talbot with Mathieson, continued to hold the lead as darkness fell at 10pm, and he was followed by the Delahaye of Mazaud/Mongin and the Delage of Gerard/Monneret, while the Bugatti was still in fourth place, a lap behind the leader. The correspondent of *Motor Sport* noted that the side spotlight on the T57C was very effective in picking up the line on right-hand corners.

At 2am, the Mazaud/Mongin Delahaye,

caught fire as it came into the pits and was burnt out, then Mathieson went off the road at Tertre Rouge when the Talbot threw a tyre tread, so at 4am, the Gerard/ Monneret Delage led the Bugatti by a lap, but shortly afterwards, the T57C stopped on the Mulsanne straight as a wheel was breaking up. After a delay, the car came slowly round to the pits and was stationary for ten minutes while the wheel was changed and the car was inspected. The delay dropped it back to sixth place, but Wimille speeded up and by 10am was back in second place, three laps behind the leading Delage. The T57C was lapping faster than the leader but had little chance of catching it, then at noon, the Delage came into the pits with the engine misfiring, the plugs were changed, but it stopped a lap later for another plug change. During the second stop, the Bugatti went by and took the lead. Gerard set off in pursuit but with little chance of regaining the lead, as the misfire had not been cured. By 4pm, Wimille and Veyron had built up a three-lap lead and to the delight of the crowd, the Bugatti was flagged off as the victor. It had covered 2,083 miles (3,349km), a record distance, and apart from the defective wheel had run faultlessly. It was the last major victory for Bugatti, the end of the road had almost been reached.

When the Munich Agreement was signed and the Sudetenland was ceded to Germany, Hitler had declared it would be his final territorial demand in Europe, but despite this, German forces occupied the remainder of Czechoslovakia on 14 March while the Czechs stood helplessly aside, realising that resistance would be pointless. Since January, Germany had been demand-

17/18 June 1939: The T57C heads the line-up at the start of the Le Mans 24-Hour race.

17/18 June 1939: Veyron brings the T57C round Mulsanne Corner.

ing that Poland should hand over the port of Danzig, which separated East Prussia from the rest of Germany. The Poles had refused and on 31 March Britain and France signed a pact guaranteeing to defend Poland against attack. Despite this pact, German demands became more strident and insistent, and there was intense diplomatic activity, but war seemed inevitable.

In England, as in the rest of Europe, there was the constant hope that war would

be averted and although some events were cancelled, the motor racing calendar continued. In November 1937, the Bugatti Owners Club had bought Prescott House, about five miles (8km) north of Cheltenham. The drive, up a steep hill to the house, about half-a-mile (800m) in length, made an ideal short hill-climb course in the British tradition. Club meetings had been held in 1938 and in the first half of the 1939 season but a more ambi-

tious international meeting was held on Sunday, 30 July. To the delight of the club, the 4.7-litre T59/50B was entered for Wimille who came to England, accompanied by Jean Bugatti. As an indication of the regard felt by Ettore Bugatti for the British enthusiasts of the marque, he had given a T51 to the Bugatti Owners Club which had made its debut at a club meeting in June. The Prescott course was too narrow for the T59/50B to give its full performance; it ran with twin rear wheels, following the fashion of most of the leading British hill-climb drivers, and set the second fastest time, climbing in 46.69 seconds, which beat the former record for the hill, but was unable to match the time of Raymond Mays with a 2-litre D-type ERA who recorded 46.14 seconds. With the twin rear wheels, the Bugatti was so wide it could not use the narrow return road to the paddock and had to return down the course.

Wimille and Jean Bugatti had stayed at the Queen's Hotel in Cheltenham for the Prescott meeting, but Wimille did not linger there afterwards, as he had a racing commitment at Comminges the following Sunday, 6 August. He was driving the T59/50B sports car in the Grand Prix du

Comminges. The organisers had attracted the best sports cars in France. The most powerful entries were two works 4½-litre Talbots, driven by Sommer and Le Bègue, which had raced in the GP de l'ACF at Reims as off-set single seaters; these had become sports cars with the addition of a

18 June 1939: Wimille and Veyron sit among the bouquets.

Jean Bugatti. A photograph taken shortly before his death.

rudimentary passenger's seat, wings and lights. There was a pair of 3-litre Delages, two T145 Delahayes and numerous private T135 Delahayes and T150C Talbots. The T145 Delahayes were withdrawn after problems in practice which was dominated by the two works Talbots. Throughout practice, Wimille waited for the T59/50B but the car did not appear until the morning of the race. The race was over 40 laps of the circuit, 272 miles (437km) and the Bugatti started from the back of the grid, the last of the 23 starters. Sommer and Le Bègue led at the end of the first lap, but Wimille had worked his way through the field into third place. On lap five he had closed the gap and went by both Talbots on the main straight. Sommer held on and repassed two laps later, then Wimille took the lead again on lap 10, but Sommer was in front on lap 12. The pair continued to exchange the lead until lap 25 when Wimille came into the pits to refuel, the stop took 55 seconds as a stone thrown up by Sommer's car had punctured the Bugatti's radiator which needed temporary repairs. Wimille rejoined the race in third place and moved up to second when Sommer stopped to change plugs. Sommer restarted but was dropping back and Wimille began to chase Le Bègue whom he caught and passed on lap 30. The Bugatti was overheating so Le Bègue was able to stay on its tail in the closing laps and on the last lap, just before the final corner, he was able to pass. The T50B engine was so hot that Wimille dared not reply and the Talbot crossed the line 0.4 seconds in front.

The day after the Comminges race, Monday, 7 August, the last Brooklands meeting of all was held, but there were no Bugatti victories. The only successes had come at the first meeting of the season on 11 March when Jack Lemon Burton won the Second March Mountain Handicap in his T51A and the Third March Mountain Handicap went to Charles Mortimer driving the red T35B formerly owned by Charles Martin. Finishing second behind Mortimer was a monoposto special, the BHW, driven by Reg Parnell which had been built around the 4.9-litre engine taken from the T54 raced by Kaye Don. Amateur drivers had found little success on the European mainland; on 28 May, Maurice Trintignant had repeated his 1938 victory with his T51 at the GP des Frontières, but that was all.

For Jean Bugatti the pleasures of the English interlude were forgotten on his return. He received a summons to join his father in Paris for a meeting with one of the company's bankers. They were informed that the bank was unwilling to give the company any more credit. It is not known which of the four bankers handling the affairs of Bugatti made the decision, it may have been the merchant bankers, Erlangers, fearing for their invested capital. The day-to-day cash account of the company was held with the Rural Bank of Strasbourg at the local Molsheim branch and all too frequently in 1938/39, Jean Bugatti had been forced to negotiate with the manager before being allowed to draw cash for the factory wages. It seems that the aviation sub-contract had not begun and the bankers must have had doubts if it would be sufficient to meet the mounting debts. Ettore Bugatti acted immediately, he drove in his Royale, with his chauffeur Toussaint, and his Paris secretary, Mme Stella Tayssédre to Laeken, the palace of King Leopold of the Belgians. As well as being a regular customer, Leopold had almost certainly been giving financial support and Bugatti asked if he would give backing to a plan to move all car production to Belgium. Leopold was willing to help and his advisers suggested that Bugatti could take over the Minerva factory at Antwerp, or probably with royal funding, build a new factory in the Antwerp suburbs. Bugatti realised that a receivership could be the next step and he

wanted to forestall this by moving car production out of a receiver's reach. He was willing to leave the remainder of the company's industrial activity at Molsheim.

Despite the imminence of war, the well-to-do French had taken their holidays in August. At La Baule, a race with entry by invitation, had been arranged for Sunday, 13 August, for cars and drivers which had competed at Le Mans in June. An invitation had been given to Wimille and the T57C was being prepared at Molsheim. Perhaps the financial anxieties had caused delays, but the preparation of the car was only completed late in the afternoon of the Friday before the race. Just before dusk, Jean Bugatti took the car out to the N420 which ran from Molsheim to Strasbourg. The road was used for testing cars at speed and had been the main straight for the 1922 GP de l'ACF. Bugatti was accompanied by Robert Aumaitre and he did several runs along the straight reaching speeds of 145mph (235kmh). Mechanics from the factory guarded the side turnings to prevent traffic joining the road when the T57C was approaching. It was 10pm and darkness was falling when Jean Bugatti decided to make a final run. Aumaitre watched from the roadside as Bugatti wanted him to observe how the car handled over a slight bump in the road, leaving the village of Duppigheim, near the site of the 1922 pits and grandstands. As the car approached at maximum speed, a cyclist pedalled on to the road from a footpath, he was struck by the car and thrown over it, escaping with broken wrists, the car ran over the bicycle, then swerved to the left, hit two pear trees, bounced back to the right and hit another tree, which split the car in two, lengthwise. Jean Bugatti, with the steering wheel still grasped in his hands, was thrown out on to the road and was killed instantly.

The news of Jean's death was telephoned to Ettore Bugatti at Laeken, and he left at once for Molsheim, driving through the night in the Royale. Ettore had refused to let Jean race fearing the consequences and appreciating his inestimable value. Despite the ban, his worst fears had been realised, as well as the grief of losing his son, it was an incalculable disaster for his company. The future of Bugatti was built around Jean, he had been trained since childhood as the heir, but just as important, he had shown a design flair and artistic genius that if given full rein, could have approached that of his father. Since 1933, he had managed the Molsheim factory and had been responsible for the major designs which had emerged during the 1930s. He had shed the natural conservatism of Ettore Bugatti and had shown an enthusiasm to embrace technical advances which would have boded well for the future of the company, despite the financial difficulties. Jean's death was mourned not just by his family and his staff at Molsheim, but throughout the motoring and motor racing world, where he was respected not only for his abilities, but also for his natural charm. In a tribute, Noel Domboy described him as the brains and soul of the company. It is probably not an exaggeration to say that when Jean died, the future of Bugatti died with him.

Jean was buried in the family vault in the cemetery at Dorlisheim about a mile (1.5km) south of Molsheim, and within sight of the factory. The remains of the T57C were taken back to Molsheim and buried in a secret site in the factory grounds. For a while the financial disasters were forgotten, and these would soon be of little importance. Three weeks later, at dawn on 1 September, German forces invaded Poland and the Second World War began.

Chapter 18

The dark years

ALTHOUGH MOLSHEIM WAS inside the protective ring of the Maginot Line, it was vulnerable to air attack, so when the war began, Ettore Bugatti was ordered by the War Ministry to strip the factory of all machinery and move it to an empty factory in Bordeaux at 363 Boulevard Alfred Daney which had been formerly used by *Compagnie Industrielle de Matériel de Transport*. The move took place during the autumn of 1939 and by February 1940, the Bordeaux factory was producing crankshafts for the Hispano-Suiza Y45 V-12 engine. When France fell after the German Blitzkreig in May and June 1940, Bugatti was in a difficult position. Although he regarded himself in every respect as a Frenchman, he was still an Italian national and when Italy entered the war as a German ally on 11 June, he became an enemy alien in France. His position improved little when France signed an armistice on 22 June, ending hostilities with Germany and Italy. As an Italian, he was then expected to give full support to the German war effort. Production at Bordeaux had stopped when France fell and German orders were given for the whole plant to be moved back to Molsheim immediately. To forestall this, Bugatti dismissed all his staff on 26 June and some returned to Molsheim.

As a term of the armistice, Alsace was taken from France and incorporated into the German Reich. The Molsheim factory had been inspected and declared suitable for German war production, Bugatti was told that he was required to sell it to a

German engineer, Hans Trippel. The price was fixed at 7.5 million Reichmarks, provided by the Luftwaffe Bank, the factory was sold on 12 August 1940 and Trippel's organisation moved in; on 15 January 1941, the Molsheim factory became Trippel Werke GMbH. Trippel had designed a range of amphibious military vehicles and these were produced, together with torpedo motor parts and some V-1 flying bombs. Bugatti's willingness to sell the factory was later to give rise to suggestions of collaboration, although he subsequently insisted that the sale was imposed on him and the price did not reflect the true value of the factory.

The Bordeaux factory had become a German Army repair shop, where some of the staff were employed until it was bombed by the RAF in November 1940, and they were dismissed. In the bombing some of the wooden patterns from the Molsheim foundry were destroyed. Shortly before the war began, Bugatti had bought the Château d'Ermenonville about 20 miles (30km) north-east of Paris. This was a substantial residence standing in a large estate and he may have hoped to establish a new Molsheim there, but it was impracticable to use it in the wartime conditions. It is possible that the purchase may have added to the financial difficulties. He returned to Paris and established a drawing office in his apartment at 20 Rue Boissière, where he was joined in October 1940 by Noel Domboy and Antonio Pichetto. Some of the staff from Bordeaux joined the work-

shop at 15 Rue Débarcadère. Ettore Bugatti's personal life was in turmoil. His relationship with his wife Barbara had cooled and this may have been a reason for his departure from Molsheim in 1932. At the beginning of the war, Barbara was established in a house at Sauveterre de Guyenne, near Bordeaux, and Ettore began a relationship with a fashion model, Genevieve Delcuze, who was nearly 40 years his junior.

In the small Paris office, new designs were prepared in the anticipation that when the war ended it would be possible to start car production again. The designs ranged from a 10cc engine to power a pedal cycle, to a 62-litre marine engine. The car designs were a mixture of the revolutionary and the conservative. The T68 was a 316/368cc overhead camshaft four cylinder engine intended to run at 12,000rpm, while the T73/73C was a high-performance 1,463cc engine, effectively a scaled-up T68 which was intended to be a high-performance unit for a range of post-war sports and racing cars. In 1942, Bugatti bought an interest in the La Licorne car factory at Courbevoie, on the Seine and some prototypes of these engines were built.

When the war began, Benoist and Wimille who were reservists, were recalled to L'Armée de l'Air. 'Williams', leaving his wife at La Baule, returned to England immediately and joined the British Army. Benoist was posted to Le Bourget outside Paris as armaments officer, and during the

1938: The machine shop at Molsheim.

French collapse in June 1940 he escaped in his T57S towards the south. He was captured by an advancing Panzer unit but seeing a side turning, he accelerated away and escaped before the German troops could open fire. He returned to Paris and joined the Resistance. He became responsible for supervising the dropping of arms and supplies to the Resistance in the Seine-et-Oise department, where his immediate superior was Captain William Grover-Williams, alias 'Williams', who had joined the Special Operations Executive in 1942 and had been parachuted into France on 30 May 1942 as a Resistance leader. They were joined by Wimille who had been demobilised when the armistice was signed. 'Williams' built up a successful circuit, formed a number of sabotage cells, and established a particu-larly effective group at the Citroën factory.

On 1 August 1943, 'Williams' was arrested by the Gestapo, the day after his radio operator had been captured, probably when his transmissions were traced. Working with him, was the husband of Stella Tayssédre who was also arrested. 'Williams' was imprisoned first in Paris, probably at Fresnes prison, then he was taken to Berlin to the notorious Gestapo headquarters in Prince Albrechtstrasse. Despite continuous torture, he gave nothing away. Finally, the Gestapo, realising that no information would be obtained, sent him to Sachsenhausen concentration camp at Oranienburg, north of Berlin, where he was shot on 3 March 1945. Tayssédre was never heard of again. 'Williams''s wife Yvonne was a courier for the circuit, she too was arrested and imprisoned at Fresnes, but survived.

Benoist took over leadership of the group after 'Williams' was arrested. He was captured, but escaped, then he was caught again on 18 June 1944. He too was taken to Fresnes for torture and interrogation, and like 'Williams' he did not break and revealed nothing. He was taken to Buchenwald concentration camp, north of Weimar, and with 34 other French, English and Canadian agents and Resistance members, was hanged on 12 September 1944. Wimille managed to evade arrest until the liberation of Paris in August 1944, then rejoined L'Armée de l'Air until the end of the war.

Epilogue

THE FIGHTING IN EUROPE finished on 8 May 1945 and with the defeat of Japan, the Second World War ended on 14 August 1945. On Sunday, 9 September, the first post-war motor race was held in the Bois de Boulogne in Paris. It was a minor low-key meeting, but of great symbolic significance. It was held on a 1.72-mile (2.7km) circuit and the first race of the day, for cars up to 1,500cc was the Coupe Robert Benoist. The principal race, the 43-lap Coupe des Prisonniers was for Formule Libre cars and was a clear indication to the French that all was well with the World and the dark days were over. First in the list was an entry from Automobiles Ettore Bugatti, the driver was Wimille and the car the 4.7-litre T59/50B. He was matched against Sommer with a works Talbot, Etancelin had appeared with his old Monza Alfa Romeo and 14 other cars made up the field including a T51, a T55 and a T57S. Wimille's car arrived too late to practice, showing that an honourable tradition was being maintained and Ettore Bugatti arrived in his Royale to watch the race. Wimille was up into second place behind Sommer after two laps, and after four laps he took the lead and went on to win by 20 seconds.

To France, Wimille's win indicated that there would be a return to the glorious days of the past, Bugatti would be restored to the former eminence and France would rule the motor racing world again. The reality was very different. Bugatti had no funds to start building cars again, the cash he had received from the sale of Molsheim was almost exhausted and his claim that Molsheim should be restored to him was not being favourably received. In October it was announced that a new racing 1,500cc Bugatti would be produced for the 1946 season, based on the T73C design, 20 would be built, 15 would be reserved for French drivers and the remaining five would be sold to British drivers. Delivery would take place between April and June 1946. Two weeks later there was a further announcement that 20 more cars would be built to satisfy the provisional orders that had been received. Sadly, it was all a delusion of grandeur. A handful of parts had been made at the Rue Débarcadère workshop but no cars were completed and there was never

7 September 1945: The T59/50B before the start of the Coupe des Prisonniers, in the Bois de Boulogne.

any evidence of an attempt to put the T73C or the T73 road car into production.

Bugatti was being hampered in his claim for the restitution of Molsheim by his Italian nationality, so on 25 February 1946 he became a French subject by naturalisation. The factory was held by the Administration des Domaines, a department of the French government and later in 1946, he made a formal claim to the court in Saverne for restitution. The claim was opposed by the communist trade unions, which wanted the factory to be a workers' co-operative, and the Court ruled against Bugatti. Bugatti's personal life had become more settled, Barbara Bugatti had died on 21 July 1944, but Genevieve Delcuze had been living with him since 1940; she had a daughter, Thérèse in 1942 and a son Michel in 1945. She was married to Bugatti on 12 October 1946. In May 1947, Bugatti went to the Cour d'Appel at Colmar and made a formal appeal against the ruling of the court at Saverne. The advocate representing the trades unions made fierce personal attacks on him, which upset Bugatti deeply and he broke down. The court adjourned to consider its decision and after the hearing he went with Toussaint in the Royale to Molsheim, where he looked at the derelict factory over the locked gates, then he drove to the scene of Jean's death and while there he collapsed. It seems probable that he had a slight stroke, exacerbated by the stress and emotion of the day. He was taken back to Paris where he had little vitality and showed little interest in life; from the account given by L'Ebé, there must have been another stroke. He entered the American Hospital in Neuilly-sur-Seine where he went into a coma, pneumonia ensued and he died on Thursday, 21 August 1947 aged 65. He did not know that on 11 June, the Cour d'Appel at Colmar had allowed his appeal and restored the Molsheim factory to him.

Ettore Bugatti's funeral was held on Monday, 25 August at the church of St Pierre-de-Chaillot in the Avenue Marceau, between the Champs Elysée and the Seine. The hearse was covered in wreaths and flowers and it was followed by a lorry also loaded with tributes. There was a requiem mass in the church and the coffin stood on a bier surrounded by ten workers from Molsheim, led by Robert Aumaitre. An oration was given by M Peyrimhoff de Fontenelle, the chairman of the sporting committee of the ACF. After the service, Roland, Lidia and L'Ebé Bugatti stood outside the church to receive the condolences of the mourners. His body was taken to Molsheim and after a simple ceremony was laid to rest in the family vault in the cemetery at Dorlisheim, where Jean had been buried. At the funeral, an elderly Molsheim worker murmured a simple epitaph to David Scott-Moncreiff, the only Briton present: 'Monsieur, he had no equal'.

Despite the countless problems of a devastated Europe, there had been a full season of motor racing in 1946, and in 1947 some of the *grandes épreuves* were reinstated. There was little room for obsolescent Bugattis in the post-war scene as new racing cars were being built and sold, particularly by Maserati, as soon as the war ended. Only in England did Bugattis still find success. Brooklands had been sold as a factory site and Donington was an army camp, so apart from two race meetings on an airfield, British drivers had to be content with sprints and hill-climbs in the two years following the war. The first post-war British speed event was a sprint on an airfield runway at Elstree, north of London on Easter Monday 1946, and the fastest time was recorded by Peter Monkhouse, driving the T51 which Ettore Bugatti had given to the Bugatti Owners Club. The T59 in which the Duke of Grafton had been killed in 1936 had been rebuilt and was driven successfully in 1946 and 1947 by George Abecassis who was then one of the leading British drivers. A British Hill-climb Championship was instituted in 1947 and in the first round on 17 May at Bo'ness, a course 22 miles (35km) west of Edinburgh, Abecassis set the fastest time. He was a consistent runner in all the rounds of the 1947 Championship and ended the season as runner-up to Raymond Mays.

Although Bugattis were no longer a force in front-line motor racing, the former works drivers were still making their mark. Wimille, after his only Bugatti drive in the Bois de Boulogne, had returned to Alfa Romeo for the 1946 season and became the leading driver of an all-conquering team. Realising that the German teams were invincible, in 1938 Alfa Romeo virtually abandoned grand prix racing and built the Tipo 158 which dominated the 1,500cc voiturette class between 1938 and 1940 when Italy entered the war. In 1947, a grand prix formula was adopted with supercharged 1,500cc and unsupercharged 4½-litre cars, this was dominated by the Tipo 158s which after a defeat in the first outing at St Cloud in June 1946, remained unbeaten until the team withdrew from racing at the end of the 1948 season. Wimille led the team and was acknowledged as the uncrowned World Champion. He was joined in the team by Varzi. Varzi had left the Auto Union team in 1936 with drug problems, but the addiction was cured shortly before the war began and in the immediate post-war seasons he had almost recovered his best form. During practice for the Grosser Preis von Europa at Berne on 30 June 1948, Varzi took out a new Tipo 158, it was wet and he slid wide on a bend, the car struck a bank and overturned at little more than walking speed. Varzi's head was crushed in the accident, Chiron who was following in a Talbot, stopped and helped to lift the car off Varzi, who died a few minutes later cradled in his old teammate's arms. Varzi was mourned throughout Italy and the traffic stopped in Milan when his body was carried through the city in a funeral cortège before being buried at his home town of Galliate, north of Milan.

As well as racing for Alfa Romeo, Wimille drove for the small but impressive Gordini team in Formula B or voiturette races. He took a Gordini to South America for the winter race series in January 1949. Practising for the Gran Premio de General Juan D. Peron on a circuit in Buenos Aires, early in the morning of 28 January 1949, Wimille had to swerve to avoid spectators who were pressing onto the circuit. The Gordini hit a straw bale and overturned, Wimille was thrown out and died of his injuries shortly afterwards. He was buried in the Paris church of St Philipe de Roule and at his funeral he was awarded a posthumous Legion d'Honneur. All his obituaries acknowledged that he was the finest grand prix driver of his time. His death caused particular sadness at Gordini where Robert Aumaitre had become chief mechanic and Antonio Pichetto was in charge of the small drawing office. In the post-war years, Pichetto had become Antoine, probably having taken French nationality.

Chiron, who had withdrawn from competition after his drives for Talbot in 1937, returned to racing after the war. He drove for Talbot between 1947 and 1949 and won the first post-war GP de l'ACF at Lyon in 1947 and repeated the success at Reims in 1949 in the GP de France, which was a substitute for the GP de l'ACF. In the early 1950s he competed with Maserati and Osca. He won the 1954 Monte Carlo Rally and his last race was for the new Lancia GP team at Monaco in 1955 when he finished sixth. He died in Monaco on 22 June 1979.

When Ettore Bugatti died, Roland Bugatti took over the reins, with Pierre Marco as works manager, but he had an impossible task. He lacked the training and experience, there was little capital and no new designs. Ettore Bugatti had died intestate so his estate was divided between his two families with his widow taking a life interest in part of the estate. There was friction between Roland and Genevieve. An attempt was made to launch a new model, the T101 which was a revised T57. It was shown at the 1951 Paris Salon, but it was out-dated and too expensive and there was no public

interest. Negotiations with Porsche to assemble cars at Molsheim fell through as the project needed capital which the company did not have. Bugatti continued by working on industrial contracts and making engines under licence for vehicles for the French Army, but Roland Bugatti still nursed the hope that the old glories could be revived by a return to grand prix racing. Genevieve Bugatti had married René Bolloré, the Rizla cigarette paper heir in 1950, so with capital provided by Bolloré and with a loan from Credit National it was decided to set out on the grand prix path again. Gioachino Colombo was asked to design a car complying with the new unsupercharged 2½-litre grand prix formula which would begin on 1 January 1954. Colombo had a remarkable record. He had been the principal designer of the Tipo 158 Alfa Romeo which had gained even greater glory when Alfa Romeo returned to racing in 1950 and had been driven by Farina and Fangio, the winners of the first two World Championships in 1950 and 1951. When he left Alfa Romeo, Colombo had designed the first V-12 Ferrari engine which had set Ferrari on the road to greatness, so his credentials were impeccable. In 1953, he had been working with the design team which produced the 250F Maserati and when this was completed, he had established a design consultancy in Milan.

The progress of the project was slowed when France abandoned Northern Vietnam to the Viet Cong and French military contracts were trimmed, thus reducing the income coming to Molsheim. The intention was to build six cars which would be raced in the 1954 season but it was not until 21 November 1955 that the first car, known as the T251, was shown to the press at Entzheim airfield about a kilometre from the 1922 GP de l'ACF circuit. The engine was a straight eight-cylinder which may have been inspired by Jano, Colombo's mentor in the 1920s and 1930s. It was effectively two 'fours' with a gear train in the middle driving the camshafts and also

driving the transmission. The dimensions were 75mm x 68.8mm and the capacity was 2,430cc. There were two valves and two plugs per cylinder fired by two magnetos and the engine was fed by four double choke Weber carburettors. The engine was behind the driver and mounted transversely across the car within a small-tube space frame with the cooling water running through the tubes from a front-mounted radiator. It is not known what power the engine developed, but it has been suggested that the first engine gave about 230bhp although it was a free revving unit and unofficial reports told of 10,000rpm being seen on the test bed. Spur gears drove a five-speed Porsche gearbox from the centre of the crankshaft and another set of spur gears connected with the final drive. A fuel tank containing an aircraft type bag tank, was mounted on each side of the frame beside the cockpit. Most unorthodox of all, there was rigid axle suspension at the front and the rear operating on the De Dion principle. A bell crank connected to the wheel uprights operated long rods, actuating coil spring/damper units mounted diagonally across the frame, while radius arms located the suspension at the front and rear. Drum brakes were fitted at the front and rear, but disc brakes were being developed and it was intended the car would race with these. The result was a very short, dumpy car with a wheelbase of 7ft 2in (2.18m) and a track of 4ft 3in (1.29m). A neat body covered the car and the front cowling was extended across the full width of the car partially fairing-in the front wheels.

It seems that when Colombo was invited to design a car, he arrived at Molsheim with an already completed design which he had been hoping to sell to a manufacturer. This had conventional coil spring independent suspension at the front and the rear. This design was rejected by Roland Bugatti who said that for the sake of tradition, any car from Molsheim must have rigid axles. Colombo redesigned the car with the unorthodox suspension which was shown to the press. The first car had a mildly tuned engine running on pump fuel as it was intended to develop the chassis and ensure good handling and roadholding before seeking a competitive power output. Colombo advised upon the design while remaining in his Milan office and only made sporadic visits to Molsheim, but Stefano Meazza, who had been chief mechanic to the Ferrari grand prix team, was engaged to supervise the building and testing of the car. Unfortunately, despite Meazza's presence, a number of detrimental changes were made to the geometry and dimensions of the suspension when the car was being built.

It was the intention to test the prototype thoroughly then build a second car, incorporating the lessons learned from the test. This would make its debut in the GP de l'ACF at Reims in July 1956. The testing began on Entzheim airfield early in 1956 and revealed many problems, particularly with the chassis. The second car was built and was fitted with modified bodywork, but as the date of the GP de l'ACF approached, Roland Bugatti, Colombo and Meazza realised the T251 would not be fit to compete. They wanted to withdraw the entry, but René Bolloré and the bankers of Credit National wanted it to race, arguing that they must keep faith with the French public which expected much of the car and also hoping that commercial benefits would accrue, even from a mildly successful debut. Marco supported Bolloré and the bankers, so there was a political split at Molsheim. Maurice Trintignant, who had become one of the leading French drivers in the post-war years, agreed to drive the car at Reims. He had been driving for the Gordini and Ferrari teams, and had been the victor at Le Mans in 1954 and at Monaco in 1955.

Both T251s were taken to Reims a week before the race for testing, Trintignant tried both cars and reported that the handling was unpredictable and there was insufficient power for the long Reims straights. He

1 July 1956: The last grand prix entry, in the Grand Prix de l'ACF, at Reims. The layout of the transverse engine of the T251 can be seen and the stubby nature of the car is emphasised.

preferred the prototype for the race and this was fitted with the race engine from the second car. In the official practice sessions Trintignant recorded a best time of 2min 42sec, 19 seconds slower than Fangio's D50 Lancia/Ferrari which was on pole position. There were 19 cars assembled for the start with two cars behind the T251 on the grid, at the end of the first lap, Trintignant was in 16th place but he picked up several places and by lap seven was lying 13th, where he stayed until lap 18, when he pulled into the pits as the throttles were jammed with dust picked up from the track. It was impossible to clean the carburettors so the car was withdrawn. When Trintignant climbed out of the T251 at the Reims pits, the story of Bugatti in grand prix racing came to an end.

Much of the blame for the complete failure of the T251 has been laid at Colombo's door and his design has been derided, but the handling and directional problems seem to have been more the fault of those at Molsheim who altered the design than that of Colombo. In recent years, a senior member of the F1 McLaren design team studied Colombo's original drawings and made a computer simulation of the T251. He concluded that the design was many years ahead of its time and if it had been built and developed properly, it could have been successful. Following the failure of the T251, there were bitter recriminations between Roland Bugatti, Bolloré and Marco. Bugatti and Bolloré resigned from their executive positions and a manager was appointed. Work continued

Trintignant in the second T251 which was only used for practice at Reims.

at the factory, with the manufacture of engines for Simca and helicopter rotors. It had been intended to market a road car, the T252, based on the T251 and fitful development of this continued for several years. Marco left in 1958 and an agreement was signed with Hispano-Suiza to make Hercules diesel engines and other parts. The agreement was not studied fully and Bugatti lost money on the contracts, and in July 1963, the family agreed to the sale of Molsheim and all the assets of the company to Hispano-Suiza. A new company was formed, Hispano-Bugatti, which continued to make diesel engines and became a subsidiary of the aircraft company SNECMA in 1968. As Messier-Bugatti, the company survives within the SNECMA group and civil and military

aircraft landing gear, defence material and carbon-fibre brakes are made at the Molsheim factory.

When Molsheim was sold, Roland Bugatti retired to Rognes, near Aix-en-Provençe where he died in 1977 aged 55, he was buried there. Lidia Bugatti had lived in the Château d'Ermenonville after the war with her husband the Comte de Boigne. The château was an asset of the company so she had to leave it after the Hispano-Suiza sale. She died at Chambery in 1972 and was buried there. L'Ebé was the last survivor of Ettore Bugatti's first family, and she died in Paris in 1980 and was buried in the family vault at Dorlisheim. It was reported that she died in straitened circumstances and the funeral costs were paid by some former Molsheim workers.

That should have been the end of the story, but in 1987, plans were revealed for the manufacture of a car in Italy, bearing the Bugatti name, which had been bought for this purpose from SNECMA. A factory was built at Campogalliano, near Modena, and Paolo Stanzani, who had previously worked for Lamborghini, was engaged as chief executive and technical director. In 1990, the project was bought by Romano Artioli, an Italian entrepreneur. A car had been designed by Marcello Gandini which was called the EB110 to mark the 110th anniversary of Ettore Bugatti's birth. The EB110 was a car into which the Bugatti might well have evolved if Automobiles Ettore Bugatti had survived successfully into the second half of the 20th century. It had a 3,499cc, 81mm x 56mm V-12 engine with five valves per cylinder, boosted by four turbochargers, which was reported to develop 611bhp at 8,250rpm. This was installed in a mid-engined coupé based on a carbon-fibre structure, with a six-speed gearbox and four-wheel-drive. The EB110 went into production and it was reported that 139 cars were made although it seems likely that this figure was an over-statement. To be a true 'super car', it was necessary to have a racing image, so a high performance version, the EB110SS was entered for Le Mans in 1994 which was nominally a private entry but had factory support and was driven by Alain Cudini, Eric Helary, and Jean-Christophe Boullion. It ran in the GT class and was slowed during the race by a leaking fuel tank and the need to change all four turbochargers. It was eliminated from the race when it crashed while leading the GT class, having covered 226 laps.

No EB110 ran at Le Mans in 1995, but a single car was taken to the United States to run in the Watkins Glen three-hour race, a World Sports Car Championship round, on 24 June driven by Gildo Pallanca-Pastor from Monaco and the very experienced and successful, former grand prix driver, Patrick Tambay, it finished the race in 19th place

18/19 June 1994: The EB110SS at speed during the Le Mans 24-Hour race.

having covered 77 laps. The car travelled across to the West Coast for the 1 hour 45 minute Championship round at Sears Point in California on 16 July. Here Derek Hill, the son of Phil Hill, the 1961 World Champion, shared the drive with Pallanca-Pastor and they finished in 16th place. The car then voyaged across the Pacific for the Championship round at Suzuka in Japan on 27 August. Pallanca-Pastor had Eric Helary as the co-driver, but their race ended after 104 laps when the gearbox broke.

Racing an EB110 became more difficult after September 1995 as Bugatti Automobili SpA went into liquidation with reported

debts of $60 million. Despite the problem of a closed factory, Pallanca-Pastor took his car to Daytona for the 24-hour race on 3 February 1996, sharing it with Derek Hill and Olivier Grouillard, but once again the gearbox failed after 154 laps. A month later, the car was entered for the Monza four-hour race but did not appear. It did go to Le Mans on 28 April for the qualifying session for the 24-hour race, but despite the skill and experience of Tambay it was not fast enough to qualify and after that it disappeared from the racing scene.

That was the end of the Bugatti racing

story. Perhaps the name will appear once more in the 21st century; in 1998, the name was bought by Volkswagen and prototype luxury Bugatti super cars have been shown at motor shows, so the name may yet be revived in the racing world. For enthusiasts all over the world, the name Bugatti will forever be remembered and revered. The memory of wondrous blue cars which captivated and conquered the motor racing world in those now far-off decades between the two world wars, and the eccentric, unique artist who produced them, is surely immortal.

Appendix 1

The drivers

LOUIS CHIRON (1899–1979)

Louis Chiron was born in Monaco on 3 August 1899. His father was *maître d'hôtel* of the Hôtel de Paris in Monte Carlo. He joined the French Army in the later years of the 1914–18 war as an artilleryman, then became driver to Marshal Pètain, the commander of the French Armies of the North on the Western Front. After the War, Chiron became a dance partner at the Hôtel de Paris and bought a T22 which was prepared and supported by Ernest Friderich, who had become the Bugatti agent in Nice. Chiron entered local sprints and hill-climbs in 1923 and his first success was a third place at the Mont Agel hill-climb in 1924. For the 1925 season, he was bought a touring T30 by a rich American woman whom he had met on the dance floor. The car was fitted with a light racing body and Chiron had many successes in local events in 1925, becoming champion of the Moto Club de Nice. His ability was noticed by Alfred Hoffmann, the heir to the Hoffmann-La Roche pharmaceutical empire, who was interested in motor racing and had formed the Nerka sparking plug company. For the 1926 season, Hoffmann bought a T35 for Chiron and after taking fourth place in the GP de Provence, his first circuit race, he won the GP du Comminges. In 1927, Hoffmann bought Chiron a T35T which was converted to T35B specification, a win at Miramas and a second place in the supporting race to the GP de l'ACF, as well as a string of hill-climb wins, brought

Chiron to the notice of Ettore Bugatti. He was reserve driver to the works team at the GP de San Sebastian and became a member of the team for the British Grand Prix at Brooklands, finishing fourth.

In 1928, he became the virtual No. 1 of the Bugatti team, mostly driving a T35C and scored wins at Rome, Reims and San Sebastian, finishing the season with a victory in the GP d'Europe at Monza, there was also a string of successes in lesser events. An unsuccessful trip to Indianapolis with a GP Delage reduced Chiron's 1929 European season, but he won at San Sebastian again and also at the Nürburgring in the sports car GP von Deutschland. The T35B and C were finding the going harder in 1930 and Chiron gained fewer victories, and one of the more controversial was at Spa where Bouriat held back to let him win. The appearance of the T51 in 1931 put Chiron back on top again and he won his local GP de Monaco, shared the car with Varzi to win the GP de l'ACF and finished the season with a win at Brno after dodging the fallen bridge. At Spa in 1931, it was noticeable that he was able to lap quicker than Nuvolari and Varzi, indicating that he may have been the fastest driver in Europe at that time. His last season with Bugatti was in 1932 and the T51 was outclassed by the P3 Alfa Romeo so he was only able to win at Nice, Dieppe and Brno.

Chiron had formed a relationship with Alice Hoffmann, Alfred's wife, and this was a contributing factor in his breach with

Bugatti at the end of 1932. In 1933, he formed a private team with Caracciola, the Scuderia CC, to race a pair of Monza Alfa Romeos, but Caracciola was badly hurt at Monaco and the venture was unsuccessful. In the middle of the season, Chiron joined the Scuderia Ferrari, and stayed with them until the end of 1935, gaining a number of wins and places, the most notable being the 1934 GP de l'ACF where he beat the new German teams at Montlhéry. His ability and his services to France were recognised when he was appointed as a Chevalier of the Legion d'Honneur in 1935. He joined Mercedes-Benz in 1936 but it was not a successful partnership and his personal life was unhappy as Alice Hoffmann had left him to marry Caracciola, so he announced his retirement at the end of the season. He was tempted back to drive sports T150C Talbots in 1937 and won the GP de l'ACF again, then retired once more.

Chiron returned to the sport after the Second World War and drove for Talbot, winning the first post-war GP de l'ACF at Lyon in 1947 and repeated the victory in 1949 at Reims. After racing an F2 Osca in 1953, he had his last grand prix drive at Monaco in 1955 when he finished sixth in a D50 Lancia. He had shown his versatility by winning the 1954 Monte Carlo Rally with a Lancia. His last racing success was in 1958 at the Vuillafans-Echevannes hill-climb when he won his class with a Porsche Carrera. Thereafter Chiron devoted himself to the organisation of the GP de Monaco and the Monte Carlo Rally. He died at Monaco on 22 June 1979. Chiron was probably at his peak in the early 1930s and at that time he may have been the fastest driver in grand prix racing; his name will always be associated with Bugatti. He had great mechanical sympathy with his cars and on several occasion he nursed a sick car home to win, while his rivals would probably have broken it.

BARTOLEMEO COSTANTINI (1889–1941)

Bartolemeo ('Meo') Costantini was born in Venice in 1889, the son of a rich family. He showed an early interest in motor cars and joined the Aquila-Italiana firm in Turin where he worked with Giulio Cesare Cappa, who later designed the transmission of the four-wheel-drive T53. Costantini seems to have started his serious competition career in 1914 when he drove an Aquila-Italiana in the Targa Florio, the Coppa Florio and in the GP de l'ACF at Lyon; he retired in these races but took fourth place in the Parma-Poggio di Berceto hill-climb. His first Bugatti drive was in the 1921 Circuito del Garda when he drove a works T13 and finished second. In 1922 he transferred his affections to Bianchi and took seventh place in the GP del Autunno on the newly opened Monza track.

After a fallow year in 1923, Costantini, who had become a close friend of the Bugatti family, was living at Molsheim and in 1924 he drove a T35 at Lyon in the GP de l'ACF but retired with the gear lever damaged by a thrown tyre tread. His true talent was shown two months later at San Sebastian where he took second place and made fastest lap, although racing against the much more powerful Sunbeams. His first triumph came in May 1925, driving a T35, in the Targa Florio. He went on to win the 1,500cc class in the touring car grand prix at Montlhéry with a T39, then took fourth place in the GP de l'ACF when the Alfa Romeo team was withdrawn after Ascari's fatal crash, and finished the season by

coming third and winning the 1,500cc class with a T39 in the GP d'Italia at Monza.

Costantini continued to show his skill in 1926. In April, he won the Targa Florio again with a T35T; then he came second in the farcical GP de l'ACF, the first *grande épreuve* of the new 1,500cc GP formula. He followed this up with a third place in the GP d'Europe at San Sebastian and a week later won the Formule Libre GP de Espana on the same circuit with a T35. At the end of the season, he would have won the GP d'Italia at Monza but while leading, with only a few laps to go, his engine tightened up and he had to slow, finishing second. A week later, he was back at Monza again for the GP di Milano and driving the T35C on its debut, he won his last race by the margin of 11 minutes.

Costantini retired at the end of the 1926 season as his health had declined, but he stayed at Molsheim and became the racing team manager, apparently working unpaid. The young Jean Bugatti became his assistant and as he matured, gradually became the joint team manager with his mentor, although Costantini seemed to retain the responsibility of negotiations with the drivers, who had a high respect for him. The break between Chiron and Bugatti at the end of 1932, may have been exacerbated by Costantini who was reported to have been taking an unduly close interest in Baby Hoffmann, Chiron's mistress. With Bugatti's decline in grand prix racing, there was no longer a job for Costantini, so he left Molsheim at the end of 1934 and returned to Italy. Since their youth, Costantini and Ugo Gobbato, the managing director of Alfa Romeo had been friends and in January 1937, he was invited by Gobbato to join Alfa Romeo as assistant to Vittorio Jano, the chief designer. Costantini organised the Alfa Romeo pit at Le Mans in 1937, and when Jano was dismissed in October 1937, carried on working with Wifredo Ricart, Jano's successor. Costantini was the pit manager at Tripoli in 1939 when the Tipo 158s were defeated by Mercedes-Benz and

some of the blame for the defeat was attributed to him. He died in Venice in 1941.

Costantini is perhaps one of the most under-rated drivers of all. His two Targa Florio victories, together with his other successes mark him out as a remarkable driver and contemporary observers noted his exceptional speed was combined with great smoothness. His victories in 1925 and 1926 helped to put Bugatti at the forefront of racing manufacturers and he showed an equal ability as the team manager. A lot of the credit for the racing successes of Bugatti lies with Costantini.

ALBERT DIVO (1895–1966)

Albert Diwo was born in the Paris district of Belleville on 24 January 1895. He changed his name to Divo in December 1928. He was the son of poor parents and became an apprentice mechanic at the age of 13. Before the First World War, he worked as a mechanic on racing power boats and enlisted as an artilleryman in the French Army in December 1914, subsequently becoming a pilot in L'Armée de l'Air. After the war he joined the Sunbeam Talbot Darracq combine and was the riding mechanic to René Thomas in the 1921 Indianapolis 500 and the GP de l'ACF and also rode with Segrave at Brooklands. Encouraged and tutored by Thomas, in 1922 he became a driver for the STD team, his first race was the Tourist Trophy in the Isle of Man where he took second place in a 1,500cc Talbot-Darracq. In 1923, he became a member of the STD grand prix team and after taking second place in the GP de l'ACF at Tours, was the winner of the GP de Espana at Sitges. Divo moved to the Delage team for 1924 and was second in the GP de l'ACF at Lyon. In 1925, he shared victory in the GP de l'ACF at Montlhéry with Benoist, and in the GP de San Sebastien with Morel. He returned to STD at the beginning of 1926 and found that the 1,500cc Talbot was not fast enough to match the new 1,500cc Delage, so only gained minor wins in 1926 and 1927.

With the withdrawal of Delage and STD from racing at the end of 1927, Divo was out of work, so he joined Bugatti at Molsheim. He seemed to be an infrequent member of the team, but showed his worth by winning the 1928 Targa Florio with a T35B, following this up with a second Targa victory in 1929 driving a T35C. In 1930, he was third with a T35C in the GP de Belgique at Spa and a year later, lost an almost certain second place in the GP de l'ACF at Montlhéry when the engine mounting bolts of the T51 he was sharing with Bouriat, loosened just before the end of the race. Sharing a T51 with Bouriat, he was third in the GP d'Italia at Monza, and he also shared a T50 with Bouriat in the disastrous Le Mans venture. In 1932 he drove both the T51 and the T54, but the P3 Alfa Romeo had appeared and it was a poor season for Bugatti. Divo was entrusted the difficult T53 at Mont Ventoux and took second place.

He was still nominally a works driver in 1933 and was entered for the GP de l'ACF with a T51, but the car was not ready and after that he took little part in the sport until he made a reappearance driving a sports Talbot in 1936/37, picking up several places. His last event was a sprint meeting at Bordeaux in 1949. After retiring from racing, Divo ran a garage in Paris; for many years Janine Jennky, the Bugatti driver was his mistress. He died at Morsang-sur-Onge on 19 September 1966. In an age when there were marked social barriers, Divo made the difficult transition from mechanic to driver. He was probably at his peak in the mid-1920s and by the time he arrived at Molsheim, he was expected to be a second string to such aces as Chiron, but his two Targa Florio victories, as well as his earlier *grande épreuve* successes, mark him out as a driver of exceptional toughness and ability.

RENE DREYFUS (1905–93)
René Dreyfus was born in Nice on 6 May 1905, the son of a prosperous linen merchant. He began racing in 1924 and won the 750cc class in his first race, the Circuit des Gattières. In 1925, he bought a touring-bodied T22 with which he gained many successes in local hill-climbs then in 1927 he graduated to a T37A receiving support from Ernest Friderich, the Bugatti agent in Nice. His first major event was the 1928 Targa Florio where the T37A finished eighth. After completing his military service, Dreyfus joined Friderich as a salesman and raced the T37A in the 1929 GP de Monaco taking fifth place. Dreyfus moved up a class when he was offered drives by Albert de Bondelli who had bought the Monaco-winning T35B and with this he scored his first major win in the GP de Dieppe, then racing against works teams he took fourth place in the GP de San Sebastien and finished third in the GP de Tunisie.

With help from Friderich, a new T35B was bought for the 1930 season, with this he won the GP de Monaco beating Chiron, then went on to win the GP de la Marne. Now regarded as a leading driver, Dreyfus joined the Maserati team in 1931 but had poor results, he stayed with Maserati until halfway through the 1932 season and then left by mutual agreement and arranged with Chiron to drive his privately owned T51 for the rest of the season, picking up places at the Nürburgring and Nice. When Chiron left Molsheim after a dispute at the end of 1932, Dreyfus took his place in the team, but it was a difficult time as the T51 was becoming outclassed and Dreyfus could only gain places during 1933, there were no wins. He became involved in the development of the T59 in 1934, and after picking up third place at Monaco, he was the winner in the GP de Belgique, the last *grande épreuve* won by a Bugatti. Dreyfus left the declining Bugatti team at the end of 1934 and went to the Scuderia Ferrari where he gained a number of places against the German teams and won at Dieppe. Political sanctions forced him out of the Scuderia, so in 1936 he drove a works Talbot in the French sports car series then moved to Delahaye in 1937. He also had voiturette victories at Tripoli and Turin with a works 6CM Maserati. As the No. 1 driver for Delahaye he became involved in a head-to-head battle with Wimille and Bugatti for the Million Franc prize, which he secured by a narrow margin.

When the new grand prix formula began in 1938, Dreyfus won the first two races at Pau, where he beat the Mercedes-Benz team, and at Cork, becoming Champion of France at the end of the season. He stayed with Delahaye for the curtailed 1939 season and was recalled to the French Army when the war began. He was granted leave to drive an 8CTF Maserati at Indianapolis in 1940 and stayed in the United States when France was defeated. He joined the US Army and after the war, opened a restaurant in New York. Dreyfus drove a Ferrari at Le Mans in 1952 and his last event was the Sebring 12-hours in 1955 with an Arnolt-Bristol, and subsequently managed Renault and Lotus teams in SCCA events. He died in the United States on 17 August 1993. Dreyfus was probably the equal of any driver in the early 1930s and it was his misfortune that all too often he had cars which were outclassed. He published his autobiography *My Two Lives* in 1983.

PHILIPPE ETANCELIN (1896–1981)
Philippe Etancelin, always known affectionately as 'Phi-Phi', was born in Rouen on 28 December 1896. His family were wool merchants and he worked in the business, which seemed to take priority over his motor racing. He began racing in 1926 with a T35A in which he gained some successes in hill-climbs. He took to the circuits in 1927 with a T35 and won his first race, the GP de la Marne, as well as more hill-climb successes. He moved up to a T35C in 1928, but only ran in few races without any results. It was a good year in 1929 with wins in the GP de la Marne, at Comminges and La Baule. He was sixth in the first GP de Monaco and was battling with Chiron

for the lead at San Sebastian when he went off the road and overturned, escaping unhurt. Etancelin's greatest season was 1930 with Bugatti, which began badly with a series of crashes and retirements, but in August he won the Circuit de Dauphine, then took the T35C to Monza for his first race outside France, where he won the first heat of the GP di Monza and came sixth in the final. Two weeks later at Pau, he achieved his first major victory when he beat the works cars to win the GP de l'ACF. He kept the T35C for the start of the 1932 season, winning the Circuit de l'Esterel Plage on the Riviera and coming second at Casablanca, but he realised that it was outclassed by the new T51 and would also be unable to equal the new 8C Alfa Romeo, so in mid-season, he bought a new Monza Alfa Romeo and abandoned Bugatti for ever. He raced Alfa Romeos until the end of 1934, winning a number of lesser races and gaining another great victory in the 1934 Le Mans 24-hour race. In 1935 and 1936 he raced Maseratis but had little success apart from a win at Pau. After a season away from the sport in 1937, Etancelin returned to drive a 4½-litre Lago-Talbot in 1938 and 1939 and was able to pick up some places behind the German teams. He returned to the sport after the war and drove the Monza Alfa Romeo in the first post-War race in the Bois de Boulogne in September 1945. After two unsuccessful seasons with Maserati and Delage, he bought a new Lago-Talbot in 1948 and for the next four seasons was a regular member of the grand prix circus, winning the 1949 GP de Paris and taking second place in the 1949 GP d'Italia at Monza. His last season was 1953, when at the age of 56, he took third place in the GP de Rouen, and after the race was decorated as a Chevalier of the Legion d'Honneur, then he shared a sports Lago-Talbot with Pierre Levegh to take third place in the 12 Heures de Casablanca. He died at Neuilly-sur-Seine on 13 October 1981.

Etancelin had the ability to be a member of a works team and on his day was capable of racing on level terms with the best of his contemporaries, but it seems he preferred to remain an independent, racing when his business commitments allowed. In his early days he had several crashes, but matured into a steady, safe driver. A cheerful, friendly man, for nearly 25 years, he was one of the outstanding personalities of the racing world, always distinctive with his soft blue cap turned back-to-front and his wheel-sawing driving style.

JULES GOUX (1885–1965)

Jules Goux drove for Bugatti at the end of a distinguished racing career. He was born at Valentigney in the Doubs department on 6 April 1885 and after training as an engineer at the Arts et Métiers in Paris, he joined Peugeot where his father was the head of the bicycle division and became a test driver. He began racing with a Peugeot voiturette in 1906, but three nephews of Armand Peugeot had started a breakaway firm Lion-Peugeot, so Goux joined them. With a Lion-Peugeot he came second in the 1907 Coupe des Voiturettes, came third in the 1908 race and won the Coppa Vetturette on the Madonie circuit in Sicily in 1909. The two branches of the Peugeot firm merged in 1912 and with a Peugeot L76, Goux won the Coupe de la Sarthe at Le Mans. In the spring of 1913, he set a World Hour record at Brooklands with an L76, then took an L76 to the United States where he won the Indianapolis 500. After taking fourth place in the 1914 GP de l'ACF, Goux joined the French Army when the First World War began and served as a lieutenant in the artillery.

Goux returned to Indianapolis in 1919 and finished third with a Peugeot, but as the firm had withdrawn from racing, he joined Ballot and after taking third place in the 1921 GP de l'ACF, he won the Gran Premio d'Italia at Brescia. Ballot was declining so after coming second in the 1922 Targa Florio, Goux joined Rolland-Pilain but he had no success and had almost retired from the sport when he was invited to join Bugatti at the beginning of 1925. The T35 was not fast enough to match the Alfa Romeo and Delage teams, but Goux was fifth in the GP de l'ACF and was leading the 1,500cc class of the Gran Premio d'Italia with a T39 when the fuel tank split. It was Goux's year in 1926; he took third place in the Targa Florio with a T35T, then won the first *grande épreuve* of the new 1,500cc grand prix formula, the farcical GP de l'ACF at Miramas with a T39. He won a much harder race with a T39 at San Sebastian when he beat the Delage team in the Grand Prix d'Europe and the following week was second in the Gran Premio de Espana with a T35T. He finished the season by taking second place behind Costantini in the GP di Milano at Monza with a T35C. In 1927, he was third in the touring car GP at Montlhéry, then driving a T37A, finished sixth in his last race, the Coupe du Commission Sportive, the Formule Libre race which preceded the GP de l'ACF.

After retiring, Goux worked in the petroleum industry, then sold cars in Paris, before rejoining Bugatti at Molsheim in 1936 as an administrator. He made the arrangements for the move to Bordeaux in 1939/40 and later in the war was responsible for the management of the Château d'Ermenonville. After the war he returned to Peugeot, but went back to work at Molsheim when the factory was recovered after the death of Ettore Bugatti and continued there until he retired in 1954. He died at Mirmande, a village south of Valence, on 6 March 1965. Goux was one of the small band of drivers who was able to make the change from the long, near open road circuits of Edwardian days to the short closed circuits, which have survived into the 21st century. His ability to shine on each is a measure of his skills.

MARCEL LEHOUX (1889–1936)

Marcel Lehoux was born at Blois on 3 April 1889. After serving in the First World War, he emigrated to the French colony of Algeria and opened a garage. In 1922, he bought a T22 which he drove in local events, and gained his first success in the 1924 Circuit d'Anfa at Casablanca. In 1925, he crossed the Mediterranean and ran the T22 at Miramas, then bought a T35A which he entered for the GP de San Sebastian, running against the full 2-litre grand prix cars and showed he had exceptional ability by keeping ahead of the works T35s of de Vizcaya and Goux, until he slowed near the end of the race. For 1926, Lehoux had a T35 and beat Chiron and 'Williams' in a heat of the GP de Provençe, but his forays from Algeria were infrequent and with a T35B in 1927 he was second in a heat of the GP de Provençe and won the San Sebastian touring car GP sharing a Georges Irat with Rost, but otherwise stayed at home and scored hill-climb successes.

Victories in the Grands Prix at Tunis and Algiers with a T35C in 1928 were followed up with another impressive drive at San Sebastian where he battled with Chiron and Benoist for the lead, finishing third. After repeating his Algiers win, Lehoux travelled to Reims in 1929 and took third place in the GP de la Marne and fought with the works drivers at San Sebastian where he was also third. At the end of the season, the 'circus' went to the GP de Tunisie and Lehoux showed he was the equal of the best independents by taking second place. In 1930, Lehoux spent the racing season in France and gained his first major victory in winning at Dieppe, he also picked up a second place at Reims, but his season was dogged by mechanical failures, although he was always up with the leaders when he retired. He was one of the first customers for a new T51 in 1931 and the pattern was much the same as in 1930 with wins at Geneva and Reims and several places, but also with retirements when well-placed.

Lehoux was a customer for a T54 in 1932, but the P3 Alfa Romeo had appeared and the going became much harder for the independents in the major races. In the

T54, he chased Varzi home in the GP de Tunisie and won at Casablanca, then relied mostly on his trusty T51 which took him to second place at Nancy and Comminges. He relied solely on the T51 in 1933 and won in a snowstorm at Pau and in high summer at Dieppe, beating the works cars in both races. In September, he took fourth place in the GP d'Italia in the morning, then won the tragic GP di Monza in the afternoon and finished the season by coming third in the GP de Espana, beating the new T59s. Despite his ability to beat the works cars, it seems he received no offers from Molsheim, but Enzo Ferrari saw the talent and in 1934 he joined the Scuderia, picking up several places in a P3 Alfa Romeo. He was invited to drive the SEFAC in 1935, but the car was not ready and he had several unsuccessful races in an 8CM Maserati of the Scuderia Subalpina. In 1936, after coming third at Pau in the T51 he joined the ERA team and ran in several voiturette races with a second place at Monaco. He drove a 2-litre ERA in the GP de Deauville on 19 July and during the race he was in a collision with Farina's Alfa Romeo, the ERA overturned and Lehoux was killed instantly. At 47 he was one of the oldest drivers racing regularly, but despite his age, he was capable of keeping up at the front of the field and gained some most creditable victories against works cars. For some years before his death, he had been living with Helene Delangle ('Hellé-Nice').

ACHILLE VARZI (1904–48)

There are many who consider that Achille Varzi was the finest driver of all in the early 1930s. He was born at Galliate, near Milan on 8 August 1904, the son of a prosperous textile manufacturer. He began racing motorcycles in 1923 and was Italian 350cc Champion in his first season with a Garelli. He moved to Sunbeam and became Italian 500cc Champion in 1926, during the season, he bought a T37 and drove in his first major car race, the GP di Milano, but returned to motorcycles for 1927 with

Moto Guzzi. His greatest motorcycle rival was Tazio Nuvolari who suggested that they should join forces as the Scuderia Nuvolari and race a pair of T35Cs in 1928. The season began well and Varzi was second at Tripoli and third at Alessandria, but a string of retirements followed and he felt that Nuvolari was not giving the car proper preparation. The Scuderia broke up before the end of the season and the resulting antipathy between Varzi and Nuvolari lasted for many years. Varzi bought a P2 Alfa Romeo and in 1929 gained victories at Alessandria, Rome, Montenero and Monza becoming Champion of Italy. In 1930 he became a works driver with Alfa Romeo when the firm returned to grand prix racing and he gained his legendary victory in the Targa Florio with a P2. Nuvolari was also a member of the team and Varzi realised that their rivalry was too destructive, so left Alfa Romeo in mid-season and joined Maserati, securing wins at Pescara, Monza and San Sebastian and being declared Champion of Italy for the second year.

Varzi joined Bugatti for 1931, becoming joint No. 1 with Chiron. It was a term of his contract that he was provided with a T51 painted red, which he could race in events where the works cars were not competing. He started well with wins in his 'private' car at Tunis and Alessandria. In the works T51 he had a third place at Monaco, but he was beaten in the Targa Florio by Nuvolari with a new 8C Alfa Romeo. In its Monza form, the Alfa Romeo was hard to defeat, but with a T51 Varzi shared victory with Chiron in the ten-hour GP de l'ACF at Montlhéry and took third place in the GP von Deutschland at the Nürburgring. For the GP di Monza, he had a T54, and won his heat taking third place in the final. Varzi drove the unfortunate T50 in the Mille Miglia where he retired and at Le Mans where the car was withdrawn.

The going was much harder in 1932 as the new P3 Alfa Romeo was too fast for the T51 and Varzi only had one victory at Tunis. He shared third place with Chiron in the

Targa Florio and his T54 broke in the GP d'Italia as did his T51 at Montlhéry. He led the Mille Miglia with a T55, but the car failed him. The situation was much happier in 1933, Chiron had departed, leaving Varzi as the undisputed leader of the Bugatti team, and Alfa Romeo had withdrawn the P3 from racing, there was also the expectation of the new T59. The season began well, with a T51, Varzi had the legendary duel with Nuvolari at Monaco and won, then repeated the victory in the controversial 'lottery' race at Tripoli. There was a win in the Avusrennen with a T54, but after that, the preparation of his cars suffered as priority was given to the completion of the T59 at Molsheim and the only consolation was a second place in the GP de Belgique. When the T59 raced in the GP de Espana, it must have been evident to Varzi that it would not be competitive, so he left Bugatti at the end of the 1933 season.

In 1934, he joined the Scuderia Ferrari and won the Mille Miglia, following this with wins at Tripoli, the Targa Florio, Montenero and Nice. Realising that Alfa Romeo was following the same decline as Bugatti, Varzi moved to Auto Union in 1935, winning at Tunis and Pescara and had another win at Tripoli in 1936. He had formed a relationship with Ilse Pietsch, the wife of another Auto Union driver and she encouraged him to experiment with drugs, an addiction followed and apart from a voiturette win at San Remo with a 6CM Maserati in 1937, Varzi disappeared from racing in the seasons before the Second World War. He recovered from the addiction during the war and in 1946 rejoined Alfa Romeo to race the Tipo 158. He won at Turin in 1946, then took a Tipo 308 Alfa Romeo to South America, winning at Rosario and Interlagos. In 1947 he won at Bari with the Tipo 158 and took three second places. On 30 June 1948, he took out an experimental Tipo 158 in practice for the Grosser Preis von Europa at Berne; he lost control in the rain, the car hit a kerb at a low speed and overturned. Varzi died

almost immediately of head injuries. In the early 1930s, Varzi was possibly the best driver of the era, Nuvolari was still approaching his peak and probably only Chiron was in the same class at that time. A quiet, elegant and introverted man, Varzi was perhaps the most talented driver ever to race a Bugatti.

PIERRE VEYRON (1903–70)

Pierre Veyron was born at Berc in the Lozere department on 1 October 1903. He trained as an engineer and was a friend of Albert Divo, who encouraged him to take up motor racing. He began with an EHP sports car in 1930 and gained class wins at La Turbie and L'Esterel hill-climbs and a class second in the Oran touring car grand prix. In 1931, he received some support from André Vagniez, an industrialist from Amiens, and a T37A was bought. Driving this for the first time in the GP de Tunisie, he finished second. The first victory came in the GP de Genève when he had an easy win and this was followed up with another second place at Comminges. Vagniez bought a Tipo 26 Maserati for the 1932 season and Veyron used this to great effect, winning at Casablanca, Nancy and Comminges and finishing second at Tunis, Oran, Nice and Brno.

Veyron's record in 1932 was noticed by Jean Bugatti and in 1933, he was invited to work at Molsheim as a test driver with the attraction that a T51A would be available for him to continue his career in voiturette racing. He lived up to Bugatti's expectations and won at the Avus, Lwow and Albi, with a third place at the Eifelrennen. The only failure was a crash in the rain at Brno when leading. He was also entered in a works T51 in some lesser grands prix. In 1934, Veyron had a full season. New cars were appearing in voiturette racing and the competition was tougher, but he won again at the Avus and at Albi, with a second place at Berne. He appeared more in full grands prix with a T51 than with the T51A in voiturette events. The T51, sometimes a works entry

and sometimes in his name, was outclassed and his best result was third at Albi. At the beginning of the season, he took International class F records at Montlhéry with a T51A and at Le Mans, he shared a T50 with Labric, which was disguised as a private entry and was in second place when it retired.

In 1935 there was a third Albi win and a class win at Nancy, while he chased the ERAs at Berne and Brno coming second in both races. With the T51 there was a second at Chimay and he was back at Le Mans sharing the T50 with Labric; it led for a short time before failing. In April, assisted by Labric and Villeneuve, he had taken the 24-hour International class record with a T51A. By 1936, there was very little room for the T51A among the voiturettes and Veyron ran only once in the class, coming second at Albi, but he was also engaged in driving one of the T57Gs. At Montlhéry, in the GP de l'ACF, he shared a car with 'Williams' and finished sixth, then came fourth in the GP de la Marne. In the late autumn, he joined Benoist and Wimille in taking International class records at Montlhéry with a T57G. Veyron had only one outing in 1937 when he shared a T57G with Labric at Le Mans but retired. In 1939, not having raced for two years, he reached the climax of his career when he shared the winning T57C at Le Mans with Wimille.

When war broke out, Veyron was recalled to the colours as a reservist and served as a quartermaster in an artillery regiment until the fall of France in June 1940. Later, he served in the Resistance and was decorated with the Croix de Guerre. At the end of the war, he joined the Gordini team and in 1948, won his class in the Spa 24-hour race and the Montlhéry 12-hour race. He had some unsuccessful drives at Le Mans with a Nash Healey and his last race was at Le Mans in 1954. He later formed his own company conducting research for the petroleum industry, and died at Cap d'Eze on 2 November 1970. Veyron was a competent and efficient driver, rather than an ace, but he made Bugatti pre-eminent in voiturette racing in the years before the arrival of the ERA. His greatest feat was to be a safe and adequate partner for Wimille in the Le Mans victory.

'WILLIAMS' 1903–45

William Charles Frederick Grover-Williams raced under the pseudonym of 'Williams'. He was known as the 'Anglo-French enigma' and it is only in recent years that his story has been discovered. He was born in the Paris suburb of Montrouge on 16 January 1903. His father was English and had worked as a groom to a Russian diplomat in London, and had moved to Paris with his employer where he settled, marrying a French woman and establishing a car-hire business. 'Williams' was brought up in Paris and as a young man, went to work for Sir William Orpen as a chauffeur. Orpen was a famous portrait painter who had enhanced his reputation as an official artist in the First World War and was living in Paris. It seems that when 'Williams' was not driving Orpen, he was allowed to use his employer's cars for discreet private hire and may also have worked for his father. 'Williams' began his competition career with a Harley-Davidson motorcycle and his first event with a car was the Gometz-Le-Chatel hill-climb in 1925. He followed this with a run in the 1926 Monte Carlo Rally driving a Hispano-Suiza, possibly owned by his father.

His first race was the GP de Provençe in March 1926 driving a T35 and he came second, having given Segrave a hard race. 'Williams' then bought the Targa Florio winning T35T and came sixth in the GP de Espana at San Sebastian. During the season he set the fastest times at the La Turbie, Mont-Agel and Esterel hill-climbs. His ability was noticed by the STD combine for whom he became a works driver in 1927, but the team was unable to match the performance of the Delage team and withdrew from racing in mid-season. In 1928,

he joined Bugatti and gained his first major victory, winning the GP de l'ACF at Comminges with a T35C, he was second at Antibes behind Chiron and ended the season with a brief flash of glory by leading the opening laps of the GP d'Europe at Monza until his car fell sick. His big year was 1929 when he only drove in few races, but won the first GP de Monaco and followed this by a second victory in the fuel consumption GP de l'ACF at Le Mans. At this time, Orpen's mistress, Yvonne Aubicq, left him and married 'Williams'. It seems the parting was amicable and she received a satisfactory settlement from Orpen who gave the couple his Rolls-Royce.

In 1930, 'Williams' and his wife had settled at La Baule, breeding dogs and he made few appearances; he shared a T35B with Divo in the Targa Florio, coming seventh and battled for the lead in the early laps of the GP de l'ACF at Pau in a T35C before retiring. The ten-hour *grandes épreuves* of 1931 needed two drivers, so 'Williams' was recalled to the works team to drive the new T51. He retired in the GP de l'ACF at Montlhéry when running third, but at Spa, in the GP de Belgique, he won, sharing the car with Conelli and ended the season winning his local GP at La Baule.

It was a difficult year for Bugatti in 1932 as the T51 was outclassed by the new P3 Alfa Romeo. 'Williams' had an active season driving both the T51 and the T54, but his best result was sixth in the GP de l'ACF with a T51 and the consolation of winning again at La Baule with a T54. The pattern was the same in 1933, the Bugatti team waited for the T59 and the T51s were poorly prepared so 'Williams' had little to show for the season apart from a hat-trick at La Baule with a T54. He drove a T59 when it made its debut at San Sebastian, but crashed in practice. 'Williams' had apparently retired from racing and did not drive in 1934 and 1935, but he was back in the Molsheim fold in 1936, driving a completely outclassed T59 at Monaco

where he finished ninth and last. His final race was in the GP de l'ACF at Montlhéry where he shared a T57G with Veyron and finished sixth. 'Williams' moved to England when the Second World War began and joined the British Army in February 1940. Initially, he was a driver, but in 1942 he was commissioned as a Lieutenant and joined the Special Operations Executive. Under the code name of 'Sebastien', he landed in France in May 1942 and organised Resistance groups in the Paris area, recruiting Robert Benoist as an assistant, together with other Bugatti employees. He built up a successful circuit of groups, including a very effective sabotage group in the Citroën factory. In July 1943, 'Williams' was captured by the Gestapo and was interrogated and tortured for over a year, at first in Paris and then in Germany, but according to official reports 'gave away no information'. He was shot in Sachsenhausen concentration camp on 18 March 1945. In his earlier racing days, 'Williams' showed an ability which could have made him a top driver, but it seems that after his marriage he was content to race for pleasure and the 'hunger' was absent. His wartime exploits and ordeals showed he was a man of astonishing courage.

JEAN-PIERRE WIMILLE (1908–49)

The son of a journalist who wrote about motoring and aviation, Jean-Pierre Wimille was born in Paris on 26 February 1908. He began racing in 1930, driving a T37A which was bought for him by Marguerite Mareuse. His first important event was the 1930 GP de l'ACF at Pau but he retired after two laps with a seized supercharger. After a few outings with the T37A at the beginning of the 1931 season, Wimille moved up in the world, in collaboration with Jean Gaupillat, he bought a T51, perhaps with Mareuse support. The pair raced it in the ten-hour *grandes épreuves* and Wimille's driving ability was noted, though they had no success, the best place was seventh in the GP de l'ACF and the season came to a premature end when Wimille crashed at Dieppe while in second place and the car caught fire. In 1932, Wimille bought a T54 but had no success with it and soon returned to the T51, scoring his first victory with it in the GP d'Oranie. In mid-season, he abandoned the T51 to Gaupillat and bought a new Monza Alfa Romeo. He won his first race with it at Nancy but had disappointing results for the rest of the season. He kept the Monza in 1933 but there were no wins and his only results were second places at Reims and Comminges and a third at Brno.

In 1934, Wimille joined the works team at Molsheim as the third driver, but it was a bad time, the T59 was outclassed by the German teams and by Alfa Romeo, he was given few drives and his results during the season were dismal. The only success came at the end when he won the GP d'Algérie. In 1935, only Wimille, Benoist and Veyron were kept on the factory payroll and he was the undisputed No. 1 driver. The T59 was mostly entered for the lesser races and Wimille had a win at La Turbie, was second at Tunis and Nancy and third at Dieppe. At the end of the season he came an impressive fourth in the GP de Espana, battling with the German teams throughout the race. His fortunes were better in 1936, when he scored excellent victories with the T57G in the GP de l'ACF and in the GP de la Marne and he also won the minor GP de Deauville with a T59. The T59/50B had appeared and after some disappointing races in Europe, Wimille took it to the United States and came a very profitable second in the Vanderbilt Cup. In the late autumn he joined Benoist and Veyron in a successful attempt on International class records with a T57G.

Wimille's first major victory came in 1937 when he won the Le Mans 24-hour race in a T57G, sharing the car with Benoist. The road-equipped T59 gave him wins at Pau, Bone and Reims, but his season was centred around the *Fonds de Course* prizes. He won the 400,000FF prize with a T59 in April, but failed in the Million Franc attempt with the T59/50B in August. During the winter of 1937/38, Alfa Romeo had been making overtures to him, and after two unsuccessful outings with the 3-litre T59/50B at Cork and Reims, Wimille drove for Alfa Corse in grands prix for the rest of the 1938 season. Political sanctions stopped him driving for Alfa Romeo in 1939, so he returned to Molsheim. He won the minor Coupe de Paris with the mono-posto T59/50B and was successful with a sports T59/50B at Luxembourg and came second with it at Comminges. His great triumph was to repeat the Le Mans victory, driving a T57C with Veyron.

Wimille enlisted in L'Armée de l'Air at the beginning of the Second World War and joined the Resistance after the fall of France. He finished the war as a liaison officer in North Africa. He won the very first post-war race in the Bois de Boulogne in September 1945, driving the T59/50B. In 1946, after two wins in the Bois de Boulogne and at Perpignan with a Tipo 308 Alfa Romeo, Alfa Corse recruited him to drive the Tipo 158. He won his heat at Geneva, was third in the final and was third at Turin. Wimille found his true form in 1947 with the Tipo 158, winning the GP von Schweiz at Berne and the GP de Belgique at Spa. He stayed with Alfa Romeo and scored three major wins in 1948, the GP de l'ACF at Reims, the GP d'Italia at Turin and the GP di Monza. He had been driving successfully for Gordini in Formula 2 races and he took a Gordini to South America for the 1948/49 winter season. He crashed while practising for the GP de Gen Peron at Buenos Aires on 29 January 1949 and died of head injuries shortly afterwards. Wimille was acknowledged as the finest driver in grand prix racing in the seasons following the Second World War and was truly an uncrowned World Champion. For Bugatti his qualities had been inestimable. The successes gained in the years immediately preceding the Second World War were due very largely to Wimille's skill.

Appendix 2

Brief specifications of the principal Bugatti competition cars

(Except where stated all models had semi-elliptic front springs and reversed quarter-elliptic rear springs and cable operated mechanical brakes)

Type 13 (8-Valve): 1910–1920
Chassis Nos
361–843 (this includes all the 8-valve models also encompassing the T15, T17, T22 & 23)

Engine
4 cyl 65mm x 100mm 1327cc, plain 3-bearing crankshaft, single ohc operating 8 valves via banana tappets

Transmission
Wet multiplate clutch, separate four speed gearbox, rear axle mounted on semi-elliptic (1910–13) or reversed quarter elliptic (1913–20) springs

Dimensions
Wheelbase 6ft 6½ ins (2.0 m)
Track 3ft 9¼ins (1.15m)
Tyre size 710 x 90
Wire wheels

Type 13 (16-Valve): 1920–1926
Chassis Nos
901–2906 (this figure includes all the 16-valve T13, T15, T22 & 23). The number of 16-valve T13s was about 100

Engine
4 cyl 66mm 68mm or 69mm x 100mm 1368cc, 1453cc or 1496cc, 3-plain bearing crankshaft (1920–23) 2-ball 1 plain 3-bearing crankshaft (1921–26), single ohc operating 16 valves via banana tappets, single or twin ignition.

Transmission
Wet multiplate clutch, separate four speed gearbox

Dimensions
Wheelbase 6ft 6½ins (2.0 m)
Track 3ft 9¼ins (1.15 m)
Tyre size 710 x 90.
Wire wheels

Type 18: 1912–1914
Chassis Nos
471–474, 714–716

Engine
4 cyl 100mm x 160mm, 5027cc, 3 or 5-plain bearing crankshaft, single ohc operating 8 inlet and 4 exhaust valves via fingers

Transmission
Wet multi plate clutch, 4-speed gearbox/countershaft, final drive by chains (One car had shaft drive)

Dimensions
Wheelbase 8 ft 4½ins (2.55m)
Track 4ft 1¼ins (1.25m)
Tyre size 880 x 120
Wire wheels

Type 30: 1922–1923
Chassis Nos
4001–4004 (Strasbourg 1922)
4014–4016 (Indianapolis 1923)

Engine
8 cyl 60mm x 88mm 1991cc, ball 3-bearing crankshaft, plain rods, single ohc operating 16 inlet and 8 exhaust valves via fingers

Transmission
Wet multi plate clutch, separate four speed gearbox (hydraulic front brakes)

Dimensions
Wheelbase 7ft 10½ins (2.4m)
Track 3ft 11¼ins (1.2m)
Tyre size 765 x 105
Wire wheels

Type 32:1923
Chassis Nos
4057–4061

Engine
8 cyl 60mm x 88mm 1991cc ball 3-bearing crankshaft, roller rods, single ohc operating 16 inlet and 8 exhaust valves via fingers.

Transmission
Wet multi plate clutch, three speed gearbox in rear axle (reversed quarter elliptics front and rear, hydraulic front brakes)

Dimensions
Wheelbase 6ft 6½ins (2.0m)
Track 3ft 11¼ins (1.2m)
Tyre size 765 x 105
Wire wheels

Type 35 & 39: 1924–1930
Chassis Nos
4323–4965. This includes all the T30s. The total number of T35s was about 350.

Engine
8 cyl 60mm x 88mm 1991cc (T35/35A/35C) 60mm x 100mm 2262cc (T35B/T35T) 60mm x 66mm, 52mm x 88mm and 54mm x 81mm 1493cc (T39/39A) ball and roller 5-bearing crankshaft with roller rods (except T35A ball 3-bearing crankshaft with plain rods) single ohc operating 16 inlet and 8 exhaust valves via fingers. T35B/35C/39A are supercharged.

Transmission
Wet multi plate clutch, separate four speed gearbox

Dimensions
Wheelbase 7ft 10½ins (2.4m)
Track 3ft 11¼ins (1.2m)
Tyre size 710 x 90, 5.00 or 5.50 x 19
Alloy wheels (wire on T35A)

Type 37: 1926–1930
Chassis Nos
37101–37388

Engine
4 cyl 69mm x 100mm 1496cc plain 5-bearing crankshaft plain rods, single ohc operating 8 inlet and 4 exhaust valves via fingers. T37A is supercharged.

Transmission
Wet multi plate clutch, separate four speed gearbox

Dimensions
Wheelbase 7ft 10½ins (2.4m)
Track 3ft 11½ins (1.2m)
Tyre size 710 x 90, 4.50 or 5.00 x 19
Wire wheels (optional alloy on T37A)

Type 43: 1927–1931
Chassis Nos
43150–43310

Engine
8 cyl 60mm x 100mm 2262cc ball and roller 5-bearing crankshaft with roller rods, single ohc operating 16 inlet and 8 exhaust valves via fingers, super-charged.

Transmission
Wet multi plate clutch, separate four speed gearbox

Dimensions
Wheelbase 9 ft 9 ins (2.97m)
Track 4ft 1¼ins (1.25m)
Tyre size 5.00 x 19
Alloy wheels.

Type 44: 1927–1930
Chassis Nos
44251–441345

Engine
8 cyl 69mm x 100mm 2991cc plain 9-bearing crankshaft with plain rods, single ohc operating 16 inlet and 8 exhaust valves via fingers.

Transmission
Wet multi plate clutch, separate four speed gearbox

Dimensions
Wheelbase 10ft 3ins (3.122m)
Track 4ft 1¼ins (1.25 m)
Tyre size 5.00 x 19
Wire wheels.

Type 45: 1930
Chassis nos
47155, 47156 and one other

Engine
Double-bank 16 cyl 60mm x 84mm 3801cc two ball and roller 9-bearing crankshafts geared together, with plain rods, two single ohc operating 16 inlet and 8 exhaust valves via fingers, two superchargers.

Transmission
Wet multiplate clutch, separate four speed gearbox

Dimensions
Wheelbase 8ft 6¼ins (2.6m)
Track 4ft 1¼ins (1.25m)
Tyre size 5.00 x 19
Alloy wheels.

Type 50: 1930–1934
Chassis Nos
50112–50176

Engine
8 cyl 86mm x 107mm 4972cc plain 9-bearing crankshaft with plain rods, twin ohc operating 8 inlet and 8 exhaust valves directly, supercharged.

Transmission
Dry multi plate clutch, 3-speed gearbox in rear axle.

Dimensions
Wheelbase 10ft 2ins (3.1m)
Track 4ft 7ins (1.4m)
Tyre size 6.50 x 20
Alloy wheels.

Type 51:1931–1936
Chassis Nos
51121-51160

Engine
8 cyl 60mm x 100mm 2262cc 60mm x 66mm 1492cc (T51A) ball and roller 5-bearing crankshaft with roller rods, twin ohc operating 8 inlet and 8 exhaust valves directly, supercharged.

Transmission
Wet multi plate clutch, separate four speed gearbox

Dimensions
Wheelbase 7ft 10½ins (2.4m)
Track 3ft 11½ins (1.2m)
Tyre size 5.00 x 19
Alloy wheels.

Type 53:1932–1935
Chassis Nos
53001–53003

Engine
8 cyl 86mm x 107mm 4972cc plain 9-bearing crankshaft with plain rods, twin ohc operating 8 inlet and 8 exhaust valves directly, supercharged.

Transmission
dry multi plate clutch, separate four speed gearbox, four wheel drive with front wheels driven from off-set drive shaft to front bevel box. Independent front suspension with twin transverse leaf springs.

Dimensions
Wheelbase 8ft 6ins (2.6m)
Track 4ft 1in (1.25m)
Tyre size 28 x 5
Alloy wheels

Type 54: 1932–1934
Chassis Nos
54201–54210

Engine
8 cyl 86mm x 107mm 4972cc plain 9-bearing crankshaft with plain rods, twin ohc operating 8 inlet and 8 exhaust valves directly, supercharged.

Transmission
Dry multi plate clutch, separate three speed gearbox

Dimensions
Wheelbase 9ft 0¼ins (2.75m)
Track 4ft 5ins (1.35m)
Tyre size 5.00 x 19 or 6.00 x 20
Alloy wheels.

Type 55: 1932–1935
Chassis Nos
55201–55238

Engine
8 cyl 60m x 100mm 2262cc ball and

roller 5-bearing crankshaft with roller rods, twin ohc operating 8 inlet and 8 exhaust valves directly, supercharged.

Transmission
Dry multi plate clutch, separate four speed gearbox

Dimensions
Wheelbase 9ft 0¼ins (2.75m)
Track 4ft 1¼ins (1.25m)
Tyre size 5.00 x 19
Alloy wheels.

Type 57: 1935–1939
Chassis Nos
57102–57841

Engine
8 cyl 72mm x 100mm 3257cc plain 5-bearing crankshaft with plain rods, twin ohc operating 8 inlet and 8 exhaust valves via fingers. (T57C supercharged).

Transmission
(T57S) Dry twin plate clutch, integral four speed gearbox.

Dimensions
Wheelbase (T57S) 9ft 9¼ins (2.98m)
Track 4ft 5ins (1.35m)
Tyre size 5.00 x 18
Wire wheels (T57S). 5.50 or 6.00 x 19
Piano wire & alloy wheels (T57G & C).

Type 59: 1934–1936
Chassis Nos
59121–59124 and four others

Engine
8 cyl 72mm x 100mm plain 5-bearing crankshaft with plain rods, twin ohc operating 8 inlet and 8 exhaust valves via fingers, supercharged.

Transmission
Dry multi plate clutch, separate four speed gearbox

Dimensions
Wheelbase 8ft 6½ins (2.6m)
Track 4ft 1½ins (1.25m)
Tyre size 5.50 or 6.00 x 19
Piano wire & alloy wheels.

Bibliography

Biaumet, André *Le Grand Prix des Frontières à Chimay* (Author, 1986)

Blight, Anthony *The French Sports Car Revolution* (G. T. Foulis, 1996)

Boddy, William *Montlhéry* (Cassel, 1961) *The Story of Brooklands* (Grenville, 1950)

Borgeson, Griff *Bugatti* (Osprey, 1981)

Bradley, W. F. *Ettore Bugatti* (Motor Racing Publications 1948) *Targa Florio* (G. T. Foulis, 1956)

Bugatti, L'Ebé *The Bugatti Story* (Souvenir Press, 1966)

Campbell, Malcolm *My Thirty Years of Speed* (Hutchinson, 1935)

Carli, Emanuele Alberto *Settant'Anni di Gare Automobilistiche in Italia* (AC d'Italia, Editrice dell Automobile, 1967)

Cholmondley-Tapper T. P. *Amateur Racing Driver* (G. T. Foulis, 1954)

Chakrabongse, Prince Chula *Road Star Hat Trick* (G. T. Foulis, 1948)

Cimarosti, Adriano *Grand Prix Suisse* (Hallwag, 1992)

Conway, Hugh *Bugatti* (G. T. Foulis, 1963) *Bugatti Magnum* (G. T. Foulis, 1989) *Grand Prix Bugatti* (G. T. Foulis, 1968)

Court, William *Power and Glory* (Macdonald, 1966) *Grand Prix Requiem* (Patrick Stephens, 1992)

Davis, S. C. H. *Motor Racing* (Iliffe, 1932)

Dees, Mark L. *The Miller Dynasty* (Barnes, 1981)

Delsaux, Jean-Paul *Francorchamps 1922–1947* (Author, 1990)

Dreyfus, René (with Beverley Rae Kimes) *My Two Lives* (Aztex, 1983)

Dumont, Pierre *Bugatti: Thoroughbreds from Molsheim* (EPA, 1975) *Peugeot* (EPA, 1976)

Earl, Cameron C. *Quicksilver* (HMSO, 1996)

Eyston, George *Flat Out* (John Miles, 1933)

Hodges, David *The French Grand Prix* (Temple Press, 1967) *The Le Mans 24-Hour Race* (Temple Press, 1963) *The Monaco Grand Prix* (Temple Press, 1965)

Hull, Peter *Prescott Speed Hill Climb 1938–1998* (Bugatti Owners Club, 1998)

Jarraud, Robert *Bugatti-Doubles Arbres* (L'Automobiliste, 1977)

Jenkinson, Denis *Motor Sport Racing Car Review 1957* (Grenville, 1957)

Kupelian, Yvette and Sirtiane, Jacques *Soixante Ans de Competition Automobile en Belgique 1896–1956* (Kupelian & De Bock)

Louche, Maurice *1895–1995 Un Siècle de Grande Pilotes Français* (Author, 1995) *Mont Ventoux* (Author, 1984)

Lurani, Giovanni *La Storia de la Mille Miglia* (Istituto Geografico de Agostini, 1979) *Racing Round the World* (G. T. Foulis, 1956)

Lynch, Brendan *Green Dust* (Portobello, 1988)

Lyndon, Barré *Grand Prix* (John Miles, 1935)

Mason, Chris *Uphill Racers* (Bookmarque, 1990)

Monza: Official Year Books 1960–1962 (SIAS, 1961–63)

Moretti, Valerio *When Nuvolari Raced* (Veloce, 1994)

Mortimer, Charles *Brooklands and Beyond* (Goose, 1974)

Nixon, Chris *Racing the Silver Arrows* (Osprey, 1986)

Nye, Doug *History of the Grand Prix Car 1945–65* (Hazelton, 1993)

Pomeroy, Laurence *The Grand Prix Car* (Temple Press, 1954)

Popely, Rick, with L. Spencer Riggs *Indianapolis 500 Chronicle* (Publications International, 1998)

Posthumus, Cyril *The German Grand Prix* (Temple Press, 1966)

Raffaelli, Antoine *Memoirs of a Bugatti Hunter* (Maeght Editeur, 1997)

Setright, Leonard *The Grand Prix Car 1954 to 1966* (George Allen & Unwin, 1968)

Sewell, David *British Bugatti Register* (Author 1989)

Sheldon, Paul and Rabagliati, Duncan *A Record of Grand Prix and Voiturette Racing* Volumes 1–4, and 6 (St Leonards Press 1987)

Taruffi, Piero *Works Driver* (Temple Press, 1964)

Venables, David *First Among Champions* (Haynes, 2000) *The Racing Fifteen-Hundreds* (Transport Bookman, 1984)

Weber, Eugen *The Hollow Years* (Sinclair-Stevenson, 1995)

Wimpffen, Janos L. *Time and Two Seats* (Motor Sport Research Group, 1999)

Wood, Jonathan *Bugatti – The Man and the Marque* (Crowood, 1992)

Wright, Gordon *France in Modern Times* (W. W. Norton, 1987)

Newspapers and periodicals
Autocar
Automobile Quarterly
L'Automobiliste
Brooklands Society Gazette
Bugantics
Le Fanatique de l'Automobile
Motor
Motor Sport
Old Motor
Omnia
Speed
Veteran & Vintage
Vintage Sports Car Club Bulletin

Index